PARLIAMENTS OF THE WORLD

A Comparative Reference Compendium

INTER-PARLIAMENTARY UNION

PARLIAMENTS OF THE WORLD

A Comparative Reference Compendium

SECOND EDITION

VOLUME I

Prepared by

THE INTERNATIONAL CENTRE FOR PARLIAMENTARY DOCUMENTATION OF THE INTER-PARLIAMENTARY UNION

Facts On File Publications
New York, New York ● Oxford, England

First edition published in the United States in 1976 by
Walter de Gruyter

Library of Congress Cataloguing in Publication Data
Main entry under title:

Parliaments of the World.

Bibliography : p.
Includes index
1. Legislative Bodies. 2. Comparative government.
I. Inter-parliamentary Union.
JF501.P36 1986   328'.3   84-26008
 ISBN 0-8160-1551-1 (Vol.I)
ISBN 0-8160-1552-X (Vol.II)
ISBN 0-8160-1186-9 2 Vol. Set

Printed in Great Britain
10 9 8 7 6 5 4 3 2 1

CONTENTS

VOLUME I

Introduction   ix

Conventions, Symbols and Abbreviations   xii

I.   **Parliaments of the World**

    The Parliaments of the World   3
    National representative bodies of all sovereign states
    throughout the world; normal term; number of Members.

II.   **Parliament and its Membership**

    Characteristics and Composition of Parliament   Table 1   13

    Eligibility for Membership and Incompatibilities   Table 2   65
    qualifications and disqualifications
    incompatibility with other offices

    Parliamentary Mandate and Cessation   Table 3   103
    of Membership
      recall
      resignation
      expulsion
      authority resolving disputed elections

    Parliamentary Immunities and Privileges   Table 4   135
      offences against Parliament

    Parliamentary Remuneration   Table 5   179
      salary
      allowances
      pension schemes

    Facilities and Amenities   Table 6   205

III.   **Parliamentary Procedure**

    Rules of Procedure and Parliamentary Budget   Table 7   235

    Sessions of Parliament   Table 8   269
      joint sittings, meetings of committees and
      other bodies in recess

CONTENTS

Presiding Officers or Collective Directing Authority	Table 9	313
Secretary General of the House	Table 10	363
Organisation of Business	Table 11	391
Debate in the House	Table 12	429
Order in the House	Table 13	459
Methods of Voting in the House	Table 14	475
Quorum Requirements	Table 15	495
Voting Majority Requirements	Table 16	515

IV. Proceedings and Debates

Publication of Debates	Table 17	549
Official Languages of Parliament	Table 18	579

V. Parliamentary Groupings

Parliamentary Parties and Groups Official Opposition rights of the Parties and the Opposition unattached Members	Table 19	589

VI. Parliamentary Committees

Committees types of committees appointment to committees	Table 20	625
Chairmen and Staff of Committees expert advisers	Table 21	653
Meetings of Committees procedure quorum	Table 22	677
Attendance at Committee Meetings government officials participation by other MPs summoning witnesses calling for documents	Table 23	699

CONTENTS

VOLUME   II

VII.   **Parliament and its Means of Information**

Parliamentary Library and   Table 24   725
Information Services

Documentation, Research and Reference   Table 25   755
Services
  information provided by the Documentation,
  Research and Reference Services

VIII. **Parliament and the Media**

Parliament and Journalists   Table 26   781
  information for the media
  rights and facilities

Broadcasting/Telecasting of   Table 27   807
Parliamentary Debates

IX.   **Legislation**

The Legislative Function   Table 28   835
  bodies sharing the legislative
  function
  extra-parliamentary consultation

Initiation of Legislation   Table 29   859
  right to initiate legislation
  conditions affecting the right
  to initiate

Legislative Function in Multi-   Table 30   881
Cameral Parliaments
  procedure and powers in
  budgetary matters

Volume of Legislation   Table 31   909

The Legislative Process   Table 32   921
  stages in the legislative process
  reconsideration of Bills and
  veto rights

Role of Committees in the   Table 33   961
Legislative Process

Amendments to Bills   Table 34   993

Delegated Legislation   Table 35   1027
  parliamentary scrutiny of delegated
  legislation

CONTENTS

X.   **The Budget**

     Nature of the Budget   Table 36   1049

     Timing of the Budget   Table 37   1067

     The Budget in Parliament   Table 38   1091

XI.   **Parliament and the Government**

     Role of Parliament in Appointing   Table 39   1115
     the Executive

     Ministerial Responsibility to Parliament   Table 40   1147

     Scrutiny of Public Expenditure   Table 41   1175

     Scrutiny of Administration   Table 42   1203

     Parliament and Foreign Affairs   Table 43   1237

XII.   **Parliament and Emergency**

     Parliament and the State of Emergency   Table 44   1273
       grounds for declaring emergency
       role of Parliament

XIII.   **Constitutionality of Laws**

     Parliament and the   Table 45   1305
     Constitutionality of Laws

XIV.   **Dissolution of Parliament**

     Dissolution of Parliament   Table 46   1325
       constitutional provisions
       authority - role of Government
       circumstances

XV.   **Judicial and Other Functions of Parliament**

     Judicial and Other Functions of Parlt   Table 47   1353
       nominations and appointments
       indictments
       economic development

   Index   1399

INTRODUCTION

Contrary to some contemporary opinions, Parliaments of sovereign States have been developing and strengthening in recent times. This appears to show that the concept of representative parliamentary institutions, as a legitimate and workable mechanism for representing the popular will in the ordering of public affairs is deeply rooted in the human mind.

Despite the universality of the basic concept, an extraordinary variety of Parliaments exists. Furthermore, they are in constant evolution in industrialised and developing countries alike. Knowledge of the situation elsewhere enables a Parliament to make useful comparisons when changes are envisaged in its structure and functioning. Published comparative studies also help to make Parliaments better known, not only to other Parliaments, but also to universities and research institutes, journalists, and indeed all those interested in the growth and functioning of political systems.

With these aims in mind, the Inter-Parliamentary Union in 1961 published a comparative study entitled "Parliaments", of which a revised and updated edition was published in 1966. The Union's International Centre for Parliamentary Documentation (CIDP), which was created in 1965 to contribute to the study and strengthening of parliamentary institutions, made it possible to carry this concept a stage further.

Thus in 1973 a study was launched by means of a further questionnaire sent to all Parliaments of sovereign states throughout the world. The result of the questionnaire covering fifty-six Parliaments appeared in the first edition of "Parliaments of the World" published in 1976. This work proceeded further than the previous studies and for the first time presented considerable detail in the form of tables to facilitate comparison and cross-reference.

Ten years later a new and revised questionnaire was sent to all of the 142 Parliaments of sovereign States throughout the world. Eighty-three replied and furnished a mass of information which served as the basis for the preparation of the draft text for the present edition which is to be published in French as well as in English. This information was supplemented as appropriate from the CIDP's large collection of material on constitutional and parliamentary matters. This includes fundamental documents such as constitutions, standing orders, electoral laws and laws pertaining to Parliaments.

INTRODUCTION

The draft text was then submitted to all responding Parliaments between June and September 1985 for comment and correction. The Parliaments were requested to ensure that the information given was correct as at 30 June 1985. The draft was also subject to a critical scrutiny by the Consultative Committee of Experts of the CIDP. This comprised Dr. G. Gude (United States of America) who is the Chairman, Dr. B.R. Bhagat (India), Professor A. Gwizdz (Poland), Dr. W. Koops (Netherlands), and Professor J. Owona (Cameroon).

Eighty-three Parliaments, as shown immediately after the list of contents, are described in the study as they existed at 30 June 1985. The systematic approach adopted in this study made it necessary to set this reference date after which no changes occurring in any of the Parliaments considered were included. In addition to covering nearly fifty per cent more Parliaments than the 1976 edition, the present work revises the format to consolidate the material and present it in a more convenient manner. Some of the detail in the first edition relating to elections has been removed as much of this is now provided in the Union's annual publication "Chronicle of Parliamentary Elections and Developments".

The present edition contains fifteen broad sections each of which deals with some major aspect of the structure, powers or procedure of Parliament. Each section comprises one or more chapters and each chapter consists of a comparative table preceded by introductory explanatory text.

There are forty-seven chapters. Each of the associated comparative tables provides basic data and statistics on the topic covered by the chapter, with each of the eighty-three Parliaments considered in turn in alphabetical order. The tables attempt to present the essential information concisely, using as far as possible the same nomenclature for the same concepts and structures, to bring out significant similarities and differences between the various parliamentary systems. In so doing, some detail and a degree of precision, inevitably, has been lost. It is accordingly recommended that those seeking greater detail or precision with respect to a given Parliament refer to the source documents. The assistance of the Union's CIDP could be sought, if required. Many helpful references to the relevant article of a Constitution will be found in the tables.

The introductory text to each chapter provides an overall assessment of the topic treated. The text comments on and explains its associated comparative table in a manner intended to be helpful for its better understanding. Some of the major features of the table are also summarised, often with the help of small subsidiary tables.

The study could not have been completed without the attentive care and collaboration of many people. Foremost among these are the Secretaries General and staffs of the Parliaments covered, who, by providing most of the material on which the study is based, and subsequently checking their respective draft entries, made an indispensable contribution to its preparation and accuracy.

INTRODUCTION

Thanks are also due to Mr. F. Ch. Jonas Condomines who analysed many of the replies to the questionnaire and prepared corresponding draft tables. Grateful acknowledgement is also made of the earlier contribution of Mr. Valentine Herman assisted by Mrs. Françoise Mendel whose work in preparing the 1976 edition provided a reliable point of departure for the present enlarged and updated edition.

This study also owes much to Mr. Michel Ameller, whose analyses prepared for the edition of "Parliaments" published by the Inter-Parliamentary Union in 1966 are still largely relevant and provided a firm base for the updated texts preceding the tables.

Many others, too numerous to be mentioned individually, helped at various stages of the project. Their contribution is acknowledged with gratitude and appreciation.

Pio-Carlo Terenzio
Secretary General
Inter-Parliamentary Union

CONVENTIONS, SYMBOLS AND ABBREVIATIONS

1. Where bicameral Parliaments are under consideration, the information given applies to both Houses, except when otherwise stated, or where two clearly separate sets of information appear against the respective House names.

2. For consistency in entries concerning bicameral Parliaments, the "Upper" House, "First" Chamber or the House representing the federated entities has been placed first. This order does not necessarily imply any special priority or importance.

3. "Member" written with a capital M denotes a Member of Parliament; "member" with a small m denotes merely the common noun.

4. Similarly "Parliament" or "Government" indicates the particular and "parliament" or "government" the general use of the noun.

5. In translating names and titles, the English synonym nearest in form to the original language has been adopted where appropriate, e.g. Assemblée - Assembly; Congreso - Congress; etc.

6. A dash (-) means "information unavailable".

7. Abbreviations:

AIPLF	=	Association internationale des parlementaires de langue française
AIPU	=	Arab Inter-Parliamentary Union
Amdt	=	amendment
APPU	=	Asian Pacific Parliamentary Union
Art.	=	article
ASEAN	=	Association of South-East Asian Nations
Const.	=	Constitution
CPA	=	Commonwealth Parliamentary Association
CPEP	=	Conference of Presidents of European Parliaments

CONVENTIONS, SYMBOLS AND ABBREVIATIONS

Cttee	=	committee
EFTA	=	European Free Trade Association
EP	=	European Parliament
Govt	=	Government
IPCCB	=	Inter-Parliamentary Consultative Council of Benelux
IPU	=	Inter-Parliamentary Union
MP	=	Member of Parliament
NA	=	not applicable
NAA	=	North Atlantic Assembly
NC	=	Nordic Council
pa	=	per annum
pd	=	per diem
pm	=	per mensem
PACE	=	Parliamentary Assembly of the Council of Europe
Parlt	=	Parliament
SO	=	Standing Orders
UAP	=	Union of African Parliaments
WEU	=	Western European Union

PART I

PARLIAMENTS OF THE WORLD

THE PARLIAMENTS OF THE WORLD

Below are listed all the national representative bodies of sovereign states throughout the world as at 30 June 1985. Those marked with an asterisk * are described in greater detail in the subsequent tables.

Country	Parliament/Houses	Term of office (years)	Member-ship
Albania	People's Assembly	4	250
*Algeria	National People's Assembly	5	282
Angola	People's Assembly	3	207
Antigua and Barbuda	Parliament/Senate House of Representatives	5 5	17 17
*Argentina	National Congress/Senate Chamber of Deputies	9 4	46 254
*Australia	Parliament/Senate House of Representatives	6 3	76 148
*Austria	Parliament/Federal Council National Council	5 or 6 4	63 183
*Bahamas	Parliament/Senate House of Assembly	5	16 43
Barbados	Parliament/Senate House of Assembly	5 5	21 27
*Belgium	Legislative Chambers/Senate House of Representatives	4 4	182 212
Belize	National Assembly/Senate House of Representatives	5 5	9 28
Benin	National Revolutionary Assembly	5	196
Bhutan	National Assembly	3	150

3

Country	Parliament/Houses	Term of office (years)	Member-ship
Bolivia	National Congress/Chamber of Senators	4	27
	Chamber of Deputies	4	130
Botswana	National Assembly	5	39
*Brazil	National Congress/Federal Senate	8	69
	Chamber of Deputies	4	479
*Bulgaria	National Assembly	5	400
Burma	People's Assembly	4	475
Burundi	National Assembly	5	65
*Cameroon	National Assembly	5	120
*Canada	Parliament/Senate	(a)	104
	House of Commons	5	282
*Cape Verde	People's National Assembly	5	63
*China	National People's Congress	5	2,978
Colombia	Congress/Senate	4	114
	House of Representatives	4	199
*Comoros	Federal Assembly	5	38
*Congo	People's National Assembly	5	153
*Costa Rica	Legislative Assembly	4	57
*Cuba	National Assembly of People's Power	5	499
*Cyprus	House of Representatives	5	50
*Czecho-slovakia	Federal Assembly/Chamber of Nations	5	150
	Chamber of the People	5	200
Democratic People's Republic of Korea	Supreme People's Assembly	4	615
*Democratic Yemen	Supreme People's Council	5	111
*Denmark	Folketing	4	179
Djibouti	National Assembly	5	65

(a) Until retirement

4

Country	Parliament/Houses	Term of office (years)	Member- ship
Dominica	House of Assembly	5	31
Dominican Republic	Congress/Senate Chamber of Deputies	4 4	27 91
Ecuador	National Congress	4	71
*Egypt	People's Assembly	5	458
El Salvador	Legislative Assembly	3	60
Equatorial Guinea	House of Representatives of the People	5	60
*Fiji	Parliament/Senate House of Representatives	6 5	22 52
*Finland	Parliament	4	200
*France	Parliament/Senate National Assembly	9 5	317 577
*Gabon	National Assembly	5	120
Gambia	House of Representatives	5	49
*German Democratic Republic	People's Chamber	5	500
*Germany (Federal Republic)	Parliament/Federal Council Federal Diet	(b) 4	45 518
*Greece	Chamber of Deputies	4	300
Grenada	Parliament/Senate House of Representatives	5 5	13 15
Guinea Bissau	National People's Assembly	5	150
Guyana	National Assembly	5	65
Haiti	Legislative Assembly	6	59
Honduras	National Congress	4	82
*Hungary	National Assembly	5	387

(b) Variable

Country	Parliament/Houses	Term of office (years)	Membership
Iceland	Parliament/Eefri Deild	4	20
	Nedri Deild	4	40
*India	Parliament/Council of States	6	244
	House of the People	5	544
*Indonesia	House of Representatives	5	460
Iran	Islamic Consultative Assembly	4	270
Iraq	National Assembly	4	250
*Ireland	The Oireachtas/Senate	5	60
	House of Representatives	5	166
*Israel	The Knesset	4	120
*Italy	Parliament/Senate	5	323
	Chamber of Deputies	5	630
*Ivory Coast	National Assembly	5	147
Jamaica	Parliament/Senate	5	21
	House of Representatives	5	60
*Japan	Diet/House of Councillors	6	252
	House of Representatives	4	511
*Jordan	National Assembly/Senate	4	30
	House of Deputies	4	60
*Kenya	National Assembly	5	173
Kiribati	House of Assembly	4	38
*Kuwait	National Assembly	4	65
*Lebanon	National Assembly	4	99
*Liechtenstein	Diet	4	15
*Luxembourg	Chamber of Deputies	5	64
Madagascar	National People's Assembly	5	137
*Malawi	National Assembly	5	101
*Malaysia	Parliament/Senate	3	69
	House of Representatives	5	177
Maldives	People's Council	5	48

Country	Parliament/Houses	Term of office (years)	Member-ship
*Mali	National Assembly	3	82
*Malta	House of Representatives	5	65
*Mauritius	Legislative Assembly	5	70
*Mexico	Union Congress/Senate	6	64
	Chamber of Deputies	3	400
*Monaco	National Council	5	18
*Mongolia	Great People's Khural	5	370
Morocco	House of Representatives	6	306
Mozambique	People's Assembly	5	226
*Nauru	Parliament of Nauru	3	18
Nepal	National Panchayat	5	140
*Netherlands	States General/First Chamber	4	75
	Second Chamber	4	150
*New Zealand	House of Representatives	3	95
*Nicaragua	National Assembly	6	96
*Norway	Storting/Lagting	4	39
	Odelsting		116
Pakistan	Parliament/Senate	6	87
	National Assembly	5	237
Panama	Legislative Assembly	5	67
Papua New Guinea	National Parliament	5	109
Paraguay	Congress/Senate	5	30
	Chamber of Deputies	5	60
Peru	Congress/Senate	5	60
	Chamber of Deputies	5	180
*Philippines	National Assembly	6	201
*Poland	Diet	4	460
*Portugal	Assembly of the Republic	4	250

Country	Parliament/Houses	Term of office (years)	Member-ship
*Republic of Korea	National Assembly	4	276
*Romania	Grand National Assembly	5	369
*Rwanda	National Development Council	5	70
St Kitts-Nevis	National Assembly	5	16
Saint Lucia	Houses of Parliament/Senate	5	11
	House of Assembly	5	17
*St Vincent and the Grenadines	House of Assembly	5	19
Samoa	Legislative Assembly	3	47
San Marino	Great General Council	5	60
Sao Tome and Principe	People's National Assembly	5	40
*Senegal	National Assembly	5	120
Seychelles	People's Assembly	4	25
Sierra Leone	House of Representatives	5	104
Singapore	Parliament	5	79
*Solomon Islands	National Parliament	4	38
*Somalia	People's Assembly	5	178
*South Africa	Parliament/House of Assembly	5	178
	House of Representatives	5	85
	House of Delegates	5	45
*Spain	General Courts/Senate	4	256
	Congress of Deputies	4	350
*Sri Lanka	Parliament	6	196
Suriname	Parliament	2.25	31
Swaziland	Parliament/Senate	5	20
	House of Assembly	5	50
*Sweden	Parliament	3	349

Country	Parliament/Houses	Term of office (years)	Member-ship
*Switzerland	Federal Assembly/States Council	4	46
	National Council	4	200
*Syrian Arab Republic	People's Council	4	195
*Thailand	National Assembly/Senate	6	243
	House of Representatives	4	324
Togo	National Assembly	5	67
Tonga	Legislative Assembly	3	28
Trinidad and Tobago	Parliament/Senate	5	31
	House of Representatives	5	36
*Tunisia	Chamber of Deputies	5	136
Turkey	Turkish Grand National Assembly	5	400
Tuvalu	Parliament of Tuvalu	4	13
*Uganda	National Assembly	5	156
*USSR	Supreme Soviet/Soviet of Nationalities	5	750
	Soviet of the Union	5	750
United Arab Emirates	Federal National Council	2	40
*United Kingdom	Parliament/House of Lords	(c)	1,183
	House of Commons	5	650
*United Republic of Tanzania	National Assembly	5	239
*United States of America	Congress/Senate	6	100
	House of Representatives	2	435
Uruguay	General Assembly/Senate	5	31
	Chamber of Representatives	5	99
*Vanuatu	Parliament	4	39
Venezuela	Congress of the Republic/Senate	5	47
	Chamber of Deputies	5	200
Viet Nam	National Assembly	5	496

(c) Continuous

Country	Parliament/Houses	Term of office (years)	Member- ship
Yemen	People's Constituent Assembly	3	159
*Yugoslavia	Assembly of the SFR/Federal Chamber	4	220
	Chamber of Republics and Provinces	4	88
*Zaire	Legislative Council	5	310
*Zambia	National Assembly	5	136
*Zimbabwe	Parliament/Senate	5	40
	House of Assembly	5	100

PART II

PARLIAMENT AND ITS MEMBERSHIP

TABLE 1

CHARACTERISTICS AND COMPOSITION OF PARLIAMENT

One of the most controversial questions in constitutional law concerns how many Chambers a Parliament should comprise. In practice, the choice seems simple enough: should there be one House or two, a unicameral or a bicameral system? (or perhaps as in the case of South Africa, more than two Houses?). While federal states, almost without exception, are spared this choice by reason of their peculiar constitutional structure, unitary states are free to choose the system they prefer. In our examination of Table 1 we consider, firstly, some of the factors which account for the existence of unicameral and bicameral systems and, secondly, some of the characteristics of these systems.

Unicameral Systems

Although any systematic attempt to examine the various reasons why so many countries have adopted a unicameral system (fifty-five countries out of eighty-three under study) is beyond the scope of this study, some important trends can be noted. Countries which are small in size are more likely to have one Chamber rather than two, as the problem of the balance of political power is less difficult to solve in them than it is in big countries. In the unitary socialist countries, the bicameral system is regarded as leading to complications, delays and expenses, with few, if any, compensating advantages. In the course of the twentieth century, the Scandinavian countries have all replaced bicameral systems with unicameral ones. The Constitution of Norway, however, originally drawn up in 1814, presents an interesting example of a Parliament possessing certain characteristics of two-Chamber Parliaments. Unicameral Parliaments are predominant in a number of countries which have recently achieved independence, and which are politically evolving in circumstances very different from those found in Western Europe when parliamentary government was born.

Evolution of Bicameral Systems

The earliest example of a bicameral system occurred in England towards the end of the thirteenth century. It began with the institution of a Chamber for the high aristocracy and brought together the feudal magnates, the Lords Spiritual and Temporal. This arrangement has been maintained to the present day, although the aristocratic character of the House of Lords has been reduced by the appointment to it of Life Peers. Furthermore, the power of the House of Lords has been greatly restricted in favour of the popular House, the House of Commons.

13

At present, the bicameral system can no longer be explained by the need for a separate aristocratic representation. It justifies itself by two main arguments:

- in federal states, the bicameralism reflects the dualist structure of the state;
- in unitary states, the adoption of bicameralism reflects the desire, either to have within the parliamentary machine an in-built mechanism in the form of a so-called "revising" Chamber to maintain a careful check on the sometimes hasty decisions of a first Chamber, or, to achieve a more stable balance between the Legislature and the Executive as the unbridled power of a single Chamber is likely to be restrained by the creation of a second Chamber on a different basis.

Federalism and Bicameralism

The relationship between federalism and bicameralism can be seen from Table 1A. It can be seen that while fifty-four of sixty-six unitary states have adopted a unicameral legislature, only one of the federal states (Comoros) has this arrangement. Why is federalism so closely associated

TABLE 1A. Federalism and Bicameralism

Structure of Parliament	Structure of State		
	Unitary	Federal	Total
Unicameral	54	1	55
Bicameral	12	16	28
Total	66	17	83

with bicameralism? In federal systems bicameralism is the obvious legislative arrangement because these systems have, by definition, a two-tier structure. One of these structures is the nation as a complete entity, the other the several states of the federation with their particular characteristics. Within the national Parliament these tiers are inevitably translated into two separate Chambers, the first emanating from the people as a whole, the second made up of members representing each state.

Historically, federal bicameralism came about as the result of a compromise between two schools of thought in the Philadelphia Convention of 1787 which, starting from the hypothesis that there was to be only one Chamber, disagreed upon the number of members in it that each State should have. The Connecticut Compromise gave rise to a bicameral system in which each State achieved equal representation (irrespective of its population) in the upper Chamber, and representation in the lower Chamber proportional to its population.

Today, the federal systems of Argentina, Australia, Brazil, Mexico, Switzerland, and United States of America, reflect this arrangement in the composition of their bicameral Parliaments. In Czechoslovakia it is maintained in the equal representation of two Republics in the Chamber of Nations, and in Yugoslavia the Republics and Autonomous Provinces are represented in both Chambers by an equal number of delegates (although differing for each Chamber) but the level on which they are elected - communal assemblies for the Federal (popular) Chamber, and Republican and Provincial Assemblies for the Chamber of Republics and Provinces - is different. In the remaining federal states with bicameral Parliaments (Austria, Belgium, Canada, the Federal Republic of Germany, India, Malaysia, Spain and USSR), the original federal principle has been modified in such a way that the various units of the federation (whether provinces, regions, autonomous republics, states or whatever) are all guaranteed some, but not equal, representation in one of the Chambers, depending on their status and population.

Unitary States and Bicameralism

In unitary states the nature of the second Chamber in some cases reflects the conscious or unconscious desires of those who framed the Constitution to temper the democratic aggressiveness of the first Chamber with a representative body of a more "conservative" character. In some countries with a unicameral Parliament advice must be sought from another assembly. For example in Comoros, Egypt and Luxembourg, the Island Councils, the popularly-elected Shoura or the Council of State, respectively, must be consulted during the legislative process (see Table 30). Similarly in Zambia the House of Chiefs may submit resolutions to Parliament on Bills and other matters. The nature of this conservatism can be further considered in two ways, firstly by comparing the powers that the two Chambers have (we postpone this comparison to Table 30) and, secondly, by comparing the composition of the Chambers.

Composition of Parliaments

From Table 1B we can examine the way in which the conservative character of federal or upper Chambers is revealed by their election or appointment. While the composition of almost all of the popular and only Chambers is determined by direct election (eighty out of eighty-three Parliaments, the exceptions being China, Cuba and Yugoslavia), the composition of the federal or upper Chambers is noticeably different. In only twelve out of twenty-eight of these Chambers are the majority of Members directly elected.

In the Bahamas, Canada, Fiji, Jordan and Thailand, all the Senators are appointed by the Head of State, as are the majority of Senators in Malaysia. In Argentina, Austria, the Federal Republic of Germany, India, Netherlands and Yugoslavia, most or all of the Members of the federal or upper Chamber are appointed by local units. In France and Zimbabwe, most or all Senators are elected by electoral colleges consisting of Members of the popular Chamber and of provincial councils; and in the United Kingdom, the majority of members of the House of Lords are hereditary Peers. In Ireland, most of the members of the Senate are elected from five panels representing vocational interests, while some Senators are elected by the Universities.

TABLE 1B. Elective and Appointive Bases of Parliament

Bases of Composition of Chambers	Number of Countries	
	Federal or Upper Chambers	Popular (or only) Chamber
Most directly elected	12	80
All or most elected by local units	6	3
Most elected by local units and the popular Chamber	1	0
Most elected by the other Chamber	1	0
Most elected by other bodies	1	0
All or most appointed by Head of State	6	0
Ex-officio Members (UK House of Lords)	1	0
Total	28	83

In Norway all Members of the Storting are popularly elected. At the first meeting of the Storting after each election, the 155 Members of the Storting choose from among themselves 39 Members to form the Lagting, the remaining 116 Members forming the Odelsting.

In Yugoslavia, a very particular system of representation is adopted for both Chambers. It is based on the principle of collective representation, in the form of a series of interdependent delegations elected one from the other at all levels of socio-political life (place of work or residence, communal assembly, provincial assembly, republican assembly, federal assembly). Delegates to the SFRY Assembly are therefore, although actually indirectly elected by either communal assemblies (Federal Chamber) or Republican and Provincial Assemblies (Chamber of Republics and Provinces), simultaneously spokesmen of the citizens to this highest assembly as well as of the delegation of which they are members. This delegation, in some particular cases of decision-making in the Chamber of Republics and Provinces, may even take position as one entity and represent one vote.

Size of Parliaments

The size of each of the two Chambers is presented in Table 1C. The number of members in the various Chambers differs considerably. The Diet of Liechtenstein (with 15 Members) is the smallest of the popular (or only) Chambers under consideration, China (2,978) the largest. The Bahamas Senate (16) is the smallest of the upper Chambers, the House of

Lords (1,183) in the United Kingdom, the largest. Two factors which influence the determination of how many members a Chamber will have are, the geographical and environmental conditions of a country and the size of the population of that country.

TABLE 1C. Number of Members of Parliament

	Number of Countries	
Number of Members	Federal or Upper Chamber	Popular (or only) Chamber
1-99	14	22
100-199	5	25
200-299	5	11
300-399	2	8
400-499	0	8
500-599	0	5
600 or more	2	4
Total	28	83

The first of these factors has an effect through desires to achieve adequate representation for both rural and urban areas, and for the different social, economic, ethnic, linguistic, religious, cultural, occupational and other groupings. No system can ideally represent all of these areas or groupings, but, other things being equal, a physically small and socially homogeneous country is likely to have a small legislature, and a physically large and socially heterogeneous country a large legislature.

Population and Size of Parliaments

In addition to a country's social and geographical features, the size of its population will also affect the size of its Legislature. Central to the theory of representational democracy is the idea that legislators represent populations, irrespective of the various social and other characteristics of these populations. The difficult tasks of the individual legislator can be much simplified by ensuring that he does not have to represent too large a section of the total population, and by ensuring that this population is not dispersed over too wide an area. The size of the various legislatures reflects these concerns. In Table 1D we present information on the average number of Members in the popular Chamber against population.

The findings are unambiguous. The larger the population of a country, the larger is its Legislature. This relationship is not perfect, and one could not expect it to be as there are ceilings on the minimum and maximum number of members which a Legislature can realistically contain.

TABLE 1D. Relationship Between Population and Size of Legislature

Population in Millions	Average Number of Members in the Popular House	Number of Countries
Up to 1	40	13
1 to 10	162	32
11 to 20	228	13
21 to 40	300	9
41 to 60	445	7
61 to 80	459	2
81 to 100	–	0
100 to 200	483	3
Over 200	1,177	4
		Total 83

Term of Office of Parliament

The statutory term of office of a Parliament is also related to repre-sentational democracy. In theory, elections to a Parliament should not be so infrequent that they fail to reflect the opinions of the electorate, nor be so frequent that they are likely to produce excessive discontinuities in the process of government. The statutory term of office of the vari-ous Chambers is presented in Table 1E, where it can be seen that almost all popular Chambers have a maximum term of office of four or five years. It is noticeable that, in about half of the bicameral Parliaments, members are elected or appointed to federal or upper Chambers for longer periods than their counterparts in popular Chambers. This is another indication of the conservative nature of these Chambers. In the United Kingdom for example, members of the House of Lords are ap-pointed for life, and in the Canadian Senate until optional or compulsory retirement (depending on when they were appointed) at the age of 75. The term of office of members of the federal Chambers in Austria and the Federal Republic of Germany is not constant. In Austria the term of office of a Member of the Federal Council is determined by the term of office (either 5 or 6 years) of the provincial Legislature which delegates him. The term of office of Members of the Federal Council in the Federal Republic of Germany is consequent on the formation of new State Govern-ments following State elections.

In fourteen of the twenty-four federal or upper Chambers with fixed terms of office, all of the members are elected (or appointed) at the same time. Members of the remaining ten upper Chambers are elected at dif-ferent times, it being usual for one-third or one-half of them to be elec-ted every two or three years. The staggering of elections enables shifts in the opinions of the electorate to be more accurately reflected, the longer term of office having the effect of not giving too great an empha-sis to these shifts.

TABLE 1E. Statutory Length of Office of Parliaments

Length of Office (in years)	Number of Countries	
	Federal or Upper Chamber	Popular (or only) Chamber
2	0	1
3	1	6
4	6	26
5	6	47*
6	7	3
7	0	0
8	1	0
9	2	0
Variable	3	0
Life or retirement	2	0
Total	28	83

* Includes South Africa 2 Chambers being counted as 1.

The Electoral System

One of the major problems of electoral systems is to determine how the parliamentary seats to be allotted to the parties and candidates reflect the votes cast by the electorate. Two main types of electoral system exist: majority systems, with one or two ballots, in which the candidate or candidates obtaining most votes are elected; systems of proportional representation in which the seats are divided up among the lists or parties in proportion to the number of votes obtained by each. The common feature of the various majority systems is that under them large parties are advantaged and small parties disadvantaged with the result that both local and national minorities obtain only indirect and approximate representation. In contrast, systems of proportional representation are considered to guarantee to both large and small parties parliamentary representation proportional to their electoral strength. The choice made between the two types of electoral systems, far from being purely technical in character, is frequently made on political grounds affecting, as it does, the nature of representation in a Parliament.

Evolution of Electoral Systems

For a long period methods of voting were not a matter of controversy. Parliamentary tradition, especially in the Anglo-Saxon countries, managed with the simplest system of all, namely, election in a single ballot by a simple majority (or plurality vote). This system can be summed up in the phrase "first past the post". But in the second half of the nineteenth century, the efforts of the supporters of proportional representation began to show results. By 1891 and 1892 it had been adopted in some of the Swiss cantons; in 1893 it was adopted in Belgium; in 1906 in Finland, and in 1909 in Sweden. Gradually, it spread throughout Europe as political systems changed following two world wars. Outside Europe, proportional representation has not become so widespread although it is used, for example, in elections for the Parliament of Israel, and for the upper Chamber of India. Any discussion of types of electoral systems must be concerned with the way the voter is asked to choose between candidates in the election as well as the formula by which the seats are attributed to the winning candidates on the basis of the votes cast by the electorate.

Categorical and Ordinal Ballots

At the polling booth the voter may be asked to cast his ballot in either a categorical or an ordinal manner. A categorical ballot requires the voter to prefer one party or candidate as opposed to all others. Whether he votes for individual candidates (as, for example, in Canada, Czechoslovakia and New Zealand) or for party lists of candidates (as, for example, in Belgium, Cameroon and Costa Rica) his vote cannot be divided between competing individuals or parties. In contrast an ordinal ballot does not require the voter to make an unequivocal choice between parties or individuals but allows him to distribute his vote among them in any way he chooses.

There are three main types of ordinal ballots:
- preferential voting within one list where the voter is required to express a preference for candidates within the list he chooses, as in Austria, and Italy (Chamber of Deputies);
- alternative voting where the voter is required to rank the candidates, from different parties, in his order of preference, as in Australia, Ireland and Malta; and
- list ballot with vote-splitting where the voter is allowed to award his preferences to candidates appearing on different lists of candidates, as in Denmark and Switzerland (National Council).

Majority Representation

The second major feature of electoral systems concerns the formula by which the seats are attributed to the winning candidates on the basis of the votes cast by the electorate (Table 1F). Different electoral systems

TABLE 1F. Types of Electoral Systems
(Popular or Only Chamber)

System	Number of Countries
Simple Majority	35
Absolute Majority	11
Alternative Transfer (preferential) Vote)	3
Proportional	30
Mixed	3
Total	82*

* Excludes Yugoslavia, where the Members of the Federal Chamber are elected by communal assemblies.

20

require different majorities. In most countries a simple majority (or plurality) of the votes cast is sufficient to win a seat; in others, this is raised to an absolute majority (as in many of the socialist countries); and in still others, to a majority achieved by the alternative transferable (or preferential) vote system, which is in fact a variation of the majority system but tending to confer on it certain characteristics of proportional representation.

Most electoral systems require the majority to be achieved on the first and only ballot, as under the simple majority and the single transferable vote systems. Other countries have provisions for a second ballot if no candidate obtains the necessary majority on the first. Where provisions exist for two ballots (as in Comoros and Monaco) a candidate must obtain an absolute majority of the votes cast in order to be elected at the first ballot. If no candidate obtains this majority at the first ballot, a second ballot is held where the candidate obtaining a simple majority is declared the winner. In many of the socialist countries the electoral law provides for a second ballot and, if necessary, more ballots if, at the first ballot, a candidate does not obtain an absolute majority of the votes cast or if the number of votes cast is less than half the number of electors on the register.

Proportional Representation

By contrast, under systems of proportional representation, the number of votes that a candidate or list must obtain is determined by the electoral formula. As these formulae are both extremely complex and differ from country to country, it is impossible to do more than to mention the main types of them. The d'Hondt highest average (found, for example, in Argentina and Belgium), and the Hagenbach-Bischoff method (Italy and Switzerland). Some countries (for example, Denmark and the Netherlands) combine those systems, and the electoral systems of the Federal Republic of Germany, Japan and Mexico combine features of both majority and proportional systems. The many variations of method testify to the difficulty of putting into practice a system which is very simple in principle.

The electoral system reflects each country's politics of which it is both cause and effect. Majority voting is frequently associated with a two-party system, proportional representation with a multi-party system. The objective of all electoral systems should be to ensure the best representation possible and, in particular, to safeguard the representation of minorities.

Filling Vacancies

The filling of seats which become vacant through reasons of death or resignation during the lifetime of a legislature, is the subject of Table 1G. Three methods of filling vacant seats are encountered:

- vacancies are filled by a substitute who is designated at the same time as the titular candidate (as in Belgium, Mexico and Sweden);

- by the next-in-line candidate of the party whose Member formerly held the seat (as in Costa Rica, Finland and Israel); and
- by holding a by-election (as in Cameroon, USSR, United Kingdom).

The first two of these methods share an element of conservatism, as vacancies are filled on the basis of the electorate's preference at the preceding election; the latter is more responsive in that it takes into account whatever shifts in the electorate's preferences might have occurred since the last election.

TABLE 1G. Electoral Systems and Filling of Vacancies

Methods of Filling Vacancies	Type of Electoral System			
	Proportional Representation	Majority	Mixed	Total
Substitutes	6	5	1	12
Next-in-line of party holding seat	14	4	4	22
By-election	6	41	0*	47
Total	26	50	5	81**

* Mexico, Republic of Korea and Switzerland may also hold by-elections.
** Information on Indonesia and Ivory Coast not available.

The method chosen to fill vacant seats is largely determined by the type of electoral system in force, as Table 1G reveals. In most of the countries with a majority electoral system, vacant seats are filled by by-elections. In only six countries with systems of proportional representation is this method used.

Proclamation and Validation of Elections

The counting of the ballot papers does not signify the end of the election. Three further processes must be completed. Firstly, the results of the election must be officially proclaimed. Secondly, some authority must validate the election of each Member. Thirdly, any disputes which may have arisen concerning the electoral regulations or irregularities in the conduct of the election must be settled. Once a candidate has been declared elected and has his election validated, he may take his seat in Parliament providing his election is not disputed, and he does not have to resolve an incompatible occupation (which is examined in Table 2).

Despite stringent precautions, there is always the risk that an election result may be falsified by some form of fraud. However rare the possibility of fraud or error in the electoral process, there must be an opportunity to question, within a specified period, the regularity of an election. The electors or the unsuccessful candidates have the right to contest the election and to obtain a decision which either confirms the result or declares it null, and which either authorises another election or provides for the direct replacement of the candidate who has been declared irregularly elected. Two distinct stages are involved here, firstly, the validation of elections, secondly, the settling of disputes concerning them.

Validation of Elections

The authorities responsible for the validation of elections are shown in Table 1H. In several countries Parliament itself performs this role.

TABLE 1H. Validation of Elections

	Number of Houses	
Authority Reponsible	Upper	Lower
Parliament or Parliamentary Committee	6	26
National Election Authority	3	26
Constituency Electoral Board or Returning Officer	4	12
Judiciary, Constitutional Court or Council	2	12
Government	0	2
State Governor or State Legislature	3	1
Other	1	2
None or NA	7	0
Total	26*	81*

* Information not available for Argentina and Spain.

Parliament is considered to be the sovereign body in the nation and, as a consequence, no interference by other public bodies, especially the Executive, is considered proper in the designation of its Members. In, for example, Algeria, Czechoslovakia, Netherlands and Romania, special committees of Parliament have been established to validate the election of Members. In Fiji, Gabon, Kuwait, Mali, Malta and Senegal, the verification of the credentials of Members is undertaken by the Supreme or Constitutional Court (or its equivalent), and in Brazil and Costa Rica by judicial authorities especially established to settle disputed elections. The publication of the election results in the Official Gazette serves the purpose of validating results in Monaco. National election authorities and constituency electoral bureaus perform this task in other countries. Generally, these bodies are additionally responsible for counting the ballots and/or proclaiming the election results. In the United Kingdom, the validation of results is undertaken by the Clerk of the Crown, and in the United States by the Governor of each State.

TABLE 1 : CHARACTERISTICS AND COMPOSITION OF PARLIAMENT

1.1 Name of country and Parliament	1.2 Name(s) of House(s)	1.3 Normal term of office (years)	1.4 a) Total membership b) Million population	1.5 Membership: a) Elected b) Appointed c) Ex-officio
ALGERIA (ALGERIE) National People's Assembly (APN) (Assemblée populaire nationale APN)	National People's Assembly (Assemblée populaire nationale APN)	5	a) 282 b) 22	a) 282 b) 0 c) 0
ARGENTINA National Congress (Congreso Nacional)	Senate (Senado)	9 (1/3 election every 3 years).	a) 46	a) 46 b) 0 c) 0
	Chamber of Deputies (Cámara de Diputados)	4 (1/2 election every 2 years).	a) 254 b) 28.5	a) 254 b) 0 c) 0
AUSTRALIA Parliament of the Commonwealth	Senate	6 (1/2 election every 3 years, often but not necessarily coincident with House of Reps elections)	a) 76	a) 76 b) 0 c) 0
	House of Representatives	3	a) 148 b) 15.6	a) 148 b) 0 c) 0

1.6 Features of electoral system or appointment	1.7 Filling casual vacancies	1.8 Authority responsible for validating elections
Universal, direct, suffrage following party proposals. APN members are elected by simple majority from a single list established by the Front de Libération Nationale (National Liberation Front FLN) which presents three times the number of candidates than seats to be filled.	By-elections	Committee for the validation of mandates (20 members) elected by the APN
Indirect election by local legis-latures, simple majority system. Senators of the Federal Capital elected by a "Junta Electoral" (d'Hondt method). Direct election, list system, proportional representation (d'Hondt method).	The Const. pro-vides for by-elec-tions but in prac-tice vacancies are filled under the electoral law by substitutes elected at the same time as the Members replaced.	
Direct election, proportional representation. Successful candidates must gain a quota determined by dividing total valid first preference votes by one more that the number of seats to be filled and adding 1 to the number so obtained. Remaining seats are filled by distribution of preferences.	Nomination by the Parliament of the State from which the Senator whose seat falls vacant was originally elected.	Governor of each State must certify election of Senators to represent State.
Direct election. Alternative transferable vote in single-member constituencies.	By-elections	Divisional Returning Officer

TABLE 1 : CHARACTERISTICS AND COMPOSITION OF PARLT (continued)

1.1 Name of country and Parliament	1.2 Name(s) of House(s)	1.3 Normal term of office (years)	1.4 a) Total membership b) Million population	1.5 Membership: a) Elected b) Appointed c) Ex-officio
AUSTRIA (ÖSTERREICH) Parliament (Parlament)	Federal Council (Bundesrat)	5 or 6 (depending on the term of the provincial legislatures which elect the Members).	a) 63	a) 63 b) 0 c) 0
	National Council (Nationalrat)	4	a) 183 b) 7.6	a) 183 b) 0 c) 0
BAHAMAS (BAHAMAS) Parliament	Senate	5 (co-terminous).	a) 16	a) 0 b) 16 c) 0
	House of Assembly		a) 43 b) 0.237	a) 43 b) 0 c) 0

1.6 Features of electoral system or appointment	1.7 Filling casual vacancies	1.8 Authority responsible for validating elections
Proportional representation system; Members and alternates elected by provincial legislatures.	By alternates	President of the relevant provincial legislature
Direct election; list system with proportional representation.	By next-in-line of party which formerly held the seat.	Central electoral authority (headed by the Federal Minister for Home Affairs).
Appointed by Governor-General on advice of Prime Minister – 9; on advice of Leader of Opposition – 4; on advice of Prime Minister after consultation with Leader of Opposition – 3.	Appointed by the Governor-General in a like manner to the way the seat was filled under 1.6 following the last dissolution of Parliament.	NA
Direct election; simple majority system.	By-elections	Returning Officer

TABLE 1 : CHARACTERISTICS AND COMPOSITION OF PARLT (continued)

1.1 Name of country and Parliament	1.2 Name(s) of House(s)	1.3 Normal term of office (years)	1.4 a) Total membership b) Million population	1.5 Membership: a) Elected b) Appointed c) Ex-officio
BELGIUM (BELGIQUE) (BELGIEN) Legislative Chambers (Chambres Législatives/Wetgevende Kamers)	Senate (Sénat/Senaat)	4 (co-terminous).	a) 182	a) 106 directly elected 50 indirectly elected b) 25 co-opted c) 1 (King's son or Crown Prince)
	Chamber of Representatives (Chambre des Représentants/ Kamer van Volksvertegenwoordigers)		a) 212 b) 9.85	a) 212 b) 0 c) 0
BRAZIL (BRASIL) National Congress (Congreso Nacional)	Federal Senate (Senado Federal)	8 (election every 4 years renewing alternately 1/3 and 2/3 Senators).	a) 69	a) 47 b) 22 (one for each State) c) 0
	Chamber of Deputies (Câmara dos Deputados)	4 (elections simultaneous with Senate).	a) 479 b) 128	a) 479 b) 0 c) 0

1.6 Features of electoral system or appointment	1.7 Filling casual vacancies	1.8 Authority responsible for validating elections
a) Direct election for the Senate and Chamber of Representatives. List system with proportional representation (d'Hondt method). Each elector votes for the head of the list or an individual candidate within the list. Seats won are allocated to candidates receiving at least the minimum number of votes required (i.e. the quota). b) Indirect election of the Senators by provincial councils. List system with proportional representation (d'Hondt method). c) Co-option by the Senate. List system with proportional representation (d'Hondt method).	For 1.6 a): appointment of a substitute elected at the same time as the sitting member or if no substitute a by-election. For 1.6 b) provincial council by-election. For 1.6 c): a fresh co-option.	Parliament (each House respectively).
Direct election. Simple majority. When 1/3 of Senate seats are open one candidate is voted for. On alternate elections, when 2/3 of Senate seats are renewed, each elector votes for two candidates.	For the relevant State, next at the previous election in number of votes.	Electoral Tribunals; Regional Electoral Tribunals; Superior Electoral Tribunal.
Direct election. Party-list system with seats alloted proportionally to lists according to method of highest average. Seats are subsequently awarded to the candidates with most preferential votes.		

TABLE 1 : CHARACTERISTICS AND COMPOSITION OF PARLT (continued)

1.1 Name of country and Parliament	1.2 Name(s) of House(s)	1.3 Normal term of office (years)	1.4 a) Total membership b) Million population	1.5 Membership: a) Elected b) Appointed c) Ex-officio
BULGARIA National Assembly (Narodno Sobranie)	National Assembly (Narodno Sobranie). The National Coun- cil is the supreme con- tinuing body of the National Assembly (see 28.1 and 39.1).	5	a) 400 b) 8.93	a) 400 b) 0 c) 0
CAMEROON (CAMEROUN) National Assembly (Assemblée Nationale)	National Assembly (Assemblée Nationale)	5	a) 120 b) 9 (1976)	a) 120 b) 0 c) 0
CANADA Parliament of Canada (Parlement du Canada)	Senate (Sénat)	Until 75 years of age	a) 104	a) 0 b) 104 c) 0
	House of Commons (Chambre des Communes)	5	a) 282 b) 24.3	a) 282 b) 0 c) 0
CAPE VERDE (CABO VERDE) People's National Assembly (Assembleia Nacional Popular)	Assembly (Assembleia)	5	a) 63 b) 0.30	a) 63 b) 0 c) 0

1.6 Features of electoral system or appointment	1.7 Filling casual vacancies	1.8 Authority responsible for validating elections
Direct election in single-member constituencies. If no candidate obtains an absolute majority on the 1st ballot, or if less than an absolute majority of registered electors have voted, subsequent ballots are held until requirements are met.	By-elections	Parliament
Direct election by universal suffrage. Simple majority vote for a party-list on which each party presents as many candidates as there are seats.	By-elections for which at least 2 seats must be vacant in the administrative region at least 1 year before end of Parlt.	Electoral Commission
Senators are summoned by the Governor-General.	Appointment by the Governor General on advice of Prime Minister and Cabinet.	NA
Direct election. Simple majority system in single-member constituencies.	By-elections	Chief Electoral Officer
Direct, free, universal ballot with simple majority, single list system where any citizen may add to or amend the list.	Next candidate on the list for the last election	National Electoral Commission

TABLE 1 : CHARACTERISTICS AND COMPOSITION OF PARLT (continued)

1.1 Name of country and Parliament	1.2 Name(s) of House(s)	1.3 Normal term of office (years)	1.4 a) Total membership b) Million population	1.5 Membership: a) Elected b) Appointed c) Ex-officio
CHINA National People's Congress (NPC)	National People's Congress of the People's Republic of China (NPC)	5	a) 2,978 b) 1,032	a) 2,978 b) 0 c) 0
COMOROS Islamic Federal Republic Federal Assembly (Assemblée Fédérale)	Federal Assembly (Assemblée Fédérale)	5	a) 38 b) 0.4	a) 38 b) 0 c) 0
CONGO People's National Assembly (Assemblée Nationale Populaire ANP)	People's National Assembly (Assemblée Nationale Populaire ANP)	5	a) 153 b) 1.5	a) 153 b) 0 c) 0
COSTA RICA Legislative Assembly (Asamblea Legislativa)	Legislative Assembly (Asamblea Legislativa)	4	a) 57 b) 2.0	a) 57 b) 0 c) 0

1.6 Features of electoral system or appointment	1.7 Filling casual vacancies	1.8 Authority responsible for validating elections
Simple majority vote of respective electoral unit, but if number of successful candidates exceeds number of seats to be filled, those obtaining most votes are considered elected; if insufficient, another election is held among unelected candidates and those obtaining most votes (provided no less than 1/3 votes cast) are elected. Electoral units are: People's Congresses of 21 provinces, 5 autonomous regions, 3 municipalities directly under Central Govt, and Armed Forces. All minority nationalities are entitled to appropriate representation.	By-elections in the electoral unit or when not in session, in its Standing Cttee.	NPC Standing Cttee (see 9.1) on basis of report from its credentials cttee.
Direct election. System of absolute majority, in two ballots, for single-member constituencies.	By-elections	Constitutional Council
Direct election by universal suffrage. Simple majority system, single constituency (one national list).	By-elections within 3 months if fewer Members remaining than 1/2 plus 1 of the seats but not 1 year before Parlt term ends.	Minister of the Interior.
Direct election. List system with proportional representation (quota is number of seats divided by total votes). First round unfilled seats distributed in order of remaining votes. Some remaining votes may be awarded by Supreme Electoral Tribunal to minorities polling more than 1/2 a quota.	By next-in-line of party which previously held the seat.	Supreme Electoral Tribunal

33

TABLE 1 : CHARACTERISTICS AND COMPOSITION OF PARLT (continued)

1.1 Name of country and Parliament	1.2 Name(s) of House(s)	1.3 Normal term of office (years)	1.4 a) Total membership b) Million population	1.5 Membership: a) Elected b) Appointed c) Ex-officio
CUBA National Assembly of People's Power (Asamblea Nacional del Poder Popular)	National Assembly of People's Power (Asamblea Nacional del Poder Popular)	5	a) 499 b) 9.7	a) 499 b) 0 c) 0
CYPRUS House of Representatives (Vouli ton Antiprosopon)	House of Representatives (Vouli ton Antiprosopon)	5	a) 50 b) 0.66	a) 50 b) 0 c) 0
CZECHOSLOVAKIA (CESKOSLO-VENSKE) Federal Assembly (Federální shromáž-dění)	Chamber of Nations (Sněmovna národů)	5 (terms end to-gether under the Const.).	a) 150	a) 150 b) 0 c) 0 (75 from Czech and 75 from Slovak Social-ist Republics)
	Chamber of the People (Sněmovna lidu)		a) 200 b) 15.5	a) 200 b) 0 c) 0
DEMOCRATIC YEMEN Supreme People's Council (Majlis Al-Sh'ab Al-A'la)	Supreme People's Council	5	a) 111 b) 1.8	a) 111 b) 0 c) 0
DENMARK (DANMARK) Folketing (Folketinget)	Folketing (Folketinget)	4	a) 179 b) 5.1	a) 179 b) 0 c) 0
EGYPT People's Assembly	People's Assembly	5	a) 458 b) 45	a) 448 b) 10* c) 0 (*by President of Republic).

34

1.6 Features of electoral system or appointment	1.7 Filling casual vacancies	1.8 Authority responsible for validating elections
Indirect election by members of the Municipal Assemblies. Absolute majority. Proportional representation system. 1 seat per 20,000 inhabitants or fraction over 10,000 in each municipality by single untransferable vote.	By-elections	Parliament
Direct election. Universal suffrage, complex system of proportional representation. Electors vote for a party indicating preference for up to 3 candidates (except leader) or for either a party or an independent. Seats subsequently allocated to parties and candidates by formula involving percentage of valid votes and party gradings after distribution of 1st and 2nd preferences.	Next-in-line after successful candidate on list of the party of the previous seat holder.	Returning Officer
Direct election for both Chambers. Absolute majority system in single-member constituencies. If an absolute majority is not obtained on the first ballot a second ballot is held within 15 days.	By-elections	Mandate and immunities cttee of each Chamber
Free, universal, equal and direct election. List system, with single transferable vote.	By-elections	Supreme Commission for Elections
Direct election, list system with proportional representation.	By substitutes	Folketing
Party-list proportional representation system with universal ballot.	Next-in-line on party-list or his substitute, or appointment as appropriate.	People's Assembly

TABLE 1 : CHARACTERISTICS AND COMPOSITION OF PARLT (continued)

1.1 Name of country and Parliament	1.2 Name(s) of House(s)	1.3 Normal term of office (years)	1.4 a) Total membership b) Million population	1.5 Membership: a) Elected b) Appointed c) Ex-officio
FIJI Parliament of Fiji	Senate	6	a) 22	a) 0 b) 22 c) 0
	House of Representatives	5	a) 52 b) 0.6	a) 52 b) 0 c) 0
FINLAND Parliament (Eduskunta)	Parliament (Eduskunta)	4	a) 200 b) 4.8	a) 200 b) 0 c) 0
FRANCE Parliament (Parlement)	Senate (Sénat)	9 (1/3 of member- ship retires every 3 years)	a) 317 (296- metropolitan departments 8-overseas departments 3-overseas territories 2-collective territories 8-represent- atives of French citi- zens living out of France)	a) 317 b) 0 c) 0
	National Assembly (Assemblée Nationale)	5	a) 577 b) 55.0	a) 577 b) 0 c) 0

1.6 Features of electoral system or appointment	1.7 Filling casual vacancies	1.8 Authority responsible for validating elections
Governor–General appoints Senators on advice: Great Council of Chiefs (8); Prime Minister (7); Leader of Opposition (6); Council of Rotuma (1).	Appointment by Governor–General on advice of relevant body (see 1.6).	NA
Universal suffrage, simple majority, by electors on 3 ethnic rolls and a national roll. MPs are elected from and by each roll as follows: Fijians 12, Indians 12, others 3, with 10, 10 and 5 respectively from national roll.	By-elections	Supreme Court
Direct election, proportional representation from party lists of candidates. Seats distributed among parties or alliances according to d'Hondt method of highest average. For distribution of seats within each list, candidates are ranked according to votes each received.	Next–in–line of Party formerly holding the seat	Central election board of each constituency
Indirect election by electoral colleges (National Assembly Deputies, General Councillors and delegates of the Municipal Councils). Absolute majority on 1st ballot, simple on 2nd in departments with 4 or less seats. Electors vote for as many candidates as constituency seats. List system with proportional representation in the 9 departments with 5 or more seats. Seats won are attributed in list order. Citizens outside France represented by Senators elected by an electoral college (High Council of French people overseas) using list system.	Next–in–line on the list (by-elections if no substitute is available or the list is exhausted). Proportional representation uses the method of highest average.	Constitutional Council
Direct election. From 1986, proportional representation from party lists of candidates. Seats distributed at departmental level between lists according to highest average method from a single ballot.	Next–in–line on the list (by-elections if the list is exhausted).	

TABLE 1 : CHARACTERISTICS AND COMPOSITION OF PARLT (continued)

1.1 Name of country and Parliament	1.2 Name(s) of House(s)	1.3 Normal term of office (years)	1.4 a) Total membership b) Million population	1.5 Membership: a) Elected b) Appointed c) Ex-officio
GABON National Assembly (Assemblée Nationale)	National Assembly (Assemblée Nationale)	5	a) 120 b) 1.5	a) 111 b) 9 c) 0
GERMAN DEMOCRATIC REPUBLIC (DEUTSCHE DEMOKRATISCHE REPUBLIK) People's Chamber (Volkskammer)	People's Chamber of the German Democratic Republic (Volkskammer der Deutschen Demokratischen Republik).	5	a) 500 b) 16.7	a) 500 b) 0 c) 0
GERMANY, FEDERAL REPUBLIC (BUNDESREPUBLIK DEUTSCHLAND) Parliament (Parlament)	Federal Council (Bundesrat)	Variable depend- ing on formation of State Councils	a) 45	a) 0 b) 41 by State Govts; 4 by Govt of W. Berlin from the respective State Councils.
	Federal Diet (Bundestag)	4	a) 518 b) 61.7	a) 496 popu- larly elected, 22 by Berlin House of Represent- atives.
GREECE (HELLAS) Chamber of Deputies (Vouli ton Ellinon)	Chamber of Deputies (Vouli ton Ellinon)	4	a) 300 b) 10.0	a) 288 (departmental list) 12 (national list) b) 0 c) 0

1.6 Features of electoral system or appointment	1.7 Filling casual vacancies	1.8 Authority responsible for validating elections
Election comprises 2 stages: Primary election by indirect suffrage with single nomination of candidate and his substitute; fol--lowed by universal, direct suffrage for candidates appearing on a regional list which may not be altered.	Substitutes	Supreme Court
Direct election. Simple majority system with each elector voting for as many candidates as there are seats to be filled in the constituency. Each elector chooses the candidates from a single list and can cross out the names of those candidates he does not favour.	By one of 179 elected successor candidates upon decision of People's Chamber	Electoral Commission
Each of the 11 States appoints as many Members as it has votes. Each State (Land) has at least 3 votes. States with more than 2 million inhabitants have 4, more than 6 million have 5.	State Govt nomination	
Direct election. Each elector has 2 votes: "First vote" for one candidate by simple majority to fill 248 seats. 'Second vote' choice of a party-list established at State (Land) level with distribution of seats by proportional representation (Niemeyer method).	Next-in-line on the party-list which formerly held the seat.	Federal Diet
Direct, universal, compulsory, ballot. Reinforced proportional representation with seats distributed in 3 successive allocations (local, regional and national levels) each of which has a different electoral quota).	Next-in-line on the list. By-elections when the list is exhausted or when a ballot is annulled by the Special Supreme Court under the electoral act.	No specific validation. An Electoral Cttee sitting in the Ministry of the interior distributes seats. Then the courts in each constituency proclaim the candidates elected.

TABLE 1 : CHARACTERISTICS AND COMPOSITION OF PARLT (continued)

1.1 Name of country and Parliament	1.2 Name(s) of House(s)	1.3 Normal term of office (years)	1.4 a) Total membership b) Million population	1.5 Membership: a) Elected b) Appointed c) Ex-officio
HUNGARY (MAGYAR) National Assembly (Országgyülés)	National Assembly (Országgyülés)	5	a) 387 b) 10.7	a) 387 b) 0 c) 0
INDIA (BHARAT) Parliament (Sansad)	Council of States (Rajya Sabha)	Permanent body not subject to dis- solution	a) 244 (250 max) 1/3 retire every 2 years	a) 232 (238 max.) b) (12 by the President of India) c) 0
	House of the People (Lok Sabha)	5	a) 544 b) 685	a) 542 b) 2 (by the President of India) c) 0
INDONESIA House of Representatives of the Republic of Indonesia (Dewan Perwalikan Rakyat Republic Indonesia)	House of Representatives of the Republic of Indonesia (Dewan Perwa- likan Rakyat Republic Indonesia)	5	a) 460 b) 147.4	a) 360 b) 100 by the President c) 0
IRELAND (EIRE) The Oireachtas	Senate (Seanad Éireann)	Elections to take place within 90 days of dissolu- tion of House of Reps.	a) 60	a) 49 b) 11 c) 0
	House of Representatives (Dáil Éireann)	5	a) 166 b) 3.4	a) 166 b) 0 c) 0
ISRAEL The Knesset (Ha-Knesset)	The Knesset (Ha-Knesset)	4	a) 120 b) 4.2	a) 120 b) 0 c) 0

1.6 Features of electoral system or appointment	1.7 Filling casual vacancies	1.8 Authority responsible for validating elections
Direct election with universal suffrage, absolute majority. At least 2 candidates must run for each of the 352 constituencies. Approximately 10 % of candidates are elected from a national list.	By-elections. Also by substitutes who have obtained at least 1/4 of the votes during election for previous seat holder.	Constituency Electoral Bureaus; Returning Offices; National Election Authority/Electoral Presidency.
Election by the elected members of State Legislative Assemblies; proportional representation by means of a single transferable vote.	By-elections	Election Commission of India
Direct election by simple majority of adult suffrage	By-elections	Proclaimed by the constituency returning officer and validated by publication in the Official Gazette.
Direct, general, free elections with proportional representation based on a party list system.	–	General Election Institution (chaired by the Minister of Home Affairs)
43 elected from panels of candidates representing vocational Interests; 6 elected by University constituencies; 11 nominated by Prime Minister. Those elected are by proportional representation by single, transferable vote.	New nomination or by-elections as appropriate	The Senate Returning Officer (Clerk of Senate) for the 43 elected from the panels; Provost or Vice-Chancellor for the 6 University members.
Universal suffrage; proportional representation system by single transferable vote.	By-elections	Returning Officer for each of the 41 constituencies.
Direct universal suffrage, list system, single constituency, proportional representation.	Next-in-line on the candidates list of relevant party or bloc	Central Elections Cttee

TABLE 1 : CHARACTERISTICS AND COMPOSITION OF PARLT (continued)

1.1 Name of country and Parliament	1.2 Name(s) of House(s)	1.3 Normal term of office (years)	1.4 a) Total membership b) Million population	1.5 Membership: a) Elected b) Appointed c) Ex-officio
ITALY (ITALIA) Parliament (Parlamento)	Senate (Senato)	5 (co-ter- minous).	a) 321 plus ex- Presidents of the Republic	a) 315 b) 6 life nominees by President of Republic c) ex- Presidents of the Republic
	Chamber of Deputies (Camera dei Deputati)		a) 630 b) 56.2	a) 630 b) 0 c) 0
IVORY COAST (COTE D'IVOIRE) National Assembly (Assemblée Nationale)	National Assembly (Assemblée Nationale)	5	a) 147 b) 8.0	a) 147 b) 0 c) 0
JAPAN (NIPPON) The Diet (Kokkai)	House of Councillors (Sangiin)	6 (half- election every 3 years).	a) 252	a) 252 b) 0 c) 0
	House of Representatives (Shugiin)	4	a) 511 b) 117.1	a) 511 b) 0 c) 0

1.6 Features of electoral system or appointment	1.7 Filling casual vacancies	1.8 Authority responsible for validating elections
Universal direct suffrage for one candidate on a list of competitors. 65 % quota ensures a seat. If quota not reached the d'Hondt system applies.	Next candidate on the same constituency list	The Senate
Universal, direct suffrage. List system with proportional representation. Allocation of seats by adjusted Hagenbach-Bischoff method. Seats not allocated by this system are assigned by a national electoral college on the basis of non allotted votes.		The Chamber of Deputies
Direct election, by universal suffrage using system of absolute majority on 2 ballots.	–	National Assembly
152 elected by direct election, simple majority system, and 100 under proportional representation system with the binding list formula.	By-elections for those directly elected, but if within 3 months of election or elected by proportional representation, the next unsuccessful candidate.	Election Management Cttees. Successful candidates are determined at the election conference. Final decision on the validity or invalidity by judicial authorities.
Direct election, simple majority system.	By-elections, but if within 3 months of election then the next unsuccessful candidate.	

TABLE 1 : CHARACTERISTICS AND COMPOSITION OF PARLT (continued)

1.1 Name of country and Parliament	1.2 Name(s) of House(s)	1.3 Normal term of office (years)	1.4 a) Total membership b) Million population	1.5 Membership: a) Elected b) Appointed c) Ex-officio
JORDAN National Assembly (Majles Al-Ummah)	House of Senate (Majles Al-ayyan)	4 (if the House of Deputies is dissolved	a) 30	a) 0 b) 30 c) 0
	House of Deputies (Majles Al-nuwab)	Senate Sessions are suspended).	a) 60 b) 2.3	a) 60 b) 0 c) 0
KENYA National Assembly (Bunge)	National Assembly (Baraza la Taifa)	5	a) 173 (including the President) b) 17	a) 158 b) 12 (Presidential appointment) c) 3 (President, Speaker, Attorney-General)
KUWAIT National Assembly (Majlis Al-Ommah)	National Assembly (Majlis Al-Ommah)	4	a) 64 b) 1.7	a) 50 b) 0 c) 14 (Ministers)
LEBANON National Assembly (Assemblée Nationale)	National Assembly (Assemblée Nationale)	4	a) 99 b) 3.1	a) 99 b) 0 c) 0
LIECHTENSTEIN Diet (Landtag)	Diet (Landtag)	4	a) 15 b) 0.026	a) 15 b) 0 c) 0
LUXEMBOURG Chamber of Deputies (Chambre des députés)	Chamber of Deputies (Chambre des députés)	5	a) 64 b) 0.36	a) 64 b) 0 c) 0

1.6 Features of electoral system or appointment	1.7 Filling casual vacancies	1.8 Authority responsible for validating elections
Appointed by Royal Decree	Appointment for remainder of predecessor's term	NA
Direct election, proportional representation, list system.	By-elections or when compelling circumstances prevent elections, by absolute majority of the Assembly.	House of Deputies
Direct election. Simple majority system in single-member constituencies.	By-elections	Election Supervisor
Simple majority list system (2 seats in 25 constituencies). Universal male suffrage.	By-elections	Constitutional Court
Direct election by universal suffrage. Simple majority list system.	By-elections within 2 months of vacancy	National Assembly
Direct election by universal suffrage. List system with proportional representation (d'Hondt method). Parties failing to obtain an 8 % vote do not qualify for distribution of seats. Their votes in each constituency are deducted from the total.	Next-in-line candidate of the party holding the seat	Diet
Direct election by universal suffrage. List system with proportional representation.	Candidate next-in-line	Chamber of deputies

TABLE 1 : CHARACTERISTICS AND COMPOSITION OF PARLT (continued)

1.1 Name of country and Parliament	1.2 Name(s) of House(s)	1.3 Normal term of office (years)	1.4 a) Total membership b) Million population	1.5 Membership: a) Elected b) Appointed c) Ex-officio
MALAWI National Assembly	National Assembly	5	a) See 1.5 b) 4.9	a) 101 b) (any number ap- pointed by the President) c) Ministers who are not elected MPs.
MALAYSIA Parliament of Malaysia (Parlimen Malaysia)	Senate (Dewan Negara)	Perma- nent body. (Sena- tors serve a maximum of 2 terms each of 3 years).	a) 69	a) 26 b) 43 (by the King) c) 0
	House of Representatives (Dewan Rakyat)	5	a) 177 b) 15.7	a) 177 b) 0 c) 0
MALI National Assembly (Assemblée Nationale)	National Assembly (Assemblée Nationale)	3	a) 82 b) 6.4	a) 82 b) 0 c) 0
MALTA House of Representatives (Kamra tad- Deputati)	House of Representatives (Kamra tad- Deputati)	5	a) 65 or 66 b) 0.3	a) 65 or 66 b) 0 c) 0
MAURITIUS Mauritius Legislative Assembly	Legislative Assembly	5	a) 70 b) 1.0	a) 62 plus 8 "best losers" b) 0 c) 0

1.6 Features of electoral system or appointment	1.7 Filling casual vacancies	1.8 Authority responsible for validating elections
Direct election by simple majority system in single member constituencies	By-elections	Electoral Commission
Indirect election of 2 Senators by a simple majority of the members of each of the 13 State Assemblies	Appointment of a replacement	State Assemblies
Direct election. Simple majority system in single member constituencies.	By-elections	Election Commission
Universal direct suffrage, simple majority system.	By-elections which are not held until the number of Members is reduced by 1/4 of by 1/2 within 12 months of a general election.	Supreme Court
Universal, direct suffrage, proportional representation system with single transferable vote.	By-elections	Constitutional Court
Direct election of 62 Members by universal suffrage, list system, simple majority vote. 8 MPs called "best losers" are drawn from unsuccessful party candidates having obtained the highest percentage of votes, to ensure fair and adequate representation.	Allocated by the Electoral Supervisory Commission to the most successful unreturned candidate	Electoral Commissioner

TABLE 1 : CHARACTERISTICS AND COMPOSITION OF PARLT (continued)

1.1 Name of country and Parliament	1.2 Name(s) of House(s)	1.3 Normal term of office (years)	1.4 a) Total membership b) Million population	1.5 Membership: a) Elected b) Appointed c) Ex-officio
MEXICO Union Congress (Congreso de la Union)	Chamber of Senators (Cámara de Senadores)	6 (simul- taneous election).	a) 64	a) 64 b) 0 c) 0
	Chamber of Deputies (Cámara de Diputados)	3	a) 400 b) 70	a) 400 b) 0 c) 0
MONACO National Council (Conseil National)	National Council (Conseil National)	5	a) 18 b) 0.03	a) 18 b) 0 c) 0
MONGOLIA (BUGD NAYRAMDAKH MONGOL ARD ULS) Great People's Khural of the Mongolian People's Republic	Great People's Khural of the Mongolian People's Re- public	5	a) 370 b) 1.7	a) 370 b) 0 c) 0
NAURU (NAOERO) Parliament of Nauru	Parliament of Nauru	3	a) 18 b) 0.007 (1977)	a) 18 b) 0 c) 0
NETHERLANDS (NEDERLAND) States General (Staten-Generaal)	First Chamber (Eerste Kamer)	4 (not necessa- rily co-	a) 75	a) 75 b) 0 c) 0
	Second Chamber (Tweede Kamer)	term- minous).	a) 150 b) 14.3	a) 150 b) 0 c) 0
NEW ZEALAND House of Representatives	House of Representatives	3	a) 95 b) 3.2	a) 95 b) 0 c) 0

48

1.6 Features of electoral system or appointment	1.7 Filling casual vacancies	1.8 Authority responsible for validating elections
Direct suffrage, simple majority system electing 2 for each state and 2 for the federal district.	Substitutes or by-elections	The Chamber
300 elected by a plurality within a system of single electoral districts and 100 elected according to proportional representation in up to 5 regions established by law.		The respective Chamber on evidence from the Federal electoral colleges and the state legislatures
Direct election, universal suffrage, absolute majority of not less than 1/4 of registered voters on 1st ballot, simple majority on 2nd vote. Each elector votes for as many candidates as there are seats. Vote splitting between lists possible.	By-elections	Results are validated by publication in the Official Gazette.
Direct election by universal suffrage, absolute majority, from equal-population constituencies.	By-elections	Parlt, on presentation of its Mandate Cttee.
Direct election, compulsory preferential vote system. Seven constituencies return 2 Members each, the eighth returns 4.	By-elections	Returning officer
Indirect election by members of the provincial councils; proportional representation; list system.	Next-in-line on the party list	The Chamber
Direct election; proportional representation.		The Chamber on report of its Credentials Cttee
Direct election of individual candidates by universal suffrage; simple majority system.	By-elections	Judiciary

49

TABLE 1 : CHARACTERISTICS AND COMPOSITION OF PARLT (continued)

1.1 Name of country and Parliament	1.2 Name(s) of House(s)	1.3 Normal term of office (years)	1.4 a) Total membership b) Million population	1.5 Membership: a) Elected b) Appointed c) Ex-officio
NICARAGUA National Assembly (Asamblea Nacional)	National Assembly (Asamblea Nacional)	6	a) 96 b) 3.0	a) 90 b) 0 c) 6
NORWAY (NORGE) Storting (Stortinget)	The unicameral Storting has 2 divisions: Lagting and Odelsting (see also Table 30).	4	a) 155 (Lagting 39, Odel- sting 116) b) 4.1	a) 155 b) 0 c) 0
PHILIPPINES (FILIPINAS) (PILIPINAS) National Assembly (Batasang Pambansa)	National Assembly (Batasang Pambansa)	6	a) 201 b) 48.1	a) 184 b) 17 c) 0
POLAND (POLSKA RZECZPOSPOLITA LUDOWA) Diet (Sejm)	Diet (Sejm)	4	a) 460 b) 37.2	a) 460 b) 0 c) 0
PORTUGAL (REPUBLICA PORTUGUESA) Assembly of the Republic (Assembleia da República)	Assembly of the Republic (Assembleia da República)	4	a) 250 b) 9.8	a) 250 b) 0 c) 0
REPUBLIC OF KOREA (TAEHAN- MIN'GUK) National Assembly (Kukhoe)	National Assembly (Kukhoe)	4	a) 276 b) 40.9	a) 276 b) 0 c) 0

1.6 Features of electoral system or appointment	1.7 Filling casual vacancies	1.8 Authority responsible for validating elections
Universal suffrage with a system of proportional representation	By substitutes or according to National Assembly Statutes 7 and 8	Supreme Electoral Council
Direct election by universal suffrage, proportional representation, list system.	By substitutes elected at the same time as the Members	Storting
Direct election by compulsory universal suffrage of 184 regional representatives by simple majority. 17 Members appointed by the President comprising 3 Cabinet members and 14 sectoral representatives.	By-elections within 60 days for the unexpired term	Provincial and District Board of Canvassers (scrutineers).
Direct election by universal suffrage. Absolute majority on the 1st ballot. Single list presented by the Council of the Patriotic Movement of National Rebirth, and regional lists of the Electoral Conventions of each "voivodie". If insufficient candidates obtain an absolute majority, or fewer than 1/2 electors vote, a 2nd ballot requiring a simple majority is held.	The Diet can decide to allocate the seat to the candidate next-in-line.	Diet
Direct election by universal suffrage, list system with pro-portional representation (d'Hondt method).	Next-in-line on the list of candidates not elected	National Electoral Commission. Results are vali-dated by publica-tion in the official journal.
Mixture of systems: 184 Members by direct election, simple majority, and 92 Members elected by proportional representation, list system.	By-elections and vacant proportion-al representation seats filled by next-in-line candi-dates of relevant political party	Election Management Committee concerned

TABLE 1 : CHARACTERISTICS AND COMPOSITION OF PARLT (continued)

1.1 Name of country and Parliament	1.2 Name(s) of House(s)	1.3 Normal term of office (years)	1.4 a) Total membership b) Million population	1.5 Membership: a) Elected b) Appointed c) Ex-officio
ROMANIA Grand National Assembly (Marea Adunare Naţională)	National Assembly (Marea Adunare Naţională)	5	a) 369 b) 22.7	a) 369 b) 0 c) 0
RWANDA National Development Council (CND) (Conseil national du développement – Inama y'Igihugu Iharanira Amajyambere)	National Development Council (Conseil natio- nal du dévelop- pement – Inama y'Igihugu Iharanira Amajyambere)	5	a) 70 b) 6.0	a) 70 b) 0 c) 0
ST VINCENT AND THE GRENADINES House of Assembly	House of Assembly	5	a) 19 or 20 (see 1.5c) b) 0.11	a) 13 b) 6 c) 1 (Attorney- General if not an elected Member)
SENEGAL National Assembly (Assemblée nationale)	National Assembly (Assemblée nationale)	5	a) 120 b) 6.0	a) 120 b) 0 c) 0
SOLOMON ISLANDS National Parliament	National Parliament	4	a) 38 b) 0.25	a) 38 b) 0 c) Attorney- General parti- cipates with- out vote
SOMALIA (JAMHUURIYADA DEMUQRAADIGA SOOMAALIYEED) Poeple's Assembly (Golaha Sharciga)	People's Assembly (Golaha Sharciga)	5	a) 178 b) 10	a) 171 b) 6 by State President c) 1 President life Member

1.6 Features of electoral system or appointment	1.7 Filling casual vacancies	1.8 Authority responsible for validating elections
Direct election by universal suffrage. If no candidate obtains a simple majority on the 1st ballot, or less than a simple majority of all registered electors have voted, subsequent ballots are held until these requirements are met.	By-elections	Assembly, on report of the Validation Cttee.
Direct elections by universal suffrage. Simple majority system in single-member constituencies.	By-elections	National Development Council
Direct election. Simple majority vote in single member constituencies. 4 of the 6 Senators are appointed by the Governor-General on advice of the Prime Minister and 2 on advice of the Leader of the Opposition.	By-election or fresh appointment as appropriate within 90 days	Supervisor of elections
Universal, direct suffrage. Half the Assembly is elected by majority vote in the respective constituency; half by proportional representation against a national list.	Next-in-line at the last election	Supreme Court
Direct election by universal suffrage, simple majority in single member constituencies.	By-elections	Returning officers
Direct election by universal suffrage. Candidates and reserves on list proposed by the Central Cttee of the Party are elected or rejected as a whole.	From 20 reserved places on the electoral list	State Cttee for Election

TABLE 1 : CHARACTERISTICS AND COMPOSITION OF PARLT (continued)

1.1 Name of country and Parliament	1.2 Name(s) of House(s)	1.3 Normal term of office (years)	1.4 a) Total membership b) Million population	1.5 Membership: a) Elected b) Appointed c) Ex-officio
SOUTH AFRICA (SUID-AFRIKA) Parliament of the Republic of South Africa (Parlement van die Republiek van Suid-Afrika)	House of Assembly (Volksraad)	5 (not necessa- rily co- ter- minous)	a) 178 b) 24.9: black 17.0 white 4.5 coloured 2.6 Indian 0.8	a) 166 (see 1.6) 8 by MPs b) 4 by State President, 1 for each province c) 0
	House of Representatives (Raad van Ver- teenwoordigers		a) 85	a) 80 (see 1.6) 3 by MPs b) 2 by State President
	House of Delegates (Raad van Afgevaar- digdes)		a) 45	a) 40 (see 1.6) 3 by MPs b) 2 by State President
SPAIN (ESPANA) General Courts (Cortes Generales)	Senate (Senado)	4 (not necessa- rily co- ter- minous)	a) 256	a) 208 b) 48 (by regional assemblies) c) 0
	Congress of Deputies (Congreso de los Diputados)		a) 350 b) 34.9	a) 350 b) 0 c) 0
SRI LANKA Parliament	Parliament	6	a) 196 b) 13.3	a) 196 (168 seats filled) b) 0 c) 0

1.6 Features of electoral system or appointment	1.7 Filling casual vacancies	1.8 Authority responsible for validating elections
Direct elections by white voters. Simple majority in 1 ballot.	For directly elec- ted Members through by-elec- tion for the unex- pired portion of the term. For nominated or in- directly elected Members by nomi- nation or election for the unexpired portion of the term.	Returning Officer for each electoral division
Direct election by coloured voters. Simple majority in one ballot.		
Direct election by the Indian community. Simple majority in one ballot.		
Direct election (208), simple majority system. Depending on number of Senators to be elected in each constituency (usually 4) electors can cast 1, 2 or a maxi- mum of 3 votes.	By-elections	–
Direct election, proportional representation, list system (d'Hondt method).	Next-in-line candidates on the list for the seat	
Direct election. Simple majority system with each elector voting for as many candidates as there are seats to be filled in the constituency.	Nomination by the Secretary of the political party of the Member vaca- ting the seat, or by-election if no nomination made within 30 days.	Commissioner of Elections

TABLE 1 : CHARACTERISTICS AND COMPOSITION OF PARLT (continued)

1.1 Name of country and Parliament	1.2 Name(s) of House(s)	1.3 Normal term of office (years)	1.4 a) Total membership b) Million population	1.5 Membership: a) Elected b) Appointed c) Ex-officio
SWEDEN (SVERIGE) Parliament (Riksdag)	Parliament (Riksdag)	3	a) 349 b) 8.3	a) 349 b) 0 c) 0
SWITZERLAND (SUISSE; SCHWEIZ; SVIZZERA) Federal Assembly (Assemblée fédé- rale; Bundesver- sammlung; Assemblea federale)	States Council (Conseil des Etats; Standerat; Consiglio degli Stati)	Fixed for the States Council by the laws of each Canton.	a) 46	a) 46 b) 0 c) 0
	National Council (Conseil national; Nationalrat; Consiglio nazionale)	Elections generally coincide with National Council elections every 4 years.	a) 200 b) 6.4	a) 200 b) 0 c) 0
SYRIAN ARAB REPUBLIC AL-JUMHURIYAH AL-ARABIYAH AL-SURIYAH) People's Council (Majles el Chaab)	People's Council (Majles el Chaab)	4	a) 195 b) 10.0	a) 195 b) 0 c) 0
THAILAND (PRATHET THAI) National Assembly (Rathasapha)	Senate (Wuthisapha)	6 (1/3 renewed every 2 years).	a) 243	a) 0 b) 243 c) 0
	House of Representatives (Saphaphuthaen Rasadon)	4	a) 324 b) 51.2	a) 324 b) 0 c) 0

1.6 Features of electoral system or appointment	1.7 Filling casual vacancies	1.8 Authority responsible for validating elections
Universal, direct suffrage. Proportional representation. Party list system.	Substitute elected at same time as the Member. Also to replace the Member elected Speaker, appointed Minister or absent for at least a month.	National Tax Board (Section for Elections)
Direct election for 46 Members with each canton (state) applying its own system: 2 Members by proportional representation; 41 by various majority systems; 3 are elected by assemblies of citizens.	Constituencies with proportional re-presentation by the candidate next-in-line, majority system by by-elections.	As specified by the respective State electoral law
Direct election. List system with proportional representation (Hagenbach-Bischhoff method) for 195 Members in multi-member constituencies. Electors cast preferential vote; vote-splitting between lists, repeating a candi-date's name, deleting names is allowed; candidates may be cho-sen from different lists to form a new list. Simple majority system in 5 single-member constituencies.		National Council
Direct, universal suffrage. Simple majority system, each elector votes for as many candidates as there are seats in the constitu-ency.	By-elections	People's Council
Appointed by the King (re-eligible).	Appointment for remainder of predecessor's term	NA
Direct election. Party list. Simple majority system.	By-elections	Judiciary

TABLE 1 : CHARACTERISTICS AND COMPOSITION OF PARLT (continued)

1.1 Name of country and Parliament	1.2 Name(s) of House(s)	1.3 Normal term of office (years)	1.4 a) Total membership b) Million population	1.5 Membership: a) Elected b) Appointed c) Ex-officio
TUNISIA (TUNISIYAH) Chamber of Deputies	Chamber of Deputies	5	a) 136 b) 7.0	a) 136 b) 0 c) 0

UGANDA
National Assembly
	National
	Assembly
		5	a) 156
			b) 12.6
				a) 126
				b) 10 specially
				elected MPs
				(by the party
				with most MPs)
				   10 by the
				President
				   10 army
				represen-
				tatives
				c) 0

UNION OF SOVIET SOCIALIST REPUBLICS (SOYUZ SOVIETSKIKH SOTSIALISTICHES- KIKH RESPUBLIK)	Soviet of the Nationalities (Sovet Natsional- nostey)	5 (co- ter- minous).	a) 750	a) 750 b) 0 c) 0
Supreme Soviet of the USSR (Verchovnyi sovet SSSR)	Soviet of the Union (Sovet Sojuza)		a) 750 b) 271.2	a) 750 b) 0 c) 0
UNITED KINGDOM Parliament	House of Lords	Life	a) 1,183	a) 0 b) 0 c) 1 (Lord Chancellor)
	House of Commons	5 (term of a Parlt).	a) 650 b) 55.5	a) 650 b) 0 c) 0

UNITED REPUBLIC
OF TANZANIA
National Assembly
(Bunge)
	National
	Assembly
	(Bunge)
		5	a) 239
			b) 21.2
				a) 111 direct
				   72 indirect
				b) 30 nomi-
				nated by the
				President
				c) 25
				(Regional
				Heads)
				   1 Vice-
				President

1.6 Features of electoral system or appointment	1.7 Filling casual vacancies	1.8 Authority responsible for validating elections
Direct, universal suffrage. Simple majority on a single ballot for a list of candidates.	By-elections	Chamber of Deputies
Direct election. Simple majority system.	By-elections	Electoral Commission
Direct, universal suffrage in single-member constituencies. Candidates receiving over 1/2 vote are considered elected. All MPs are elected as candidates of a single bloc of the Communist and non-Party list.	By-elections	Election Commission comprising representatives of mass organisations
NA (see 2.3).	NA	NA
Direct election by universal suffrage. Simple majority system in single-member constituencies.	By-elections	Clerk of the Crown
156 by direct universal suffrage. Simple majority in single-member constituencies. 15 to women elected by the Assembly. 5 elected by the Zanzibar House of Representatives.	By-elections for elected members; new appointments for those appointed.	Electoral Commission

TABLE 1 : CHARACTERISTICS AND COMPOSITION OF PARLT (continued)

1.1 Name of country and Parliament	1.2 Name(s) of House(s)	1.3 Normal term of office (years)	1.4 a) Total membership b) Million population	1.5 Membership: a) Elected b) Appointed c) Ex-officio
UNITED STATES OF AMERICA Congress of the United States	Senate	6 (1/3 election every 2 years).	a) 100	a) 100 b) 0 c) 0
	House of Representatives	2 (Elec- tions for both Houses held simulta- neously).	a) 435 popularly elected; 4 elected district Delegates; 1 elected commis- sioner for Puerto Rico b) 226.5	a) 440 b) 0 c) 0
VANUATU Parliament (Parlement, Parlemen)	Parliament (Parlement, Parlemen)	4	a) 39 b) 0.12	a) 39 b) 0 c) 0
YUGOSLAVIA Assembly of the Socialist Federal Republic of Yugoslavia (Skupština Socijalističke Federativne Republike Jugoslavije)	Federal Chamber (Savezno veće)	4 (Members limited to 2 terms).	a) 220	a) 220 (30 from each Republic; 20 from each Province) b) 0 c) 0
	Chamber of Republics and Provinces (Veće republika i pokranjina)		a) 88 b) 22.4	a) 88 (12 from each Republic; 8 from each Province) b) 0 c) 0
ZAIRE Legislative Council (Conseil législatif)	Legislative Council (Conseil législatif)	5	a) 310 b) 30	a) 310 b) 0 c) 0

1.6 Features of electoral system or appointment	1.7 Filling casual vacancies	1.8 Authority responsible for validating elections
Each State directly elects 2 Senators by universal suffrage. Simple majority system.	By-elections called by the Executive of the State where the vacancy occurs.	Secretary of State or other chief election officer of the relevant State
Direct election, universal suffrage. Simple majority in single-member constituencies.		
Direct election, universal suffrage. Proportional representation system.	By-elections	Electoral office
Indirect election by secret simple majority vote on the basis of a candidate list proposed by self-management and socio-political organisations and communities and compiled by the communal assemblies on the territory of the respective autonomous regions (6 Republics and 2 Provinces).	Supplementary elections	Republican (Provincial) Election Commission.
Indirect election by all the Chambers of the respective regional assemblies at a joint session by secret vote		Respective Provincial Assembly
Direct, universal suffrage in a system of proportional representation.	Replacement by the substitute next-in-line	Legislative Council

TABLE 1 : CHARACTERISTICS AND COMPOSITION OF PARLT (continued)

1.1 Name of country and Parliament	1.2 Name(s) of House(s)	1.3 Normal term of office (years)	1.4 a) Total membership b) Million population	1.5 Membership: a) Elected b) Appointed c) Ex-officio
ZAMBIA National Assembly	National Assembly	5	a) 136 b) 6.0	a) 126 b) 10 (by President) c) 0
ZIMBABWE Parliament of Zimbabwe	Senate	5 (co-ter-minous).	a) 40	a) 34 b) 6 (by President) c) 0
	House of Assembly		a) 100 b) 7.5	a) 100 b) 0 c) 0

1.6 Features of electoral system or appointment	1.7 Filling casual vacancies	1.8 Authority responsible for validating elections
Direct election, universal suffrage. Simple majority system in single-member constituencies.	By-elections	Electoral Commission
14 elected by 80 common roll seat members of the House of Assembly and 10 by white roll Members; 10 Chiefs elected by Council of Chiefs.	By-elections or fresh appointment as appropriate	Chief Electoral Officer
80 elected by common roll (simple majority) and 20 by white roll (preferential vote). Single-member constituencies (after 1980 election which was on party list for the common roll).	By-elections (after single-member constituency elections).	

TABLE 2

ELIGIBILITY FOR MEMBERSHIP AND INCOMPATIBILITIES

In countries which have parliamentary government, eligibility, like the franchise, should be as wide as possible. Whatever limitations on eligibility that are in force in a country should not unduly limit the choice of an elector to be a candidate, but should be dictated by practical considerations and be free of political motives. In a democracy every elector should, in theory, be eligible for election to Parliament. In practice, however, because it is considered that the purpose of an election is to choose an assembly which is capable of representing the people and looking after the affairs of the nation, it is thought reasonable to ask for certain qualifications from the candidate which are more demanding than those from the ordinary elector. In the majority of countries, the criteria of eligibility for candidates to Parliament are more exacting than those required of voters. The differences between the two sets of conditions apply mainly to age, nationality, residence, personal conduct and ability, and the holding of public office.

Age and Eligibility

Age is the major restriction on eligibility for candidature, as Table 2A reveals.

TABLE 2A. Eligibility and Age

Minimum Age for Candidature	Federal or Upper Chambers	Popular (or only) Chamber	Total
18	4	23	27
20	1	3	4
21	7	27	34
23	0	5	5
24	0	1	1
25	0	17	17
28	0	3	3
30	8	3	11
35	3	0	3
40	3	0	3
Variable	2	1	3
Total	28	83	111

For half of the federal or upper Chambers, some experience of life is felt to be indispensable and a higher minimum age requirement is accordingly demanded.

Nationality and Eligibility

A second restriction upon eligibility is nationality. Prospective Members of Parliament must show that they belong to the country whose destiny will be in their hands and for this reason many States apply stricter conditions of nationality to candidates than to electors. Citizenship is an almost universal requirement and sometimes citizenship from birth is required as, for example, in the Philippines. Where naturalisation is not an absolute bar, a relatively long period of citizenship has to be established, as in Costa Rica and Senegal (10 years), Argentina (6 years for the Senate, 4 years for the Chamber of Deputies), Jordan (5 years), and the United States (9 years for the Senate, 7 years for the House of Representatives).

Residence and Eligibility

The qualification of nationality is frequently supplemented by a condition of residence. Candidates in Argentina, Brazil, Cameroon, the Canadian Senate, Cape Verde, Congo, Liechtenstein, Luxembourg, Nauru, New Zealand, Philippines, Rwanda, St Vincent, Tunisia and the United States of America must all be ordinarily resident in the local unit (whether constituency, state, or province) in which they seek election. This is not the case in other countries, where candidates need not meet such an exacting residence condition. However, in many other countries candidates must reside in the country for a minimum period before seeking election. Candidates for "Scheduled Castes/Tribes" in the Indian House of the People must belong to such Castes/Tribes. Similarly, candidates for the Irish Senate elected from a panel, must have knowledge and experience relevant to the panel.

Other Conditions for Eligibility

In addition to these qualifications, candidates must satisfy certain other conditions. In fifty-nine countries insanity, gross handicap or legal incapacity is a bar whilst in fifty-seven, criminal conviction of various degrees of severity also renders a candidate ineligible, sometimes for a period of years after a penal sentence has been completed. Sometimes the above conditions are embraced by a condition of deprivation of political rights under the law and this applies in twenty-six countries. In thirty-two countries undischarged bankrupts are ineligible for office and in fourteen allegiance to a foreign power or acquisition of foreign citizenship constitutes a bar. In nineteen countries candidates for office must meet certain literacy requirements. Additional conditions of oral and personal fitness for office can be found in Thailand (where candidates must not be drug addicts), and in Denmark (where those convicted of actions unworthy of a Member cannot seek membership of Parliament). These kinds of examples could be multiplied. They serve to illustrate that in many countries the electoral law seeks to ensure that candidates for parliamentary office are called upon to have a higher standard of moral and personal fitness than are electors.

Ineligibility and Incompatibility

Ineligibility must be distinguished from incompatibility. The two are often confused because the rules governing them have the same objective, that is, to ensure that Members of Parliaments are not subject to pressures either from the Executive or from private interests. This common objective is achieved in different ways. Ineligibility constitutes an absolute legal bar to being elected as it nullifies the election of a candidate. Incompatibility of occupation, on the other hand, does not affect the validity of an election but is rather a matter for subsequent choice. It follows that more candidates are likely to be ruled out on grounds of ineligibility than of incompatibility.

Incompatibility of Occupations and Professions with Membership of Parliament

In most countries, it has been considered necessary to protect the independence of Members either by drawing up a list of persons who are ineligible or by making rules governing incompatibility or both. There are three main objectives governing these rules:

- not to jeopardise the separation of powers by ensuring that a Parliament consists of Members who are in no economic or occupational sense subordinated to or dependent on the Government;
- to guarantee the freedom of the elector by preventing certain persons from profiting by the influence which they have acquired from the positions they hold in particular constituencies;
- to secure the independence of Members of Parliament from private interests.

The principle of incompatibility forces a Member to choose within a predetermined, and generally quite short, period between his membership and the occupation which is held to be incompatible with it. If his choice is in favour of the former he must resign (or not accept) the latter, and vice versa. Most countries have rules on incompatibilities. Only thirteen countries (Bahamas, Bulgaria, Cuba, Democratic Yemen, Denmark, German Democratic Republic, Hungary, Mongolia, Poland, Romania, Somalia, Sweden and USSR) have no rules.

Categories of Occupations Incompatible with Membership of Parliament

The major categories of incompatible occupations are presented in Table 2B. The nature of these incompatibilities reveals two objectives. On the one hand, a desire to ensure the separation of powers between the executive, legislative, and judicial branches of Government and hence the incompatible nature of occupations in the public service, judiciary, armed forces and police, and ministerial office. On the other hand, there is a desire to ensure economic and financial independence between members of the Legislature and the Government and hence the incompatible position of public contractors and executives of public corporations.

TABLE 2B. Occupations Incompatible with Membership of Parliament

Incompatible Occupations	Number of Countries where Incompatibility Exists
Membership of other Assemblies	43
Public Servant	35
Public Office or Office of Profit under the Government	30
Member of Armed Forces, Police, etc.	29
Member of the Judiciary	29
Ministerial Office	26
Executive of Public Corporation or Government Instrumentality	18
President of the Republic	15
Senior Regional Administrator	10
Electoral Officer	9
Public Contractor	9
Minister of Religion	9
Auditor-General or Member of Audit Board	7
Official of Foreign or International Organisation	6
Ombudsman	4
Company Executive	4
Teacher	3

Incompatibility of the Public Service

In many countries where incompatible occupations exist, public servants, and holders of public office are excluded from membership of Parliament. In some countries election to Parliament does not harm the careers of public servants. They retain their former status, but are suspended from duty during their term as Members, and placed on leave or secondment which does not affect their rights of promotion or superannuation. In some countries, only senior public servants or certain officers are excluded. In many countries, the criterion used is nomination by the Government or payment from public funds. In practice, this has the effect of excluding all of the public services. Specific offices are designated as being incompatible in certain countries. In Austria, for example, this covers the President and Vice-President of the Court of Audit, in Cameroon, Members of the Social and Economic Council; and in the Netherlands and Sri Lanka, staff of the Parliament.

Incompatibility of the Judiciary and Other Occupations

Another category of incompatibility covers judges and magistrates. Here it is considered that law-making should be kept distinct from the application of the law. In some countries (e.g. Austria, Czechoslovakia, Finland and Gabon), this incompatibility applies only to senior judges, while in others it applies to the whole Judiciary. For reasons similar to those which prohibit members of the public service from accepting parliamentary office, membership of the armed and security forces is deemed incompatible in many countries. Public contractors, executives of public and semi-public corporations and certain ministers of religion (particularly when assisted by public funds) have been declared incompatible occupations in a number of countries.

Incompatibility with Membership of Other Assemblies

An important aspect of the incompatibility rule is the way it affects other public elective offices. In bicameral systems, for example, it is forbidden to be a Member of both Chambers at the same time. In most countries, Members are generally allowed to be elected representatives of local units, but there are exceptions to this. In Argentina, Australia, Belgium, Brazil, Canada, India, Spain and the United States of America no Member of Parliament can simultaneously be a member of a State or provincial legislature. In other countries such as Algeria, Cyprus, Egypt, the Republic of Korea and Uganda no Member of the National Assembly can be a member of a local assembly.

Incompatibility of a Ministerial Office with Membership of Parliament

In twenty-six countries, the office of Minister is held to be incompatible with membership of Parliament. The extension of the incompatibility rule to cover ministerial office raises constitutional problems which are fundamental to the organisation of a regime. Incompatibility between ministerial office and membership of Parliament is a usual feature of those countries which have formal separation of powers, and is typical of presidential regimes such as Brazil, Costa Rica and the United States. This incompatibility is not generally recognised in parliamentary regimes (although France, the Netherlands, Norway and Sweden are among notable exceptions to this) where the holding of both offices is not only authorised but is positively encouraged in order to strengthen the bonds between the Legislature and the Executive. Although discussed in more detail later (Table 39) some comments warrant attention at this stage. In some countries which model themselves on the British system (e.g. Fiji and Malta) there is a constitutional requirement that Ministers also be Members of Parliament. In Australia and India they must either be Members on appointment to ministerial office, or acquire such membership within three or six months respectively. In Kuwait and Malawi, Ministers who are not elected Members of Parliament are considered to be ex-officio Members. Although there is sometimes no statutory requirement that Ministers be Members of Parliament, they usually are in countries such as Belgium, Canada, the Federal Republic of Germany and the United Kingdom. This derives from the fundamental principle of parliamentary governments in which a close link between the Legislature and the Government is established on either a legal or a customary basis.

TABLE 2: ELIGIBILITY FOR MEMBERSHIP/INCOMPATIBILITIES

| Country and House(s) | Qualifications for Membership | | |
	2.1 Age (years)	2.2 Residence	2.3 Education/other
ALGERIA National Assembly (APN)	28	In Algeria	None
ARGENTINA Senate	30	Born in or, at least, 2 years residence in constituency.	Must have Argentinian citizenship for at least 6 years for Senate, 4 years for Chamber.
Chamber of Deputies	25		
AUSTRALIA Senate	18	Residence in country for at least 3 years	British subject; qualified elector.
House of Representatives			
AUSTRIA Federal Council	21	Yes	None
National Council			
BAHAMAS Senate	30	One year immediately prior to nomination	One year citizenship prior to nomination
House of Assembly	21		

70

2.4 Disqualifications: On grounds of insanity, insolvency, conviction, etc.	2.5 Incompatibility of Membership: a) Membership of other assemblies b) Ministerial office c) Other offices or professions
Insanity; conviction for a crime or offence leading to a prison term; conduct during war of national liberation contrary to the national interest; contumacy; insolvency; convicts and exiled persons.	a) Yes b) Yes c) Senior regional administrators; magistrates; public servants with authority in the constitutency
None	a) Yes (provincial or municipal) b) Yes (ministerial office and govt office – if not allowed by the relevant House) c) Provincial Governors; practising lawyers; clergymen belonging to Catholic orders
Insolvency; criminal conviction to imprisonment of 1 year or more; attaint of treason; conviction of bribery or undue influence at an election within 2 years; allegiance to foreign power.	a) Members of State Legislatures b) A Minister must become a member of either House within 3 months c) Public servants; public contractors
Conviction for a criminal offence of more than 12 months imprisonment; legal incapacitation.	a) Membership of the other Council b) No c) Federal President; members of the Constitutional Court, the Supreme Court and the Administrative Court; President and Vice-President of the Court of Audit; executives of joint stock companies, banking, commerce, industry, transport and industrial private limited companies, public companies, savings banks and mutual insurance companies, if so decided by the relevant Council cttee
Insanity; insolvency; conviction.	a) Membership of the other House b) No c) Other public office; undisclosed contractor to Govt

TABLE 2: ELIGIBILITY FOR MEMBERSHIP/INCOMPATIBILITIES (cont.)

| Country and House(s) | Qualifications for Membership | | |
	2.1 Age (years)	2.2 Residence	2.3 Education/other
BELGIUM			
Senate	40	Residence in Belgium	Belgian by birth or full naturalisation and enjoying full civil and political rights. Only certain categories of citizens having demonstrated civic or educational qualifications or who have rendered conspicuous service to the nation are eligible for election to the Senate.
Chamber of Representatives	25		
BRAZIL			
Federal State	35	Nationality and residence within State for which campaigning	Must be literate and have party affiliation (see 19.3).
Chamber of Deputies	21		
BULGARIA			
National Assembly	18	None	None
CAMEROON			
National Assembly	23	On electoral roll, with residential qualifications.	Read and write French or English

2.4 Disqualifications: On grounds of insanity, insolvency, conviction, etc.	2.5 Incompatibility of Membership: a) Membership of other assemblies b) Ministerial office c) Other offices or professions
Conviction for a criminal offence; insanity; persons suffering certain mental or moral deficiency; persons sentenced to corrective punishment for less than 3 years, or for 3 months or less, are disqualified for a period of 12 years or 6 years respectively.	a) Membership of the other House or of a provincial council b) No c) Salaried govt office except Minister; public officials paid by the State; ministers of religious sects subsidised by the State; lawyers in public service; agents of the State Bank; inspectors of limited companies
Insanity; conviction.	a) Yes b) Yes c) Govt or public office; directorship of banks or State-owned companies
Persons placed under judicial disability for incapacity to act with full responsibility	a), b), c) None
Conviction for a felony; conviction to 3 months imprisonment without remission of sentence or to 6 months imprisonment; under warrant of arrest; bankruptcy; mentally defective; conviction for threat to State security disqualifies for 10 years.	a) Members of the Economic and Social Council b) Yes c) Executives and members of the board of state enterprises; members of police, security and military forces and civil servants responsible for national security, until at least 6 months have passed since they left office

TABLE 2: ELIGIBILITY FOR MEMBERSHIP/INCOMPATIBILITIES (cont.)

| Country and House(s) | Qualifications for Membership | | |
	2.1 Age (years)	2.2 Residence	2.3 Education/other
CANADA Senate	30	Must reside in the Province or Territory for which appointed.	Must have real estate worth $ 4,000 net and total assets of at least $ 4,000.
House of Commons	18	None	None
CAPE VERDE People's National Assembly	21	For at least 6 months before the election	None
CHINA National People's Congress (NPC)	18	None	None
COMOROS Federal Assembly	23	None	–
CONGO People's National Assembly (ANP)	18	Residence of at least 3 months in the constituency	None
COSTA RICA Legislative Assembly	21	Citizen with 10 years residence but need not reside in constituency.	Able to read and write

2.4 Disqualifications: On grounds of insanity, insolvency, conviction, etc.	2.5 Incompatibility of Membership: a) Membership of other assemblies b) Ministerial office c) Other offices or professions
Bankruptcy or insolvency; attaint of treason or conviction for felony; or any infamous crime.	a) Membership of the other House b) No c) None
Conviction for certain electoral offences; penal conviction and insantiy.	a) Membership of the Senate or of Provincial Assemblies b) No c) Sheriff; registrar of deeds; clerk of the Peace or County or Crown Attorney; Chief Electoral Officer; Assistant Chief Electoral Officer; returning officers of each district; judges appointed by the Governor in Council
Legal incapacity	a) No b) Prime Minister c) President of the Republic
Deprivation of political rights according to law	a) and b) No c) A Member of the standing cttee of the NPC may not hold any post in the administrative, judicial or procuratorial State instrumentalities
Permanent disqualifications; conviction for crime; contumacy; undischarged bankruptcy; gross handicap. For maximum of 5 years: those convicted of offences with imprisonment of up to 3 months.	a) – b) Office of Prime Minister or Minister incompatible with Assembly Membership c) The President of the Republic or an Island Governor may not hold any other elected office
Conviction for crime; undischarged bankruptcy; insanity; under judicial disability.	a) No b) Yes c) Persons engaged in commerce
Persons under detention; relatives of the President of the Republic.	a) No b) Yes c) Supreme Court of Justice; Supreme Tribunal of Election; President of the Republic; public servant; member of the police service; military on active service; Director of Civil Registrar; managers of autonomous institution or any other elective office

TABLE 2: ELIGIBILITY FOR MEMBERSHIP/INCOMPATIBILITIES (cont.)

| Country and House(s) | Qualifications for Membership | | |
	2.1 Age (years)	2.2 Residence	2.3 Education/other
CUBA National Assembly of People's Power	18	None	None
CYPRUS House of Representatives	25	In Cyprus	None
CZECHOSLOVAKIA Chamber of Nations	21	None	None
Chamber of the People			
DEMOCRATIC YEMEN Supreme People's Council	24	-	-
DENMARK Folketing	18	Candidates need not reside in the constituency but must reside in the country.	None
EGYPT People's Assembly	30	None, but must be an enrolled elector and Egyptian of an Egyptian father.	Must be literate, have completed or be exempt from military service, and not have had membership of the Assembly withdrawn.
FIJI Senate	21	None	None
House of Representatives			

2.4 Disqualifications: On grounds of insanity, insolvency, conviction, etc.	2.5 Incompatibility of Membership: a) Membership of other assemblies b) Ministerial office c) Other offices or professions
Legally certified mentally deficient; legally disqualified for criminal offences.	a) and b) No c) None
Conviction of offence involving dishonesty or moral turpitude; disqualification for any electoral offence; certified mental incapacity.	a) Member of a communal chamber or a municipal council b) Yes c) Public office; members of the armed forces
In custody; serving prison sentence or declared legally incompetent.	a) Membership of the other Chamber b) No c) Member of Constitutional Court; President of the Republic
Insanity; under guardianship, detention, conviction.	a) and b) No c) None
Those convicted of actions unworthy in the public view of a Folketing member.	a) and b) No c) None
Insanity; loss of qualifications under 2.3.	a) Member of the Shoura Advisory Council or local popular councils b) No c) Post of Governor, mayor or sheik; holding public office in Govt or public sector; appointment in foreign companies or projects applying the law on investment of Arab and foreign capital; members of board of joint-stock companies
Insanity; insolvency; conviction exceeding 12 months prison; conviction for election offences; allegiance to a foreign power.	a) Membership of the other House b) No c) Public servants; electoral office within previous 3 years; public contractors

TABLE 2: ELIGIBILITY FOR MEMBERSHIP/INCOMPATIBILITIES (cont.)

| Country and House(s) | Qualifications for Membership | | |
	2.1 Age (years)	2.2 Residence	2.3 Education/other
FINLAND Eduskunta	18	None	None
FRANCE Senate	35	None	None
National Assembly	23		
GABON National Assembly	28	Registered voter	–
GERMAN DEMOCRATIC REPUBLIC People's Chamber	18	None	None

2.4 Disqualifications: On grounds of insanity, insolvency, conviction, etc.	2.5 Incompatibility of Membership: a) Membership of other assemblies b) Ministerial office c) Other offices or professions
Conviction for electoral offences; under tutelage.	a) – b) No c) Chancellor of Justice and his deputy; members of the Supreme Court; members of the armed forces on active service; Ombudsman and his Deputy
Loss of eligibility by reason of judicial decision. The substitute for an MP who enters the Govt cannot stand against him in the following election.	a) Membership of the other House b) Yes c) Ombudsman in the whole territory; Members on mission longer than 6 months; Prefects, Deputy Prefects, heads of administrative services of the State or Department (county) in the constituency where they have exercised their functions and for variable prior period; members of the armed forces, the Constitutional Council, the Economic and Social Council or the Supreme Broadcasting Authority; judges; holders of public functions under foreign states and officials of international organisations; public servants; executives of State enterprises; State-assisted companies; savings and credit organisations; companies holding Govt contracts and real-estate companies
Insanity; conviction involving loss of civil and political rights.	a) Members of Economic and Social Council b) Yes c) Members of the Supreme Court; paid positions with a foreign state or international organisation; public office; executives of public enterprises; senior public servants
Persons declared legally incapable; persons deprived of their civil rights by Court decision.	a) and b) No c) None

TABLE 2: ELIGIBILITY FOR MEMBERSHIP/INCOMPATIBILITIES (cont.)

| Country and House(s) | Qualifications for Membership | | |
	2.1 Age (years)	2.2 Residence	2.3 Education/other
GERMANY Federal Council	Dependent on State Assembly	None	Dependent on State Assembly
Federal Diet	18	None	German citizen for 1 year
GREECE Chamber of Deputies	25	None	None
HUNGARY National Assembly	18	None	None
INDIA Council of States	30	None	Elector of the constituency represented
House of the People	25	Candidates need not reside in the constituency except for certain seats.	Candidates for seats reserved for "Scheduled Castes/ Tribes" must belong to such Castes/ Tribes.
INDONESIA House of Representatives	21	Indonesian territory	Secondary school or equivalent

2.4 Disqualifications: On grounds of insanity, insolvency, conviction, etc.	2.5 Incompatibility of Membership: a) Membership of other assemblies b) Ministerial office c) Other offices or professions
Dependent on State Assembly	a) Member of the Federal Diet b) Member of Federal Govt c) Judges and as determined by each State
Judicial deprivation of voting rights (1 year or more imprisonment); legal incapacity or guardianship; mental deficiency.	a) Members of the Federal Council b) No c) Federal President; judges; public servants; members of armed forces
Persons disfranchised pursuant to legal prohibition or criminal conviction for an offence defined in the common penal or military code.	a) Yes, such as local boards, but not European Parlt for first 2 Members of each recognised party b) No c) Members of the Board, governors or directors of public or semi-public enterprises; members of armed and police forces, certain public offices, notaries, and registrars of mortgages must resign before officially announcing their candidature
Conviction; mental derangement.	a) and b) No c) None
Insanity; bankruptcy; allegiance to a foreign State; defection (see Const. 52nd Amdt Act 1985); disqualification by law.	a) Membership of the other House or of a State Legislature b) No c) Holders of office of profit under the Indian or a State Govt except those exempt by law
Insanity; insolvency; conviction; membership of a prohibited organisation.	a) Supreme Advisory Council b) Minister; Attorney General c) President; Deputy President; High Court; Supreme Audit Board

TABLE 2: ELIGIBILITY FOR MEMBERSHIP/INCOMPATIBILITIES (cont.)

Country and House(s)	Qualifications for Membership		
	2.1 Age (years)	2.2 Residence	2.3 Education/other
IRELAND Senate	21	None	Candidates elected from a panel must have knowledge and experience relevant to the panel.
Dáil			
ISRAEL The Knesset	21	None	None
ITALY Senate	40	None	Must be literate.
Chamber of Deputies	25		
IVORY COAST National Assembly	23	None	None
JAPAN House of Councillors	30	None	None
House of Representatives	25		

2.4 Disqualifications: On grounds of insanity, insolvency, conviction, etc.	2.5 Incompatibility of Membership: a) Membership of other assemblies b) Ministerial office c) Other offices or professions
Imprisonment for more than 6 months with hard labour or penal servi- tude; bankruptcy; unsound mind.	a) Membership of the other House b) Prime Minister must be member of Dáil, no more than 2 Ministers may be Senators c) The President; Comptroller and Auditor- General; judges; members of the Defence or Police Force on full pay; public servants unless terms of employment permit; certain offices such as chairman or director of a semi- state body
Deprivation of rights by a Court under electoral law; within 5 years of serving a 5 year or greater prison term for offence against national security.	a) – b) – c) President of the State; State comptroller; salaried rabbis; judges; senior public servants and army officers must leave their positions at least 100 days before election (juniors are suspended during their mandate)
Insanity; conviction.	a) Member of the other House; regional depu- ties or councillors; President of regional commissions b) Govt representatives for Sardinia and Sicily; regional governors c) Mayors of towns of over 20,000 inhabitants; senior police officers; senior public servants; senior officers of the armed forces in the constituency where they hold office; public contractors or officers of subsidised organi- sations; office directly or indirectly remuner- ated by the State
Removal of eligibility rights by a Court of Law; persons under legal guardianship.	a) and b) No c) Senior public servants; members of the armed forces; police and firemen
Conviction; disqualifi- cation for electoral crime; legal incompetency.	a) Membership of the other House b) No c) Public servants in office (except as pro- vided by law); officers of a public corpor- ation; various other offices may be filled provided both Houses agree

| Country and House(s) | Qualifications for Membership | | |
	2.1 Age (years)	2.2 Residence	2.3 Education/other
JORDAN Senate House of Deputies	40	Jordanian for at least 5 years	Registered elector. A Senator must also be, under the Const., a prominent person who has rendered service to the nation.
KENYA National Assembly	21	None	Literate in Swahili and English, Member of the Kenya Africa National Union.
KUWAIT National Assembly	30	Resident in one of the constituencies	Literate in Arabic; male; qualified elector of Kuwaiti origin.
LEBANON National Assembly	21	Not specified	Literate
LIECHTENSTEIN Diet	20	In Liechtenstein	Male citizens
LUXEMBOURG Chamber of Deputies	21	In Luxembourg	None

2.4 Disqualifications: On grounds of insanity, insolvency, conviction, etc.	2.5 Incompatibility of Membership: a) Membership of other assemblies b) Ministerial office c) Other offices or professions
Loss of citizenship; foreign protection; bankruptcy; conviction exceeding 1 year for non-political offence and not pardoned; interdiction; insanity; blood relationship with the King.	a) Membership of the other House b) No c) Municipal office; any Govt office with a salary paid from public funds; material interest in a Govt contract except for lease of land and property or mere shareholders in a company of more than 10 members; public office for profit
Insanity; bankruptcy; conviction exceeding 6 months; allegiance to a foreign state.	a) and b) – c) Public or civic office
Conviction; loss of civil rights.	a) Yes b) No c) Public office (except permitted by the Const.); Board members or company directors; armed forces and police
Insanity; conviction which includes loss of civil rights.	a) Yes b) No c) Mayors; senior executives of public agency; senior public servants must tender resignation 6 months before election
Deprivation of voting rights by Court decision; conviction and prison term; under guardianship; committal to a closed institution.	a) – b) Yes c) Members of the Courts, the Administrative Court, the Supreme Court
Deprivation of rights under the law; criminal conviction; bankruptcy; keepers of disorderly houses.	a) Council of State b) Yes c) District Commissioners; Receivers of Public Monies; Magistrates of the Judicial Order; members of the Audit Office; members of the armed forces on active service; public servants; primary school teachers; ministers of State-supported religions

Country and House(s)	Qualifications for Membership		
	2.1 Age (years)	2.2 Residence	2.3 Education/other
MALAWI National Assembly	25 or 21 in special cases specified by the President	None	Able to read and speak English. Member of the Malawi Congress Party.
MALAYSIA Senate	30	In Malaysia	Must be literate.
House of Representatives	21		
MALI National Assembly	25	1 year residence in the country	Able to read and write French.
MALTA House of Representatives	18	In the Maltese Islands	None
MAURITIUS Legislative Assembly	18	Commonwealth citizens having resided in Mauritius for not less than 2 years immediately prior to nomination	Competent in written and spoken English
MEXICO Chamber of Senators	30	In the State at least 6 months before the elections	None
Chamber of Deputies	21		

2.4 Disqualifications: On grounds of insanity, insolvency, conviction, etc.	2.5 Incompatibility of Membership: a) Membership of other assemblies b) Ministerial office c) Other offices or professions
Insanity; bankruptcy; conviction to death, imprisonment or for an electoral offence prescribed by Parlt (7 year limit); subject to a detention order; allegiance to another country.	a) and b) No c) President of the Republic; offices prescribed by Parlt; members of armed or police forces
Insanity; bankruptcy; conviction with sentence exceeding 1 year or fine greater than M$ 2,000; failure to lodge a timely return of election expenses; acquired citizenship of a foreign country.	a) The other House, but Members except Presiding Officers, Ministers and Deputy Ministers may serve Legislative Assemblies b) No c) Office of profit under the Govt; public office, Presiding Officers may not exercise a private profession
Insanity; insolvency; conviction for electoral offences.	a) and b) Yes c) All paid non-elective public offices
Bankruptcy; insanity; legal incapacity; conviction exceeding 12 months or for an electoral offence; allegiance to a foreign power.	a) and b) No c) Public office; members of the armed forces
Bankruptcy; of unsound mind; conviction, or under sentence of death; adherence to a non-Commonwealth State.	a) and b) No c) Public and Parastatal bodies; public or local govt officers; contractors to the Govt (undeclared)
–	a) The other Chamber or local councils b) – c) Public office; ministers of religion; those on active military service or holding command in the police or rural gendarmerie; offices of profit under the Federation or State

TABLE 2: ELIGIBILITY FOR MEMBERSHIP/INCOMPATIBILITIES (cont.)

| Country and House(s) | Qualifications for Membership | | |
	2.1 Age (years)	2.2 Residence	2.3 Education/other
MONACO National Council	25	None	None
MONGOLIA Great People's Khural (GPKh)	18	None	None
NAURU Parliament	20	At least a month in the constituency	None
NETHERLANDS First Chamber	21	None	None
Second Chamber			
NEW ZEALAND House of Representatives	18	Yes, for at least 1 year in New Zealand.	Citizenship, permanent residence or registration as an elector on 22nd August 1975.
NICARAGUA National Assembly	21	None	None

2.4 Disqualifications: On grounds of insanity, insolvency, conviction, etc.	2.5 Incompatibility of Membership: a) Membership of other assemblies b) Ministerial office c) Other offices or professions
None	a) Council of the Crown; Council of State b) Yes c) Public or elective office in a foreign country; public officials, members of the Judiciary, Royal Household and security forces
As prescribed by law	a) and b) No c) None
Bankruptcy or insolvency according to the law; insanity or mental derangement; conviction or subject to sentence for an offence punishable by death or at least 1 year imprisonment.	a) and b) – c) Holders of office of profit in the service of Nauru
Conviction for an offence indicated as such by law to imprisonment for at least 1 year with loss of right to elect or be elected; mental disability.	a) Membership of the other Chamber b) Yes, but see 39.4 c) Membership of the Council of State, General Board of Auditors and any other public office that may be declared incompatible; judges or public prosecutors of the Supreme Court, Clerk or other staff of either Chamber; such public servants as are excluded by law; military on active service
Oath of allegiance to, or acquisition of citizenship of, a foreign state; conviction of a crime punishable by imprisonment for 2 or more years; corrupt electoral practice; mental disability.	a) and b) No c) Public servants; holders of public office; Crown agents for land purchase
Suspension of civil rights; conviction for a major crime since 19th July 1979; deprivatiion of rights and privileges of Member.	a) – b) No c) None

TABLE 2: ELIGIBILITY FOR MEMBERSHIP/INCOMPATIBILITIES (cont.)

Country and House(s)	Qualifications for Membership		
	2.1 Age (years)	2.2 Residence	2.3 Education/other
NORWAY Storting	18	10 years residence in Norway but not necessarily resident at time of election	None
PHILIPPINES National Assembly	25, except representatives of Youth sector must be between 18 and 25.	Natural-born citizen and not less than 6 months residence in the province, city or district in which he shall be elected, except for the Youth sector which is 1 year.	Able to read and write; registered voter.
POLAND Diet	21	None	Eligible to vote
PORTUGAL Assembly of the Republic	18	Not specified	None
REPUBLIC OF KOREA National Assembly	25	None	None
ROMANIA Grand National Assembly	23	None	None

2.4 Disqualifications: On grounds of insanity, insolvency, conviction, etc.	2.5 Incompatibility of Membership: a) Membership of other assemblies b) Ministerial office c) Other offices or professions
Insanity; conviction carrying loss of electoral rights.	a) No b) Yes c) Diplomatic post; public office in govt departments and at Court
Conviction for rebellion, sedition, violations of anti-subversion and firearms laws, crimes against national security.	a) – b) No c) Public appointive office except for govt members; employment in any govt instrumentality including govt-owned, controlled, corporations
Insanity; deprivation of civil rights under the law.	a) State Tribunal b) No c) None
Insanity; those serving sentences for fraud; deprivation of political rights by judicial decision.	a) No b) Yes c) Ambassadors; Ombudsman; head of regional govt; magistrates; State public servants; armed forces on active service; directors of a public institute; head of a Minister's office; members of the National Electoral Commission; ministers of religion
Insanity; bankruptcy; imprisonment; conviction of election offence; suspension or deprivation of voting rights by judicial decision.	a) Local Assemblies b) No c) President of the Republic, members of Presidential Electorate Body, Const. Cttee, and Election Management Cttee; judges; certain public servants; employees of govt corporations, Agricultural, Fisheries and Livestock Cooperatives; teachers; journalists; military personnel
Insanity; judicial deprivation of electoral rights.	a) No b) No c) None

Country and House(s)	2.1 Age (years)	2.2 Residence	2.3 Education/other
		Qualifications for Membership	
RWANDA National Development Council	21	At least 6 months in the Constituency	At least 4 years of secondary studies
ST VINCENT House of sssembly	21	1 year residence	Able to speak and read English
SENEGAL National Assembly	25	Resident for a period in Senegal	10 years citizenship for naturalised persons
SOLOMON ISLANDS	21	None	None
SOMALIA People's Assembly	21	Resident in Somalia	Must be active in social affairs.

2.4 Disqualifications: On grounds of insanity, insolvency, conviction, etc.	2.5 Incompatibility of Membership: a) Membership of other assemblies b) Ministerial office c) Other offices or professions
Bankruptcy; conviction for murder, attack on State security or military desertion; imprisonment for 1 to 5 years in the last 10 years or more than 5 years in the last 20 years; insanity; deprivation of civil rights under the law.	a) – b) Yes c) President of the Republic; magistrates; members of the armed forces; public servants; officers of public instrumentalities; paid occupation in the private sector
Insanity; insolvency; conviction (except in default of a fine); adherence to a foreign power.	a) – b) No (but no more than 2 Senators) c) Judges; members of the armed forces; ministers of religion (except as Senator); public servants; holders of public office
Outstanding military service obligations; conviction which impedes electoral registration; deprivation of civil rights by law.	a) No b) Minister or State Secretary c) The General Treasurer; State Inspectors-General and Inspectors; Secretaries General of Ministers; directors of Govt instrumentalities; members of the Economic and Social Council; members of police, penitentiary and customs services; armed forces on active service; regional governors; magistrates; municipal treasurers; non-elective public office; paid positions with a foreign or international organisation
Insanity; bankruptcy; conviction to death or imprisonment exceeding 6 months (except in lieu of a fine); allegiance to a foreign power; disqualification for electoral offences.	a) – b) No c) Office of Governor-General or Speaker; holders of public or electoral office
Insanity; criminal conviction.	a) and b) No c) None

TABLE 2: ELIGIBILITY FOR MEMBERSHIP/INCOMPATIBILITIES (cont.)

Country and House(s)	Qualifications for Membership		
	2.1 Age (years)	2.2 Residence	2.3 Education/other
SOUTH AFRICA House of Assembly	18	At least 5 years in the Republic	Registered voter for the respective House (see 1.6).
House of Representatives			
Congress of Deputies			
SPAIN Senate	18	None	None
Congress of Deputies			
SRI LANKA Parliament	18	Candidates need not reside in the Consti-tuency.	None
SWEDEN Riksdag	18	None	None
SWITZERLAND States Council	Varies with the canton	According to cantonal laws	None
National Council	20	None	
SYRIAN ARAB REPUBLIC People's Council	25	None	Must be literate

94

2.4 Disqualifications: On grounds of insanity, insolvency, conviction, etc.	2.5 Incompatibility of Membership: a) Membership of other assemblies b) Ministerial office c) Other offices or professions
Unsound mind; insolvency; conviction to imprisonment for not less than 12 months within the last 5 years.	a) Yes b) No, but a person appointed Minister must become a Member within 12 months c) Local public office; justice of the peace; members of the Defence Force on active service
–	a) Membership of the other House or Autonomous Community Assembly b) No c) High State Administration Office; members of the Constitutional Court and Electoral Commission; Ombudsman; magistrates, judges, public prosecutors; members of the defence, security and police forces
Insanity; bankruptcy; within 7 years of completing a period of penal conviction of more than 2 years; imposition of civic disability; conviction for bribing MPs.	a) – b) No c) President of the Republic; judges, certain State officers; parliamentary staff; Commissioner of Elections; member of Public Service Commission; Auditor–General; members of armed and police forces
Under tutelage.	a) No b) If an MP is appointed Minister his substitute is called c) None
Insanity or feeble mindedness; holders of foreign decorations.	a) Membership of the other Council b) Yes c) Govt office in some States; Federal public servants; Federal judges; ministers of religion; State electoral laws may specify other incompatibilities
Insanity; criminal conviction.	a) and b) No c) Membership of the Supreme Constitutional Court; public servants, except university professors

TABLE 2: ELIGIBILITY FOR MEMBERSHIP/INCOMPATIBILITIES (cont.)

| Country and House(s) | Qualifications for Membership | | |
	2.1 Age (years)	2.2 Residence	2.3 Education/other
THAILAND			
Senate	35	None	No educational qualifications for Thai born. Those with alien father require Thai secondary education or university degree.
House of Representatives	25		
TUNISIA			
Chamber of Deputies	28	In the Constituency	None
UGANDA			
National Assembly	18	In Uganda	To educational level Senior 4 or equivalent
UNION OF SOVIET SOCIALIST REPUBLICS			
Soviet of Nationalities	21	None	None
Soviet of the Union			
UNITED KINGDOM			
House of Lords	21	None	Peer of the Realm, Archbishop or Bishop.
House of Commons			None

2.4 Disqualifications: On grounds of insanity, insolvency, conviction, etc.	2.5 Incompatibility of Membership: a) Membership of other assemblies b) Ministerial office c) Other offices or professions
Insanity; deafness; dumbness and illiteracy; legal disenfranchisement; drug addiction; conviction to prison or within 2 years of completion of sentence of 2 years or more (except for offences committed through negligence); bankruptcy.	a) Membership of the other House b) No c) Buddhist priests, novices, monks or clergy; permanent or salaried govt officials or officials of a State agency; contractors to the State. Senators may not be members of any political party
Deprivation of civil rights under the law	a) No b) No c) Paid public office; employment paid by a foreign State or international organisation; senior officers of a public or govt instrumentality
Insanity; bankruptcy; conviction and imprisonment for 6 months for criminal offence 5 years previously.	a) Membership of a district or urban authority b) No c) Public office except Minister
Insanity only	a) Membership of the other Soviet, but members of one Soviet may participate in the deliberations of the other and exercise a "consultative" vote b) No c) None
Bankruptcy; conviction for treason.	a) Membership of the House of Commons b) No c) None
Insanity; bankruptcy; conviction for treason; detention for longer than 1 year; guilty of corrupt election practices.	a) Membership of the House of Lords or legislature outside the Commonwealth b) No c) Offices of profit under the Crown as listed in the House of Commons Disqualification Act of 1975. Includes public servants, police, armed forces, certain clergy

TABLE 2: ELIGIBILITY FOR MEMBERSHIP/INCOMPATIBILITIES (cont.)

| Country and House(s) | Qualifications for Membership | | |
	2.1 Age (years)	2.2 Residence	2.3 Education/other
UNITED REPUBLIC OF TANZANIA National Assembly	21	In Tanzania	Membership of the Party of the Revolution (Chama Cha Mapinduzi – CCM).
UNITED STATES OF AMERICA Senate	30	In the State in which election is sought	9 years citizenship
House of Representatives	25		7 years citizenship
VANUATU Parliament	25	None	None
YUGOSLAVIA Federal Chamber	18	In the country	None
Chamber of Republics and Provinces			
ZAIRE Legislative Council	25	In Zaire	4 years post-primary education or adequate political or administrative experience
ZAMBIA National Assembly	21	None	Read and write English. Candidature must be retained by the Central Cttee of the United National Independence Party.

2.4 Disqualifications: On grounds of insanity, insolvency, conviction, etc.	2.5 Incompatibility of Membership: a) Membership of other assemblies b) Ministerial office c) Other offices or professions
Insanity; allegiance to a foreign power; preventive detention; conviction or deportation order exceeding 6 months; receipt of 2 or more salaries; disqualification from voting.	a) and b) No c) Company shareholders; private company directors; persons receiving rent for buildings; govt contractors
None	a) Membership of the other House and in practice of State assemblies b) Yes c) Federal govt officials; holders of public office
Insanity; insolvency; conviction.	a) Membership of Councils of Chiefs (National, Regional, Island and Local) b) No c) President of the Republic; judges and magistrates; policemen; public servants, including teachers
None	a) – b) Yes c) Federal Secretary; judges of the Constitutional Court and members of the Presidency of the Assembly. Public office holders relinquish the office on election
Bankruptcy; insanity; penal conviction of more than 1 year in the last 5 years or more than 3 years in the last 10; prisoners deprived of political and civil rights.	a) Yes b) Yes c) Incompatible with all other public functions or elected position, or post in an international organisation
Insanity; insolvency; within 5 years of conviction or completion of a prison sentence; allegiance to a foreign power.	a) Membership of the House of Chiefs b) No c) President of the Republic; Electoral Commission members and election officers; members of the armed forces

TABLE 2: ELIGIBILITY FOR MEMBERSHIP/INCOMPATIBILITIES (cont.)

| Country and House(s) | Qualifications for Membership | | |
	2.1 Age (years)	2.2 Residence	2.3 Education/other
ZIMBABWE Senate	White Senators: 40; Black Senators and Senator Chiefs: 30.	10 years residence	None specified but use of English is essential.
House of Assembly	21	5 years residence	

2.4 Disqualifications: On grounds of insanity, insolvency, conviction, etc.	2.5 Incompatibility of Membership: a) Membership of other assemblies b) Ministerial office c) Other offices or professions
Insanity; insolvency; conviction involving imprisonment of 6 months or more; preventive detention of 6 months or more.	a) and b) No c) President of the Senate; Speaker; public officers; employees in statutory body or the Public Services

TABLE 3

PARLIAMENTARY MANDATE AND CESSATION OF MEMBERSHIP

Whatever the nature of the mandate, the Member of Parliament is elected to fulfil certain functions and, consequently, is invested, by virtue of moral, political or juridical criteria, with responsibilities towards the electorate and citizens in general. These responsibilities, which may vary in relative importance or substance in each country, are of three types:

- participation in the elaboration and control of national policies in the light of certain options;
- explaining to citizens his personal actions or those of Parliament; and
- giving assistance and advice to citizens.

Imperative Mandate

In the socialist countries, the law not only establishes that the Member of Parliament is responsible to the electors but also contains two provisions which guarantee the effective exercise of that responsibility. The first of these is that the Member must account regularly to his electors for his personal actions and the activities of the assembly of which he is a Member. In some cases the law lays down the minimum which the Member must do to carry out this obligation. The second provision in law is that the Member may be recalled by his electors if he betrays their confidence or if he commits an action unworthy of his office.

The procedure for recall varies somewhat from country to country. In Hungary, the mandate of a Member can be revoked at the initiative of 10% of his or her constituency, or a proposal for recall put forward by the National Council of the Popular Patriotic Front. A polling date is set by the Presidential Council and recall confirmed by majority vote in secret ballot with more than half the constituency voting. In the case of Members elected from the national list, the decision is taken by the National Assembly on a proposal of the Popular Patriotic Front. Similar procedures exist in Bulgaria, China, Congo, Cuba, Czechoslovakia, Democratic Yemen, German Democratic Republic, Malawi, Mongolia, Poland, Romania, USSR and Yugoslavia.

In Indonesia, political factions have the right to recall their members, and in Liechtenstein, where the small size of the country facilitates intimate contact, a Member may be recalled by his electoral group.

Non-imperative Mandate

Table 3A shows that in most of the countries under consideration the mandate of a Member cannot be revoked by his electors. In these countries, the mandate does not take on the same meaning as it does in the so-

TABLE 3A. Revocation of Mandate and Expulsion of Members from Parliament

Number of Countries in which Members:	
Can have their mandate revoked by the electorate	18
Cannot have their mandates revoked by the electorate	67
Can be expelled by Parliament	70
Cannot be expelled by Parliament	13

cialist countries because Members are not bound to their constituents by any legal obligation. Their independence is reflected in the absence of any procedure for recall and the fact that the imperative mandate has no validity. The only opportunity which the electors have to remove a Member is when he presents himself before them for re-election.

Expulsion of Members from Parliament

As can be seen from Table 3A above, in all but thirteen of the countries under consideration, Members can be expelled by Parliament, and in only seven (Belgium, Ireland, Kenya, Mauritius, Mexico, Monaco and the Netherlands) are there no provisions cited for either recall or expulsion. The major reasons cited for expulsion are presented in Table 3B which shows that an incompatible occupation or loss of eligibility are grounds for expulsion in an aggregate of 39 countries. However, the introduction to Table 2 shows that these are widely applied grounds for ineligibility and are likely to be implicit for many other countries.

Absence from parliamentary sessions or neglect of duties is a reason for expelling Members in twenty-nine countries. In Australia, for example, a Member who fails to attend any session of Parliament for two consecutive months without permission loses his seat, as does a Member of Parliament in the United Republic of Tanzania or Vanuatu who is absent from three consecutive sittings without permission. Twenty-six countries (including Cyprus, India and the Republic of Korea) provide for expulsion when the House decides he is guilty of misconduct and other offences of an unparliamentary nature. In fifteen countries, when a Member is convicted of a criminal offence by a court of law and loses his civil rights, he can be expelled from Parliament. In some instances this expulsion follows automatically from the conviction, in others it is

TABLE 3B. Reasons for Expelling Members from Parliament

Reasons for Expulsion	Number of Countries
Failure to remedy an incompatible occupation	5
Loss of eligibility	34
Failure to attend sessions or neglect of duties	29
Misconduct and unparliamentary activity	26
Conviction of crimes, loss of rights, etc.	15
Loss of party membership or change of affiliation	7

dependent on a decision of the Chamber in addition to the judicial decision. In five countries (Cameroon, Gabon, Sri Lanka, Vanuatu and Zambia) a Member is expelled from Parliament if party membership is lost. Party membership is also a condition of eligibility in certain other countries such as Malawi and the United Republic of Tanzania. In Portugal, transfer of party allegiance is a ground for expulsion, whilst in Thailand membership of Parliament lapses on loss of party membership unless new party membership is obtained within 60 days.

Special Procedures for Expulsion

The ways in which Members can be expelled from Parliament differ considerably. In many countries (for example Argentina, Israel, Jordan, the United States of America and the Republic of Korea), a two-thirds majority at least is required to expel Members. A majority of three-fourths is required in Rwanda and Thailand, and five-sixths in Finland. Frequently the decision to expel a Member from Parliament is based on the recommendation of a committee which will have had the matter referred to it and been instructed to report back to the House. In Czechoslovakia, for example, a decision to expel a Member is based on a recommendation of the Mandate and Immunities Committee, in Denmark on the Committee of Scrutineers, and in the Republic of Korea on the Legislative and Judicial Committee. Different procedures are found in Austria, where a decision to expel a Member is taken by the Constitutional Court on the basis of a recommendation from Parliament, and in the Federal Republic of Germany, where Members are expelled by the Council of Elders for loss of eligibility or following a decision by a court of law.

Resignation from Parliament

Nearly all countries give the Members of their Parliaments the option of resigning their seats as Table 3C reveals. In the majority of countries a Member informs the presiding officer or Parliament of his intention to resign his seat, and this is automatically accepted on behalf of the House. In other countries, however, a Member's resignation can only

TABLE 3C. Resignation of Members from Parliament

Form of Resignation	Number of Countries
Automatic, at request of Member	46
Conditional, with approval of Parliament	25
Conditional, with approval of electing body	4
No provisions	4
Total	79*

* Excludes China, Democratic Yemen, Nicaragua and Vanuatu for reasons of missing data.

take effect if it is accepted by Parliament. In Finland, for example, a Member can only resign from the Eduskunta if he can show some legal obstacle or other acceptable impediment to his continued membership. In Cuba and Yugoslavia a resignation must be submitted to the body electing the Member, and in Indonesia and the German Democratic Republic the party or mass organisation represented must be consulted. A unique and curious practice is found in the United Kingdom, where a Member cannot resign from the House of Commons, but, by convention, if he wishes to leave the House, may apply for and is normally granted, an appointment to posts which are technically offices of profit under the Crown, and hence incompatible with membership. His acceptance of such an office (Steward of the Chiltern Hundreds or of the Manor of Northstead, both of which are purely formal and without either duties or remuneration) disqualifies him from membership of the House. In four countries, Mexico, Norway, Philippines and Mongolia, no formal provisions are made for resignation.

Settling of Disputed Elections

Whereas many countries leave the task of verifying the credentials of Members to Parliament, frequently on advice of a committee or other body, the settlement of contested elections is usually left to the Judiciary, as can be seen from Table 3D. In the majority of countries where the Judiciary settles disputed elections, the highest court in the land takes on this responsibility. In Australia, Brazil, Costa Rica and Greece, for example, special judicial bodies have been established to deal with these matters. The existence of these bodies reveals a recognition of the importance of the electoral process. Other countries leave the settling of disputed election to Parliament (Norway and the United States of America) or to national or regional election authorities (Cape Verde, Czechoslovakia, Philippines). In the Congo it is the Minister of the Interior who has the responsibility.

TABLE 3D. Settling of Disputed Elections

Authority Responsible	Number of Countries
Judiciary	38
Special Judicial Body	8
National Election Authority	7
Parliament	24
Constituency Electoral Bureau	3
Regional or Local Assembly	2
Minister of the Interior	1
Total	83

TABLE 3: CESSATION OF MEMBERSHIP - BY RECALL, EXPULSION
RESIGNATION/INVALIDATION OF ELECTIONS

Country and House(s)	3.1 Recall provisions: procedure and grounds	3.2 Resignation procedure and acceptance
ALGERIA National People's Assembly (APN)	None	Request addressed to the APN President who submits it to the APN Bureau for ratification. It is communicated to the APN and the Govt notified.
ARGENTINA Senate Chamber of Deputies	None	A Member can resign from the House if the latter accepts his resignation by an absolute majority vote.
AUSTRALIA Senate House of Representatives	None	In writing to the President of Senate or Speaker of House of Representatives. In absence of the Presiding Officer, resignation may be addressed to the Governor-General.
AUSTRIA Federal Council	None	By announcement to the provincial legislature which delegated him. The President of the provincial legislature informs the Chairman of the Federal Council of this decision.
National Council		By announcement to the Central Electoral Authority which informs the National Council President of this decision.
BAHAMAS Senate House of Assembly	None	In writing to the Speaker who accepts or rejects.

3.3 Expulsion procedure and grounds	3.4 Authority resolving disputed elections
The APN can withdraw a Member's mandate for failure to meet eligibility requirements, betrayal of the people's trust or comitting an act unworthy of his office. A request for expulsion is submitted by the APN President on advice of the Bureau, or request of the Govt, or 1/3 APN membership. It is transmitted to the Legal and Administrative Cttee which must hear the MP concerned and has 30 days to report to the Bureau. Expulsion is pronounced by the majority of APN membership.	The Supreme Court
2/3 majority decision of the relevant House, for physical disability or moral turpitude.	The respective House
A Senator or Member can be expelled from Parliament for misconduct if House so decides. Seat is declared vacant on failing to attend any sitting of Parlt for 2 consecutive months without permission, or on becoming subject to disqualifications in 2.4.	Court of Disputed Returns (High Court of Australia).
A member can be expelled from either Council if he does not participate in the oath-taking ceremony; fails to take his seat 30 days after an election, or is absent for 30 consecutive days, and does not heed a public announcement to attend in the next 30 days; loses his eligibility; or fails to remedy an incompatible occupation. In all cases, if a simple majority of the Council so decides, the respective President reports the matter to the Constitutional Court, which may expel the member.	Constitutional Court
For loss of qualifications (see 2.4).	Election Court

Country and House(s)	3.1 Recall provisions: procedure and grounds	3.2 Resignation procedure and acceptance
BELGIUM Senate	None	In writing to the appropriate Presiding Officer or, during recess, to the Minister of Interior.
Chamber of Representatives		
BRAZIL Federal Senate	None	In writing to the Management Board of the House or declaration on floor of House. Takes effect on publication.
Chamber of Deputies		
BULGARIA National Assembly	Effected on proposal of the public organisation that nominated the candidate or of at least 1/5 of the electors of the relevant constituency. Grounds are systematic failure to perform duties, betrayal of election programme, or conduct incompatible with parliamentary office.	Resignation possible when Deputy objectively incapacited from exercising his functions. Parlt decides.
CAMEROON National Assembly	None. Ineligibiity arising during the mandate. Exclusion from the party.	Letter addressed to President of the Assembly and accepted by the Assembly
CANADA Senate	NA	By writing under his hand addressed to the Governor—General resigning his place in the Senate.
House of Commons	None	By written declaration, attested by 2 witnesses to the Speaker, or announcement in the House.
CAPE VERDE People's National Assembly	Any citizen may appeal to the National Electoral Commission within 24 hours after proclamation of election results.	Formal notarised letter to the President of the Assembly. Acceptance is by the Assembly in plenary session.

3.3 Expulsion procedure and grounds	3.4 Authority resolving disputed elections
NA	The respective House
Each ground has a particular procedure laid down in rules for each House. Grounds include: destructive attitude to Const.; loss of political rights; breaking party rules; absence at 1/3 of sessions.	Electoral Justice either at local or national level
NA	Parliament
Loss of eligibility (see 2.4, 2.5, 2.6); exclusion from party; forfeiture is established by the Bureau of the Assembly.	Electoral Commission
Seat declared vacant by Senate resolution if absent for 2 consecutive sessions; he violates his oath of Allegiance; or ceases to qualify for membership under 2.3 or 2.4.	NA
Expelled by order of the House for offences against the House, misdemeanours, or conviction of treason or other grave offences. When legally convicted of offences warranting expulsion, the record of conviction is laid before the House.	Judge, Supreme Court of Canada.
Members may be expelled for legal incapacity; insanity; absence from the country; or neglect of duties. Procedure is based on an investigatory process founded in law.	National Electoral Commission

Country and House(s)	3.1 Recall provisions: procedure and grounds	3.2 Resignation procedure and acceptance
CHINA National People's Congress (NPC)	Recall of Deputies possible by the relevant electoral unit that elected them (see 1.6), or when not in session, by a simple majority vote of its Standing Cttee.	–
COMOROS Federal Assembly	–	Any deputy may resign.
CONGO People's National Assembly (ANP)	Electors may request recall, by written petition to ANP President. The ANP Bureau appoints an inquiry cttee to report within a month. The Member concerned has the right to submit a written defence. Final decision is taken by the ANP plenary.	Request submitted to ANP President; inquiry by the Bureau; acceptance by ANP; and Head of State advised.
COSTA RICA Legislative Assembly	–	Announcement to the Assembly

3.3 Expulsion procedure and grounds	3.4 Authority resolving disputed elections
Not specified	The Presidium of the People's Congress of the respective province, autonomous region or municipality directly under Central Govt. The NPC Standing Cttee confirms the qualification of Deputies or declares their election invalid on the basis of report from the Credentials Cttee.
Absence during 3 consecutive sittings without justification	Supreme Court
Same procedure as for recall, but if no defence is submitted the Member is discharged without debate. Grounds are: use of name and position in commercial publicity; betrayal of the people's trust; behaviour unworthy of the office. The political Bureau also has power to expel.	Minister of Interior
2/3 majority of the Assembly if convicted of a common crime	Supreme Electoral Tribunal

Country and House(s)	3.1 Recall provisions: procedure and grounds	3.2 Resignation procedure and acceptance
CUBA National Assembly of People's Power	May be proposed by another Member or the electing Municipal Assembly. When the Municipal Assembly receives the request, it is admitted on 20 % vote. The National Assembly then expresses its view. The Member is considered recalled if a majority of the Municipal Assembly present vote in favour. Grounds are: repeated failure to meet obligations; electors' loss of confidence; criminal offence that mars public's conception; unworthy conduct.	Written request to the electing Municipal Assembly which informs the National Assembly (or Council of State in recess); the latter responds and the Municipal Assembly then accepts or rejects.
CYPRUS House of Representatives	None	Written request to the President of the House
CZECHOSLOVAKIA Chamber of Nations Chamber of the People	By public vote of electors for loss of their confidence or through an act incompatible with the mandate	Resignation submitted to the President of the relevant Chamber
DEMOCRATIC YEMEN Supreme People's Council	At the request of 1/4 of the constituents, subject to majority vote of MPs.	–
DENMARK Folketing	None	A Member can resign by notifying the Folketing President.

3.3 Expulsion procedure and grounds	3.4 Authority resolving disputed elections
None (but see 3.1).	The Municipal Assembly with appeal to the National Assembly
The seat of a MP becomes vacant on conviction of an offence involving dishonesty or moral turpitude; disqualification for an electoral offence; loss of citizenship; contraction of incapacitating mental illness.	Electoral Court (i.e. the Supreme Court).
Decision taken by the Chamber on proposal of the Mandate and Immunities Cttee for loss of eligibility	District Election Commission
–	Parliamentary Cttee for Contest of Elections and the Supreme Commission for elections
Loss of eligibility is ground for expulsion. Decision is by simple majority of the Folketing on recommendation of Cttee of Scrutineers.	Folketing

Country and House(s)	3.1 Recall provisions: procedure and grounds	3.2 Resignation procedure and acceptance
EGYPT People's Assembly	None	Under the Const. only the Assembly may accept the resignation of Members.
FIJI Senate	NA	In writing to the President, who advises the appropriate authority (see 1.6). A resigning President advises the Clerk.
House of Representatives	None	Notification in writing to the Speaker
FINLAND Eduskunta	None	A Member can only resign on showing some legal obstacle, or other acceptable impediment to membership.
FRANCE Senate National Assembly	None	Letter to the President, who notifies the House and Government.
GABON National Assembly	None	Letter addressed to Head of State
GERMAN DEMOCRATIC REPUBLIC People's Chamber	Electors, Parties and mass organisations with concurrence of the National Council of the National Front of the G.D.R. can recall a Member for gross neglect of duty. Recall is decided by the Chamber.	A Member may request, after consultation with the Party or mass organisation represented, that his seat be declared vacant.

3.3 Expulsion procedure and grounds	3.4 Authority resolving disputed elections
Grounds under the Const. include: no-confidence motion, change in category (e.g. worker, farmer) under which elected; failing to discharge parliamentary duties. On grounds being reported to the Speaker, matter is referred to the Cttee on Constitutional and Legislative Affairs, which must hear the Member concerned for report to the Assembly Bureau. The Bureau also hears the Member concerned and may refer the matter to the Cttee on Values. Final decision is taken by 2/3 majority of the Assembly in the light of cttee reports.	Under the Const. contested membership is investigated by the Court of Cassation and decided by 2/3 majority of Assembly Members.
President advises seat vacant after absence from 4 consecutive meetings without leave. Other grounds are loss of citizenship or sentencing to more than 12 months in prison, but subject to extension of membership pending legal appeal. As above, except absence for 3 consecutive days.	Supreme Court
Grounds are repeated absence from Parlt without authorisation of the House, loss of eligibility or conviction of a serious crime. In this last case, Eduskunta may expel the Member by a 5/6 majority vote.	Supreme Administrative Court
Failure to remedy an incompatible occupation or conviction of a crime involving loss of civil rights or imprisonment, on proclamation by the Constitutional Council.	Constitutional Council
Exclusion from Gabon Democratic Party	Supreme Court
Party or mass organisations may ask for revocation of membership. Decision is by the Chamber.	People's Chamber

117

Country and House(s)	3.1 Recall provisions: procedure and grounds	3.2 Resignation procedure and acceptance
GERMANY Federal Council	By the appointing State Government	Application for recall
Federal Diet	None	Declaration to the President of Bundestag or a public notary for transmission to the President
GREECE Chamber of Deputies	None	In writing (which cannot be withdrawn) to the President of the Chamber
HUNGARY National Assembly	On initiative of 10 % of the electors or proposals of the National Council of the Popular Patriotic Front. Recall is valid if more than 1/2 electors vote and majority is in favour. If MP elected from the national list then recall can be made by the Assembly on proposal of the Popular Patriotic Front.	In writing to the President of the National Assembly
INDIA Council of State House of the People	None	In writing to the Chairman or Speaker, as appropriate, who is empowered to accept.
INDONESIA House of Representatives	Factions (see 19.1) have the right to recall their Members.	In writing to the Leader of the relevant Faction
IRELAND Senate Dáil	None	In writing to the Chairman who makes announcement to the House.
ISRAEL The Knesset	None	Membership ceases 48 hours after receipt of a letter of resignation by the Chairman unless withdrawn within this time.

3.3 Expulsion procedure and grounds	3.4 Authority resolving disputed elections
None	NA
Decision of the Council of Elders for loss of eligibility or if the Federal Court declares Member's party unconstitutional.	Federal Diet on proposal of its Scrutiny of Elections Cttee
Lapse of mandate for incompatibility according to the Const. (see 2.5), or invalidation of the election.	Special superior Court, as provided in the Constitution.
By the Assembly on recommendation of Cttee on Immunities and Incompatibilities for loss of eligibility	National Assembly in light of reports from the National Electoral Presidency and the Mandate and Immunity Cttee
Gross contempt of the House or acts unbecoming to a Member may be investigated by the Cttee of Privilege or a Special Cttee and may lead to expulsion on a motion of the Leader of the House.	High Court of the various States and the Supreme Court of India
See 3.1	General Election Institution chaired by Minister of Home Affairs
Members cannot be expelled.	High Court
By a 2/3 majority resolution on complaint of 10 House cttee members following sentence to prison for one year or more provided the Member has been heard in defence.	The Knesset

Country and House(s)	3.1 Recall provisions: procedure and grounds	3.2 Resignation procedure and acceptance
ITALY Senate	None	Resignation accepted by the relevant House
Chamber of Deputies		
IVORY COAST National Assembly	None	In writing to the President of the Assembly
JAPAN House of Councillors	None	In writing to the Presiding Officer, who submits it to the plenary for decision without debate. When Diet not in session, resignation is accepted by Presiding Officer.
House of Representatives		
JORDAN Senate	None	In writing to the Speaker who notifies the House for acceptance.
House of Deputies		
KENYA National Assembly	None	In writing to the Speaker
KUWAIT National Assembly	None	In writing to the President of the Assembly accepted by the Assembly
LEBANON National Assembly	None	Assembly accepts or refuses resignation.
LIECHTENSTEIN Diet	By the Member's electoral group for compelling reasons	Notification to the President of the Diet, the Member's parliamentary group and party.
LUXEMBOURG Chamber of Deputies	None	Notified in session to the Chamber; otherwise to the Government.

3.3 Expulsion procedure and grounds	3.4 Authority resolving disputed elections
Only in case of incompatibility (see 2.5 and 2.6) or electoral invalidation.	Electoral Junta appointed to each House but invalidation is debated and decided by the respective House.
Expulsion declared by the Assembly for failure to attend the sittings of 2 consecutive sessions without leave.	Supreme Court for electoral disputes. National Assembly for invalidation of elections.
By resolution of 2/3 of MPs present for loss of qualifications. An MP who disturbs order in a House can be expelled by a 2/3 majority (see 13.1).	High Court
By 2/3 majority resolution and, for Senators, Royal approval, for loss of qualifications.	2/3 majority. Any voter may present a petition within 15 days of election result.
None	High Court
Majority resolution of the Assembly if qualifications lost (see Table 2).	Constitutional Court
By a Court composed of judges and parliamentarians, for high treason or crime.	National Assembly
If recalled or convicted of a major offence	Supreme Court
A Member absent for more than 1/2 sittings of 2 consecutive ordinary sessions is automatically considered to have deserted his mandate.	Chamber of Deputies

Country and House(s)	3.1 Recall provisions: procedure and grounds	3.2 Resignation procedure and acceptance
MALAWI National Assembly	Seat must be vacated if confidence and support of a majority of constituents is lost, or if appointed, the President withdraws the appointment.	If elected, by writing to the Speaker; if appointed, to the President.
MALAYSIA Senate House of Representatives	None	In writing to the Presiding Officer of the respective House.
MALI National Assembly	None	In writing to the Presiding Officer who advises the Assembly for acceptance.
MALTA House of Representatives	None	In writing to the Speaker. The Speaker may resign by announcement to the House or in writing to the Clerk of the House.
MAURITIUS Legislative Assembly	None	In writing to the Speaker. Seat falls vacant on receipt by the Speaker.
MEXICO Chamber of Senators Chamber of Deputies	None	Members may not resign but special concessions may be granted by the respective Chamber.
MONACO National Council	None	In writing to the President of the National Council who transfers the request to the State Minister to inform the Prince.

3.3 Expulsion procedure and grounds	3.4 Authority resolving disputed elections
Seat must be vacated under the Constitution for loss of qualifications (see Table 2); absence for 3 successive meetings without the Speaker's permission; or on voting against the President if as a candidate he declared his support.	High Court
Substantive motion to the respective House for loss of qualifications (see Table 2).	High Court of Malaysia
Absence for 2 successive ordinary sessions	Supreme Court
On motion of the House for loss of qualifications	Constitutional Court
No provisions	Supreme Court
No provisions	Federal Electoral Committee
Members cannot be expelled.	Courts of Law

Country and House(s)	3.1 Recall provisions: procedure and grounds	3.2 Resignation procedure and acceptance
MONGOLIA Great People's Khural (GPKh)	The electors of a constituency may request recall of their representative. The request is considered by the GPKh Presidium which convenes a public meeting to be attended by not less than 2/3 of the constituents. Recall is decided by vote.	NA (except see 3.1).
NAURU Parliament	None	In writing to the Speaker, or in case of the Speaker, to the Clerk of Parliament. Resignation is effective on delivery and subject to acceptance.
NETHERLANDS First Chamber Second Chamber	None	In writing to the President of the Chamber or, in the Second Chamber during recess, to the Central Voting Office.
NEW ZEALAND House of Representatives	None	Letter of resignation addressed to the Speaker
NICARAGUA National Assembly	As established in the Fundamental Statutes	As established in the Fundamental Statutes
NORWAY Storting	None	A Member cannot resign.
PHILIPPINES National Assembly	None	No constitutional or other legal provision
POLAND Diet	Electors may recall an MP failing to discharge his responsibilities or having lost their confidence. They address a proposal to the Diet through the MP's sponsoring organisation or by the Patriotic Movement of National Rebirth. Approval is required by 2/3 majority of at least 1/2 Diet members.	In writing to the Diet Presidium which informs the Diet through the Presiding Officer.

3.3 Expulsion procedure and grounds	3.4 Authority resolving disputed elections
Application lodged giving reasons, together with an account to the constituency. Acceptance is by the GPKh.	Election disputes are considered by the constituency and district electoral commissions. Invalidity of elections is decided by the GPKh on advice of its Mandate Cttee.
Parlt derives its power to expel Members from practice at Westminster introduced originally through the Constitution.	Court of Disputed Elections (Supreme Court of Nauru).
No provisions	The Chamber
Disqualification occurs on failure to attend Parlt for 1 year without permission.	High Court
For crimes under procedure of the Immunity Law	Supreme Electoral Council
Loss of membership only occurs on relevant conviction by a law court or on appointment to an incompatible public office.	The Storting
By the House for disorderly behaviour, with the concurrence of 2/3 membership.	Commission for Elections
No provisions	The Diet and the Council of State at the request of the electors

TABLE 3: CESSATION OF MEMBERSHIP – BY RECALL, EXPULSION
RESIGNATION/INVALIDATION OF ELECTIONS (continued)

Country and House(s)	3.1 Recall provisions: procedure and grounds	3.2 Resignation procedure and acceptance
PORTUGAL Assembly of the Republic	None	In writing to the President of the Assembly, becoming effective on publication in the official journal.
REPUBLIC OF KOREA National Assembly	None	Presentation of resignation for decision by plenary. During a recess the Speaker may accept a resignation.
ROMANIA Grand National Assembly	Members can be recalled at any time for failure to discharge their duty, actions contrary to socialist ethics or fairness, loss of confidence of their constituents.	In writing to the Bureau of the Grand National Assembly for approval by the Assembly
RWANDA National Development Council (CND)	None	Const. provides for resignation but procedure is not specified. The CND accepts.
ST VINCENT House of Assembly	None	In writing to the Speaker to take effect when received.
SENEGAL National Assembly	None	In writing to the Assembly President who advises the Assembly for acceptance, and the President of the Republic after acceptance.
SOLOMON ISLANDS National Parliament	None	In writing to the Speaker
SOMALIA People's Assembly	None	In writing with reasons. Accepted by simple majority of the Assembly.

3.3 Expulsion procedure and grounds	3.4 Authority resolving disputed elections
Declared by the Assembly Bureau on advice from the Rules and Mandates Cttee with appeal to the Assembly (secret ballot). Grounds are loss of qualifications; unjustified absence beyond provisions of SO; transfer of party allegiance; judicial sentence for participation in fascist organisations.	Judicial Tribunals
On decision of the Assembly following request by 20 or more Members or a cttee and referral to Legislative and Judicial Cttee; for insult, malice, obstruction, disorderly behaviour, violation of secrecy, abuse of position or failure to resolve incompatibilities of membership (see Table 2).	Supreme Court
No provisions (but see 3.1).	Assembly, on report of Validation Cttee.
Only for loss of qualifications by 3/4 majority of CND membership	State Council (special judicial body).
By loss of qualifications, e.g. bankruptcy, serious court conviction.	Court of Law
Temporary suspension of warrant issued for arrest and immunity lifted. Assembly may expel a Member after a hearing, for absence without leave during 2 ordinary sessions.	Supreme Court
A Member shall vacate his seat if he becomes disqualified (see Table 2) or if absent from 2 consecutive meetings without leave or justifiable reasons.	High Court
Any Member may be relieved of his responsibilities for failure to fulfil membership conditions in the electoral law or to discharge his duties.	State Cttee for Election

Country and House(s)	3.1 Recall provisions: procedure and grounds	3.2 Resignation procedure and acceptance
SOUTH AFRICA House of Assembly	None	In writing to the Secretary to Parliament
House of Representatives		
House of Delegates		
SPAIN Senate	None	Request to the Presiding Body of the House
Congress of Deputies		
SRI LANKA Parliament	None	In writing to the Secretary General of Parliament
SWEDEN Riksdag	None	No Member or substitute may resign without consent of the Riksdag.
SWITZERLAND States Council	None	In accordance with the relevant Cantonal Law
National Council		In writing to the Council President. The Secretariat of Parlt advises the State Government.
SYRIAN ARAB REPUBLIC People's Council	None	A Member can resign if resignation accepted by absolute majority of the Council.

3.3 Expulsion procedure and grounds	3.4 Authority resolving disputed elections
Parlt has power to expel but never yet exercised. The Minister of Justice, on the advice of an advisory cttee, may require a Member to resign, who is judged to be a threat to State security or the maintenance of law and order. Absence without leave for a whole session entails forfeiture of membership.	Division of the Supreme Court having jurisdiction
Expulsion is only possible on judicial sentence, but indictment and prosecution require authorisation of the House. This is obtained on petition to the House President, referred to the Cttee on the Status of Deputies within 5 days and reported to the House for decision within a further 30 days. A petition is rejected if the House fails to pronounce on it within 60 calendar days of its presentation.	Judiciary
A Member's seat becomes vacant on being declared legally void; on the Member losing party membership or becoming subject to disqualification (see 2.4 and 2.5); on his being continuously absent from sittings without leave for 3 months.	Election Judge (the Chief Justice or a judge of the Supreme Court).
Decided by a court, should a Member, through a criminal act, prove to be manifestly unfit for office.	Election Review Cttee appointed by the Riksdag
Loss of eligibility. Procedure not specified in the Constitution or legislation.	Respective State Government National Council
Only in the case of flagrante delicto and with prior authority of the Council President	People's Council, following investigation by the High Constitutional Court.

TABLE 3: CESSATION OF MEMBERSHIP - BY RECALL, EXPULSION
RESIGNATION/INVALIDATION OF ELECTIONS (continued)

Country and House(s)	3.1 Recall provisions: procedure and grounds	3.2 Resignation procedure and acceptance
THAILAND Senate	None	In writing to the Speaker of the respective House
House of Representatives		
TUNISIA Chamber of Deputies	None	In writing to the Chamber President who advises the Executive.
UGANDA National Assembly	None	In writing to the Speaker
UNION OF SOVIET SOCIALIST REPUBLICS Soviet of Nationalities Soviet of the Union	By a majority in the constituency for failure to justify the electors' trust or unworthy actions. Mass organisations may raise the matter, notifying the Member, with the Credentials Commission of the relevant Soviet, for the preparation of findings and eventual vote by the electorate.	Personal application of the Member in connection with circumstances interferring with the execution of his mandate. Decision is by the Supreme Soviet or its Presidium.
UNITED KINGDOM House of Lords	NA	All lay members are members for life. Archbishops and bishops appointed since 1976 retire at age 70.
House of Commons	None	Members wishing to resign apply for posts which technically disqualify for membership. The Chancellor of the Exchequer has the gift of these posts.

3.3 Expulsion procedure and grounds	3.4 Authority resolving disputed elections
Membership of a Senator terminates on joining any political party. 1/10 membership of either House can lodge a complaint with its Speaker seeking termination of membership of any MP for loss of qualifications. The matter is decided by the Constitutional Tribunal. 1/4 membership can seek termination of an MP for jeopardising the dignity of the House with decision by resolution of 3/4 membership of the House. Membership of the House of Representatives lapses on loss of party membership unless a new party membership is obtained within 60 days or on being absent without leave throughout a session.	Judiciary
Absence without leave for 3 consecutive months can entrain forfeiture of remuneration and expulsion by secret vote of the Chamber.	Chamber of Deputies through a special post-election cttee elected by the Chamber
The Attorney General petitions the High Court, on failure to attend 30 consecutive sittings or failure to take the oath of allegiance.	High Court
On decision of the Supreme Soviet or its Presidium in connection with a court indictment	The respective Soviet on submission by its elected Credentials Commission
A person succeeding to a peerage may disclaim it for life within 12 months by disclaimer delivered to the Clerk of the Crown in Chancery.	Claims of peerage are considered by the Committee of Privileges.
By the House, on complaint of being unfit for membership (e.g. corruption, fraud, perjury) usually after examination and report by a select committee.	Courts of Law with the House giving effect to judicial decisions

Country and House(s)	3.1 Recall provisions: procedure and grounds	3.2 Resignation procedure and acceptance
UNITED REPUBLIC OF TANZANIA National Assembly	None	In writing to the Speaker who can accept the resignation.
UNITED STATES OF AMERICA Senate	None	In writing to the President of the Senate
House of Representatives		By notification to the House and the executive of the relevant State
VANUATU Parliament	None	-
YUGOSLAVIA Federal Chamber	Yes, according to the same procedure as for election.	Resignation is submitted to the electorate, i.e. the body electing the MP.
Chamber of Republics and Provinces		
ZAIRE Legislative Council	None	Request addressed to the Council Bureau for acceptance by the Council
ZAMBIA National Assembly	None	Submitted in writing to the Speaker who informs the Assembly for acceptance.
ZIMBABWE Senate	None	In writing to the President of the Senate or the Speaker as appropriate, or to the Secretary to Parliament.
House of Assembly		

3.3 Expulsion procedure and grounds	3.4 Authority resolving disputed elections
Seat becomes vacant (except Heads of Regions) on failing to attend 3 consecutive sittings without permission.	High Court and Appeal Court
2/3 majority of the House; no grounds specified.	Respective House
2/3 majority of the House for disorderly conduct	
Seat becomes vacant on absence from 3 consecutive sittings, loss of qualifications, resignation from party.	Judiciary
None	Courts
Loss of mandate can follow absence without leave for 1/4 of a session; loss of nationality or qualifications; grave transgression of the rules of the Popular Revolution Movement.	Supreme Court of Justice
At the decision of the House on an MP ceasing to be a Party member for gross misconduct, or loss of qualifications.	High Court
By motion of a majority of the relevant House membership, if absent for 21 consecutive sittings in a session without leave, or sentenced to death or imprisonment for 6 or more months.	Judiciary

TABLE 4

PARLIAMENTARY IMMUNITIES AND PRIVILEGES

Immunities

The objective of parliamentary immunities is to protect Members of Parliament from legal actions by the Government or by private persons. Historically, their purpose was to safeguard the precarious position of elected assemblies against powerful Governments. While their original purpose has considerably changed, they are, nonetheless, still justifiable in the contemporary world as their existence also facilitates the smooth running and complete independence of Parliament. For this reason, immunities relate primarily to the exercise of parliamentary duties.

Non-accountability of Members

Immunity applies to anything spoken or written, or any act committed, by a Member of a Legislature in the ordinary course of his official duties. Immunity covers speeches delivered in Parliament or its committees, interruptions in debate, motions or bills proposed, voting, oral or written questions, etc. In short, any action which presupposes that the person carrying it out is doing so in the course of his parliamentary duties and which no person other than a Member could do. The protection afforded by this immunity is absolute and permanent. A Member cannot have any criminal charge or civil case brought against him for these actions even after he has ceased to be a Member.

Inviolability of Members

In addition to non-accountability, Members may also benefit from "inviolability" or protection from legal processes. This ensures that Members are protected against legal action brought against them for civil and/or criminal acts committed outside the orbit of their office, even though the ordinary citizen does not benefit from a similar protection. This is a privilege with less obvious justification than non-accountability and, as Table 4A reveals, it does not meet with the same unanimous approval in all Constitutions or legal systems.

In most Western European and socialist countries, Members are immune from arrest for criminal offences but not for civil offences. In ten Parliaments which model themselves on the United Kingdom system, the pattern is reversed: Members are immune from arrest for civil offences but not for criminal offences. In Malaysia, Mauritius, the Netherlands and Zimbabwe, Members are not immune from arrest for either civil or for criminal offences.

TABLE 4A. Immunity from Arrest

Immunity	Number of Countries
Total Immunity	26
Except in Flagrante Delicto	42
In Civil Cases only	10
No Immunity	4
Total	82*

* Solomon Islands excluded for reasons of missing data.

Extent of Inviolability

Fear of encroachment by the Executive upon the liberty of Members of Parliament has given rise to the principle of inviolability. Whether it covers Members from arrest for civil and/or criminal offence, its purpose is to protect Members of Parliament from false accusations by Governments and other persons. In most countries this protection does not cover what are regarded as major offences such as treason, felony, sedition or subversion; nor does it apply (in forty-two countries) to offenders discovered in flagrante delicto. In general, Constitutions and legal systems provide that cases of flagrante delicto fall outside the ambit of parliamentary immunity, which makes possible the immediate arrest and prosecution of a Member against whom a charge is made without recourse to any other form of proceedings. The essential feature of flagrante delicto is that the person committing the offence can be identified unequivocally, ruling out any risk of mistaken identity or tendentious interpretation of facts.

With this exception, the lifting of a Member's immunity is entrusted to Parliament itself (except Cyprus where it is the Supreme Court) or to its directing authority when Parliament is not in session. Parliamentary immunity cannot be lifted under any circumstances in Australia, Cuba, Fiji, the Indian House of the People, Indonesia, Malta, Mongolia, the Netherlands, Norway, the Republic of Korea, Tanzania and the United States of America.

Duration of Inviolability

The duration of parliamentary inviolability varies from country to country, as can be seen from Table 4B. In several countries, it is permanent, so that Members are protected by their legislatures for the whole term of their office. A number of other countries limit it to the duration of the parliamentary session. Between sessions the Member is answerable to the law in the same way as ordinary citizens.

A variant on this practice is found in Australia, Canada, India, Nauru and the United Kingdom where inviolability extends to the session and to 40 days before and after. In Indonesia, Members of Parliament are immune from arrest only whilst on parliamentary premises. In Fiji,

Ireland, Norway, Malawi, the Philippines and the United States of America they are also immune whilst going to and from Parliament. In Uganda, this concept extends to any time that a Member is on parliamentary duty.

TABLE 4B. Duration of Parliamentary Inviolability

Period of Inviolability	Number of Countries
Term of Office	46
Duration of Session	19
Duration of Session and an Additional Period	5
On Parliamentary Premises	2
In Parliament and Coming and Going	7
Total	79*

* Excludes Malaysia, Mauritius, the Netherlands and Zimbabwe, where the concept of inviolability does not apply.

Offences against Parliament

Among the privileges enjoyed by Parliaments and their Members is the protection from offences against Parliament. The countries under consideration fall into two groups: those which do not recognise the concept of offences against Parliament and those which do. In the first group of countries (which includes Belgium, Cape Verde, France and Hungary) no distinction is made in law between offences against Parliament and offences against other public authorities. Parliament is not protected for its own sake, but because it is part of the machinery of government which has to preserve its dignity in all circumstances. In the second group of countries (which includes Canada, Ireland, Japan, Jordan, Norway and the United States of America) Parliament has granted itself special protection against offences which may be committed against it.

Offences against Parliament normally fall under the heading of breach of privilege or contempt. While no formal definition of such breaches or contempts can be advanced here, the following are typical examples of such offences:

- assaulting, obstructing, molesting or insulting Members or officers of Parliament in the course of their duty;
- bribery of Members;
- refusal to obey an order of Parliament or its committees for attendance or for the production of papers, books, documents or records;
- creating disturbances likely to interfere with the proceedings of Parliament;
- uttering or publishing slander or libel on Parliament or its Members;

137

- attempting to influence by fraud, threat, or intimidation the vote, opinion, judgement or action of Members;
- presenting false evidence before Parliament or its committees;
- using force or the threat of force prematurely to end a sitting of Parliament, etc.

From this partial list, it can readily be seen that the purpose of this protection is to safeguard the work of Parliament from all manner of interferences, whether these come from the Executive or from the general public.

Judgement of Offences against Parliament

In those countries which do not give special recognition to offences against Parliament, persons committing such offences are tried by courts of law in the usual manner. Where offences against Parliament are given special recognition in law they may be dealt with as shown in Table 4C, either by Parliament itself, acting as a court of law and using special procedures (as in Australia, Malaysia and the United Kingdom), or by the ordinary courts of law in the usual manner (as in Fiji, the Federal Republic of Germany, Israel and the Netherlands), or by either Parliament or the courts of law, depending upon the nature of the offence (as in India and St Vincent). In the case of Cameroon, Czechoslovakia and Indonesia, the directing authority of Parliament considers the matter. In many countries a committee of Parliament such as the Privileges Committee, the Committee on Mandatees and Immunities, or the Constitutional Affairs Committee, makes a first examination and reports its findings and recommendations.

TABLE 4C. Adjudicating Authority for Offences against Parliament

Adjudicating Authority	Number of Countries
Parliament	20
Directing Authority of Parliament	3
Parliament and/or Courts	8
Courts of Law	10
Not Defined (Republic of Korea)	1
No Offences Specified	21
Total	63*

* Algeria, Austria, Comoros, Congo, Democratic Yemen, Denmark, Finland, Gabon, Greece, Hungary, Kuwait, Mexico, Romania, Rwanda, Senegal, Solomon Islands, Somalia, Syrian Arab Republic, Vanuatu and Yugoslavia, excluded for reasons of missing data.

Penalities Prescribed

The penalties that exist for offences against Parliament (whether administered by Parliament or the courts) typically involve reprimands, fines and prison sentences. In nine countries (which include India and the United Kingdom), offenders can receive an admonishment or reprimand formally pronounced by the Speaker at a sitting of the House. In several countries (which include the Federal Republic of Germany and Malta) offenders can receive fines, often in addition to prison sentences. In twenty-three countries, offenders against Parliament can be sent to jail for varying periods of time: in the Netherlands, the maximum sentence is 20 years, in Japan 10 years, in the Federal Republic of Germany and the Ivory Coast 5 years. Other countries can impose maximum prison terms varying from 60 days (Malaysia and the Philippines) to 4 years (Zimbabwe).

TABLE 4: IMMUNITIES AND PRIVILEGES

Country and House(s)	4.1 Guarantees: a) Freedom of speech b) Freedom from arrest c) Other	4.2 Institutions and persons granted privileges and immunities	4.3 Duration of immunity or privilege
ALGERIA National People's Assembly (APN)	a) Yes b) Yes	Members	Term of office
ARGENTINA Senate Chamber of Deputies	a) Yes b) Except in flagrante delicto, c) Freedom from criminal trial (except if a 2/3 majority previously waives the immunity)	Members	Freedom of speech for life; freedom from arrest and trial only during mandate.
AUSTRALIA Senate House of Representatives	a) Yes b) For civil matters only c) Exemption from service as juror; exemption from attendance in Court as witness	Houses of Parlt; their cttees and Members. (Certain immunities extend to witnesses and officers of either House, e.g. exemption from jury duty when prior duty to business of Parliament).	a) and c) Indefinite b) During session and 40 days before and after
AUSTRIA Federal Council National Council	a) Yes, in plenary and cttees b) Except in flagrante delicto crimes (i.e. during the very act of committing the crime) and for offences manifestly unconnected with political activities. The authority concerned must seek a ruling (see 4.4)	Members	Term of office
BAHAMAS Senate House of Assembly	a) Yes b) Yes	House; cttees; Members and Officers of Parlt.	When in Parliamentary precincts

140

4.4 Waiving immunity or privilege	4.5 Offences against Parliament	4.6 Adjudicating authority for offences against Parliament. Procedure followed	4.7 Penalties prescribed
Majority of APN members	-	-	-
Respective House, by 2/3 majority.	Disorderly conduct; contempt of Parliament.	Parliament, except for crimes established in the Penal Code.	If crimes, those of the Penal Code.
None	Contempt of Parliament	Parliament; Committee of Privileges of relevant House usually meets to decide action to recommend.	Both Houses may reprimand or imprison and, in the case of their members, expel them.
The respective Council, on demand of 1/3 of the Cttee on Immunity or the Member concerned, may decide whether an offence was committed "in connection with the execution of the MP's political activities".	-	-	-
Parliament	Misleading Parliament	The respective House by censure motion	Suspension for a period depending on nature and gravity of offence

141

Country and House(s)	4.1 Guarantees: a) Freedom of speech b) Freedom from arrest c) Other	4.2 Institutions and persons granted privileges and immunities	4.3 Duration of immunity or privilege
BELGIUM Senate Chamber of Representatives	a) Yes b) During sessions, except with the authorisation of his House or in case of flagrante delicto	Members	a) Term of office b) During sessions
BRAZIL Federal Senate Chamber of Deputies	a) Yes b) Yes, except for offences against national security	Houses and Members	Term of office
BULGARIA National Assembly	a) Yes b) Freedom from detention for civil offences. For criminal offences only, a court or Prosecutor's Office can determine freedom from arrest	Members	Term of Parliament (5 years).
CAMEROON National Assembly	a) In Assembly and its cttees b) Freedom from prosecution for criminal and civil matters, except with previous authorisation of Assembly or in case of flagrante delicto or threat to state security	Members in the exercise of their mandate	Term of office (5 years).

142

4.4 Waiving immunity or privilege	4.5 Offences against Parliament	4.6 Adjudicating authority for offences against Parliament. Procedure followed	4.7 Penalties prescribed
Respective House	No distinction between offences against Parlt and offences against other public authorities.	Courts of law	Fines or imprisonment
Respective House	Breaking of decorum	Respective House, through floor procedure of accusation and defence.	Naming; suspension of mandate; loss of mandate.
Parliament or, during recess, the State Council.	None specified	NA	None
Assembly or Assembly Bureau	Contempt the Assembly or President of Assembly; appeal to violence in public sitting.	Bureau of Assembly which hears the Member.	Censure; censure and suspension with cancellation of Mandate allowance for up to 6 months.

Country and House(s)	4.1 Guarantees: a) Freedom of speech b) Freedom from arrest c) Other	4.2 Institutions and persons granted privileges and immunities	4.3 Duration of immunity or privilege
CANADA Senate House of Commons	a) In Parliament b) Under civil process, but not in any criminal action or indictable offence c) MPs are not compelled to attend as witnesses before any court when the House is in session and are exempt from jury service	Parlt; cttees; and MPs. Every person engaged in a proceeding in Parlt enjoys the same immunity as MP and receives protection from the House (witness, petitioners, counsel, etc.).	For MPs, during sessions and forty days before and after sessions, or after a dissolution. A parliamentary officer or other person required to attend Parlt is immune from civil arrest and jury duty during relevant period.
CAPE VERDE People's National Assembly	a) In Parliament and its cttees b) Except in flagrante delicto of crime punishable by 2 years prison or more	Members	Term of office
CHINA National People's Congress	a) Freedom of speech and vote in NPC meetings b) Freedom from arrest or criminal trial, except in case of flagrante delicto unless the NPC Presidium (or when not in session its Standing Cttee) consents	Members	Term of office

4.4 Waiving immunity or privilege	4.5 Offences against Parliament	4.6 Adjudicating authority for offences against Parliament. Procedure followed	4.7 Penalties prescribed
Respective House	Offences against the authority and dignity of Parlt, invasion of its rights, disobedience to its orders; disorderly conduct before or in it; uttering or writing words calculated to bring it into disrepute, etc.; breach of an established privilege of Parliament.	Penalties may be imposed on a Member or non-Member by resolution of the House concerned.	Committing a Member to prison (never yet exercised). The House of Commons may suspend or expel a Member. A Member found guilty of breach of privilege or contempt may be admonished or reprimanded by the Speaker.
Assembly or Permanent Bureau between sessions	Insult, as defined in the Penal Code, against public authorities.	Supreme Court	2 years imprisonment if offence has been publicised, 6 months if not.
NPC Presidium or Standing Cttee	None specified	NA	None

TABLE 4: IMMUNITIES AND PRIVILEGES (continued)

Country and House(s)	4.1 Guarantees: a) Freedom of speech b) Freedom from arrest c) Other	4.2 Institutions and persons granted privileges and immunities	4.3 Duration of immunity or privilege
COMOROS Federal Assembly	a) Freedom of speech and vote in exercice of functions b) Freedom from arrest, pursuit, detention or trial except with authorisation of Assembly in case of flagrante delicto	Members	Term of session. Authorisation to arrest only becomes effective at end of the session.
CONGO People's National Assembly (ANP)	a) Yes b) Except in flagrante delicto or with authorisation of ANP	Members	Term of Parliament
COSTA RICA Legislative Assembly	a) Yes b) For criminal offences except flagrante delicto	Members	Term of office (duration of session for civil proceedings).
CUBA National Assembly of People's Power	a) In Parlt and its cttees b) Freedom from arrest and detention for civil and criminal offences	Members	Term of office
CYPRUS House of Representatives	a) In Parlt and cttees b) Arrest, prosecution and imprisonment except by leave of the Supreme Court	Members	Term of office

4.4 Waiving immunity or privilege	4.5 Offences against Parliament	4.6 Adjudicating authority for offences against Parliament. Procedure followed	4.7 Penalties prescribed
Federal Assembly	–	–	–
ANP	–	–	–
2/3 majority of Legislative Assembly	None specified	NA	NA
None	None specified	NA	NA
Supreme Court	None specified	NA	NA

Country and House(s)	4.1 Guarantees: a) Freedom of speech b) Freedom from arrest c) Other	4.2 Institutions and persons granted privileges and immunities	4.3 Duration of immunity or privilege
CZECHOSLOVAKIA Chamber of Nations Chamber of the People	a) Yes b) Yes, unless the Chamber consents. If the Chamber refuses, prosecution is denied irrevocably. If a Member is arrested in flagrante delicto, the Presidium of Federal Assembly must be notified and if not approved the Member must be released immediately	Members	Term of office
DEMOCRATIC YEMEN Supreme People's Council	a) Yes b Yes	Members	Term of office
DENMARK Folketing	a) Yes b) Except in flagrante delicto	Members	Term of office
EGYPT People's Assembly	a) Yes b) Yes, except in flagrante delicto and with consent of the Assembly	Assembly; cttees; Members.	Term of Parliament

4.4 Waiving immunity or privilege	4.5 Offences against Parliament	4.6 Adjudicating authority for offences against Parliament. Procedure followed	4.7 Penalties prescribed
Both Chambers and the Presidium of the Federal Assembly	MPs subject to the disciplinary authority of the respective Chamber for statements made in the exercise of their office which offend the Chamber or its organs.	Presidium of the respective Chamber on the recommendation of the Mandate and Immunities Cttee	-
Supreme People's Council, or the Presidium if Council not in session.	-	-	-
Folketing	Attack on security or freedom of Parlt is an act of high treason.	-	-
Assembly	Affronting the Assembly or one of its parliamentary organs; resorting to violence within the Assembly in addressing Speaker, Prime Minister or MPs.	Cttee on Constitutional Affairs, or Cttee on Values or an ad hoc cttee. Testimony heard by cttee which reports to the Assembly. The accused Member may choose a colleague to help his defence.	Deprival of attending 2 sittings or if violence involved, up to 10 sittings or withdrawal of Membership.

Country and House(s)	4.1 Guarantees: a) Freedom of speech b) Freedom from arrest c) Other	4.2 Institutions and persons granted privileges and immunities	4.3 Duration of immunity or privilege
FIJI Senate House of Representatives	a) In Parlt b) When going to or from or within the precints of Parlt c) As in parliamentary powers and privileges Act	Senators and Members	Term of office. See also 4.1 b).
FINLAND Eduskunta	a) While carrying out parliamentary mandate b) In session, unless a tribunal has ordered arrest or in flagrante delicto for an offence punishable by at least 6 months imprisonment	Members	Term of Parlt
FRANCE Senate National Assembly	a) Yes b) Freedom from prosecution and arrest for penal matters	Members	a) Term of office b) Period of session
GABON National Assembly	a) In Parlt and cttees b) For criminal and civil offences (not in flagrante delicto)	Members	Term of Parlt (5 years).

4.4 Waiving immunity or privilege	4.5 Offences against Parliament	4.6 Adjudicating authority for offences against Parliament. Procedure followed	4.7 Penalties prescribed
None	Contempt of authority of Parlt; disrespect to MPs; misconduct of visitors; bribery or obstruction of MPs; interference with MPs' activities; interrupting proceedings of Parlt; withholding documents; influencing witnesses before Parlt; etc.	Judiciary	Fine and/or 2 years imprisonment
Parlt by 5/6 majority, if the matter concerns opinions expressed or parliamentary procedure.	−	−	−
Respective House or Bureau during recess	No distinction is made between offences against Parlt and offences against other public authorities.	Courts of law	−
National Assembly	−	−	−

Country and House(s)	4.1 Guarantees: a) Freedom of speech b) Freedom from arrest c) Other	4.2 Institutions and persons granted privileges and immunities	4.3 Duration of immunity or privilege
GERMAN DEMOCRATIC REPUBLIC People's Chamber	Immunity from limitation of personal liberty, house searches, confiscation and prosecution. Entitled to refuse testimony on matters communicated in confidence.	Members	Term of office
GERMANY Federal Council	Immunities and privileges as Members of the State Assemblies	Members	Term of mandate in State Assembly
Federal Diet	a) In House and cttees but not for defamation b) Except in flagrante delicto c) May refuse evidence concerning privileged information	a) and b) are privileges of the House c) Members	Term of Parlt (4 years).
GREECE Chamber of Deputies	a) Yes b) For infamous calomny with Chamber's authorisation or in flagrante delicto	Members	Until the subsequent Parlt is declared.
HUNGARY National Assembly	a) Yes b) Yes	MPs and members of the Constitutional Law Cttee	Term of office

4.4 Waiving immunity or privilege	4.5 Offences against Parliament	4.6 Adjudicating authority for offences against Parliament. Procedure followed	4.7 Penalties prescribed
People's Chamber on proposal of the Credentials Cttee	No provisions	N A	None
Dependent on State Assembly Diet	Use or threat of force against Parlt; restraining MPs from meeting or voting; demonstrating in Parliamentary precincts.	Courts through application of ordinary law	Maximum sentence of 5 years imprisonment or fine
Parliament	–	–	–
National Assembly or, during recess, the Presidential Council.	Same as offences against public authorities	–	–

Country and House(s)	4.1 Guarantees: a) Freedom of speech b) Freedom from arrest c) Other	4.2 Institutions and persons granted privileges and immunities	4.3 Duration of immunity or privilege
INDIA Council of States House of the People	a) Yes b) In civil cases during session and 40 days before and after. Prohibition of arrest and service of legal process within the precincts of the House without Presiding Officer's permission c) Freedom from obstruction or molestation while in performance of duties as a Member	Parlt; MPs; cttees. Civil cases in 4. 1 b) also applies to officers of Parlt on duty. Immunity to a person from proceedings in any court in respect of publication by or under the authority of either House, of any report, paper, votes or proceedings.	Term of office. See also 4.1 b).
INDONESIA House of Representatives	a) In Parlt and Cttees b) In Parliament building for civil and criminal offences	Members	Term of office. See also 4.1 b).
IRELAND Senate Dáil	a) Answerable only to Parliament b) Going to or coming from and within either House except for treason, felony or breach of peace c) All official documents of Parlt are privileged	The Houses collectively and Members	Term of office. See also 4.1 b).

154

4.4 Waiving immunity or privilege	4.5 Offences against Parliament	4.6 Adjudicating authority for offences against Parliament. Procedure followed	4.7 Penalties prescribed
Council of States: the House; House of the People: cannot be waived.	Breaches of privileges or contempt of Parlt; deliberately misleading the House or its committees; casting aspersions on the House or its Members; publication of false report of proceedings of secret sessions; premature publication of proceedings, evidence or report of a cttee; obstructing or molesting MPs, witnesses, or officers of Parlt.	The respective House, or the matter may be referred to a Court of Law if it involves an offence at Law and the House considers that a proceeding at Law is necessary.	Admonition or reprimand by the Presiding Officer; imprisonment; Member's expulsion.
None	Breach of state secrecy	House leadership	On decision of Faction
Respective House	Each House makes rules and SO with penalties for infringement, to ensure free debate, protection of documents, itself and Members from molestation, and corruption.	Respective House	Not defined

155

Country and House(s)	4.1 Guarantees: a) Freedom of speech b) Freedom from arrest c) Other	4.2 Institutions and persons granted privileges and immunities	4.3 Duration of immunity or privilege
ISRAEL The Knesset	a) Yes, in relation to the mandate b) Yes, except in flagrante delicto involving violence, disturbance of the peace or treason. c) Immunity from search, prosecution, compulsory military service and restriction of movement	Members	Term of office
ITALY Senate Chamber of Deputies	a) Yes b) Except in flagrante delicto c) Immunity from arrest and imprisonment following sentence	Members	a) Unlimited b) and c) Period of mandate
IVORY COAST National Assembly	a) Yes b) Except when authorised by the National Assembly or in case of flagrante delicto	Members	Term of Parlt
JAPAN House of Councillors House of Representatives	a) In Parlt b) Except in flagrante delicto unless House gives consent. MPs arrested before a session starts must be freed during session at request of House	Members	Freedom of speech during and after term of office; freedom from arrest during sessions.

4.4 Waiving immunity or privilege	4.5 Offences against Parliament	4.6 Adjudicating authority for offences against Parliament. Procedure followed	4.7 Penalties prescribed
Knesset	Carrying arms in the Knesset Building	The Courts but charges require the sanction of the Knesset chairman.	Liability to imprisonment for 2 years
a) Cannot be waived b) and c) By the respective House	Contempt of Parlt	Courts of Law with authorisation of Parlt: 1. if offence committed outside the Chamber; 2. President of the Chamber and the Bureau if during the sessions.	1. Imprisonment for 6 months to 3 years 2. Suspension from sittings; censure; exclusion from parliamentary activities
National Assembly	Outrage or violence towards the President of the Assembly or a Member	National Assembly lifts immunities and expels. Courts apply the law.	Up to 5 years prison and up to 2 million CFA francs fine.
Immunity is constitutionally secured and cannot be waived except as in 4.1.	Refusal to give testimony or submit documents without good reason; refusal to swear an oath; making a false statement.	Indictment by House, cttee or joint examination council, followed by Court judgement in accordance with law.	False statement 3 months to 10 years hard labour; other cases imprisonment for a year or less or a fine not exceeding 10,000 yen.

Country and House(s)	4.1 Guarantees: a) Freedom of speech b) Freedom from arrest c) Other	4.2 Institutions and persons granted privileges and immunities	4.3 Duration of immunity or privilege
JORDAN Senate House of Deputies	a) Yes b) In session, except in flagrante delicto or the respective House resolves by majority that sufficient reason exists for detention or trial. Between sessions the Prime Minister reports to the relevant House on reassembly	Members and cttees	During sessions of the Assembly
KENYA National Assembly	a) Yes b) Yes Under the Const. Parlt may provide for privileges and immunities necessary for effective functioning	Parlt; Members; officers of the Assembly; witnesses before cttees.	During sessions
KUWAIT National Assembly	a) Yes b) During session except in flagrante delicto	Members	Term of office. See also 41.1 b).
LEBANON National Assembly	a) In Parlt and cttees b) Except in flagrante delicto	Members	During sessions
LIECHTENSTEIN Diet	a) In the Diet and Cttees b) Except in flagrante delicto	Members	During sessions
LUXEMBOURG Chamber of Deputies	a) Yes b) Except in flagrante delicto or by authorisation of the Chamber	Members	During sessions, which is effectively the term of office (see 8.1).

4.4 Waiving immunity or privilege	4.5 Offences against Parliament	4.6 Adjudicating authority for offences against Parliament. Procedure followed	4.7 Penalties prescribed
Parliament	Damage to the prestige of Parlt or the Speaker	House of Deputies	–
See 4.1	Contempt of Parlt	Privileges Cttee	3 months imprisonment, 100 Kenya shillings fine or both.
National Assembly	–	–	–
National Assembly	None specified	NA	NA
Diet	None specified	NA	NA
Chamber of Deputies	None specified	NA	NA

Country and House(s)	4.1 Guarantees: a) Freedom of speech b) Freedom from arrest c) Other	4.2 Institutions and persons granted privileges and immunities	4.3 Duration of immunity or privilege
MALAWI National Assembly	a) Yes b) Proceeding to and from Parlt and in its precincts	President of the Republic; Ministers; Speaker; Members.	Term of office. See also 4.1 b).
MALAYSIA Senate House of Representatives	a) Yes b) No c) Exemption from jury service and civil court attendance as witness during sittings	Both Houses, cttees, Members and officers of Parlt in respect of authorised parliamentary publications.	Term of office
MALI National Assembly	a) Yes b) Except in flagrante delicto	Members	Term of office
MALTA House of Representatives	a) Yes b) For civil debt not in contravention of the criminal code	Members and Officers of Parlt in carrying out their duties in the House	Term of office

4.4 Waiving immunity or privilege	4.5 Offences against Parliament	4.6 Adjudicating authority for offences against Parliament. Procedure followed	4.7 Penalties prescribed
-	None specified	NA	None
Parliament	Refusal of evidence; wilful obstruction; offering bribes to Members or Officers; assault, insult or menace to Members; disturbance of proceedings, tempering with witnesses; libel; wilful misrepresentation; failure of Members to reveal pecuniary interests.	Parliament with the respective House sitting as a court.	Fine not exceeding M\$ 1,000 and imprisonment not exceeding 60 days
The Assembly	None specified	NA	None
Cannot be waived.	Perjury by a witness; misleading the House; contempt of Parlt by word or gesture; bribery or obstruction of Members; threat or assault; tampering with witnesses; disturbance in the House precincts.	Parliament	Reprimand, fine and or imprisonment.

Country and House(s)	4.1 Guarantees: a) Freedom of speech b) Freedom from arrest c) Other	4.2 Institutions and persons granted privileges and immunities	4.3 Duration of immunity or privilege
MAURITIUS Legislative Assembly	a) Yes b) No	Members; cttees.	Term of office
MEXICO Chamber of Senators Chamber of Deputies	a) Yes b) Yes	The President of the Republic	Term of office
MONACO National Council	a) Yes b) Except in flagrante delicto	Members	During session
MONGOLIA Great People's Khural	a) Guaranteed to all under the Constitution b) Yes, except with permission of the GPkh or its Presidium c) A Member cannot be dismissed from work or an agricultural collective as a result of disciplinary measures without permission of the GPKh or its Presidium	Members	Term of office

4.4 Waiving immunity or privilege	4.5 Offences against Parliament	4.6 Adjudicating authority for offences against Parliament. Procedure followed	4.7 Penalties prescribed
The Speaker	Wilful disobedience of an authorised cttee order relating to evidence, answering questions, production of documents or offering or accepting bribes.	The Speaker who reports to Parlt, which moves to request the Attorney-General to institute proceedings.	Imprisonment not exceeding 3 months or a fine not exceeding 1,000 rupees.
The respective Chamber	–	–	–
National Council	Obstruction or interruption of parliamentary proceedings	Court of Law	One month to 1 year in prison and/or a fine of 1,000 to 20,000 francs.
None	None specified	NA	NA

Country and House(s)	4.1 Guarantees: a) Freedom of speech b) Freedom from arrest c) Other	4.2 Institutions and persons granted privileges and immunities	4.3 Duration of immunity or privilege
NAURU Parliament	a) Parlt and cttees b) For any civil debt while, going to, attending or returning from Parlt and for offences in parliamentary precincts, except with the Speaker's consent c) Exemption from jury service or summons to give evidence	Parlt, cttees, Members, Officers of Parliament.	During sessions and 40 days before and after a session. See also 4.1 b).
NETHERLANDS First Chamber Second Chamber	a) Yes b) No	Members; Ministers; persons who participate in deliberations of the Chamber or cttees.	Unlimited
NEW ZEALAND House of Representatives	a) Yes b) For civil offences only c) Freedom from attendance at inferior courts and ability to be excused at superior courts as parties or witnesses	Parlt and cttees; c) also extends to officers of Parlt.	During sessions
NICARAGUA National Assembly	a) Yes, in Parlt and cttees b) Yes	Members	Term of office

4.4 Waiving immunity or privilege	4.5 Offences against Parliament	4.6 Adjudicating authority for offences against Parliament. Procedure followed	4.7 Penalties prescribed
Parliament	Breach of privilege; contempt for or misleading Parlt; reflections upon Parliament; acceptance of bribes.	Parlt, usually following a report from the Cttee of Privileges.	Reprimand from the Chair; suspension; expulsion; imprisonment.
None	Use or threat of violence; obstructing an MP.	Ordinary procedure in Court of Law	Imprisonment of maximum 20 years and minimum 1 day
Parliament	Deliberately misleading the House; disclosing prematurely cttee proceedings; reflecting on Speaker's impartiality, etc.	House, following a report from its Privileges Cttee.	Imprisonment, suspension from House or cttees, admonition.
Parliament in plenary sitting	As established in the Fundamental Statutes	Parliament	Expulsion and other penalties depending on the offence

Country and House(s)	4.1 Guarantees: a) Freedom of speech b) Freedom from arrest c) Other	4.2 Institutions and persons granted privileges and immunities	4.3 Duration of immunity or privilege
NORWAY Storting	a) Yes, in plenary and cttees b) Except for clear guilt in serious crime	Members	a) Indefinite b) In the Storting and going to and from
PHILIPPINES National Assembly	a) Yes b) Yes, for offences punishable by less than 6 years imprisonment	Members	a) Term of office b) During attendance at sessions and while coming and going
POLAND Diet	a) Yes b) Except by authorisation of the Diet or, be- tween sessions, the State Council (see 8.5)	Members	Term of office from the day of the elections
PORTUGAL Assembly of the Republic	a) Yes b) Except for major crimes or in flagrante delicto	Members	Term of office
REPUBLIC OF KOREA National Assembly	a) Yes, in Parlt and cttees b) Yes, except in flagrante delicto c) Not liable outside National Assembly for votes cast in Parlt or its cttees	Members	a) and c) Indefinite b) During session

4.4 Waiving immunity or privilege	4.5 Offences against Parliament	4.6 Adjudicating authority for offences against Parliament. Procedure followed	4.7 Penalties prescribed
None	Ordinary offences against Members; failure to attend, participate, observe SO, provide information, or observe secrecy pledge. Disturbance of the liberty and security of the Storting is an act of treason.	The Odelsting prosecutes in the Court of Impeachment (Riksretten) comprising 2/3 members of the Lagting and 1/3 Supreme Court Justices.	Variable according to the offence (fine, imprisonment, loss of office, etc.).
The Member himself	Disorderly behaviour	The House with concurrence of 2/3 membership following investigation by the Cttee of Privileges	Suspension not exceeding 60 days, or expulsion.
2/3 majority of at least 1/2 the Diet members on proposal of the Mandates and Rules Cttee or, between sessions, the State Council.	Failure to discharge responsibilities as an MP or conduct unbecoming a Member.	The Diet refers the matter to the Mandates and Rules Cttee for report.	Suspension for one or more sittings
Assembly of the Republic	None specified	NA	None
None	Breach of privilege and contempt of Parlt	No special procedure	No special penalties

Country and House(s)	4.1 Guarantees: a) Freedom of speech b) Freedom from arrest c) Other	4.2 Institutions and persons granted privileges and immunities	4.3 Duration of immunity or privilege
ROMANIA Grand National Assembly	a) Yes b) Except in flagrante delicto unless the Assembly (or in recess, the State Council) consents	Members	Term of office
RWANDA National Development Council (CND)	a) Yes b) During sessions except in flagrante delicto and with the authorisation of 3/4 majority of the CND	The CND and its cttees; the President of the Republic; Ministers and State secretaries.	Term of office
ST VINCENT House of Assembly	a) Yes, in Parlt and cttees b) For civil offences	Members	Term of office
SENEGAL National Assembly	a) Yes b) During sessions except with Assembly authorisation or in flagrante delicto; between sessions except with Bureau authorisation or in flagrante delicto	Members	Term of office
SOLOMON ISLANDS National Parliament	a) Yes b) –	–	Term of office
SOMALIA People's Assembly	a) Yes b) Except in flagrante delicto	Members	Term of office

4.4 Waiving immunity or privilege	4.5 Offences against Parliament	4.6 Adjudicating authority for offences against Parliament. Procedure followed	4.7 Penalties prescribed
The Assembly or, during recess, the State Council.	–	–	–
The National Development Council	–	–	–
The Assembly	Disrespect towards representative of Monarch or Heads of friendly States; raising of sub-judice matters.	The Assembly, via a cttee of the House. Court of Law in serious cases.	As recommended by the cttee or provided by law
The Assembly or Assembly Bureau	–	–	–
Parliament	–	–	–
Parliament	–	–	–

Country and House(s)	4.1 Guarantees: a) Freedom of speech b) Freedom from arrest c) Other	4.2 Institutions and persons granted privileges and immunities	4.3 Duration of immunity or privilege
SOUTH AFRICA House of Assembly House of Representatives House of Delegates	a) Yes b) For civil matters only during sessions, except in Cape Town c) Exemption from court attendance as witness or defendant during sessions, except in Cape Town	Members; Counsel; attorneys and witnesses before Parlt or its cttees; officers of Parlt.	While in attendance on Parliament
SPAIN Senate Congress of Deputies	a) Yes b) Yes, except in flagrante delicto	Houses of Parlt; cttees; Members.	Term of office
SRI LANKA Parliament	a) Yes b) For any act committeed in carrying out the parliamentary mandate and for civil offences	President of the Republic; Members.	Term of office
SWEDEN Riksdag	a) Yes b) Yes, in respect of acts and statements pursuant to his mandate except with consent of 5/6 membership or in flagrante delicto of crime with minimum penalty of 2 years imprisonment	Speaker; Members and substitutes fulfilling mission as members.	Unlimited in respect of mandate; term of office for other criminal acts.

4.4 Waiving immunity or privilege	4.5 Offences against Parliament	4.6 Adjudicating authority for offences against Parliament. Procedure followed	4.7 Penalties prescribed
Resolution of Parlt	Contempt of Parlt which in- cludes dis- obedience to an order of Parlt; offer or accep- tance of bribes; assaulting, obstructing or insulting any Member; dis- turbance in Parlt or its vicinity.	The complaint is presented to Parlt by the Member, if possible with evidence. If a prima facie case has been estab- lished, the Speaker allows a motion for full inquiry by a Select Cttee to recommend action.	Fine; imprison- ment; admonition; or reprimand.
a) Cannot be waived b) See 3.3	None specified	NA	NA
Parliament	Breach of privilege	Parlt and Courts of Law	Warning; fines; and penal sentences.
See 4.1 b)	None specified	NA	NA

TABLE 4: IMMUNITIES AND PRIVILEGES (continued)

Country and House(s)	4.1 Guarantees: a) Freedom of speech b) Freedom from arrest c) Other	4.2 Institutions and persons granted privileges and immunities	4.3 Duration of immunity or privilege
SWITZERLAND States Council National Council	a) Yes b) For matters pertaining to Parlt only with authori- sation of both Councils. For other matters, during sessions, except in flagrante delicto or with authority of the respective Council	Members	Term of office. See also 4.1 b).
SYRIAN ARAB REPUBLIC People's Council	a) Yes b) Penal proceed- ings require authorisation of the Council Presi- dent except in flagrante delicto	Members	Term of office
THAILAND Senate House of Representatives	a) Yes b) Except in fla- grante delicto or with permission of the House c) Criminal trial of an MP may not take place during a session without House permission or unless attend- ance at sittings is unhindered	Members; wit- nesses before Parlt; printers and publishers of parliamentary documents.	a) Absolute privilege b) During sessions
TUNISIA Chamber of Deputies	a) Yes b) Except in flagrante delicto or if Parlt waives immunity	Members	Term of office
UGANDA National Assembly	a) Yes b) For civil matters	Members and parliamentary officials	When on parliamentary duty

4.4 Waiving immunity or privilege	4.5 Offences against Parliament	4.6 Adjudicating authority for offences against Parliament. Procedure followed	4.7 Penalties prescribed
Parliament (and see 4.1).	None specified	NA	None
See 4.1 b). If during recess, the President advises the Council at the next session start.	-	-	-
The respective House	None specified	NA	NA
Majority of Members, on report of Cttee on Immunity which hears the Member concerned, within 15 days.	None specified	NA	None
National Assembly	Wilful breach of privilege and contempt of Parlt	Cttee of Privileges and Assembly as a whole	Reprimand; suspension from sittings; etc.

Country and House(s)	4.1 Guarantees: a) Freedom of speech b) Freedom from arrest c) Other	4.2 Institutions and persons granted privileges and immunities	4.3 Duration of immunity or privilege
UNION OF SOVIET SOCIALIST REPUBLICS Soviet of Nationalities Soviet of the Union	a) Yes, in plenary and other parliamentary bodies b) Except with consent of the Supreme Soviet during sessions or the Presidium between sessions c) Guarantee of unhindered exercise of a Member's duties	Members	Term of office
UNITED KINGDOM House of Lords House of Commons	a) Yes b) Freedom from interference in attending or going to or from Parlt except for a criminal charge c) Exemption from jury service or giving evidence	a) b) and c) MPs and Officers of Parliament a) and b) Witnesses and other persons attending Parlt	Effectively continuous for Members Session of Parlt and 40 days before and after
UNITED REPUBLIC OF TANZANIA National Assembly	a) Yes b) For civil offences c) Exemption from service as court assessor	Members; parliamentary cttees; officers of Parlt.	Session of Parlt or cttee
UNITED STATES OF AMERICA Senate House of Representatives	a) Yes b) Yes, for misdemeanours c) Absolute immunity for all legislative actions and qualified immunity for official actions	Members House; Members; officers; cttees; employees.	During session and travel to and from a session

4.4 Waiving immunity or privilege	4.5 Offences against Parliament	4.6 Adjudicating authority for offences against Parliament. Procedure followed	4.7 Penalties prescribed
Supreme Soviet during sessions or the Presidium between sessions	No special crimes against Parlt specified	NA	NA
The respective House	Contempt of the House	The House	Reprimand; fine; imprisonment; but fine or imprisonment not imposed in recent years.
	Breach of Privilege or contempt e.g. misleading the House, acceptance of bribes, disobedience to House orders, reflections upon the House.	The House, usually after report from the Cttee of Privileges.	Reprimand or admonition; suspension; expulsion; imprisonment.
No provision	None specified	NA	NA
None	Disorderly conduct; breach of privilege.	The House	Censure or expulsion
		The House on recommendation of Cttee on Standards of Official Conduct	Various, including reprimand; censure; fine; expulsion.

Country and House(s)	4.1 Guarantees: a) Freedom of speech b) Freedom from arrest c) Other	4.2 Institutions and persons granted privileges and immunities	4.3 Duration of immunity or privilege
VANUATU Parliament	a) Yes b) Unless otherwise decided by Parliament	Members in parliamentary precincts	During sessions
YUGOSLAVIA Federal Chamber Chamber of Republics and Provinces	a) Yes, in the Chamber b) Yes, for criminal offences	Members; Federal Executive Council; Federal Secretaries; Presidents of Federal Cttees; members of the Constitutional Court.	Term of office
ZAIRE Legislative Council	a) Yes b) Except in flagrante delicto or with Council authorisation	Members	Term of office
ZAMBIA National Assembly	a) Yes b) Yes	Members	Duration of session
ZIMBABWE Senate House of Assembly	a) Yes b) No	Houses; cttees; Presiding Officers and Members; officers of Parlt.	Term of office

4.4 Waiving immunity or privilege	4.5 Offences against Parliament	4.6 Adjudicating authority for offences against Parliament. Procedure followed	4.7 Penalties prescribed
Parliament	–	–	–
The respective Chamber	–	–	–
Legislative Council	None specified	None specified	None specified
National Assembly	Breach of privilege	National Assembly	Reprimand; suspension; fine; imprisonment.
Parliament through an Act	Refusal to supply oral or docu- mentary inform- ation; revealing evidence before Parlt without permission; voting on matters having direct pecuniary interest; accep- ting gift or reward for promoting a parliamentary matter.	The relevant House decides following inves- tigation by a cttee.	Fine up to $ 6,000 or an imprison- ment up to 4 years, or both with recovery of gift or reward.

TABLE 5

PARLIAMENTARY REMUNERATION

In virtually all countries it is accepted that Members of Parliament be provided with a salary and/or allowaances. While the forms of such payments vary greatly from country to country, the growing claims of parliamentary life, coupled with the increasing frequency and duration of sessions, have led to the introduction of emoluments designed to provide Members of Parliament with the means of livelihood which they can no longer earn from their former occupation, especially where it proves incompatible with membership. Consequently, the nature of parliamentary remuneration has gradually changed. Instead of being a mere reimbursement of expenses it has, to some extent, become a salary. Reimbursement, either on a monthly or a yearly basis, nevertheless remains the practice in the socialist countries, where Members continue to carry on their profession or occupation while serving in Parliament and continue to receive their ordinary salaries.

The variety and complexity of methods used in calculating parliamentary emoluments makes it very difficult to advance generalisations about them. Three main reasons can be put forward for this. The first of these relates to differences in the economic and social conditions of the countries under examination. The second arises because payments may consist of two distinct parts, i.e. salaries and the reimbursement of out-of-pocket expenses. It is accordingly difficult to determine a balance between the two. The final factor which confounds comparative analysis is that, besides a salary, Members may be provided with a wide variety of facilities and services which are considered necessary for them to perform their parliamentary duties efficiently.

Special Allowances

Apart from a basic salary, emoluments are often supplemented by additional allowances which may either be a fixed amount designed to cover a variety of purposes or a specific sum for a particular purpose. Allowances paid to Members for each day that Parliament meets are found in many countries including Costa Rica, Liechtenstein, Poland, Rwanda and the USSR. In a number of countries (which include Finland, Israel and Portugal) the exact amount paid to each Member for attending sittings of Parliament depends upon the distance of his residence in his home constituency from the Parliament. The size of travel allowances that Members receive in countries such as Austria, Israel, Portugal and the United States of America is also dependent on the relative distance of their constituencies from Parliament.

Additional examples of special allowances include constituency allowance (Australia), family allowance (Greece), the cost of daily meals and lodging in the capital (Switzerland), entertainment allowances (Nauru), and secretarial assistance (Cyprus and the United Kingdom). In the socialist countries, such costs are usually covered by Members receiving general reimbursement for office-connected expenses. Some countries such as Italy, Poland and Senegal provide special allowances for parliamentary positions such as committee chairman.

Taxation

A Member's basic salary and subsequent allowances are taxed in different ways in different countries, as shown in Table 5A. In Finland, India, Malawi and New Zealand, for example, only the basic salary is taxed. By contrast, in Greece one half of the salary is taxed, and in Israel all of the emoluments are taxed. In the majority of the countries considered, salary is taxed but not the allowances. In countries where Members are reimbursed for expenses but do not receive a fixed salary, the emoluments are not usually subject to taxation.

TABLE 5A. Parliamentary Salary, Allowances and Taxation

Salary and Allowances	Number of Countries
Salary Only Received - Tax-free 5, Taxed 7	12
Allowances Only Received - Tax-free 9, Taxed 3	12
Salary and Allowances - Tax-free 7, Taxed 8	15
Salary Tax-free, Allowances Taxed	0
Salary Taxed, Allowances Tax-free	34
Total	73*

* China, Congo, Costa Rica, Democratic Yemen, Indonesia, Mali, Mexico, St Vincent, Senegal and Solomon Islands excluded for reasons of missing data.

Pension Schemes

Parliamentary pension schemes exist in nearly half the Parliaments under study, as shown in Table 5B. Four Parliaments offer a terminal grant on completion of service. Pension schemes are usually based on contributions from Members' salaries. Typically, a fixed percentage (in Japan 9.7%, in Australia 11.5%) is deducted from their monthly salaries. Members receive pension benefits proportional to this monthly contribution, as well as on the basis of a certain number of years of parliamentary service and/or on reaching a specified age of retirement. Each of

TABLE 5B. Pension Schemes

Type of Pension Scheme	Number of Countries
Parliamentary (Contributory and Non-Contributory)	39
State	14
Terminal Grant	4
Under Study	3
None	18
Total	78*

* Algeria, Argentine, China, Democratic Yemen and Mali, excluded for reasons of missing data.

these factors may be low. Pensions are payable to former Members of the Cyprus House of Representatives after only 4 years of service provided they have reached the age of 60. A former Member of the Israeli Knesset receives a pension upon reaching 40 years of age, provided he has been a Member of the Knesset for at least 4 years. In the Federal Republic of Germany pensions are payable after 6 years service at 65. In Denmark, the required 8 years parliamentary service need not necessarily be consecutive for a Member to receive a pension.

In the case of a Member's death, the beneficiaries of retirement pensions are often the surviving spouse and children. Such provisions are found, for example, in Norway and the United Kingdom. Disability pensions are a further possibility. In Australia, these payments are made where the Member's infirmity arose during his term of office.

TABLE 5: PARLIAMENTARY REMUNERATION

Country and House(s)	5.1 Annual salary (US$ approximately)	5.2 Allowances (US$ approximately)
ALGERIA National People's Assembly (APN)	Members, in addition to a continuation of their salary before election receive a parliamentary allowance.	4,500
ARGENTINA Senate	10,000	None
Chamber of Deputies		
AUSTRALIA Senate	28,800	Electoral: Senator 10,200 pa; Member, constituency smaller than 5,000 sq.km. 10,200 pa; Member, electorate of more than 140,000, 12,400 pa; Member, constituency larger than 5,000 sq.km. 14,800 pa. Travel: daily where including overnight stay away from headquarters in capital cities 67, other cities 54.
House of Representatives		
AUSTRIA Federal Council	According to term of office 15,070 to 19,370	Expenses: 4,850 pa.
National Council	30,140 to 38,740	Expenses: 9,700 pa; travel for Members living outside Vienna: 3,850, 5,800 or 7,700 pa depending on distance.
BAHAMAS Senate	10,000	Duty travel: 100 pd.
House of Assembly	21,000	Duty travel: 100 pd limited to 3 times pm.
BELGIUM Senate	33,700	Family allowances according to scale for public servants
Chamber of Representatives		

182

	5.3 Taxation	5.4 Pension Schemes
	Salary and allowances taxable	–
	Salary tax free	–
	Salary only is taxable.	Contributions are 11.5 % of salary. Pension payable after 8 years' service on defeat, ill health, or retirement at the age of 60 and after 12 years' service on resignation. Pension is 50 % of final salary for 8 years' service, increasing with each year to 75 % for 18 or more years of service.
	Only expense and travel allowances exempt from taxation	Members contribute 13 % of their salary. At age of 55 and after 10 years' service, former Members entitled to a pension of 48 % of last salary plus 1.6 % for each additional year of membership subject to the total not exceeding 80 % of final salary.
	No tax on earnings in the Bahamas	None
	50 % of salary is taxable.	Contribution of 6.5 % of salary entitles contributor to pension at age 58, after at least 5 years service at end of mandate. Contribution of 6.5 % of salary entitles contributor to pension at 55, after at least 8 years service at end of mandate. Those with less than 8 years receive reduced pension at 65. Pension is proportional to service for both Houses.

Country and House(s)	5.1 Annual salary (US$ approximately)	5.2 Allowances (US$ approximately)
BRAZIL Federal Senate	27,000	600 pa, in two instalments.
Chamber of Deputies		
BULGARIA National Assembly	None	Variable, to meet parliamentary expenses.
CAMEROON National Assembly	No salary. Basic parliamentary allowance 9,105.	Mandate allowance to cover expenses: 240 pa.
CANADA Senate	40,900, annual sessional indemnity.	Expenses: 6,700 pa.
House of Commons		Expenses: 13,800 pa.
CAPE VERDE People's National Assembly	No salary, except for President of the Assembly (315).	Accommodation; travel; compensation for income lost whilst attending Parlt; social security benefits.
CHINA National People's Congress (NPC)	Same as salary or remuneration received before election	Allowances and material facilities required to discharge duties
COMOROS Federal Assembly	3,430	–
CONGO People's National Assembly (ANP)	None	Daily allowance during sessions: 32.
COSTA RICA Legislative Assembly	–	Sitting allowance

Approx. 80 % of remuneration exempt from taxation	"Members Pension Institute"
Allowances taxable	None
Mandate allowance is not taxable.	Contribution of 6 % of basic parliamentary allowance. Assembly's contribution is 12 %.
Expense allowance exempt	Pension after resignation or retirement if 6 years of service, based on length of service and average salary over best six years up to a max. of 75 % of that average. Minimum contribution 6 % of sessional indemnity. Additional pension awarded for periods of extra duties. Pension after 6 years minimum service, amount depending on length of service, up to 75 % of annual average indemnity. Additional pension in case of holding other offices. Compulsory contribution of 10 % of indemnities and salaries.
Salary of President not taxable	President only has pension entitlements.
Tax free	None. All welfare entitlements at their nomrmal place of work are, however, by their being elected.
All remuneration taxable	MPs are affiliated to civil service pension fund, with Federal Assembly contributing at rate of 26 % calculated on total parliamentary remuneration.
–	None
Sitting allowance is taxable.	Full State pension after 30 years service and on reaching age 50. Otherwise proportional to years of service. Pensions are based on aver age salary over last 5 years of service.

Country and House(s)	5.1 Annual salary (US$ approximately)	5.2 Allowances (US$ approximately)
CUBA National Assembly of People's Power	None	MPs enjoy a licence with no salary, receiving an allowance equivalent to salary and additional expenses incurred.
CYPRUS House of Representatives	2,690	Representation: 3,285 pa; secretarial: 800 pa; travel.
CZECHOSLOVAKIA Chamber of Nations Chamber of the People	Members do not have a salary	Reimbursement of expenses connected with execution of mandate
DEMOCRATIC YEMEN Supreme People's Council	All MPs receive salaries, etc., according to prescribed scales.	
DENMARK Folketing	20,272	Supplementary expenses: 1,853 pa for residents in or less than 45 km from Copenhagen; 2,988 for residents of Zealand; 5,772 for other Members; special allowance of 925 pa for those living in the Faroe Islands and Greenland.
EGYPT People's Assembly	740	Sitting: 37.50 for each sitting and 12.50 for each cttee meeting attended.
FIJI Senate	4,250	Daily sitting; accommodation; travel.
House of Representatives	10,000 (plus office salary).	Constituency; travel; accommodation; select cttee sitting.
FINLAND Eduskunta	18,375 to 23,677, depending on years of service.	Sitting allowance: 18 pd if living 30 to 60 km from the capital; 27 pd if living further away.

5.3 Taxation	5.4 Pension Schemes
Untaxed	None
Allowances are tax free.	Pension entitlement at age 60 provided office held for at least 48 months. Contributions are 1.75% of emoluments. Annual pension is 3/660 of annual emoluments on retirement, multiplied by months of service, but not exceeding 66% of final emoluments.
Expense allowances are tax free.	No special pension scheme. MPs are covered by normal social security.

All MPs receive salaries, etc., according to prescribed scales.

Salary only is taxable.	Retirement pension at age 67, after 8 (not necessarily consecutive) years service, 13,572 per year maximum. Also a pension for surviving spouse and children of a deceased Member of 10,987 per year.
Salary and allowances tax free	Currently under study
Salary only is taxable.	Through Fiji National Provident Fund
Salary only is taxable.	State pension payable at age 60. Full pension of 66% salary payable after 15 years service. Family of a deceased Member also receive pension benefits.

Country and House(s)	5.1 Annual salary (US$ approximately)	5.2 Allowances (US$ approximately)
FRANCE Senate	23,000	Function: 8,000 pa; accommodation: 1,200 pa.
National Assembly		
GABON National Assembly	17,150	Session allowances to cover hotel and transport expenses
GERMAN DEMOCRATIC REPUBLIC People's Chamber	Deputies continue professional activity after their election and are released in so far as is necessary to fulfil their mandate. Normal salary continues.	Deputies and successor candidates receive an expense allowance.
GERMANY Federal Council	No remuneration ex-officio (State salary continues)	Daily sitting allowance: 32.
Federal Diet	35,000	20,000 pa
GREECE Chamber of Deputies	17,740	Monthly family allowance of 10 % salary for spouse and 5 % for the first 2 children, 7 % for the 3rd and 10 % for the 4th.
HUNGARY National Assembly	None	Allowances to reimburse expenses
INDIA Council of States	900	Allowances for housing, postage, secretarial facilities, etc: 1,200 pa.
House of the People		Sitting: 7.50 pd. Various allowances for travel.
INDONESIA House of Representatives	6,120	3,333 pa
IRELAND Senate	10,587	None
Dáil	19,039	

5.3 Taxation	5.4 Pension Schemes
55 % of salary taxable	A former MP receives a normal pension at age 55. Pension depends on a minimum period of service and is proportional to the years of service in Parlt but amount of contribution is double for first 15 years of service. Reduced pension or annuity is payable on request at age 50.
Salary only is taxable.	Lump sum pension provided on contributions representing 6 % of salary
Allowances are tax free.	None
Allowance tax free	None
	Pension at age 65 of 25 % basic salary for the first 6 years service, increased by 5 % for each additional year. Additional service lowers eligible retirement age. Non-contributory.
50 % of salary taxable	Pension at age 55, and after 4 years service up to 80 % of salary depending on service. No contributions by MP to pension fund.
Allowances are tax free.	Pension of approx. $ 100 pm
Salary only is taxable.	Non-contributory. Annual benefits range from $ 360 after 5 years service increasing $ 60 for each additional year up to $ 600 max.
-	Pension from 6 % to 75 % of basic salary, depending on length of service.
Salary is taxable.	Contributory at 6 % salary; pension 1/40 salary for each year of service up to 26 2/3 %. Widows' pension 1/2 that of MP. Minium service 8 years.

189

Country and House(s)	5.1 Annual salary (US$ approximately)	5.2 Allowances (US$ approximately)
ISRAEL The Knesset	15,300	Monthly allowance: 129 for 9 months; per diem allowance: 14 or 89 (depending on location) for cttee meetings on non-sitting days; car allowance 341 to 380 according to distance of residence from Jerusalem.
ITALY Senate	37,800	Allowances for special functions such as cttee chairman
Chamber of Deputies		
IVORY COAST National Assembly	Salary	Expense allowances
JAPAN House of Councillors	46,710	Term-end 18,490 pa; documents, correspondence and travelling: 31,330 pa; special travelling for Members Commended for Long Service (25 years): 12,050 pa; miscellaneous sessions expenses for certain offices of each House: 18.1 pd.
House of Representatives		
JORDAN Senate	11,000	None
House of Deputies		
KENYA National Assembly	288	Sitting: 140; responsibility: 290; constituency: 180; travelling: 3 Kenya shillings per km.
KUWAIT National Assembly	33,120	None
LEBANON National Assembly	42,000	–

5.3 Taxation	5.4 Pension Schemes
Salary and allowances taxable	Non-contributory. Benefits payable on leaving Parlt following at least 4 years service and after age 40.
30 % of salary taxable	Contribution 5.6 % of salary. Pension entitlement depends on years of service.
Salary is taxable.	Yes
Allowances are tax free.	Contribution 9.7 % of salary. Eligible for retirement pension from age 60.
Salary is taxable.	None
Salary only is taxable.	None
None	Contributory at 5 % salary. Benefits vary with service: 1 year provides for notional 15 years; 4 years for 75 % of salary increasing with longer service.
Salary is taxable.	Benefits range from 55 % to 75 % of salary.

Country and House(s)	5.1 Annual salary (US$ approximately)	5.2 Allowances (US$ approximately)
LIECHTENSTEIN Diet	400	Sitting: 70 pd. Reimbursement of travel costs.
LUXEMBOURG Chamber of Deputies	23,300. (Deductions are made for absence without leave).	Head of family allocation as appropriate. Travel in Luxembourg and subsistence when in other countries.
MALAWI National Assembly	2,506	Mandate allowance: 119 pm.
MALAYSIA Senate	None	Senate allowance: 845 pm.
House of Representatives		House allowance: 1,267 pm; subsistence: 21 pd; sitting: 21 pd; hotel: 42 pd; private car: 0.21 per km; driver's: 106 pm; travel: 63 pm.
MALI National Assembly	None	Session allowance
MALTA House of Representatives	5,900	Sitting allowance for the 5 Members for Gozo: 20 per sitting.
MAURITIUS Legislative Assembly	5,000 for ordinary Members rising with various offices to 11,600 for the Prime Minister.	None
MEXICO Chamber of Senators	12,000	–
Chamber of Deputies		
MONACO National Council	None	Expenses 1,300
MONGOLIA Great People's Khural (GPKh)	Remuneration from usual place of work continues.	Expenses connected with duties are reimbursed by the GPKh.

5.3 Taxation	5.4 Pension Schemes
Salary and allowances are tax free.	None
1/2 salary is tax free.	A pension scheme for parliamentarians and their surviving spouses was adopted in July 1985.
Salary only is taxable.	Contributions are 5 % of salary.
Allowances are tax free.	Non-contributory scheme under the MPs' (Remuneration) Act 1980.
–	–
Salary is taxable.	Contributions under the National Insurance Act (Members of Parliament Pensions Act 1979).
20 % exempt from tax	4 % of gross salary payable under the Legislative Assembly (Retiring Allowances) Act.
–	As for public servants
Allowances are tax free.	None
Reimbursement of expenses tax free	No special scheme for parliamentarians who are covered by the State pension.

Country and House(s)	5.1 Annual salary (US$ approximately)	5.2 Allowances (US$ approximately)
NAURU Parliament	3,000	Entertainment allowance: 130 pa.
NETHERLANDS First Chamber	None	Travel: 2,780; expenses 2,100; sitting allowance varies from 50 to 100 depending on distance of residence from Parlt.
Second Chamber	Indemnification of 29,125 for income lost due to parliamentary duties minus 1/2 the amount by which additional income exceeds 3,630 to a minimum indemnity of 18,540.	Travel allowance: 2,780; hotel expenses depending upon distance from the Member's residence.
NEW ZEALAND House of Representatives	23,000	Basic expenses: 1,775; electorate: 6,600 to 9,250 depending on electorate; day attendance: 8.50; night: 18.50.
NICARAGUA National Assembly	33 pm	Expenses for travel
NORWAY Storting	25,000	Sitting: 13.30 pd or 26.30 if residing more than 40 km. from Oslo; cttee sitting: 7pd; telephone: 157 pa.
PHILIPPINES National Assembly	6,300	Travelling expenses reimbursed
POLAND Diet	Pre-election occupation and salary continue. Members are released as necessary for parliamentary activities.	Parliamentary: 15,000 zlotys pa; cttee chairman: 5,000 zlotys pm; daily sitting fee: 500 zlotys.

5.3 Taxation	5.4 Pension Schemes
No tax on personal income in Nauru	None
Allowances are tax free.	None
Tax free	Members entitled to State pensions on retirement at age 65 with additional benefits depending on length of service. State pension contribution of 11.7 % of indemnity. Also severance pay varying with length of service.
Allowances are tax free.	Compulsory superannuation provides 1/32 of salary at date of pension eligibility, for each year of service up to a maximum of 2/3 of salary. Members contribute 11 % of salary.
Salary is taxable.	Members receive normal State pension.
Salary and allowances are taxable.	Pension starts after 3 years service. Full pension (66 % salary) after 12 years, at age 65, or when age and years of service total 75, but no pension if other corresponding salary received. Widow's pension of 60 % Member's pension.
Salary only is taxable.	Contributory optional Govt Service Insurance Scheme which grants gratuity pay on completion of a given period of service or a 5-year lump sum and life pension after 5 years.
Allowances are tax free.	No special parliamentary scheme. Members are entitled to normal State pension.

Country and House(s)	5.1 Annual salary (US$ approximately)	5.2 Allowances (US$ approximately)
PORTUGAL Assembly of the Republic	7,500	Reimbursement for use of private car on duty. Sitting: 8.30 pd (resident more than 30 km. from Lisbon: 25); subsistence: 25 per week only if resident more than 30 km. from Lisbon.
REPUBLIC OF KOREA National Assembly	12,900	Special activities: 15,400 pa; legislative activities: 1,129; sitting 11 pd; private car on duty 316 pm; telephone 86 pm.
ROMANIA Grand National Assembly	Pre-election occupation and salary continue. Members are released as necessary for parliamentary activities.	Monthly and sessional allowance, and travel expenses are fixed by the Assembly.
RWANDA National Development Council	6,500	Daily sitting allowance: 22.
ST VINCENT House of Assembly	Members: 500 pm; Ministers: 1,200 pm.	Members: 230; Ministers: 420.
SENEGAL National Assembly	Members: 650; Bureau members and cttee chairmen: 750.	Representation allowance. Bureau members and cttee chairmen also receive an accommodation allowance.
SOLOMON ISLANDS National Parliament	–	Personal: 200; overseas: 250; constituency: 1,200; car: 720; appointment grant: 200.
SOMALIA People's Assembly	None	Plenary: 0.67 per sitting; cttee: 2 per sitting.
SOUTH AFRICA Houses of Assembly, Representatives, and Delegates	8,400	13 pd

Salary only is taxable.	State pension similar to public servants after 5 years service. Contribution is 6 % of salary.
Allowances are tax free.	None
Salary only is taxable.	Members are entitled to a pension from their non-parliamentary employment.
Salary and allowances are taxable.	Under study
Taxation allowances for entertainment and transport expenses	Non-contributory scheme providing gratuity of 2 years highest salary plus pension of 1/3 monthly salary after 9 years service, rising with length of service to a maximum of 3 years highest salary and 1/2 monthly salary.
–	Pension scheme to which Members make a monthly partial contribution, the balance being contributed by Parlt.
Taxable	No pension but a US$ 4,000 taxable terminal grant is payable.
Allowances are tax free.	Pension scheme for Members
Salary only is taxable.	Contributory scheme of 10 % of salary provides pension and gratuity after 8 years service. Maximum pension and gratuity after 15 years.

Country and House(s)	5.1 Annual salary (US$ approximately)	5.2 Allowances (US$ approximately)
SPAIN Senate	1,300	None
Congress of Deputies		
SRI LANKA Parliament	None	4,000 per annum
SWEDEN Riksdag	18,000	Session: 3,900 pa maximum (depending on distance of permanent residence); compensation: 1,700 pa for Members with allowances; 2,500 for those few without allowances.
SWITZERLAND States Council	6,875 (National Councillors are paid by the Confederation; States Councillors by their respective Cantons).	Daily sitting: 104; daily subsistence: 29; compensation for serious loss of normal income may be paid.
National Council		
SYRIAN ARAB REPUBLIC People's Council	3,600	350 at the start of each session
THAILAND Senate	4,200	None, except for cttee meetings.
House of Representatives	9,400	
TUNISIA Chamber of Deputies	8,900	None
UGANDA National Assembly	750	Daily subsistance when Assembly sits; daily sitting; travelling between constituency and Assembly.
UNION OF SOVIET SOCIALIST REPUBLICS Soviet of Nationalities	Pre-election occupation and salary continue. Members are released as necessary for parliamentary activities.	Expenses: 276 p.m.; daily duty: 21.
Soviet of the Union		

198

5.3 Taxation	5.4 Pension Schemes
Salary is taxable.	Social Security and Mutual Association contributions are paid out of the Parliamentary Budget.
30 % of allowances is taxable.	Ex-Members with over 5 years service and widows
Salary and compensation are taxable.	State pension scheme applied. In addition, Members benefit from non-contributory Riksdag scheme providing US$ 2,300. Other forms of pension payable before age 65 also apply.
85 % of salary is taxable.	None
Revenue tax applies.	None
Taxable	None
Salary is tax free.	Contributions are 10 % of salary to the National Pension Fund.
Salary and allowances are tax free.	Non-contributory scheme providing 30 % of salary as yearly gratuity and 1 year's basic salary as death gratuity
Salary and allowances are taxable.	No special parliamentary scheme. Members are entitled to the same pension as other citizens.

TABLE 5: PARLIAMENTARY REMUNERATION (continued)

Country and House(s)	5.1 Annual salary (US$ approximately)	5.2 Allowances (US$ approximately)
UNITED KINGDOM House of Lords	None, except for Govt Ministers, Leader of the Opposition and various parliamentary offices.	Reimbursement of expenses within the following daily limits: overnight accommodation: 56; subsistence and local travel: 23; general office secretarial and research: 23.
House of Commons	21,700 plus 15,000 for Ministers	Reimbursement of actual expenses for general office, secretarial and research up to 17,000 p.a.; London supplement: 1,200 p.a. for MPs with Inner London constituencies.
UNITED REPUBLIC OF TANZANIA National Assembly	3,050	Subsistence: 15 p.d. during sittings.
UNITED STATES OF AMERICA Senate	75,100	Administrative and clerical: 645,897 to 1,297,795 p.a. depending on respective State population; legislative assistance: 200,328 p.a.; office expenses and travel: 36,000 to 156,000 p.a. depending on State.
House of Representatives		Free postage and reimbursement of telephone and telegraph; annual travel allowance; office expenses.
VANUATU Parliament	713	None
YUGOSLAVIA Federal Chamber	3,800 to 7,700	Function: 542 p.a.; For various offices: 65 to 100 p.m.; separation: 120 p.m. (those living outside Belgrade). Per diem expenses for duty visits.
Chamber of Republics and Provinces		
ZAIRE Legislative Council	8,400	None

5.3 Taxation	5.4 Pension Schemes
Allowances are tax free.	None, except for those in 5.1.
All remuneration is taxable except travel between London and constituency.	All MPs, except Speaker and Prime Minister, contribute 6 % of salary of ordinary MP to receive pension accruing at 1/60 final salary for each year of service.
Allowance is tax free.	Non-contributory pension after 10 years' service. If less than 10 years a gratuity of 1/4 total emoluments.
Salary only is taxable.	Members contribute to the national Social Security system. They may also contribute 8 % of salary to the Civil Service Retirement System for which benefits are payable after 5 years service.
Salary is not taxable.	None. Severance payment only.
Salary taxed if it exceeds average personal income of employees in the respective Republic.	No special parliamentary scheme. Members covered by State pension insurance.
None	Under study

Country and House(s)	5.1 Annual salary (US$ approximately)	5.2 Allowances (US$ approximately)
ZAMBIA National Assembly	3,864	Special: 1,136 p.a.; constituency: 284 to 324 p.a. depending on size (243 p.a. for nominated MPs); subsistence: 97 or 292 p.a. depending on whether residence less or more than 40 km from Lusaka respectively; postal: 40 p.a.; attendance: 10 or 4 p.d. depending respectively on whether or not staying at National Assembly Motel; duty: 4 p.d. on duty in Zambia other than sittings.
ZIMBABWE Senate House of Assembly	5,200	Constituency, travelling and cttee attendance allowances vary but may aggregate 1,000 p.m.

5.3 Taxation	5.4 Pension Schemes
Salaries are taxed but allowances and gratuity are tax free.	At least 3 years continuous service entitles MPs to a gratuity of 25 % basic salary.
Allowances are tax free.	Members contribute 5 % of salary.

TABLE 6

FACILITIES AND AMENITIES

In addition to the basic salary and allowances, there are various benefits (secretarial and research assistance, office premises, posts and telecommunications, transportation and housing, etc.) attached to a seat in Parliament which are designed to help the Member to perform his duties efficiently. As a rule, the directing authorities of Parliament and other high parliamentary officials profit from these benefits to a greater extent than ordinary Members. This is especially the case where they are frequently granted housing facilities, or reimbursed for their lodging expenses. Ordinary Members may have hotels or apartments belonging to Parliament put at their disposal, as in the Federal Republic of Germany, India, Japan, Poland, Senegal and Sweden.

Because of the nature of their work it is important to grant Members of Parliament facilities for transport. These take various forms, ranging from reduced fares for journeys between a Member's constituency and Parliament to free travel throughout the country. Typical benefits include free public transport, free travel on trains, and the provision of an automobile for the directing authority of Parliament.

In most countries, Members are allowed free postage for correspondence which is either directly connected with their parliamentary duties or which originates from the parliamentary premises. The same conditions generally apply to the use of the telephone and cable services. Exceptions to the provision of these facilities are found in countries where it is believed that it is incumbent upon a Member to pay for the cost of these out of his emoluments. This assumption is widespread in connection with the provision of office premises and private secretaries. In most countries, secretaries and offices are only granted to Members in pool form. In the rarer case (found, for example, in Australia, Brazil, Canada, the Federal Republic of Germany, France, Japan and the United States of America) each individual Member is provided with an office and a secretariat, or receives additional yearly allowances specifically to cover the cost of these. In Australia, Canada and Sri Lanka an office is provided in the constituency. In Greece an allowance is granted for this purpose.

Country and House(s)	6.1 a) Secretarial assistance b) Research and reference assistance c) Office premises and facilities	6.2 Postal and tele-communication facilities
ALGERIA National People's Assembly (APN)	a) Vice-President of the APN and Chairmen of Standing Cttees have a personal secretariat; other Members have access to a typing pool b) All MPs can use a research and documentation service; standing cttees have research assistants c) Individual offices are not provided but MPs have desks in large rooms	Post office in Assembly building
ARGENTINA Senate Chamber of Deputies	a) Provided through each parliamentary group (individual secretariats are projected) b) Provided through the Parliamentary Information Directorate c) Provided to each MP	Free of charge
AUSTRALIA Senate House of Representatives	a) and b) Each Member is entitled to employ 3 staff on secretarial or research tasks at discretion. Also access to research and reference service and facilities of Parliamentary Library c) For each MP in Parlt and in constituency	Office mail free. Free telephone from Parliament House and constituency office. 15% of calls from residence.
AUSTRIA Federal Council National Council	a) b) and c) Within the parliamentary group which is subsidised	None
BAHAMAS Senate House of Assembly	a) and b) From each House Secretariat c) Use of House facilities	House facilities made available

6.3 Travel and transport	6.4 Residential accommodation	6.5 Restaurant facilities	6.6 Medical or other facilities
Duty travel expenses are reimbursed.	Reimbursement of living expenses for Members non-resident in the capital.	Subsidised	Medical services, prayer hall and hairdresser in Parlt House
Free transport by air and land	None	Subsidised	Medical facilities; free parking.
Free transport for official duties; allowances for private cars on parliamentary or electoral business; also official car transport.	None, but accommodation allowances granted (see 5.2).	Availability of parliamentary refreshment rooms; meals are subsidised.	Certain recreation facilities at Parlt House.
Free rail and ship travel in Austria; air tickets provided from Member's domicile to Parlt.	None	Indirectly subsidised (nominal rent charged for premises; furniture, crockery and cutlery supplied by Parlt).	Medical services in Parlt House (only during plenary sittings).
Reimbursement of duty air fares	None	None	None

Country and House(s)	6.1 a) Secretarial assistance b) Research and reference assistance c) Office premises and facilities	6.2 Postal and tele-communication facilities
BELGIUM Senate Chamber of Representatives	a) In constituency b) No individual research or reference assistance c) Available in new extension to Parlt House	Free correspondence with public services and 1,000 letters per year. Telephone free of charge from Parlt.
BRAZIL Federal Senate Chamber of Deputies	a) 3 secretarial staff per MP b) Access to pool of adviser and reference assistance at Document-ation and Information Centre c) Office suite (2 rooms plus toilet)	Provided up to a budgeted maximum
BULGARIA National Assembly	a) None b) From the Library c) Club and study in Parlt House	Post-office and telecommunica-tions facilities in Parlt build-ing, but corres-pondence charged to MPs.
CAMEROON National Assembly	a) Yes b) Yes c) Offices are allocated temporarily as required for research	Yes

6.3 Travel and transport	6.4 Residential accommodation	6.5 Restaurant facilities	6.6 Medical or other facilities
Free of charge for all State-owned transport	None	Subsidised	Physician in Parliament
To State headquarters (air tickets twice monthly) or business elsewhere (once per month).	Free	Subsidised	Full medical facilities for MPs and partial aid for their dependents. School transportation refund for dependents.
Rail, boat and bus transport free of charge, but not air travel.	None	None	None
Free transport between the Assembly and the respective administrative region (once per session).	Only for President, Vice-Presidents, Treasurers of the Assembly and Group Presidents. Support is given in session to some MPs on a rotation basis.	Subsidised during sessions	Medical facilities and travel for Overseas Medical treatment

Country and House(s)	6.1 a) Secretarial assistance b) Research and reference assistance c) Office premises and facilities	6.2 Postal and tele-communication facilities
CANADA Senate	a) Secretaries are assigned to one or more Senator, but are usually in pool accommodation b) From Library c) Provided by Parlt in Ottawa with room for staff	Free postage for ordinary mail inside Canada. Free phone calls inside Canada.
House of Commons	a) and b) Budget of $ 97,000 provided for secretarial, research, administrative and other support staff c) In Ottawa for each Member and staff. Budget also provides for office in constituency	As above. Members may also send four general mailings to their constituents every fiscal year.
CAPE VERDE People's National Assembly	a) and b) Yes c) -	Yes
CHINA National People's Congress	a) b) and c) Facilities and amenities are provided by the State as required to discharge the duties of Deputies	See 6.1
COMOROS Federal Assembly	-	Telephone facilities available
CONGO People's National Assembly (ANP)	a) b) and c) None	Telephone facilities in ANP during sessions only
COSTA RICA Legislative Assembly	a) b) and c) Yes	Postal services
CUBA National Assembly of People's Power	a) Yes b) Information on request c) When required	To communicate with Parlt.
CYPRUS House of Representatives	a) b) and c) None	None

6.3 Travel and transport	6.4 Residential accommodation	6.5 Restaurant facilities	6.6 Medical or other facilities
Travel provided on the basis of 52 "points" per year where one trip to constituency and return to Ottawa by MP counts 1 point. Trips by staff or spouses have different points value depending on class of travel. 10 points per year may be used by MP to travel anywhere in Canada.	Official residences provided for Prime Minister and Leader of Opposition of House of Commons as well as country residences for Prime Minister and Speaker of House of Commons.	Subsidised	Qualified nurses are on staff; barber's shop, shoe shine, steam room, masseur, hairdresser, exercise and recreation rooms; support services (procedural and legal, translation, printing and computer); language training.
Yes	Fully subsidised during sessions	Fully subsidised during sessions	Medical services
See 6.1	See 6.1	See 6.1	See 6.1
-	-	-	Ambulance service and some assistance in case of illness
Free transport during sessions only	None	None	Medical facilities during sessions only
-	-	-	-
Free of charge for official activities	Free when required for official activities	When on official duty	Medical facilities are free of charge for all citizens.
Duty-free car during 5 year term of office	None	None	Medical facilities

TABLE 6: FACILITIES AND AMENITIES (continued)

Country and House(s)	6.1 a) Secretarial assistance b) Research and reference assistance c) Office premises and facilities	6.2 Postal and tele-communication facilities
CZECHOSLOVAKIA Chamber of Nations Chamber of the People	a) Yes b) Yes c) Yes	During session
DEMOCRATIC YEMEN Supreme People's Council	a) For the 4 Standing Cttees b) Provided if required c) Yes	Yes
DENMARK Folketing	a) and b) Political groups granted sums to a maximum of $ 6,941 per year per member, with $ 15,265 for the group chairman; individual MPs have a grant to partly cover secretarial assistance c) Office with telephone and typewriter provided for each Member	Free phone calls from the Folketing
EGYPT People's Assembly	a) b) and c) From the General Secretariat of the Assembly	None
FIJI Senate House of Representatives	a) b) and c) None	US$ 750 per annum allowance (not taxable).

6.3 Travel and transport	6.4 Residential accommodation	6.5 Restaurant facilities	6.6 Medical or other facilities
Free use of surface transport, and in some cases of aeroplanes.	Not subsidised	Not subsidised	Medical services during sessions
Yes	None	None	Yes, including treatment abroad.
Free travel by Danish State Railways; first class travel by ferry; free domestic flights; free travel by the Metropolitan transport services; and free taxis from city air terminals to domestic airports.	None	Not subsidised	Free tickets to Tivoli, the Zoo, race and trotting courses and the Royal Theatre.
Free season-ticket (railway, planes, etc.) from constituency to capital; acquisition of a private car facilitated by the Assembly.	None	Subsidised during Assembly Sessions.	Comprehensive medical care
Direct to and from meetings	Daily allowance of US$ 60	None	No medical facilities for MPs, but Ministers enjoy subsidised treatment similar to civil servants

Country and House(s)	6.1 a) Secretarial assistance b) Research and reference assistance c) Office premises and facilities	6.2 Postal and tele-communication facilities
FINLAND Eduskunta	a) Provided through the parliamentary groups, which receive allowances for each affiliated MP b) Yes c) For each Member	Free phone calls from Parlt
FRANCE Senate National Assembly	a) Allowance for secretarial expenses of US$ 1,600 pm b) 2 research assistants for each Member c) For each Member	Free phone calls in Paris and to constituency. Partially subsidised telephone calls in constituency. Free postage for official mail.
GABON National Assembly	a) From the Secretariat b) None c) None	None
GERMAN DEMOCRATIC REPUBLIC People's Chamber	a) b) and c) MPs are assisted by the Chamber Secretariat; MPs' employers and parties are under obligation to assist them, as are mass organisations, Govt agencies and scientific institutions	Yes
GERMANY Federal Council	a) and b) Provided by States offices in the Federal Capital c) Provided in Federal Council for each State represented	At Federal Council
Federal Diet	a) and b) Monthly allowances for secretarial and research assistance c) For each Member	Free telephone calls from Parlt

6.3 Travel and transport	6.4 Residential accommodation	6.5 Restaurant facilities	6.6 Medical or other facilities
Free first-class rail transport; reimbursement of air, rail (sleeping cars) boat or bus fares for MPs living outside the capital; free taxis and buses in the capital.	None	None	Medical station in Parlt
Free rail transport; up to 60 air return journeys annually between constituency and capital; 6 free air journeys annually to other parts of France. Cars available in Paris.	Some apartments available for rent in Paris. Housing loans available, repayable over 10 years.	Yes	Medical services. Gymnasium, hairdresser. Free subscription to Official Journal.
Allowances provided (see 5.2).	Allowances provided (see 5.2).	-	-
Free travel on all public transport	Met by Expense allowance (see 5.2). Costs incurred by activities of House cttees are partly re-imbursed.	Yes	Medical office in the Parlt. Travel and hotel reserva-tion service.
Official travel expenses re-imbursed	None	None	None
Cars available in the Federal capital; free rail transport.	Low rent accommodation near Parlt for about 1/3 MPs.	Subsidised	Medical facilities

215

Country and House(s)	6.1 a) Secretarial assistance b) Research and reference assistance c) Office premises and facilities	6.2 Postal and tele-communication facilities
GREECE Chamber of Deputies	a) and b) US$ 2,700 pa for personal assistant (social charges met by House) c) Allowance for office in constituency (10 % of salary for Athens and Pireaus, 15 % elsewhere)	US$ 680 pa for postal costs; telephone free of charge (up to 2,500 telephone units pm for Athens and Piraeus, 2,700 pm elsewhere).
HUNGARY National Assembly	a) None b) From Parlt and Central Office of Statistics c) None	Free of charge
INDIA Council of State House of the People	a) Yes b) By LARRDIS of Lok Sabha Secretariat c) Individual offices are not provided but are available to major parties and groups	Post-office in Parlt House; telegram; telex; Postal allowance (see 5.2); each MP has 2 free telephones and 15,000 free local calls per year.
INDONESIA House of Representatives	a) b) and c) Yes	Yes
IRELAND Senate Dáil	a) For each Member b) From Library, information and reference service c) Only for office holders and political groups	Up to 300 official envelopes per week; free phone calls within the country not exceeding 6 minutes; 20 free telegrams a month (16 words maximum).
ISRAEL The Knesset	a) Annual allowance of US$ 1,571 for secretarial research or reference assistance; some further assistance from the relevant parliamentary group b) From the Library and Information Service c) Rooms are shared with 2 MPs per room	Free mailing from the Knesset post-office within the country; free telephone installation with a number of free calls annually.

216

6.3 Travel and transport	6.4 Residential accommodation	6.5 Restaurant facilities	6.6 Medical or other facilities
Free surface travel plus 52 return air journeys yearly from constituency to Athens.	None	None	Social services; first aid medical care in the Parliament.
Free of charge on public transport	–	Subsidised	Medical facilities
Special buses from New Delhi residences to Parlt House; 1st class fare plus one 2nd class fare by rail; 1/4 air fares; other travel allowances.	Residential units with rent rebates available.	Subsidised Parliamentary refreshment rooms; refreshment bars in Parlt House; canteens in residential localities.	First aid post in Parlt House; Medical Centre in Annexe. Banking, travel, shopping, recreation and other facilities in Parlt House.
Yes	Yes	Yes	Medical facilities
1st class railway; repayment of public transport fares; car costs repaid against prescribed mileage rates.	Daily allowance to cover meetings of House or Cttees when normal residence is outside Dublin area.	Subsidised	Medical clinic and doctor in Parlt; official stationery; 500 free photocopies a month.
Free railway and bus within the country	Two nights in a hotel per wek for MPs living outside Jerusalem	None	None

TABLE 6: FACILITIES AND AMENITIES (continued)

Country and House(s)	6.1 a) Secretarial assistance b) Research and reference assistance c) Office premises and facilities	6.2 Postal and tele-communication facilities
ITALY Senate Chamber of Deputies	a) Provided through the parliamentary groups b) None c) Offices provided for 200 Deputies and 100 Senators	Yes
IVORY COAST National Assembly	a) and c) For Bureau members and cttee chairmen only b) None	For Bureau members and cttee chairmen
JAPAN House of Councillors House of Representatives	a) 2 secretarial assistants per MP b) Provided through Parliamentary groups by subsidy and through Parliamentary services c) For each Member	Allowances provided
JORDAN Senate House of Representatives	a) Indirect secretarial assistance b) Library staff offers reference assistance c) One office for each region represented	None
KENYA National Assembly	a) Yes b) From the Library c) Yes	Postal services and telephone
KUWAIT National Assembly	a) and b) From the Assembly Secretariat c) Office and secretary for each MP	None
LEBANON National Assembly	a) and b) From the Assembly Secretariat c) Yes	Yes
LIECHTENSTEIN Diet	a) and b) From the Diet Secretariat c) -	-
LUXEMBOURG Chamber of Deputies	Offices and facilities are provided together with funding proportional to the strength of groups. Assistance is provided by the Chamber Secretariat.	No postage assistance but free official telephone calls may be made from Parliament House.
MALAWI National Assembly	a) b) and c) None	Each Member is provided with a postal frank.

6.3 Travel and transport	6.4 Residential accommodation	6.5 Restaurant facilities	6.6 Medical or other facilities
Free air, train and road travel in Italy	–	Subsidised	Medical facilities
Free of charge on duty; official cars for Questors.	Only Questors receive residential allowances.	None	Medical facilities and Health Insurance
Free passes for Japanese railways	Members' apartments available in Tokio for rent	Not directly subsidised (fuel, light and water charges borne by state treasury).	Medical offices for first-aid
None	None	None	Medical facilities
Travel to constituency by official transport	Subsidised	Subsidised	Free medical facilities
None	None	None	Medical facilities as for every citizen
For duty journeys (driver available).	On duty	None	Medical insurance
Reimbursement of travel costs	–	–	–
Travel allowance when on official duty	None	None	Collective parliamentary accident insurance
Reimbursement of duty travel expenses	None	–	Free medical services

Country and House(s)	6.1 a) Secretarial assistance b) Research and reference assistance c) Office premises and facilities	6.2 Postal and tele-communication facilities
MALAYSIA Senate House of Representatives	a) To Presiding Officers, their Deputies, Ministers and Deputy Ministers, Parliamentary Secretaries and Opposition Leader b) From the Library c) Every Member has an office with telephone	Office mail is free. Telephone provided in residence. Free calls up to US$ 84 per month.
MALI National Assembly	a) From the Assembly Secretariat b) None c) None	None
MALTA House of Representatives	a) Leader of the Opposition only has a secretarial allowance b) From the House staff c) Offices for Ministers and Opposition Leader. 2 large halls are available for Govt and Opposition Members, respectively	Free on parliamentary business within the Maltese islands
MAURITIUS Legislative Assembly	a) Partial assistance b) Information provided but no research yet c) Cttee rooms available	Yes
MEXICO Chamber of Senators Chamber of Deputies	a) Yes b) Yes c) Yes	Yes
MONACO National Council	a) and b) From the Council Secretariat c) None	Postal and telephone services provided
MONGOLIA Great People's Khural (GPKh)	a) b) and c) From the GPKh Secretariat and social authorities staff	Free of charge

6.3 Travel and transport	6.4 Residential accommodation	6.5 Restaurant facilities	6.6 Medical or other facilities
Duty travel expenses are reimbursed. Assistance with car purchase.	Assistance with housing loans	Available but not subsidised	Free treatment. Reimbursement of medical charges incurred overseas.
None	None	None	None
NA	None	Available but not subsidised	None
For ministers only	None	None	None
Duty traval expenses reimbursed; discount available on private travel.	None	Provided for working meetings; discounts available in some restaurants.	Medical services
None	None	–	–
Free transport by all available means on duty	–	Free meals during sessions and official events	Free medical service (as for all citizens). Local bodies arrange for priority service for Members in social, cultural and communal fields.

Country and House(s)	6.1 a) Secretarial assistance b) Research and reference assistance c) Office premises and facilities	6.2 Postal and tele-communication facilities
NAURU Parliament	a) Typing assistance from Parlt office b) Advice and assistance on procedure and drafting of Bills, motions, etc. c) Common lounge available	None
NETHERLANDS First Chamber	a) Very limited b) Small library and documentation service c) Each political group has a room	Free use of telephone within Chamber building
Second Chamber	a) Chamber reimburses up to US$ 900, the monthly cost of a personal assistant engaged by Member b) Chamber bears cost of assistants engaged by political groups, pro-portional to their respective strength c) For each Member	
NEW ZEALAND House of Representatives	a) One secretary for each MP at Parlt and in the electorate b) Each party group has a research unit of 10 researchers. Parliamentary Library also provides reference facilities c) For each MP: assistance for premises in the electorate	Free postage from Parlt. Free telecom-munications within New Zealand from Parlt and from home.
NICARAGUA National Assembly	a), b) and c) Yes	Yes
NORWAY Storting	a) and b) From the parliamentary party group c) For each Member	Post office in Parlt but Mem-bers pay full rates. Free telephone calls from Parlt.
PHILIPPINES National Assembly	a), b) and c) Yes	Yes
POLAND Diet	a) From the Secretariat of the Diet Chancellery b) From the Diet Library, and secretariats of groups and regional groupings c) For groups and cttees in the Diet and in regional office buildings	Specially marked stationery provided

6.3 Travel and transport	6.4 Residential accommodation	6.5 Restaurant facilities	6.6 Medical or other facilities
None	None	None	Free medical consultation, treatment and hospitalisation for all citizens.
Travel allowance (see 5.2).	Indemnification for hotel expenses	Yes	Free parking
Free air and rail transport within New Zealand	None	Subsidised meals	None
Expenses reimbursed	No	Subsidised meals	Free public medical service
Travel agency in Parlt. Free public transport.	Furnished flats available for normal rent	Subsidised to extent of staff and building costs	Free medical services during sessions
Yes	No	Subsidised	Medical and sports facilities
Free bus, train, city and air travel.	Free hotel accommodation	Subsidised in the hotel	Free public health scheme

TABLE 6: FACILITIES AND AMENITIES (continued)

Country and House(s)	6.1 a) Secretarial assistance b) Research and reference assistance c) Office premises and facilities	6.2 Postal and tele-communication facilities
PORTUGAL Assembly of the Republic	a) and b) None c) Parliamentary groups have offices and work rooms for Members	Yes
REPUBLIC OF KOREA National Assembly	a) 3 secretaries per Member b) From the Legislative Research and Reference Service c) In the Parlt buildings	Yes
ROMANIA Grand National Assembly	a) From the Assembly Secretariat b) Advisers from the Secretariat c) Yes	Yes
R W A N D A National Development Council	a) Yes b) No c) Yes	Yes
ST VINCENT House of Assembly	a) No b) No c) No	None
SENEGAL National Assembly	a) For Bureau members and cttee chairmen b) No c) For Bureau members and cttee chairmen, other Members have shared facilities	Yes
SOLOMON ISLANDS National Parliament	a) From Parlt Secretariat b) No c) Yes	Yes
SOMALIA People's Assembly	a) No b) No c) No	None

6.3 Travel and transport	6.4 Residential accommodation	6.5 Restaurant facilities	6.6 Medical or other facilities
Free transport throughout the country. Reimbursement for use of private car on duty.	Daily subsistence allowance if resident more than 30 km. from Lisbon	None	Assistance with costs when Members are covered by a medical insurance scheme.
Travel expenses paid; free railway transport on official business.	None	Yes	Assistance with costs by a medical insurance scheme
Free transport by air, land and water.	None	None	Free public medical service
Yes	Yes	Yes	-
Travel allowance	None	None	None
On official business. Free air travel. Bureau members, cttee chairmen and Budget Rapporteur General have official cars.	Residences for Bureau members and cttee chairmen. Members are lodged at "Hôtel des Députés".	Yes	Members pay 1/5 of medical fees. Remainder is paid by the Assembly. Access cards to State instrumentalities.
Yes	In the capital for meetings	None	Medical facilities
Travel at 1/2 rate after 15 years consecutive service	Residential accommodation and hotel at 1/2 rate after 15 years consecutive service	None	Medical facilities

Country and House(s)	6.1 a) Secretarial assistance b) Research and reference assistance c) Office premises and facilities	6.2 Postal and tele-communication facilities
SOUTH AFRICA House of Assembly House of Representatives House of Delegates	a) Secretarial allowance US$ 250 per month for each Whip and US$ 20 for each Member during sessions b) Yes c) For each Member	60 minutes per week free trunk line calls and unrestricted local calls during sessions; free official mail.
SPAIN Senate Congress of Deputies	a) To parliamentary groups b) From the Documentation and Library c) Joint offices	Free of charge
SRI LANKA Parliament	a) Allowance provided b) - c) Offices in the constituency	Free of charge
SWEDEN Riksdag	a) One secretarial facilitity per 6 members of a party group plus assistance from the Riksdag Secretariat b) From the Library the Research Service and party groups c) Yes	Post office in the Riksdag. Free telephone calls in Sweden.
SWITZERLAND States Council National Council	a) From the Secretariat b) From the Documentation Service and cttee secretariat c) 21 offices available for typewriting (11 with 2 desks)	Free official mail. Free telephone calls from Parlt.
SYRIAN ARAB REPUBLIC People's Council	a) Yes b) Yes c) Yes	Yes
THAILAND Senate House of Representatives	a) and b) From the Secretariat as necessary c) For political parties but not individual MPs	Post office and telegraph at Member's expense
TUNISIA Chamber of Deputies	a) Yes b) Through cttee activity c) Yes	Yes

6.3 Travel and transport	6.4 Residential accommodation	6.5 Restaurant facilities	6.6 Medical or other facilities
Free train pass. 36 internal air journeys free, 80 % discount on rest; duty travel during recess reimbursed.	Limited number of Govt houses available	Yes	Medical facilities; free parking and recreational facilities in Parlt; auditorium with TV, film projector and video equipment; free stationery.
Free of charge	None	Subsidised	The Houses have a doctor.
Free public transport	At nominal rent in the capital for Members from distant areas	Subsidised	–
Free transport	Free accommodation or office in Parlt. Nominal fee for hotel services.	Available, partly subsidised.	Preventive health care provided. Medical service available once a week in Parlt. Recreational facilities.
Free rail travel; other duty travel reimbursed.	None	None	First aid post
Yes	–	No	Medical facilities
Transportation facilities provided	None	None	Health service provided
Free travel on public transport	–	Subsidised	Medical treatment through the national Social Security service

TABLE 6: FACILITIES AND AMENITIES (continued)

Country and House(s)	6.1 a) Secretarial assistance b) Research and reference assistance c) Office premises and facilities	6.2 Postal and tele-communication facilities
UGANDA National Assembly	a) b) and c) Yes	Yes
UNION OF SOVIET SOCIALIST REPUBLICS Soviet of Nationalities	a) - b) Provided free of charge c) Premises for meetings with electors and activities as Members	Reimbursable up to 200 roubles (US$ 276 p.m.).
Soviet of the Union		
UNITED KINGDOM House of Lords	a) and b) Reimbursed (see 5.2) c) Available without charge	Free telephone calls on business in the United Kingdom from Parlt
House of Commons		As above, also calls from constituency can be included in general office expenses. Business postage in United Kingdom free.
UNITED REPUBLIC OF TANZANIA National Assembly	a) and b) None c) Yes	Yes
UNITED STATES OF AMERICA Senate	a) Allowances are provided (see 5.2) b) As above c) In the Capitol, the Senate and the State	Allowances are provided (see 5.2).
House of Representatives	a) Yes b) Yes c) Yes	
VANUATU Parliament	a) Yes b) and c) No	Yes

6.3 Travel and transport	6.4 Residential accommodation	6.5 Restaurant facilities	6.6 Medical or other facilities
Yes	Rental assistance	Yes	Free hospital treatment
Free use of all internal transport except taxis	Daily allowance (see 5.2).	–	Free medical services as for all citizens
Reimbursement of travel costs between residence and London	None, but allowance for overnight accommodation (see 5.2).	Restaurant, cafeteria and 2 bars in Parlt.	Medical surveillance service
Free travel by public transport. Car allowance payable on duty.	Reimbursement for actual expenses (except those with Inner London constituencies) up to US$ 9,100 p.a.	Dining rooms, restaurants, cafeterias, bars in Parlt partially subsidised.	Medical surveillance service; gymnasium; travel agent; gentleman's hairdresser.
Yes	None	Yes	Medical facilities
Allowances are provided (see 5.2).	None, but taxation concessions granted for costs in the capital.	Available but not subsidised	Medical facilities
Annual travel allowance	None		
Yes, to sessions.	No	No	None

229

Country and House(s)	6.1 a) Secretarial assistance b) Research and reference assistance c) Office premises and facilities	6.2 Postal and tele- communication facilities
YUGOSLAVIA Federal Chamber Chamber of Republics and Provinces	a) For Chairman of working bodies b) From Assembly services c) For some Members living in Belgrade	Free of charge in the Assembly building
ZAIRE Legislative Council	a) and b) Yes c) No	No
ZAMBIA National Assembly	a) None b) and c) Yes	Yes
ZIMBABWE Senate House of Assembly	a) Parliamentary staff available for parliamentary or constituency matters b) From the Library and research unit c) All Members have shared offices	Free of charge

6.3 Travel and transport	6.4 Residential accommodation	6.5 Restaurant facilities	6.6 Medical or other facilities
Free of charge by air, sea and land.	–	In the Assembly building, not subsidised.	General practitioner on duty; other medical facilities.
Free travel between Parlt, residence and constituency. Offical cars for Bureau members and cttee chairmen.	Residence for the President of the Legislative Council	No	Medical services
Travel allowance on duty	Subsidised	Subsidised	Medical facilities
Air travel paid by Parlt; milage reimbursed for vehicle travel.	Allowance for MPs non-resident at seat of Parliament	Yes	Public Service Medical Aid Association for nominal fee; clinic in Parliament.

PART III

PARLIAMENTARY PROCEDURE

TABLE 7

RULES OF PROCEDURE AND PARLIAMENTARY BUDGET

Procedural Independence

The autonomy of Parliament is revealed in the control that it exercises over its own rules of procedure (or standing orders). Autonomy, in this context, means that, within the framework of its constitutional functions, a Legislature is able to decide on its own method of working. Not only do the rules of procedure exist to ensure that Parliament functions smoothly, but they also modulate the relationship between Parliament and Government. Besides being a kind of manual of parliamentary practice, the rules of procedure give direct and concrete effect to the most important constitutional principles on which the machinery of government in general, and the legislative machinery in particular, is founded.

Location of Rules of Procedure

Efforts to limit the procedural independence of Parliament fall into three categories:

- the first of these is concerned with how the rules of procedure are determined;
- the second, with the referral of these to a Constitutional Court or other similar body; and
- the third, with the ways in which these rules can be amended.

The determination of the rules of procedure is considered in Table 7A. In twenty-four countries (including Austria, Japan, Senegal

TABLE 7A. How the Rules of Procedure are Determined

Determination of Rules of Procedure	Number of Countries
Basic provisions in Constitution or other Law and Rules separately adopted by the House	24
Rules adopted by the House	59
Total	83

and the USSR) the basic provisions of Parliament are laid down in the Constitution or other law, and the rules of procedure are separately adopted by the Parliaments themselves. In the remaining countries the Legislatures determine their own rules of procedure. In the latter group of countries each rule consists of one or more resolutions adopted by the Legislature and the amount, if any, of interference by the Government depends to a great extent on whether or not the Government is in the House and whether or not it uses its majority to impose procedural changes. In this respect rules of procedure differ quite considerably from statutes which are ordinarily the product of a combination of the legislative and executive branches.

Rules of Procedure and the Constitutional Court

A second indication of the procedural independence of Parliament can be ascertained from whether or not the rules of procedure can, under certain circumstances, be referred to a Constitutional Court or similar non-legislative body. This is the practice in fifteen countries, including Jordan, where the rules are referred to the King for ratification in the same way as Acts of Parliament. In France, the Constitution provides that before they are put into effect the rules of procedure must be submitted to the Constitutional Council, which has to consider whether they conform to the Constitution. In Austria, Cameroon, the Federal Republic of Germany, Gabon, Kenya, Mali, Malta, Monaco and Senegal, the Constitutional or Supreme Court can rule whether or not the rules of procedure contradict the Constitution. In Kuwait, the rules may be referred to the Constitutional Court at the request of the National Assembly, the Council of Ministers, or the Courts of Justice. In Argentina, the rules can be referred to a Court of Law if they are considered unconstitutional. In Hungary the Law, Legislation and Administrative Board may advise. In the Republic of Korea the rules of procedure may be referred to the Constitutional Committee of the Supreme Court when their validity is questioned in a trial. The situation in all of these countries differs from the French one, in that there is no automatic referral of the rules to the Court, but only referral when there is doubt as to their constitutional validity.

Amendment of Rules of Procedure

In some countries motions to amend the rules of procedure are regarded as a serious enough matter to warrant special safeguards, such as the approval of a judicial or executive body, or the approval of a special parliamentary majority. In France, as we have already noted, the Constitutional Council must approve any changes in the rules of procedure of the two Chambers.

In many countries, the rules are usually amended on the advice or recommendations made by a special Committee of Procedure. Such committees exist on a permanent basis in forty-one countries and on an ad hoc basis in a further thirteen. In fourteen countries which do not have a specially constituted Committee of Procedure, other parliamentary committees or bodies often perform the same role, such as the Committee on

Constitutional Law, Legislation and General Administration in France; the House Steering Committee in the Republic of Korea; the Legal Committee of the Bureau in Kuwait; and the Speaker, assisted by the Speaker's Conference, in Finland.

Financial Independence

One of the most important corollaries of the sovereignty of Parliament is its financial independence. If Parliament is to be completely independent from the Executive, it must have at its disposal adequate financial resources to meet its needs and to ensure its freedom of action. To achieve this result the financial autonomy of Parliament should be reflected, firstly, in the preparation of its own budget and, secondly, in the auditing of its own expenditure.

Preparation of Parliament's Budget

The authorities responsible for the preparation of the budget of Parliament differ from country to country, as shown in Table 7B. In

TABLE 7B. Preparation of Parliamentary Budget

Parliamentary Budget Prepared by	Number of Countries
Parlt or Parliamentary Cttee	23
Secretariat of Parliament	23
Directing Authority or Bureau	19
Parliamentary Questors	6
Government	11
Total	82*

* Excludes China for reasons of missing data.

twenty-three countries including Fiji, Malta, New Zealand and Sri Lanka, for example, this is undertaken by the Clerk of Parliament; in Finland by the Office's Committee of the Eduskunta; and in Cameroon, France, Italy, Ivory Coast, Senegal and the Belgian Senate by Questors. The general pattern revealed in most remaining countries is that the estimates are drawn up by the directing authority of Parliament, or by a special committee, on the basis of figures prepared by the administrative authorities and then approved by the Chamber as a whole. The major problem that this procedure involves is how far the Executive is to have a hand in the estimates of Parliament. This arises because the expenditure of public money is involved and at one stage or another it must be included in the national estimates.

In the majority of countries the budget of Parliament is not subject to any modification by the Executive and its financial independence is guaranteed. Typically, the Minister of Finance enters the sums required by

Parliament into the national estimates without questioning them or consulting the Government about them. In many countries the estimates for Parliament go through the same channels as the estimate for any ministerial department. Before they can form part of the national estimates they require the concurrence of the Minister of Finance (as, for example, in Costa Rica and India). In the Bahamas, Bulgaria, Ireland, Japan, Kenya, Mongolia, Solomon Islands, Switzerland, the USSR, Yugoslavia and Zambia, the parliamentary budget is prepared by the Government. The practice of including parliamentary expenditure in the national estimates is found in almost all countries. In theory, it enables the figure to be debated in Parliament in the same way as the expenditure for any ministerial department. In practice, this seldom happens because the estimates will have been drawn up by a parliamentary body where any objections to them will have already been discussed in detail.

Auditing of Parliamentary Expenditure

It is evident that, with a few exceptions, Parliaments have a certain measure of independence in the drawing up of their estimates of expenditure. The amount and type of control they have over the ensuing expenditure produces a different picture. In the same way that it is reasonable that Parliament should be allowed to decide, without interference, what expenditure is necessary for its functioning, so it is reasonable to expect that, like any other public funds, those allotted to Parliament should be audited to ensure that they have been used for their proper purpose and administered wisely and efficiently. This is the theory in a number of countries which draw the logical conclusion that Parliament's expenditure should be subject to the normal accounting procedure and should be scrutinised not only by a special parliamentary body, such as the directing or administrative authority or a committee, but also by some body with experience in financial matters which is both unconnected with Parliament and independent of the Executive.

The authorities responsible for the auditing of parliamentary expenditure are presented in Table 7C. In many countries the sovereignty of Parliament is vigorously upheld in that it controls its own accounts, and

TABLE 7C. Control of Parliament's Accounts

Control of Accounts by	Number of Countries
Parliament	19
Directing or Administrative Authorities of Parliament	14
Comptroller-General or Auditors	45
Government	1
Total	79*

* Excludes Bulgaria, China, Lebanon and Mongolia, for reasons of missing data.

no other authority is permitted to interfere in its financial affairs. This does not imply a lack of control but rather means that such control is exercised by a parliamentary body such as a specialist committee. Some Parliaments leave the control of their accounts to the directing or administrative authorities, such as the Secretary General in Somalia, the President of the Assembly in Gabon, the Council Bureau in Zaire, the Chairmen of the Soviets and the Presidium of the Supreme Soviet in the USSR. A number of Parliaments have their accounts audited by external authorities. In Denmark, Finland and Sweden these are appointed by Parliament or elected specifically for this purpose. In forty-five countries the accounts are audited by the Comptroller-General, the Audit Officer or other independent audit authority.

Country and House(s)	7.1 Determination of rules of procedure	7.2 Referral of rules to another body	7.3 Amendment of rules of procedure
ALGERIA National People's Assembly (APN)	Originally established by the APN	No	Same as for adoption of a Bill (see 32.1)
ARGENTINA Senate	Some rules appear in the Const. but most are included in each House's SO.	Supreme Court of Justice in case of unconstitutionality	By the relevant House
Chamber of Deputies			
AUSTRALIA Senate	Each House	No	By resolution of appropriate House
House of Representatives			
AUSTRIA Federal Council	By resolution passed by a 2/3 majority with not less than half the Members present	–	By resolution of the Council as in 7.1
National Council	By law passed by a 2/3 majority with not less than half the Members present. Basic provisions are laid down in the Constitution.	The Constitutional Court can pronounce on the constitutionality of the Rules as they take the shape of a Federal Law.	By law as 7.1. The initiative must originate among Members (private Members' Bill).
BAHAMAS Senate	Each House	No	By resolution
House of Assembly			

7.4 Name and composition of committee on procedure	7.5 Parliamentary budget prepared and modified by	7.6 Accounts audited by
Standing Orders Cttee which was dissolved after approval of the SO by APN.	Proposals for the coming APN budget are drawn up by the Bureau of the APN (comprising the APN President and 4 Vice-presidents) and voted upon during the second ordinay session for the year.	A special seven-member "Accounts Cttee" is elected at the start of each year's first ordinary session to examine and report to the APN on expenditure and the use of funds. Since 1980 the accounts have been audited by the Audit Office.
Committee on Constitutional Matters Committee on Petitions, Powers and SO.	Theorically, by the Secretariat of each House. In practice the general Budget of the State includes the Congress budget.	National Accounts Tribunal
Standing Orders Cttee of each House (10 Members in Senate, 11 in House of Representatives).	Each department of Parlt prepares own budget, which is presented to Parlt in a separate Appropriation Bill (Parliamentary Departments).	Auditor General
Committee on Procedure of the respective Council	President of the National Council in consultation with his deputies and the President of the Federal Council	Court of Audit
NA	Ministry of Finance	Auditor General

Country and House(s)	7.1 Determination of rules of procedure	7.2 Referral of rules to another body	7.3 Amendment of rules of procedure
BELGIUM Senate	Each House	No	By resolution of the respective House
Chamber of Representatives			
BRAZIL Federal Senate	Each House	No	House, by approved resolution.
Chamber of Deputies			
BULGARIA National Assembly	National Assembly	No	By Parliament
CAMEROON National Assembly	National Assembly in the form of a law	May be submitted to Supreme Court should Assembly and Executive disagree.	By Assembly, at the request of at least 16 MPs.

7.4 Name and composition of committee on procedure	7.5 Parliamentary budget prepared and modified by	7.6 Accounts audited by
SO Cttee comprising the Bureau (see 9.1) and 7 Senators appointed by the Bureau.	The Questors: considered, amended and passed by the Bureau; submitted to the Senate for final approval.	Each House
Special SO and Amendment of Parliamentary Work Cttee comprising President of Chamber and 23 Members.	The Accounts Cttee with advice from the Questors and presented to the Chamber for approval.	
Constitution and Justice Cttee	Each House	Tribunal of Accounts, which reports to the Congress.
New and amended rules usually referred to an Ad hoc Cttee	National Assembly Budget included in Budget of the State Council, which is approved by Parlt.	–
At the beginning of a Parlt: Ad hoc Cttee of 30 members elected by secret ballot. During a Parlt: Cttee on Constitutional Law, Justice, Legislation and SO, Administration and Armed Forces.	Prepared by the Assembly Questors but subject to amendment by the Finance Cttee sitting as a budgetary accounting cttee.	Auditor of the National Assembly

Country and House(s)	7.1 Determination of rules of procedure	7.2 Referral of rules to another body	7.3 Amendment of rules of procedure
CANADA Senate	Each House	No	By a resolution of the respective House
House of Commons			
CAPE VERDE People's National Assembly	People's National Assembly	No, unless any citizen raises question of constitutionality when matter is referred to the Cttee on Constitutional and Legal Affairs.	By Assembly on written proposal from Permanent Bureau, or a specialised Standing Cttee, or a Member.
CHINA National People's Congress (NPC)	Rules of procedure of NPC and its Standing Cttee established by Organisational Law of the NPC.	See 7.1	See 7.1

7.4 Name and composition of committee on procedure	7.5 Parliamentary budget prepared and modified by	7.6 Accounts audited by
Cttee on Standing Rules and Orders (20 Members).	Prepared by the Staff of the Senate, reviewed by the sub-cttee (Budgets) of the Standing Cttee on Internal Economy, Budgets and Administration, and presented to a plenary meeting of the Main Cttee. After concurrence of the Main Cttee, the Estimates are signed by the Chairman and approved by the Speaker.	Auditor General of Canada
Standing Cttee on Procedure and Organisation (12 Members).	Prepared by House Administration, reviewed and approved by the Speaker and Commissioners of Internal Economy, transmitted to the Treasury Board via the Minister for Finance for inclusion in the annual estimates to be tabled in Parlt.	
Special Standing Parliamentary Cttee on Legal and Constitutional Affairs	Prepared by Secretariat General, approved by Administrative Council, adopted by Permanent Bureau, passed by plenary of Assembly.	Accounts are examined by Administrative Council, Permanent Bureau and plenary of Assembly.
See 7.1	See 7.1	See 7.1

Country and House(s)	7.1 Determination of rules of procedure	7.2 Referral of rules to another body	7.3 Amendment of rules of procedure
COMOROS Federal Assembly	Federal Assembly	No	Proposed by at least 1/4 of MPs, with the whole archipelago represented.
CONGO People's National Assembly (ANP)	People's National Assembly	No	By the ANP at the request of the Bureau or of 2/3 Members
COSTA RICA Legislative Assembly	Basic provisions given in the Constitution are amplified by rules adopted by the Assembly.	No	2/3 majority of the Assembly
CUBA National Assembly of People's Power	By the Constitution and Parliament	No	By Parliament
CYPRUS House of Representatives	The House	No	By simple majority of all MPs
CZECHOSLOVAKIA Chamber of Nations	Prescribed by Constitution and SO	No	By an Act of the Federal Assembly
Chamber of the People			
DEMOCRATIC YEMEN Supreme People's Council	Supreme People's Council	No	By Parliament
DENMARK Folketing	Folketing	No	By vote of Parliament

7.4 Name and composition of committee on procedure	7.5 Parliamentary budget prepared and modified by	7.6 Accounts audited by
–	Assembly Bureau (see 7.6) in agreement with the Government.	Assembly Bureau (comprising President, 3 Vice-Presidents, a Questor, and 4 Secretaries elected by the Assembly).
None	The Assembly	Committee of Accounts (5 Members).
Examined by the Cttee on Judicial Affairs	Prepared by the Assembly Secretariat and incorporated by Ministry of Finance into National Budget Bill	General Comptroller of the Republic
None	Prepared by President of the Assembly and approved by the Assembly	Parliament
Rules of procedure and Members' Rights Cttee (8 members).	The President of the House	The Auditor General of the Republic
None	Office of the Federal Assembly; approved by the Presidium of the Assembly.	Federal Assembly
NA	The Secretariat	Parliament
SO Cttee consists of the Presidium (5 members) and 16 other members elected by the Folketing.	SO Cttee upon recommendation of the Presidium	1 or 3 auditors appointed by the SO Cttee on recommendation of the Presidium

TABLE 7: RULES OF PROCEDURE AND PARLIAMENTARY BUDGET (cont.)

Country and House(s)	7.1 Determination of rules of procedure	7.2 Referral of rules to another body	7.3 Amendment of rules of procedure
EGYPT People's Assembly	People's Assembly	No	By Assembly, on request of its Bureau or at least 50 Members.
FIJI Senate House of Representatives	Each House	No	By each House on its own or on select cttee recommendation
FINLAND Eduskunta	Basic rules laid down in the Parlt Act which forms part of the Const. Detailed rules adopted by Parlt.	No	By resolution of Parlt unless change required to Parlt Act which must be treated as a Const. amdt.
FRANCE Senate National Assembly	Each House	Constitutional Court	Resolution of respective House
GABON National Assembly	National Assembly	Supreme Court for advice	Ad hoc cttee appointed by the Assembly
GERMAN DEMOCRATIC REPUBLIC People's Chamber	General rules laid down by the Const. are given detail in SO by Parlt.	No	By the Chamber with advice of the SO Cttee

248

7.4 Name and composition of committee on procedure	7.5 Parliamentary budget prepared and modified by	7.6 Accounts audited by
No specific cttee, but proposals may be referred to the General Cttee or Constitutional and Legislative Affairs Cttee for examination and report.	Assembly Bureau comprising the Speaker and 2 Deputy Speakers	Assembly Accounting Cttee
SO Cttee	Clerk to Parliament	Auditor General
Procedural matters considered by the Speaker assisted by the Speaker's Conference	The Office's Cttee of the Eduskunta	4 auditors elected by the Parliamentary Electors
No specific cttee but considered by Cttee on Constitutional Law, Legislation and General Administration of the Republic.	A cttee composed of the questors of both Houses and a chairman of the Audit Office transmits a draft budget to the Ministry of Finance for inclusion, without modifications, in the Finance Bill.	A cttee of each House verifies the accounts.
No permanent SO Cttee. Members of relevant ad hoc cttees chosen from among members of 6 most important cttees.	President of Assembly, with assistance of Secretary-General, Finance Administrator and Questors.	President of Assembly
SO Cttee comprising 8 members and 1 successor candidate	Draft budget submitted to the Presidium of the People's Chamber, for approval, by the Director of the Secretariat of Parlt.	State Auditing Agency

249

TABLE 7: RULES OF PROCEDURE AND PARLIAMENTARY BUDGET (cont.)

Country and House(s)	7.1 Determination of rules of procedure	7.2 Referral of rules to another body	7.3 Amendment of rules of procedure
GERMANY Federal Council	Each House	Federal Constitutional Court may decide on compatibility with the Basic Law.	By resolution of each House
Federal Diet			
GREECE Chamber of Deputies	Current SO drafted in 1975 by a special cttee of members and approved by Parlt	No	By Parliament
HUNGARY National Assembly	National Assembly	No, but Law, Legislation and Administrative Board may advise.	Resolution of National Assembly
INDIA Council of States	Const. makes basic provisions. Detailed rules of procedure are adopted by the respective House.	No, but opinion of the Attorney General may be sought.	Adoption of a report from the Cttee on Rules of each House
House of the People			
INDONESIA House of Representatives	The House	No	By the House, on proposal of 20 MPs, if possible by consensus.

7.4 Name and composition of committee on procedure	7.5 Parliamentary budget prepared and modified by	7.6 Accounts audited by
No SO Cttee as such, but 11 member Permanent Consultative Council considers.	Permanent Consultative Council. Budget is referred to Finance Minister for inclusion in Federal Budget.	Federal Court of Accounts
Cttee on Rules of Procedure of 13 members nominated in proportion to group strength.	Draft prepared by the Council of Elders for incorporation in the Federal Budget. The Government submits the Budget to Parliament which decides by a law.	
SO Cttee comprising Chamber President (Chairman), 5 Govt members, 4 opposition.	Drafted by parliamentary accountant and considered by the Chamber Accounts Cttee, before presentation to Parliament.	Court of Accounts
Ad hoc Cttee on Procedure when necessary	National Assembly	National Assembly
Cttee on Rules chaired by the respective Presiding Officer	Respective Secretariat with concurrence of the Ministry of Finance	Pay and Accounts Office of the respective House and Comptroller and Auditor General of India
Ad hoc cttee on Rules of Procedure (composition reflecting House Factions).	Draft prepared by House Leadership assisted by the Secretariat and presented for approval through the Household Cttee (forms part of State Budget).	State Audit Board; Department of Finance; Household Cttee.

Country and House(s)	7.1 Determination of rules of procedure	7.2 Referral of rules to another body	7.3 Amendment of rules of procedure
IRELAND Senate	Each House	No	By resolution of the House, usually on a report of the Cttee on Procedure and Privileges.
Dáil			
ISRAEL The Knesset	The Knesset	No	Any MP may propose an amdt to the House Cttee. After tabling in the House, MPs have 14 days for objections. Those not accepted by the Cttee may be defended in the House when voted.
ITALY Senate	Each House by absolute majority of Members	No	By an absolute majority of Members
Chamber of Deputies			
IVORY COAST National Assembly	National Assembly	No	By National Assembly, on proposal of, at least, 5 MPs.
JAPAN House of Councillors	Fundamental principles by Const. Diet Law enacted by National Diet. Rules of each House by the relevant House.	No	Diet Law amended as for any other ordinary law and SO by the respective House
House of Representatives			

7.4 Name and composition of committee on procedure	7.5 Parliamentary budget prepared and modified by	7.6 Accounts audited by
Senate Cttee on Procedure and Privileges (Chairman and Deputy Chairman of the Senate and 10 Senators). Dáil Cttee on Procedure and Privileges (Chairman of Dail and 17 other members, representatively selected).	Department of Finance	Department of Finance
House Cttee comprising 25 MPs, proportional to party group strength.	The Knesset Chairman assisted by the accountant. Approval is by a Knesset cttee.	The Accountant-General of the Finance Ministry. Post-audit control is by the Knesset's Auditor, or by the State Comptroller at the Chairman's request.
SO Junta of the respective House comprising 10 members appointed by the respective House President who chairs the Junta.	Prepared by a college of Senators or Deputies respectively (called Questors); confirmed by the respective Presiding Officer's Cttee and approved by the respective House.	The President, Questors and Secretary General.
None	Questors assisted by the Secretary General, prepare a draft which is approved by the Finance Cttee before approbation of the plenary.	Economic and Financial Affairs Cttee of the Assembly
Standing Cttee on Rules and Administration in each House. 25 members allocated proportionally to party strength except that in House of Councillors the party must have at least 10 members.	The Cabinet, with advice from the Presiding Officer.	Board of Audit

Country and House(s)	7.1 Determination of rules of procedure	7.2 Referral of rules to another body	7.3 Amendment of rules of procedure
JORDAN Senate House of Deputies	Each House, subject to confirmation by the King.	Confirmation by the King	Petition by 10 MPs, referred to the Legal Cttee and adopted by majority vote.
KENYA National Assembly	National Assembly	Only if constitutionality in doubt	By SO Cttee
KUWAIT National Assembly	National Assembly	To the Constitutional Court, if requested by National Assembly, Council of Ministers, Courts of Law.	By National Assembly
LEBANON National Assembly	National Assembly	No	By majority vote of the Assembly
LIECHTENSTEIN Diet	Diet	No	By the Diet
LUXEMBOURG Chamber of Deputies	Chamber of Deputies	No	By resolution of the Chamber
MALAWI National Assembly	Const. provides basic provisions. Detailed rules are adopted by the Assembly.	No	By resolution of the Assembly
MALAYSIA Senate House of Representatives	Each House	No	Adopted by House on recommendation of SO Committee
MALI National Assembly	National Assembly	Supreme Court	National Assembly

7.4 Name and composition of committee on procedure	7.5 Parliamentary budget prepared and modified by	7.6 Accounts audited by
Legal Cttee	The Speaker, 2 Deputy Speakers and 2 assistants.	Audit Office
SO Cttee comprising the Speaker and 10 Members	The Executive	Comptroller and Auditor General
Legal Cttee of the Assembly's Bureau	National Assembly	Audit and Control Commission
SO Cttee of 8 members	The Assembly	–
None	The Diet	The Diet
If necessary an ad hoc cttee (or the Bureau) may consider proposals.	Chamber Bureau comprising President, 3 Vice-Presidents, 5 Secretaries elected by the Chamber.	Accounts Cttee
Cttee on Parliamentary Procedure comprising a Chairman and 5 members appointed by the Speaker.	The National Assembly	Auditor General
SO Cttee comprising Presiding Officer and 6 members nominated by Cttee of Selection.	Secretary General of Parlt who is also Clerk of the House of Representatives for approval by Parlt.	Auditor General
Cttee on Home Affairs, Justice and Security.	Assembly Bureau comprising President, 4 Vice-Presidents, 4 Secretaries, 2 Questors elected by the Assembly.	Finance Cttee

255

Country and House(s)	7.1 Determination of rules of procedure	7.2 Referral of rules to another body	7.3 Amendment of rules of procedure
MALTA House of Representatives	Basic provisions in the Const. are amplified by rules adopted by the House.	Constitutional Court	By resolution of the House usually after report by a select cttee
MAURITIUS Legislative Assembly	Basic provisions in the Const. are amplified by rules adopted by the Assembly.	No	Adoption of notice of motion; referral to cttee; consideration of cttee report and vote.
MEXICO Chamber of Senators	The respective Chamber	No	By the respective Chamber
Chamber of Deputies			
MONACO National Council	National Council	Supreme Court can rule on constitutionality.	By resolution of the National Council
MONGOLIA Great People's Khural (GPKh)	Basic provisions in the Const. are amplified by rules adopted by the GPKh.	No	GPKh by simple majority decision
NAURU Parliament	Based on Const. and SO of the Australian House of Representatives	No	By motion approved by a majority
NETHERLANDS First Chamber	The Chamber itself within the limits stipulated by the Constitution	No	The Chamber
Second Chamber			Proposed by an MP or the Cttee on Procedure and treated as an MP's bill. If approved it becomes part of SO.

256

7.4 Name and composition of committee on procedure	7.5 Parliamentary budget prepared and modified by	7.6 Accounts audited by
A select cttee chaired by the Speaker may be formed as required.	Clerk of the House in consultation with the Ministry of Finance for approval of Parlt in Cttee of Supply	Director of Audit
SO Cttee comprising the Speaker, Deputy Speaker and 4 Members nominated by Cttee of Selection.	Clerk of the Assembly	Director of Audit
–	Parliament	Cttee of Administration of the Chamber of Senators
Ad hoc Cttee on Procedure when necessary	The National Council	Finance Cttee of the Council and the Supreme Audit Commission
Cttee on Procedure	Included in the State Budget which is adopted by the GPKh.	The GPKh Presidium
SO Cttee comprising Speaker, Deputy Speaker, Cabinet Chairman, 2 other Members.	By the Clerk in consultation with the Speaker, approved by the House and Library Cttee, included in Govt's General Budget for presentation to Parliament.	Director of Audit
None	The respective Chamber	The General Board of Auditors
Cttee on Procedure with all parliamentary groups having at least 1 member and by tradition presided over by Chairman of the Chamber		

Country and House(s)	7.1 Determination of rules of procedure	7.2 Referral of rules to another body	7.3 Amendment of rules of procedure
NEW ZEALAND House of Representatives	The House	No	By resolution of the House
NICARAGUA National Assembly	National Assembly	No	By Parliament in plenary sitting
NORWAY Storting	The Storting	No	By simple majority of the Storting
PHILIPPINES National Assembly	National Assembly	No	2/3 majority resolution
POLAND Diet	Basic provisions in the Const. are amplified by rules adopted by the Assembly.	No	By the Diet on proposal of the Bureau, the Mandates and Rules Cttee or at least 15 Members.
PORTUGAL Assembly of the Republic	Assembly of the Republic	No	Resolution by absolute majority of Members present
REPUBLIC OF KOREA National Assembly	National Assembly	No	Attendance of at least 1/2 membership and by absolute majority of those present
ROMANIA Grand National Assembly	Grand National Assembly	No	Grand National Assembly
RWANDA National Development Council (CND)	Basic provisions in the Const. are amplified by rules adopted by the CND.	No	The CND on report of Parliamentary Activities Cttee

7.4 Name and composition of committee on procedure	7.5 Parliamentary budget prepared and modified by	7.6 Accounts audited by
SO Cttee set up periodically, consisting of senior Members.	Clerk of the House	Controller and Auditor General
Economic Affairs, Finance and Budget Cttee.	National Assembly	Controller
Amdts usually prepared by an ad hoc cttee appointed by the Presidium (see 9.1).	The Storting	Auditor General (under a management board with 5 members elected by the Storting).
Cttee on Rules comprising the Majority Floor Leader as Chairman, the Minority Floor Leader and 13 other members.	The Speaker assisted by the Accounts Cttee	Audit Commission
Mandates and Rules Cttee (17 members).	The Diet	The Diet
Rules and Mandates Cttee	The Administrative Council. Submitted for Assembly approval by the President.	The Administrative Council. Submitted for Assembly approval by the President.
House Steering Cttee comprising 21 Members including leaders of parliamentary parties	National Assembly Secretariat and modified by Economic Planning Board	Board of Audit and Inspection
None	Grand National Assembly	Grand National Assembly
Parliamentary Activities Cttee comprising chairmen of the permanent cttees	CND Bureau (see 11.1) and approved by the CND.	Court of Accounts

Country and House(s)	7.1 Determination of rules of procedure	7.2 Referral of rules to another body	7.3 Amendment of rules of procedure
ST VINCENT House of Assembly	The House	No	The House
SENEGAL National Assembly	National Assembly. Basic provisions are laid down in the Constitution.	Supreme Court in case of unconstitutionality or difference with the Govt	By the Assembly on initiative of Members or the President of the Republic, after report by the cttee in 7.4.
SOLOMON ISLANDS National Parliament	By Parliamentary Cttee	No	By Parliamentary Cttee
SOMALIA People's Assembly	The Assembly	No	–
SOUTH AFRICA House of Assembly House of Representatives House of Delegates	The respective House	No	Cttee on Standing Rules and Orders of each House makes recommendations to the respective House for adoption.
SPAIN Senate Congress of Deputies	Each House	No	By absolute majority of the House
SRI LANKA Parliament	Parliament	No	By resolution of Parliament

7.4 Name and composition of committee on procedure	7.5 Parliamentary budget prepared and modified by	7.6 Accounts audited by
The House may appoint an ad hoc cttee as required.	Finance Department and House Finance Cttee	Director of Audit
Cttee for Legislation, General Administration and Standing Orders	Questors assisted by the financial adviser	Financial adviser makes immediate checks. Subsequent audit by the Accounts and Audit Cttee.
Standing Select Cttee on Procedure	Minister of Finance	Auditor General
Legislative Cttee	President of the Assembly	Secretary General
Cttees on Standing Rules and Orders of the three Houses meeting jointly.	Chief Accountant	Auditor General
Cttee on Rules and Procedure comprising the House Presiding Body (see 9.1) and Members appointed by parliamentary groups proportionally to their strength.	Presiding Body	Const. (Art. 72) provides for autonomous approval of the parliamentary budget.
SO Cttee (7 members).	Secretary General of Parliament, examined by relevant cttee and forwarded to Govt for approval before adoption by Parliament.	Auditor General

Country and House(s)	7.1 Determination of rules of procedure	7.2 Referral of rules to another body	7.3 Amendment of rules of procedure
SWEDEN Riksdag	Basic provisions in the Const. and the Riksdag Act.	No	By amdt to the Const. (see 16.2) or the Riksdag Act or other supplementary legislation (see 32.1).
SWITZERLAND States Council National Council	Each Council	No	By the relevant Council on proposal of the respective Bureau or a Member
SYRIAN ARAB REPUBLIC People's Council	People's Council	–	On proposal of the Council Bureau or at least 10 Members
THAILAND Senate House of Representatives	Basic provisions in the Const. are amplified by rules adopted by each House.	No, Const. (Art. 141) places power of interpretation with respect to the Const. in Parliament.	By resolution of the House
TUNISIA Chamber of Deputies	By the Chamber with advice of a special cttee	No	By absolute majority on written proposal of 1/3 Members
UGANDA National Assembly	Basic provisions in the Const. are amplified by rules adopted by the Assembly.	–	By resolution of the Assembly and adoption of recommendations from the Rules and Orders Cttee

7.4 Name and composition of committee on procedure	7.5 Parliamentary budget prepared and modified by	7.6 Accounts audited by
Standing Cttee on the Const. (15 elected members).	Office of Administration and Services of the Riksdag, examined by Standing Cttee on Const. and approved by the Riksdag.	Auditors of the Riksdag
No permanent cttee	Finance Ministry in collaboration with the Secretary General of Parlt	Auditor General (Contrôle des finances).
None	Bureau of the Council	Bureau of the Council
House may appoint a cttee to consider a proposal or examine it in Cttee of the Whole House.	Secretariat of the National Assembly	Auditor of the Secretariat of the National Assembly first; then by the Auditor General of Thailand.
A special non-permanent cttee may be elected as required.	Chamber Bureau comprising the President, 2 Vice-Presidents, permanent cttee Chairman and Rapporteurs.	Chamber Bureau
Rules and Orders Cttee (10 members, pro-portional representation of parties).	Clerk to the National Assembly as accounting officer	Auditor General

TABLE 7: RULES OF PROCEDURE AND PARLIAMENTARY BUDGET (cont.)

Country and House(s)	7.1 Determination of rules of procedure	7.2 Referral of rules to another body	7.3 Amendment of rules of procedure
UNION OF SOVIET SOCIALIST REPUBLICS Soviet of Nationalities Soviet of the Union	Basic provisions in the Const. are amplified by rules adopted by Supreme Soviet in 1979 or approved by a law of the same date. Many procedural matters are resolved by the Supreme Soviet or the respective Soviet.	No	By amdt to the establishing Act; exceptions to the rules may be decided when necessary by majority vote.
UNITED KINGDOM House of Lords	By orders of the House or reference to established practice	No	By resolution of the House
House of Commons			
UNITED REPUBLIC OF TANZANIA National Assembly	Basic provisions in the Const. are amplified by SO adopted by the Assembly.	No	By resolution of Parlt usually after cttee deliberation
UNITED STATES OF AMERICA Senate House of Representatives	Basic provisions in the Const. are amplified by rules adopted by the respective House.	No	By resolution of the relevant House
VANUATU Parliament	Parliament	No	By Parliament

7.4 Name and composition of committee on procedure	7.5 Parliamentary budget prepared and modified by	7.6 Accounts audited by
None as such. Proposals may receive preliminary examination by a Council of Elders of each Soviet comprising groups of MPs on a constituency basis elected by the respective Soviet.	The budget of each Soviet is a share of the Supreme Soviet budget which forms part of the State Budget.	Chairman of each Soviet and the Presidium of the Supreme Soviet (see 8.5).
Select Cttee on Procedure proposed by the Cttee of Selection	Clerk of the Parliament, subject to agreement of the Finance Sub-Cttee of the House of Lords' Offices Cttee.	Comptroller and Auditor General
Select cttee appointed from time to time as required	House of Commons Commission, comprising Speaker, Leader of the House, member nominated by Leader of the Opposition, 3 other members.	
Standing Orders Cttee (14 members including Speaker and Deputy Speaker).	The Assembly Secretariat	Comptroller/Auditor General
Cttee on Rules and Administration (12 members). Cttee on Rules (13 members).	Each House which transmits it to the Office of Management and Budget of the President's Executive Office for inclusion in the Budget.	Each House subject to auditing by the General Accounting Office
Standing Orders Cttee	Prepared by Cttee of the Budget and modified by Parliament	Auditor General

TABLE 7: RULES OF PROCEDURE AND PARLIAMENTARY BUDGET (cont.)

Country and House(s)	7.1 Determination of rules of procedure	7.2 Referral of rules to another body	7.3 Amendment of rules of procedure
YUGOSLAVIA Federal Chamber Chamber of Republics and Provinces	Each Chamber	Only if they are not in conformity with the Constitution.	By the Chamber
ZAIRE Legislative Council	Adopted by the Council on proposal of cttee	No	On request of 2/3 Members
ZAMBIA National Assembly	National Assembly	No	The Standing Orders Cttee circulates draft amdts based on proposals. They are deemed approved if no objection raised.
ZIMBABWE Senate House of Assembly	Each House	No	By the House on cttee report (see 7.4).

7.4 Name and composition of committee on procedure	7.5 Parliamentary budget prepared and modified by	7.6 Accounts audited by
Commission for Controlling the implementation of the Rules of Procedure and Rules on Joint Activities of the Assembly Chambers	Budget drawn up by the Government and adopted by the Federal Chamber	Administration Commission of the Assembly (joint working body of both Chambers).
Policy, Administrative and Legal Cttee.	Council Bureau comprising President, 2 Vice-Presidents, 2 secretaries elected by the Council.	President of the Council Bureau
Standing Orders Cttee comprising 8 members with Speaker in the chair	Minister of Finance	Auditor General
Standing Rules and Orders Cttee of each House chaired by respective Presiding Officer and comprising House and party leaders	Parliamentary staff under the Speaker's supervision	Comptroller and Auditor General

TABLE 8

SESSIONS OF PARLIAMENT

Should the independence of Parliament give it the option of deciding
for itself how and when sittings should take place and how long it should
continue to sit? Or should sittings be delineated by a constitutional provision or decided by an authority other than Parliament? The answers to
these questions are pertinent because to a large extent they determine
the functions of a Parliament and its influence on the political life of a
country. It is important to define carefully the terms used in this context. A session is the period during the year when Parliament has the
legal right to meet and to transact its business. There may be more than
one session a year, and their lengths may vary. A sitting is the period
from when Members meet to conduct business until they adjourn. Usually, there is one sitting on a single day.

Legal Provision for Sessions

There are two contradictory constitutional answers to the questions
raised above. The first of these is what can be called the "authori-
tarian" tendency to curb the actions of Parliament by making the frequency and length of sessions a matter for the Government to decide.
The second is the "democratic" tendency which protects the sovereignty
of Parliament and gives it a free hand to choose the period in which its
sittings are held. In nearly all of the countries under consideration,
legal provisions are made in the Constitution for the holding of parliamentary sessions. Forty-nine of these countries have additional provisions for either a fixed date for the commencement of these sessions, for
the minimum or maximum periods of time that Parliament can meet when it
is summoned, or for Parliament itself to determine the dates of sitting.

The "Permanent Assembly" System

The "permanent assembly" system does not imply that sittings are
uninterrupted or continuous but that there is power to sit for an unlimited duration. Legally, there are no sessions, but only a legislature
whose duration corresponds to the lifetime for which a Parliament is
elected. This is the practice found, for example, in the German Democratic Republic, Italy, Luxembourg and the Netherlands. The Greek
Parliament operates an interesting system whereby a "Holiday Section"
ensures continuity of activity. The permanent assembly system is often
combined with the use of annual sessions in which, under the Constitution or by practice, the close of one session is determined by the opening
of the next session. Provided that it is not abused, the permanent

269

session system enables Parliament to devote as much time as it chooses to the effective performance of its duties and at the same time ensures that it remains independent of the Executive. There is the danger, however, that problems may arise if it puts no limit on the length of its sittings. A Parliament which can sit for an unlimited period is not necessarily a better functioning Parliament than one which meets for a pre-specified period. Party bickering may become rife, political problems may give rise to artificial feuds which do not reflect public opinion in the country, and the Government may be hamstrung by a constant battery of questions and motions of censure which leave little time for steady administration and can have unfortunate consequences for ministerial stability.

Sessions Fixed by the Executive

In direct contrast to the permanent assembly system is the system under which sessions of Parliament are fixed by the Executive. This latter system is monarchical in origin, and is based on the principle that Parliament should meet only when necessary to transact legislative business and to approve the national budget. The Head of State, or in his name the Government, summons Parliament to meet and decides when to brings its sessions to an end. In theory, a legislature should be free to scrutinise the actions of the Government without the Government's permission, although in some countries the Government does control when Parliament will sit. Specific provisions are made in the Constitutions of several countries (for example, Hungary, Jordan and India) to ensure regular meetings of Parliament where the opening and closing of sessions is the prerogative of the Executive. In the United Kingdom, a proclamation to dissolve the House of Commons contains the date when the new House will meet.

Constitutional Delineation of Sessions

Between the two extremes of the permanent session and the session fixed by the Executive, there is room for a number of practices which attempt to strike a balance between two contradictory principles: on the one hand, the principle of the sovereignty of Parliament, on the other hand, the exigencies of effective government and parliamentary scrutiny. A method frequently encountered is to lay down in the Constitution the periods during which Parliament may meet and transact business. These provisions have the effect of binding the Executive as well as the Legislature in the amount of time available to pass laws and to complete financial business and other matters. As a rule, these provisions are known as ordinary sessions, and they not only commence each year as a matter of course on a fixed date, but additionally contain a closing date for the sessions so that it is impossible for Parliament to sit on a permanent basis. This practice is found in several Parliaments, which include Argentina, the National Council of Austria, France, Lebanon, Mexico, the Republic of Korea and Sweden.

The number of ordinary sessions for which Parliament is summoned each year is the subject of Table 8A. Most countries, it can be seen, have provisions for (at least) one session to be held each year, but several countries divide their legislative year into two sessions. In

TABLE 8A. Number of Sessions Per Year

Number of Sessions	Number of Countries
One	39
Two	27
Three or more	10
"Permanent Assembly"	5
Total	81*

* Does not include Thailand which may have 1 or 2 ordinary sessions per year and the Bahamas which has no fixed legal provisions.

Bulgaria, Democratic Yemen, India, Liechtenstein, Malaysia, Nicaragua, Switzerland, the Syrian Arab Republic, the United Republic of Tanzania, and Yugoslavia, three or more sessions are held each year.

Length of Sessions

While the regulations governing the provision of parliamentary sessions are of undoubted importance (as can be seen from their frequent inclusion in Constitutions), the length of the sessions themselves is equally important, as it is a revealing indication of the contribution which Parliament makes in any country. The average number of days of plenary sittings over the last five years is the subject of Table 8B.

TABLE 8B. Average Number of Plenary Sittings

Number of Sitting Days	Popular or Only Chamber
1-24	3
25-49	15
50-74	8
75-99	7
100-124	9
More than 125	6
Total	48*

* Does not include Brazil, Bulgaria, Comoros, Congo, Costa Rica, Cuba, Democratic Yemen, Egypt, Fiji, Gabon, Indonesia, Italy, Ivory Coast, Jordan, Kenya, Lebanon, Luxembourg, Mali, Mexico, Monaco, Mongolia, Nauru, Nicaragua, Norway, St Vincent, Senegal, Solomon Islands, Somalia, Syrian Arab Republic, Thailand, Uganda, USSR, Vanuatu, Yugoslavia and Zimbabwe, for reasons of missing data.

The number of sitting days of each Parliament gives an idea, if not of the quantity or quality of work done, at least of that Parliament's place in the machinery of Government. It is noticeable that, with the exception of the Senates of Australia, Italy and the United States, the Upper Chambers in bicameral systems meet for fewer days than the Lower Chambers. In few of the socialist countries does Parliament meet for more than twenty-five days a year, but as the basic legislative work of these Parliaments is undertaken by committees which meet between sessions (see 8.3), this figure needs to be interpreted with considerable caution.

Extraordinary Sessions

During recesses events may occur which are grave enough to justify the recall of Parliament, and to cater for this eventuality most Constitutions or rules of procedure allow for the possibility of extraordinary sessions. In practice, as would perhaps be expected, extraordinary sessions are rarely called. The bodies with the initiative in calling extraordinary sessions are presented in Table 8C. In most of the countries

TABLE 8C. Initiative in Calling Extraordinary Sessions

Sessions Called at Initiative of	Number of Countries
Head of State	40
Government	21
Directing Authority of Parliament	20
Units of Federation	5
Parliament	51
Electoral Groups (Liechtenstein)	1

where provisions are made for the calling of extraordinary sessions, they can be initiated by either the Head of State or the Government. This is a reasonable practice because the Executive is in the best position to judge whether in a given situation an extraordinary session of Parliament is called for. Exceptions are Bahamas, Bulgaria, China, Cyprus, Liechtenstein, Nauru and St Vincent.

How far should Parliament be at liberty to call for an extraordinary session? This is an incontestable right of Parliament, though one which needs qualification if the drawbacks of the permanent assembly system are to be avoided. Extraordinary sessions are quite obviously superfluous in Parliaments where ordinary sessions last for a relatively long time, and are of limited value when called by Members if the order of business is determined in advance by the Executive.

In a number of countries (which include China, Italy and the USSR) the initiative in the recalling of Parliaments is in the hands of their directing authorities. As a general rule, a request for an extraordinary session has to be made by a given number of Members, a provision which emphasises the serious nature of such sessions. The number varies from country to country. In Israel, Japan and Switzerland, for example, one quarter of the Members of Parliament can request an extraordinary session, while in Cameroon, Mexico and Monaco, such a request must be made by two-thirds of the Members. The rights of minorities are heeded in twenty-five countries where extraordinary sessions can be requested by less than an absolute majority of the Members of Parliament.

Bodies Exercising Parliamentary Powers in Recess

In some countries arrangements are made for various parliamentary powers to be exercised between sessions by certain bodies. In some cases, particularly in socialist countries, the powers available may be extensive. In others, for example Austria, Denmark, the United Kingdom and Zambia, they are severely circumscribed or limited to urgent matters as in Bulgaria and Sweden. Table 8D summarises the situation.

TABLE 8D. Bodies Exercising Parliamentary Powers in Recess

Type of Power	Number of Countries
None	47
Permanent Assembly or Equivalent	5
Severely Circumscribed	5
Urgent Matters	2
Other	19
Total	78*

* Excludes Costa Rica, Monaco, Sri Lanka, Thailand and Zimbabwe, for reasons of missing data.

Subsidiary Bodies and Joint Sittings

It has already been seen that ordinary or annual sessions do not cover the entire year and that in many countries there are long periods when Pariament is in recess. Usually, these recesses are for vacations, but we have had occasion to note that in the socialist countries, particularly, the work of Parliament carries on outside the regular session. Table 8 also examines the provisions made, firstly for meetings of subsidiary bodies of Parliament during recesses and, secondly, for joint sittings of the Houses of Parliament in bicameral systems.

Meetings of Subsidiary Bodies

The number of countries in which subsidiary bodies of Parliament can meet during recesses is presented in Table 8E. Many of the countries under consideration make provisions for their directing authorities and/or their committees to meet outside the regular session. The former meet to plan the timetable of Parliament and control its administrative services, the latter meet to continue their legislative, financial and control functions. When this activity is taken into account with the number of plenary sittings held in each country, a much fuller appreciation of

TABLE 8E. Provisions for Subsidiary Bodies
to meet during Recesses

Subsidiary Bodies which can meet during Recesses	Number of Countries
Directing Authorities	22
Permanent Committees	51
Special Committees or with Permission	23
None	8

Information for the Federal Republic of Germany and
St Vincent not available.

the work of Parliament can be obtained. In Belgium, Comoros, Congo,
Costa Rica, Cyprus, Gabon, Jordan and Senegal, none of the subsidiary
bodies of Parliament are permitted to meet outside the ordinary sessions.

Joint Sittings of Parliament

In all but three of the bicameral legislative systems under consideration (Ireland, Malaysia and the United Kingdom) joint sittings of the two
Chambers can be held. The various circumstances under which such
sittings take place are listed in Table 8F. These fall into seven general
categories:

TABLE 8F. Circumstances for Holding of Joint Sittings

Type of Circumstance	Number of Countries
Ceremonial Occasions	14
Elections and Appointments	11
Legislative Matters	6
Receiving Messages from the Executive	4
Revisions of Constitution	3
Declaration of War or Emergency	3
Resignation of Head of State, Impeachments, Dismissals	3

The first of these is concerned with ceremonial occasions, such as to
witness the oath-taking ceremony of the President of the Republic, as in
Austria and the Federal Republic of Germany, and on the opening or
closing of the parliamentary sessions, as in Australia, Brazil, Fiji,
Malaysia, Mexico, the Netherlands, Thailand and Zimbabwe.

The second category of joint sittings covers elections and appointments, as some examples will illustrate. In Czechoslovakia and Italy, for example, joint sittings are held to elect the Head of State; in the USSR to elect the Presidium of the Supreme Soviet and to form the Council of Ministers; in Switzerland to elect the the Federal Council (Government); in Italy and Switzerland to elect members of the higher Courts; in the United States to count the electoral vote for the President and Vice-President; and in Belgium and the Netherlands to designate a Regent if circumstances require it.

A third category of joint sittings is held in six countries and covers legislative matters. In Australia, India, Jordan and the USSR, both Houses of Parliament may meet to seek compromises on a Bill. In Thailand the Houses may meet to reconsider a Bill, and in Brazil Congress may meet in joint sessions to vote on the National Budget Bill.

A fourth category of circumstances giving rise to joint sittings of Parliament covers the receiving of messages or policy statements from the Executive, which take place in, for example, Brazil, Czechoslovakia, Thailand and the United States.

A fifth category of joint sittings is when the two Houses of Parliament must meet to consider revisions to the Constitution, as provided for in Brazil, France and Thailand.

Some countries require a joint sitting to declare a state of war or other emergency. This occurs in Austria, the Netherlands and Thailand.

Finally, in Italy and Zimbabwe, a joint sitting is required to impeach the Head of State, or in Mexico to receive his resignation.

TABLE 8: SESSIONS OF PARLIAMENT

Country and House(s)	8.1 a) Legal provisions for sessions b) Average number of sitting days per year	8.2 Provisions for extraordinary sessions
ALGERIA National People's Assembly	a) Const. (Art. 146) provides for 2 annual sessions of 3 months maximum in: Spring (starting in April); Autumn (starting in October) b) 39	If necessary, called by the President of the Republic or on request of 2/3 of the members or by the APN President. Only matters on the agenda may be considered.
ARGENTINA Senate	a) Const. (Art. 55) provides for 1 session a year (1 May to 30 Sept. 3 sittings a week) b) Extraordinary sessions (Dec. 83 to Apr. 84) 21; ordinary sessions (May to Sept. 84) 31	The National President may convene extraordinary sessions.
Chamber of Deputies	a) As a) above b) Extraordinary sessions (Dec. 83 to Apr. 84) 22; ordinary sessions (May to Sept. 84) 29	
AUSTRALIA Senate	a) Const. (Chap. 1 Art. 6) provides for at least one session per year such that 12 months do not intervene between the end and beginning of sessions b) 66	No distinction is made between extraordinary and ordinary sessions.
House of Representatives	a) As a) above b) 53	

8.3 Committee meetings during recess	8.4 Other parliamentary bodies meeting in recess	8.5 Bodies exercising parliamentary powers in recess	8.6 Provisions for joint sittings in bicameral Parliaments
Yes	None	None	NA
Yes	NA	None	Scrutiny of Presidential election; resignation, election (if necessary) and oath taking of President and Vice-President; opening of Parlt by the National President; visits by foreign Heads of State or important ceremonial events.
Senate legislative and General Purpose Standing Cttees. Other Senate cttees may meet if so empowered. House of Representatives do not meet during recess.	None	None	If Senate twice rejects a proposed law both Houses may be dissolved and an election called. If, following the election, House of Representatives again passes and Senate rejects the proposed law, Governor General may convene a joint-sitting. Joint sitting also to appoint a Senator to any vacant Territory seat. Ceremonial occasions such as opening of Parlt.

Country and House(s)	8.1 a) Legal provisions for sessions b) Average number of sitting days per year	8.2 Provisions for extraordinary sessions
AUSTRIA Federal Council	a) Permanently in being; individual sittings convened by the Presiding Officer; obligatory if more than a quarter of Members or the Govt ask for it b) 13	See 8.1
National Council	a) Annual session convened by the Head of State (to begin not before 15 Sept. and not to last beyond 15 July of following year) b) 40	Called on demand of Govt, Federal Council or 1/3 of the members of the National Council.
BAHAMAS Senate House of Assembly	a) No provisions b) 30	By resolution of House empowering Speaker to issue notice
BELGIUM Senate	a) Summoned under the Const. (Art. 70) on the second Tuesday of Oct. to sit for at least 40 days. Each session lasts 1 year b) 62	At the same time as dissolving the Parlt for a general election, the King summons Parlt for an extraordinary session to finish pending legislative work.
Chamber of Representatives	a) As a) above b) 70	
BRAZIL Federal Senate Chamber of Deputies	a) and b) Under the Const., sessions are held from 1 March to 30 June and from 1 July to 5 December	Extraordinary sessions may be convened by President of Senate if state of emergency has been decreed, or by President of Republic, or by 2/3 of Members of House of Deputies and Senate.

8.3 Committee meetings during recess	8.4 Other parliamentary bodies meeting in recess	8.5 Bodies exercising parliamentary powers in recess	8.6 Provisions for joint sittings in bicameral Parliaments
NA (see 8.1). If decision taken before the end of the session	None	In a very limited way, the Main Ctte and its Standing Sub-Cttees. The Main cttee may be called to meet during the recess of the National Council, if necessary, where under Federal Law agreement of the Cttee is necessary for certain ordinances.	The Federal Assembly, composed of all the members of the two Councils, meets for the swearing-in ceremony of the Federal President and in theory for adoption of a resolution on a declaration of war, etc.
Cttees may meet provided appointed to sit during the recess.	None	None	None
No	None	None	Joint sittings of Parlt are held to designate a Regent when necessary.
No	Management Board of each House	Management Board of each House	For inaugural sessions; starting of recess; reading of Executive messages (which are transformed into Congress Bills); vote on National Budget Bill; vote on Constitutional amdts; appreciating Executive-initiated Bills on request.

Country and House(s)	8.1 a) Legal provisions for sessions b) Average number of sitting days per year	8.2 Provisions for extraordinary sessions
BULGARIA National Assembly	a) Under the Const. (Art. 71) Parlt is convened by the State Council at least 3 times a year and when more than 1/5 of MPs so request b) –	No special provision but 1/5 of MPs may request a session.
CAMEROON National Assembly	a) and b) Under the Const. (Art. 15) and SO 2 sessions a year of 30 days maximum each b) 50	At request of the President of Republic or 2/3 MPs, on a specific matter for 15 days maximum.
CANADA Senate House of Commons	a) The Const. (Art. 20) requires at least 1 session per year b) 148	The Const. does not provide for calling extraordinary sessions, thus, they are called by the Governor General in the same manner as regular sessions.
CAPE VERDE People's National Assembly	a) Const. (Art. 56) provides for 2 sessions a year b) 30	Article 56 of the Const.; whenever necessary.
CHINA National People's Congress (NPC)	a) Const. (Art. 61) provides for 1 session a year convened by the NPC Standing Cttee b) 75	May be convened at any time by the Standing Cttee or on request of at least 1/5 of the MPs.
COMOROS Federal Assembly	a) Const. (Art. 27) provides for 2 ordinary sessions per year (in April and October), convened by a govt decree b) –	At request of President of Republic or majority of MPs for a definite agenda. Maximum length of session is 15 days.

8.3 Committee meetings during recess	8.4 Other parliamentary bodies meeting in recess	8.5 Bodies exercising parliamentary powers in recess	8.6 Provisions for joint sittings in bicameral Parliaments
Yes	None	State Council can issue urgent decrees which require subsequent ratification.	NA
No	Bureau of the Assembly	None	NA
Standing Cttees of the House may meet and other cttees if authorised. Senate cttees may meet by order of the Senate.	None	None	On special occasions, such as Throne Speech or an address to both Houses by a foreign Head of State or distinguished visitor.
Yes	Permanent Bureau, Administrative Council, Consultative Cttee.	Permanent Bureau	NA
NPC Standing Cttee	Special cttees of the NPC	NPC Standing Cttee	NA
No	None	None	NA

Country and House(s)	8.1 a) Legal provisions for sessions b) Average number of sitting days per year	8.2 Provisions for extraordinary sessions
CONGO People's National Assembly (ANP)	a) Const. (Art. 49) provides for 2 ordinary sessions per year starting 2nd Tuesday in May and 1st Tuesday in November b) Each session is not to exceed 2 months.	Convened by the President of the Republic or at the request of 2/3 members of ANP for a defined agenda.
COSTA RICA Legislative Assembly	a) Const. (Art. 116) provides for an ordinary 6 month session divided into 2 parts b) 1 May to end July and 1 Sept. to end November	Called by Govt under the Const. when business confined to matters in decree of convocation
CUBA National Assembly of People's Power	a) Const. (Art. 76) provides for 2 ordinary sessions per year b) -	Under the Const. when requested by 1/3 of the MPs or called by the Council of State
CYPRUS House of Representatives	a) Const. provides for 1 ordinary session of 3 to 6 months each year. (In practice from Sept. to July) b) 40	Const. provides for the President of the House to summon on request of 10 Members.
CZECHOSLOVAKIA Chamber of Nations Chamber of the People	a) Const. (Art. 32) provides for the President of Republic to convene a spring session by the end of April, and an autumn session by the end of October b) 123	Convened by the President of Republic on request of a least 1/3 of the members of each Chamber
DEMOCRATIC YEMEN Supreme People's Council	a) 3 sessions per year called by the Presidium b) -	Convened by the Presidium, the Council of Ministers or on request of 2/3 MPs.

8.3 Committee meetings during recess	8.4 Other parliamentary bodies meeting in recess	8.5 Bodies exercising parliamentary powers in recess	8.6 Provisions for joint sittings in bicameral Parliaments
No	None	None	NA
No	–	–	NA
Yes	Council of State comprising its President, 5 Vice-Presidents, a Secretary and 23 members all elected by and from the National Assembly.	Under the Const. the Council of State represents the National Assembly between sessions.	NA
No	None	None	NA
Yes	The Presidium of the Federal Assembly	The Presidium of the Federal Assembly	Election of President of the Republic, of Chairman and Vice-Chairman of Federal Assembly; discussion of Govt policy statements; when the Chambers so decide.
Before or after sittings	–	The Presidium	NA

Country and House(s)	8.1 a) Legal provisions for sessions b) Average number of sitting days per year	8.2 Provisions for extraordinary sessions
DENMARK Folketing	a) The Const. (Art. 36) lays down a sessional year starting 1st Tuesday in October till the corresponding day the following year b) 106	Convened by Folketing President on request of the Prime Minister or 2/5 Members.
EGYPT People's Assembly	a) Const. (Art. 101) provides for 1 session per year, convened by the President of the Republic before the second Thursday in November b) Session lasts at least 7 months	Under the Const. (Art. 102) convened by the President of the Republic when necessary or at the request of a majority of Members. He also announces its termination.
FIJI Senate House of Representatives	a) Const. (Art. 69) provides for sessions of Parlt at a time and place proclaimed by the Governor-General. Period between sessions must not exceed 6 months. Meetings of the Senate are called by the President in consultation with the leader of Govt. Business in the Senate. Meetings of the House of Representatives are called by Speaker after consultation with Prime Minister b) -	Const. provides for the Governor-General to convene Parlt on request of 1/4 of Members of House of Representatives or if he considers the Govt has lost the confidence of the majority, or in case of urgent matters of public importance. He also announces its termination.
FINLAND Eduskunta	a) and b) Under the Parliament Act from the beginning of February for 120 days with or without interruption. A summer recess starts in June or July and usually lasts until September	Called by the President of the Republic

8.3 Committee meetings during recess	8.4 Other parliamentary bodies meeting in recess	8.5 Bodies exercising parliamentary powers in recess	8.6 Provisions for joint sittings in bicameral Parliaments
Yes	None	None, but Finance Cttee exercises customary powers concerning appropriations against expenditure.	NA
Yes	The Assembly Bureau	None	NA
Yes	–	None	To hear Governor-General's address at opening of annual session
The Foreign Affairs and the Finance Cttees	None	None	NA

Country and House(s)	8.1 a) Legal provisions for sessions b) Average number of sitting days per year	8.2 Provisions for extraordinary sessions
FRANCE Senate National Assembly	a) Const. (Art. 28) provides for 2 ordinary sessions each year. One, beginning on 2. Oct. lasts for 80 days. The other, beginning on 2 Apr. lasts for not more than 90 days b) Senate: 121 National Assembly: 149	Under the Const. extraordinary sessions of Parlt can be called by the President of the Republic to hear his messages, by the Prime Minister or a majority of Members of the National Assembly.
GABON National Assembly	a) and b) The Const. (Art. 35) provides for 2 sessions per year: from the 3rd Tuesday in April for 50 days maximum; budget session from 1st Tuesday in Oct. to at latest 3rd Friday in Dec.	Convened by President of Assembly at request of President of Republic or absolute majority of MPs for a fixed agenda not exceeding 15 days.
GERMAN DEMOCRATIC REPUBLIC People's Chamber	a) Under the Const. (Art. 62) convened by the Council of State not later than the 30th day after the election. Subsequent sessions convened by the Presidium of the People's Chamber when necessary b) 30	No distinction is made between extraordinary and ordinary sessions as the Chamber does not go into recess but meets according to its own schedule. Thus the Presidium of the People's Chamber convenes a session if Parlt so decides or on request of 2/3 of the Members.
GERMANY Federal Council Federal Diet	a) Under the Basic Law Parlt determines the opening and closing of sessions. Sessions are convened by the President of the Federal Diet. The Council is convened by its President b) Federal Council: every 3 weeks. Federal Diet: 66	Convened by the Council President on request of 2 States or Federal Govt. Convened by the Diet President on request of 1/3 Members, the Federal President, or the Federal Chancellor.

8.3 Committee meetings during recess	8.4 Other parliamentary bodies meeting in recess	8.5 Bodies exercising parliamentary powers in recess	8.6 Provisions for joint sittings in bicameral Parliaments
Yes	The Bureau comprising President, 4 Vice-Presidents (6 in the Assembly) 3 Questors, 8 Secretaries (12 in the Assembly).	None	To revise the Const.
No	None	None	NA
Yes	Presidium of the People's Chamber	NA (see 8.2).	NA
–	–	None	Held under the Basic Law when a newly elected Federal President takes the oath of office and for urgent Bills during a state of defence.
With approval of the Diet President	Presidency and Council of Elders		

TABLE 8: SESSIONS OF PARLIAMENT (continued)

Country and House(s)	8.1 a) Legal provisions for sessions b) Average number of sitting days per year	8.2 Provisions for extraordinary sessions
GREECE Chamber of Deputies	a) Const. (Arts 40 and 64) provides for 1 ordinary session a year convened by the President of the Republic, or in default starting the 1st Monday of Oct. and not shorter than 5 months b) 224	May be convened as required by the President of the Republic.
HUNGARY National Assembly	a) Const. (Art. 22) requires at least 2 sessions each year, convened by Presidential Council of the Republic or 1/3 MPs. Assembly may determine dates b) 12	Not provided by the Constitution
INDIA Council of States House of the People	a) Const. (Art. 85) provides for the President to summon Parlt as he thinks fit but period between sessions not to exceed 6 months. Council fo States usually has 4 sessions per year and House of the People 3 b) House: 97	No distinction is made between extraordinary and ordinary sessions.
INDONESIA House of Representatives	a) SO provide for the session year of 12 months divided into 4 sessions to start 16 August b) -	Called on request of the President of the Republic, or, with approval of the Steering Cttee (see 11.1), by the House Leadership or 20 Members.
IRELAND Senate Dáil	a) Const. (Art. 15.7) provides for at least 1 session a year; sittings usually from Feb. to mid-July with an Easter recess and from Oct. to Dec. b) Senate: 85; Dáil: 33	Summoned by the Chairman Summoned by the Chairman at request of the Prime Minister

8.3 Committee meetings during recess	8.4 Other parliamentary bodies meeting in recess	8.5 Bodies exercising parliamentary powers in recess	8.6 Provisions for joint sittings in bicameral Parliaments
Those of the "Holiday Section" only. (See 8.5).	"Holiday Section" comprising 1/3 Members	The Const. provides for the business of Parlt to be carried on in recess by the "Holiday Section" (see 8.4).	NA
Yes	Presidential Council elected by Parlt from MPs.	Presidential Council which is accountable to the Assembly at the next session, comprising President, 2 Vice- Presidents, Secretary and 17 MPs.	NA
Yes	None	None	Irreconcilable disagreement on a Bill other than a money Bill, or lapse of 6 months since passage by only one House.
On request of Steering Cttee	On request of Steering Cttee	House Leadership with Faction Leaders	NA
Yes	None	None	No special provisions, although Houses have exceptionally held joint sittings.

Country and House(s)	8.1 a) Legal provisions for sessions b) Average number of sitting days per year	8.2 Provisions for extraordinary sessions
ISRAEL The Knesset	a) Basic Law on the Knesset provides for 2 sessions per year with a total duration at least 8 months b) 111	Called by the Chairman of the Knesset on request of 1/4 of House or of Govt
ITALY Senate Chamber of Deputies	a) Parlt is regarded as a permanent body. Under the Const. (Art. 62) Houses are convened annually on othe 1st working day of February and October b) –	Houses may be convened for extraordinary meetings by their respective Presidents, the President of the Republic or 1/3 of their membership. When one is convened for an extraordinary meeting, the other is convened by right.
IVORY COAST National Assembly	a) Const. (Art. 31) requires 2 ordinary sessions a year b) –	Convened for a specific agenda by the President of the Assembly, at the request of the President of the Republic or an absolute majority of MPs.
JAPAN House of Councillors House of Representatives	a) Const. (Art. 52) provides for 1 ordinary session per year b) House of Councillors: 32; House of Representatives: 43	According to Const. to be called by the Cabinet (must determine the convocation) and at the request of 1/4 of the members of either House. A so-called "special session" is also called within 30 days of an election for House of Representatives

8.3 Committee meetings during recess	8.4 Other parliamentary bodies meeting in recess	8.5 Bodies exercising parliamentary powers in recess	8.6 Provisions for joint sittings in bicameral Parliaments
On prior decision of House Cttee, on request of Govt or 1/3 Cttee.	The Knesset Presidium	None	NA
Parlt does not go into recess.	See 8.3	See 8.3	Election and oath of President of Republic; election of 1/3 of the Superior Council of the Magistrature; election of 1/3 of Constitutional Court; impeachment of President of Republic and Govt members; election of 45 nominees 16 of whom provide the Court which hears impeachment of President of Republic or Govt members.
Yes	–	Bureau of the Assembly	NA
Yes	–	None	No joint sittings are held.

Country and House(s)	8.1 a) Legal provisions for sessions b) Average number of sitting days per year	8.2 Provisions for extraordinary sessions
JORDAN Senate House of Deputies	a) Const. (Art. 77) provides for 1 ordinary session per year summoned by the King annually on 1 Oct. (subject to postponement by up to 2 months). If not summoned Parlt shall assemble as summoned. Duration 4 months but King may extend up to 3 months. Houses meet simultaneously b) -	The King may independently or on request of an absolute majority of Deputies convene an extraordinary session for a specific purpose and dissolve it by royal decree.
KENYA National Assembly	a) Const. (Art. 58.2) provides for at least 1 session every year b) -	Const. provides for Parlt to determine sessions in accordance with SO (i.e. on Govt request).
KUWAIT National Assembly	a) Const. (Art. 85) provides for 1 annual session of at least 8 months. SO provide for a sitting every Thursday unless otherwise decided b) 54	Called under the Const. (Art.88) by the Amir or a majority of Members for a particular agenda.
LEBANON National Assembly	a) Const. (Art. 32) provides for 2 sessions per year from 15 March to end May and from 1st Tuesday after 15 Oct. to end of the year b) -	Convened by Govt decree or at the request of a majority of Members for a fixed agenda.
LIECHTENSTEIN Diet	a) Const. (Art. 60) provides for the Prince to summon the Diet. It meets for 1 or 2 days every 4 to 5 weeks according to need b) 9	Const. provides for Diet President to convene a session at request of 600 electors, 3 parish councils or 3 Members.

8.3 Committee meetings during recess	8.4 Other parliamentary bodies meeting in recess	8.5 Bodies exercising parliamentary powers in recess	8.6 Provisions for joint sittings in bicameral Parliaments
No	None	None	Const. provides that when one House twice rejects a Bill accepted by the other, a joint sitting is held. Decision is then by 2/3 majority. Joint sessions may also be held at request of Prime Minister.
Yes	None	None	NA
Yes	Bureau of the Assembly	None	NA
Yes	None	None	NA
Yes	National Cttee	National Cttee comprising the Diet President and 4 MPs.	NA

Country and House(s)	8.1 a) Legal provisions for sessions b) Average number of sitting days per year	8.2 Provisions for extraordinary sessions
LUXEMBOURG Chamber of Deputies	a) Const. (Art. 72) provides for 1 ordinary session each year. (In practice this opens each 2nd Tuesday in October and runs until just before the next session starts b) -	Called by the Grand Duke and by him on request of 1/3 MPs. (Normally only called immediately after an election to swear MPs, elect officers, etc.)
MALAWI National Assembly	a) Const. (Art. 44) provides for at least 1 session per year convened by he President of the Republic, also as determined by the Assembly (usually 3 per year) b) 45	May be called at any time by the President of the Republic.
MALAYSIA Senate House of Representatives	a) Under the Const.(Art. 55) 6 months shall not elapse between sessions b) Senate: 30; House of Representatives: 65	Called under SO by the respective Presiding Officers on advice of the Prime Minister.
MALI National Assembly	a) Const. (Art. 44) provides for 2 sessions per year, each not to exceed 2 months b) -	Convened at request of the President of the Republic or a majority of MPs for a fixed agenda and 12 days maximum.
MALTA House of Representatives	a) Const. (Art. 76) provides for a session at least once each year such that 12 months shall not intervene between sessions. (The 3rd and 4th Parlts - 1971/76 and 1976/81 each consisted of one 5-year session) b) 77	Called by the President on advice of the Prime Minister
MAURITIUS Legislative Assembly	a) Const. (Art. 56) requires a session from time to time such that 12 months shall not intervene between sessions b) 30	All sessions are called by vote of proclamation signed by the Governor-General.

8.3 Committee meetings during recess	8.4 Other parliamentary bodies meeting in recess	8.5 Bodies exercising parliamentary powers in recess	8.6 Provisions for joint sittings in bicameral Parliaments
Permitted	NA (see 8.1).	NA (see 8.1).	NA
Yes	Yes	Public Accounts Cttee	NA
Yes	None	None	Official opening of each session by the King
Ad hoc cttees	None	None	NA
Select cttees	None	None	NA
Yes	None	None	NA

Country and House(s)	8.1 a) Legal provisions for sessions b) Average number of sitting days per year	8.2 Provisions for extraordinary sessions
MEXICO Chamber of Senators Chamber of Deputies	a) Const. (Arts 65 and 66) provides for the annual session to start on 1 Sept. and continue till all business is disposed of but not beyond 31 Dec. b) –	Convened for a special purpose by the President of the Republic on a resolution of 2/3 of the Permanent Cttee
MONACO National Council	a) Const. (Art. 58) provides for 2 sessions not exceeding 2 months per year (from 1st working day in May and Nov.) b) –	Convened by the Prince or at request of 2/3 of Members for a fixed agenda
MONGOLIA Great People's Khural (GPKh)	a) Const. (Art. 25) provides for 1 session a year b) –	Convened by the GPKh Presidium on its own initiative or at request of 1/3 of the Members
NAURU Parliament	a) Const. (Art. 43) requires 1 session to be held within 12 months of the preceding session or 21 days after declaration of election results b) –	Convened by the Speaker on request of 1/3 of Members, representing at least 3 of the 8 constituencies.
NETHERLANDS First Chamber Second Chamber	a) Under the Const. from the 1st sitting after an election to 1st sitting of the next newly elected Chamber b) First Chamber: 40; Second Chamber: 100	None
NEW ZEALAND House of Representatives	a) Required annually consequent upon Executive need for parliamentary authority for appropriation of public money b) 100	May be called at any time by the Governor-General.

8.3 Committee meetings during recess	8.4 Other parliamentary bodies meeting in recess	8.5 Bodies exercising parliamentary powers in recess	8.6 Provisions for joint sittings in bicameral Parliaments
The Permanent Cttee only	None	Permanent Cttee comprising 14 Senators and 15 Deputies	Opening of an ordinary session (as the Electoral College); designation of an interim President; resignation of the President of the Republic; to close a session.
Yes	The Council can meet in recess as a general Study Cttee.	–	NA
Yes	GPKh Presidium	GPKh Presidium	NA
SO Cttee, Library and House Cttee.	–	None	NA
Yes	None	NA (see 8.1).	Under the Const. for matters such as Speech from the Throne; succession to the Throne (see 39.1); declaration of war; state of emergency; etc.
Yes	None	None	NA

TABLE 8: SESSIONS OF PARLIAMENT (continued)

Country and House(s)	8.1 a) Legal provisions for sessions b) Average number of sitting days per year	8.2 Provisions for extraordinary sessions
NICARAGUA National Assembly	a) Parlt meets every 2 weeks b) -	The Directive Board and the Executive Branch in certain cases specified by the Delegation of Legislative Power
NORWAY Storting	a) Const. (Art. 68) provides for an annual session. Length is determined by the Storting (usually 1 Oct. to 15 June) b) -	Const. provides for the King to call extraordinary sessions.
PHILIPPINES National Assembly	a) Under the Const. (Art. VIII. 6) once a year, from 4th Monday in July to a date determined by the Assembly b) 103	May be called by the President at any time to consider matters as he may determine.
POLAND Diet	Const. (Art. 22) provides for at least 2 sessions per year (at latest 1 April and 31 Oct.). Each is of 4 to 6 months, comprising 5 to 6 sittings b) 25	Convened by the State Council on its own initiative or on written request of 1/3 Diet membership
PORTUGAL Assembly of the Republic	a) Under the Const. (Art. 177) 1 session per year beginning 15 Oct., continuing normally until 15 June. Sittings are usually held 4 times per week between 3 and 8 p.m. b) 108	The Assembly in plenary meeting, the Permanent Cttee, or more than 1/2 membership may prolong the session period. Exceptionally, the President of the Republic can convene a session for a fixed agenda.

8.3 Committee meetings during recess	8.4 Other parliamentary bodies meeting in recess	8.5 Bodies exercising parliamentary powers in recess	8.6 Provisions for joint sittings in bicameral Parliaments
Yes	None	The Executive Branch of Power	NA
Yes, with agreement of the Presidium.	None	None	NA (but see Table 30).
Only when authorised by the Speaker	None	None	NA
Yes	Diet Bureau (see 9.1). Council of Sages comprising Bureau, group chairmen and that of Diet Economic and Social Council.	None, but continuity of certain business is assured by the State Council (see 39.1).	NA
Yes, in case of need and with Assembly agreement. The Assembly President may call a cttee to meet within 15 days of session start to prepare business.	The Permanent Cttee comprising Assembly President, Vice-President and Members representing parties in Parlt.	The Permanent Cttee (see 8.4). The Cttee ceases its activitiy during sessions.	NA

Country and House(s)	8.1 a) Legal provisions for sessions b) Average number of sitting days per year	8.2 Provisions for extraordinary sessions
REPUBLIC OF KOREA National Assembly	a) Const. (Art. 83) and National Assembly Act provide for a session per year starting 20 Sept. for a period not longer than 90 days. Const. provides that annually total days of meetings shall not exceed 150, except extraordinary session convened upon the request of the President b) 36	Convened at request of the President of the Republic or 1/3 membership and not to exceed 30 days
ROMANIA Grand National Assembly	a) Const. (Art. 54) provides for 1 ordinary session each half year convened by the State Council on proposal of the Assembly Bureau b) 10 to 12	Convened on initiative of the State Council, the Assembly Bureau or 1/3 Members.
RWANDA National Development Council (CND)	a) Const. (Art. 57) provides for 2 ordinary sessions a year starting the 3rd Tuesday in April and October. The 1st session of a new Parlt opens 8 days after the elections b) 120	Convened at the initiative of the CND President, a majority of Members or the President of the Republic for a fixed agenda.
ST VINCENT House of Assembly	a) Const. (Art. 47) provides for each session to begin within 1 month of an election or not more than 6 months from the preceding session, times are otherwise fixed by the House b) -	The Clerk shall summon a special meeting within 21 days of a written notice of motion of no-confidence in the Govt if the House has not disposed of the matter within this time.
SENEGAL National Assembly	a) Const. (Art. 52) provides for 2 sessions each year, one starting in the 1st 2 weeks of April, the other in the last quarter of the year b) -	Called by the President of the Republic or a majority of Members, addressed in writing to the Assembly President. Limited to 15 days maximum.

8.3 Committee meetings during recess	8.4 Other parliamentary bodies meeting in recess	8.5 Bodies exercising parliamentary powers in recess	8.6 Provisions for joint sittings in bicameral Parliaments
Yes	None	None	NA
Yes	Bureau of the Grand National Assembly	State Council comprising the President of the Republic, Chairman, Vice-Chairmen and Members elected by and from the Assembly.	NA
Yes	None	None	NA
–	–	None	NA
No	None	None	NA

TABLE 8: SESSIONS OF PARLIAMENT (continued)

Country and House(s)	8.1 a) Legal provisions for sessions b) Average number of sitting days per year	8.2 Provisions for extraordinary sessions
SOLOMON ISLANDS National Parliament	a) Const. (Art. 72.2) requires sessions to be held such that 12 months do not intervene between them b) -	-
SOMALIA People's Assembly	a) Const. (Art. 64) provides for 2 sessions annually b) -	May be convened by the President of the Republic, by resolution of the Standing Cttee or on request of 1/3 membership.
SOUTH AFRICA House of Assembly House of Representatives House of Delegates	a) Const. (Art. 38) provides for at least 1 session per year such that 13 months shall not intervene between the start of successive sessions. Sessions run from mid-January to end May or 30 June latest b) 90	The State President may call sessions of Parlt at his discretion. He may also summon any House to consider matters relating solely to the group concerned.
SPAIN Senate Congress of Deputies	a) Const. (Art. 73) provides for 2 ordinary sessions per year (Sept.to Dec. and February to June) b) 88	Convened by the House President on request of the Govt, the House Permanent Cttee or an absolute majority of Members for a specific agenda.
SRI LANKA Parliament	a) Const. (Art. 70) requires at least 1 session per year b) 86	The President of the Republic may summon Parlt by proclamation.

8.3 Committee meetings during recess	8.4 Other parliamentary bodies meeting in recess	8.5 Bodies exercising parliamentary powers in recess	8.6 Provisions for joint sittings in bicameral Parliaments
Public Accounts Cttee only	None	None	NA
Yes	Standing Cttee comprising chairman, vice-chairman, secretary and 10 Members elected by Assembly.	None	NA
Yes	None.	None	The State President may call a joint sitting, but must do so if requested by all 3 Houses. The Speaker may call joint sitting for 2nd reading speeches. No resolution may be passed. The Speaker of Parlt presides.
No	Permanent Cttee of each House comprising its President and 21 MPs in proportion to parliamentary group strength.	The Permanent Cttee (see 8.4).	Const. (Art. 74) provides for joint sessions to exercise non-legislative competences authorised by the Crown.
Yes	–	–	NA

Country and House(s)	8.1 a) Legal provisions for sessions b) Average number of sitting days per year	8.2 Provisions for extraordinary sessions
SWEDEN Riksdag	a) Const. Chapter 4 (Art. 1) provides for 1 session per year. This is held from 1st Tuesday in October to 31 May or 15 June b) 138 of which 13 shorter than 10 minutes (1st readings)	Convened by the Govt or the Speaker (or by the Speaker on request of 115 Members).
SWITZERLAND States Council National Council	a) The Law on Relations Between the Councils provides for 4 sessions per year b) 52 (57 including extraordinary sessions)	Called by the Govt when considered necessary, or when requested by 1/4 members of the National Council or 5 Cantons (States).
SYRIAN ARAB REPUBLIC Poeple's Council	a) SO provide for 3 ordinary sessions per year b) 1st Tuesday in October to 31 December, mid-February to end March, mid-May to end June	On decision of the Council President who fixes the dates; on written request of the President of the Republic; on written request of 1/3 member-ship.
THAILAND Senate House of Representatives	a) Const. (Art. 115) provides for 1 or 2 ordinary sessions of about 90 days each year of the National Assembly as determined by the House of Representatives. The Senate may not sit during expiration of term or dissolution of the House of Representatives except to approve a declaration of war b) -	Convened by the King in the interest of the State. Either House or 1/3 membership of Parlt may petition the King for an extraordinary session.

8.3 Committee meetings during recess	8.4 Other parliamentary bodies meeting in recess	8.5 Bodies exercising parliamentary powers in recess	8.6 Provisions for joint sittings in bicameral Parliaments
Yes	Speaker's Conference and Board of Administration may meet.	The Cttees on Finance and on Taxes may meet jointly to determine urgent tax matters under the law.	NA
Yes (see also 22.2).	Each Council Bureau and the Group Presidents' Conference of the National Council	None	For election of the Govt and Federal Court and for pardons
Yes		The President of the Republic (see 35.1).	NA
By resolution of the respective House, or after a session closes, with the Speaker's permission.	–	–	To open and close a session; consider questions of royal succession; reconsider a Bill; hear announcement of and generally debate Govt policy; interpret the Const. with respect to Parlt; approve certain treaties; amend the Const.; appoint the Constitutional Tribunal; approve a declaration of war. Senate rules apply.

Country and House(s)	8.1 a) Legal provisions for sessions b) Average number of sitting days per year	8.2 Provisions for extraordinary sessions
TUNISIA Chamber of Deputies	a) Const. (Art. 29) provides for 1 annual session from October to July. (Each new Parlt sits first early in November) b) 44	Called by the Chamber President on request of the President of the Republic or a majority of Members
UGANDA National Assembly	a) Const. (Art. 61) provides for at least one session a year so that 12 months shall not intervene between sessions b) -	Called by the President in emergency under Const. (Art. 61).
UNION OF SOVIET SOCIALIST REPUBLICS Soviet of Nationalities Soviet of the Union	a) Const. (Art. 112) provides for 2 sessions per year b) -	Convened by the Presidium of the Supreme Soviet or on proposal of a Union Republic or not less than 1/3 membership of one of the Soviets
UNITED KINGDOM House of Lords	a) Annual sessions are appointed by communication from the Crown. Times of sitting and adjournment within a session are fixed by each House b) 140	The Lord Chancellor or, in his absence, the Chairman of Cttees in consultation with the Govt, can recall the House if the public interest so requires it. The Lord Chancellor or, in his absence, the Senior Lord of Appeal in Ordinary can recall the House for judicial business.
House of Commons	a) As above b) 170	The Speaker, on Govt representation and in the public interest.

8.3 Committee meetings during recess	8.4 Other parliamentary bodies meeting in recess	8.5 Bodies exercising parliamentary powers in recess	8.6 Provisions for joint sittings in bicameral Parliaments
Yes, for preliminary agreement of Presidential decrees requiring ratification at the next session.	None	None	NA
Yes	None	None	NA
Yes	Presidium of the Supreme Soviet	Presidium of the Supreme Soviet elected by and from MPs at a joint sitting, comprising President, First Vice-President, 15 Vice-Presidents, Secretary, 21 members.	See 8.5. Also to form a Council of Ministers; settle disagreements between the Soviets; form a People's Control Cttee; elect a Supreme Court; appoint a Procurator General; hear replies to MPs' questions; resolve any matter submitted by the Supreme Soviet.
Judicial sittings may take place during a prorogation.	None	During a dissolution provision may be made for the Lords of Appeal to act in the name of the House.	None for legislative or deliberative purposes. The Houses may meet together on ceremonial occasions. Joint cttees are regularly appointed.
Select cttees when so empowered		The Speaker may issue writs for by-elections.	

Country and House(s)	8.1 a) Legal provisions for sessions b) Average number of sitting days per year	8.2 Provisions for extraordinary sessions
UNITED REPUBLIC OF TANZANIA National Assembly	a) 4 sessions per year. Const. (Art. 43.2) provides for Parlt itself to appoint its meeting dates b) 42	The President may summon Parlt at any time.
UNITED STATES OF AMERICA Senate House of Representatives	a) Const. (Art. 1 Sect. 4) provides for at least 1 session per year (commences 3rd January until adjournment in autumn or early winter) b) Senate: 152; House: 144	The President of the USA may convene one or both Houses in extraordinary circumstances, also the leadership of Congress if authorised by resolution.
VANUATU Parliament	a) Const. (Art. 19.1) provides for 2 ordinary sessions per year b) –	At the request of the Speaker, Prime Minister, or a majority of Members.
YUGOSLAVIA Federal Chamber Chamber of Republics and Provinces	a) Const. (Art. 311) provides for sessions to be convened by the President of the Assembly or the Presidents of the Chambers on their own initiative or on request of the Presidency, Federal Executive Council. President of the Chamber of Republics and Provinces convenes sessions on request of a delegation of the Chamber and President of the Federal Chamber on request of a specified number of delegates. Sittings are held as necessary, usually once a month b) –	As defined in SO of the respective Chamber

8.3 Committee meetings during recess	8.4 Other parliamentary bodies meeting in recess	8.5 Bodies exercising parliamentary powers in recess	8.6 Provisions for joint sittings in bicameral Parliaments
Yes	None	None	NA
Yes	None	None	To count the Presidential electoral vote; receive Presidential messages; hold formal ceremonies.
Standing cttees	None	None	NA
Yes, if necessary.	None	None	Joint sittings can be held on issues envisaged in the Constitution.

Country and House(s)	8.1 a) Legal provisions for sessions b) Average number of sitting days per year	8.2 Provisions for extraordinary sessions
ZAIRE Legislative Council	a) Const. (Art. 80) provides for 2 ordinary sessions a year starting on the 1st Monday in April and October b) 40	Convened by the President of the Republic for a fixed agenda
ZAMBIA National Assembly	a) Const. (Art. 92) provides for at least 1 session per year b) 43	No constitutional provision
ZIMBABWE Senate House of Assembly	a) Const. (Art. 62.2) provides for a session in every calendar year so that no more than 180 days intervene between the end and beginning of successive sessions b) –	–

8.3 Committee meetings during recess	8.4 Other parliamentary bodies meeting in recess	8.5 Bodies exercising parliamentary powers in recess	8.6 Provisions for joint sittings in bicameral Parliaments
No, except the Public Property and Financial Scrutiny Cttee.	None	Bureau of the Legislative Council	NA
Sessional cttes meet.	None	Some sessional cttees consider certain organisational matters.	NA
Yes	–	–	For special occasions such as opening of Parlt or address from the Head of State; impeachment of the President (see 47.4).

TABLE 9

PRESIDING OFFICERS OR COLLECTIVE DIRECTING AUTHORITY

The primary function of the directing authority is the responsibility for conducting debates as impartially as possible. This duty is of paramount importance because debate is the lifeblood of a Parliament. The directing authority has to see that the rules of procedure are observed, that order is maintained in the Chamber, and that his (or its) own rulings are enforced. Besides having responsibility for the conduct of debates, the directing authority performs a variety of other functions essential for the smooth running of Parliament, such as giving rulings on matters of parliamentary procedure and having responsibility for the administration of Parliament.

Individual Directing Authorities

The individual and collegiate nature of the various directing authorities can be seen from Table 9A. In forty-six countries one person has

TABLE 9A. Directing Authority of Parliament

Directing Authority	Number of Countries
President or Speaker	46
Bureau, Presidium, etc.	37
Total	83

responsibility for the functions described above although he may be assisted by one or more deputies. In thirty-seven countries these are undertaken by a collective body, such as a Bureau or Presidium. The office of Speaker (which has historical roots in the British House of Commons going back to at least 1376) is found in countries which have been influenced by the parliamentary traditions and practices of the United Kingdom, as well as in, for example, Israel, Jordan, the Republic of Korea and the United States House of Representatives. Although the essential feature of the British system is the concentration of authority in the hands of a single individual, in many other Parliaments, by contrast, the President is surrounded by a collegiate body which, under various names, shares with him the reponsibility for the working of Parliament.

313

Collective Directing Authorities

The size of these collective directing authorities varies from four members in Monaco to forty in Czechoslovakia. The existence of these collective bodies can be explained partly by the President's desire to distribute, among his colleagues, the various duties he has to perform, and partly by the desire to associate representatives of all major political groupings in his more important decisions. The Bureau, or its equivalent, is often regarded as a consultative body and is designated solely to assist the President and not to act as a check on his work nor to take decisions in his place. The Bureau is generally concerned with administrative and financial matters, while the President assumes responsibility for the conduct of parliamentary business.

A collective directing authority will typically consist of members of a number of political groups which are represented in the House. The directing authority may also include officers known as secretaries (who are Members of Parliament) whose main function is to assist the President during meetings. They check the number of Members present at debates, oversee the preparation of the minutes of proceedings and reports of debates, receive the names of Members who wish to speak, maintain order, supervise the counting of votes, and read out items which have to be communicated to Parliament.

The Bureau may also include Questors (who are also Members of Parliament), as in Belgium, Cameroon, France, Greece, Italy, Ivory Coast, Senegal and the Syrian Arab Republic, who deal with practical, financial and administrative matters of Parliament, such as the terms of employment and promotion of parliamentary officials and the control of the accounts of Parliament. The chairmen of committees are included in the Bureau of some countries (e.g. Algeria, Finland, Kuwait, Mali and Tunisia) and in others, Leaders of Parliamentary Groups (e.g. Austria, Italy, Luxembourg, Mexico, Norway and Switzerland).

Election of the Directing Authority

The principle of an elected directing authority is recognised in almost all Parliaments. Some notable exceptions to this are the following:

- the presidency of the Austrian Federal Council, which rotates in the alphabetical order of Länder among Members nominated by their respective States;
- the Speaker of the Canadian Senate, who is appointed by the Governor-General on the advice of the Prime Minister;
- the President of the Jordan Senate and the directing authorities of the Parliaments of Malawi and Thailand, who are appointed by the Head of State;
- the Speaker of the British House of Commons, whose appointment (after being elected by the House) is subject to confirmation by the Queen which, in modern times, is more or less a formality; the directing authority of the House of Lords, the Lord Chancellor, is a Member of the Government and is appointed by the Queen on advice of the Prime Minister.

In Malaysia, Malta and Zambia, the Speaker may be a Member elected by the House, or a person nominated and elected by the House from the electorate. In the United States, the Vice-President of the nation is the de jure directing authority of the Senate, and the Vice-President of India is de jure Chairman of the Council of States.

In at least forty-four of the popular chambers where the directing authority is elected, an absolute majority of votes is required in order to broaden the bases of his authority. In many of the countries under consideration, the directing authority is elected by secret ballot so that the successful candidate will not be under any obligation to those who voted for him. This is an important feature in view of the impartiality demanded by the office.

Term of Office of the Directing Authority

The term of office of the directing authority is presented in Table 9B.

TABLE 9B. Term of Office of Directing Authority

Term of Office	Number of Countries	
	Popular Chamber	Other Chamber
One Session	6	1
Term of Parliament	57	13
One Year	11	4
Two Years	2	3
Three Years	1	3
Four Years	1	0
Five Years	5	2
Six Years	0	1
Rotating	0	1
Total	83	28

In most countries the authority is elected for the life of the legislature (although the other members of the Bureau may be elected for a shorter period), as in the socialist countries, countries following the British model, and for example, Algeria, Finland, France, Greece, Ivory Coast, Kuwait and Switzerland. Several countries elect their directing authority for one session of the legislature as, for example, Belgium, Denmark, Egypt, Finland, Liechtenstein and Portugal. A number of countries limit the term of office of the directing authority to a fixed time period. In Argentina, Cameroon, Jordan, Lebanon, Monaco, Nicaragua, Senegal, Switzerland, the Syrian Arab Republic, Tunisia and Yugoslavia, this is one year, in Brazil and the Republic of Korea two years, in Mexico three years, in Thailand four years, and in the Bahamas, Cape Verde, Fiji, Ivory Coast and Kenya 5 years.

Impartiality of the Directing Authority

One measure of the impartiality of the directing authority is the legal or customary restrictions placed on his taking part in debate and voting (Table 9C). In the popular House of more than half of the countries under consideration, the directing authority is either not permitted or not expected to speak on important matters in the House. In twenty-one countries (which include Belgium, Ivory Coast, Hungary, Japan and the United States) he may only speak if he vacates the Chair and is replaced by another Member.

TABLE 9C. Directing Authority of the Popular House Taking Part in Debates and Voting in Parliament

Debates	Number of Countries	Voting	Number of Countries
Permitted	19	Permitted	33
Permitted if Vacates the Chair	21	Permitted if Vacates the Chair	2
Not Permitted	43	Casting Vote Only	22
		Not Permitted	26
Total	83	Total	83

Nineteen countries (which include Cyprus, Gabon, Mexico, Poland and the USSR) place no restrictions on the speaking rights of the directing authority of the popular House, who may participate in all debates in the same way as other Members of Parliament. Similar patterns can be found in the conditions under which the directing authorities can vote in Parliament. In some countries (e.g. Belgium, Bulgaria, Indonesia and Lebanon) there are no restrictions on the directing authorities. In Egypt and the Republic of Korea they may vote only if they vacate the Chair. In twenty-two countries (e.g. Canada, Hungary, Jordan and Switzerland), the directing authorities have a casting vote in the case of a tie. Finally, some countries (e.g. Italy, the Solomon Islands, Tunisia and Zimbabwe) do not permit their directing authorities to vote under any conditions.

TABLE 9: PRESIDING OFFICERS OR COLLECTIVE DIRECTING
AUTHORITY

Country and House(s)	9.1 Presiding Officer(s) or collective directing authority	9.2 Method of election or appointment	9.3 Term of office (years)
ALGERIA National People's Assembly (APN)	The Presidents' Conference comprising the President; the Vice-Presidents and the chairmen of the standing committees.	Elected by the APN.	President: term of Parliament (5 years). Other Conference members: 1 year, re-eligible.
ARGENTINA Senate	Chaired by the Nation's Vice-President; provisional President; 2 Vice-Presidents and 2 Secretaries.	Elected by absolute majority of the respective House	One year (starting 30 April).
Chamber of Deputies	President; 2 Vice-Presidents; 2 Secretaries.		
AUSTRALIA Senate	President	Elected by absolute majority of votes cast	3 years
House of Representatives	Speaker	Elected by absolute majority of votes cast by ballot	Term of Parlt (3 years).

9.4 Presiding Officer's position and status a) Precedence b) Succession list	9.5 Presiding Officer's a) Annual salary b) Allowances (US$ approx.)	9.6 Functions and powers
–	–	Preside over deliberations of APN; coordinate work of Bureau and relationship of APN to Executive; coordinate work of cttees and chair meetings of chairmen; represent APN on official or ceremonial occasions; manage administrative services of Assembly with help of Secretary General; assure security of Assembly; establish relationships with other Parlts.
a) and b) Succession list: 1. Vice-President (ex-officio President of the Senate) 2. President of Chamber of Deputies	No special remuneration (President of the Senate receives salary as National Vice-President. The President of the Chamber receives salary as a Deputy but enjoys greater security, a secretariat and official car).	Presidents of Houses: convene sessions; establish order of business (Senate: after consultation with group leaders; Chamber: from participation in the Committee on Parliamentary work); maintain order in the House; may participate in debates if they leave the chair; vote only in case of tie; appoint and discharge House staff; represent the House.
a) Warrant of precedence: President of Senate and Speaker of House after Governor-General, State Governors, PM and State Premier in his own State b) None	a) Basic salary of 28,820; additional salary of 16,600 b) Special allowance of 5,800 pa; staff additional to normal electoral staff entitlement of 2; unrestricted transport within Australia on official business	Maintain order in their respective Houses; participate in debate (but do so rarely); vote (Speaker has a casting vote only. The President of the Senate usually exercises a deliberative vote, but has no casting vote); ex-officio chairman of a number of parliamentary "domestic" cttees. Appoint or promote all officers within his Department, except the Clerk (appointed by the Governor General in Council); share joint responsibility for staff and administration of the three other parliamentary departments. Other functions are laid down in various Acts of Parliament.

TABLE 9: PRESIDING OFFICERS OR COLLECTIVE DIRECTING
AUTHORITY (continued)

Country and House(s)	9.1 Presiding Officer(s) or collective directing authority	9.2 Method of election or appointment	9.3 Term of office (years)
AUSTRIA Federal Council	President; 2 Vice-Presidents; Presidents' Conference (consultative body comprising the President; his deputies and the leaders of parliamentary groups).	President: see 9.3; 2 Vice-Presidents elected for 6 months by the Council.	Presidency rotates in alphabetical order of provinces among Members nominated by their respective provincial legislative assemblies.
National Council	President; 2 Vice-Presidents; President's Conference (consultative body formed by the President; his deputies and the Leaders of parliamentary groups).	President and Vice-Presidents elected by the Council (secret ballot) by an absolute majority.	Term of the National Council (4 years).
BAHAMAS Senate	President	Elected by the Senate	5 years
House of Assembly	Speaker	Elected by House	

9.4 Presiding Officer's position and status a) Precedence b) Succession list	9.5 Presiding Officer's a) Annual salary b) Allowances (US$ approx.)	9.6 Functions and powers
a) Ministerial rank b) None	a) Federal Council: 54,000; National Council: 108,000 varying according to seniority b) Both: car, free transport 1st class, staff, allowances for accommodation	Presidents of both Houses: convene sittings (within the annual session convened for the National Council); establish order of business; call Members to order; participate in debates (in theory); take part in voting; appointment of Secretary General (for both Councils) and other staff is prerogative of the President of the National Council. He is also (customarily) chairman of the "Main Committee" pertaining to executive power.
a) After the Federal President and the Cardinal-Archbishop of Vienna, par with the Federal Chancellor b) If the Federal President is unable to discharge his functions for longer than 20 days the President and 2 Vice Presidents of the National Council form a collegiate body to discharge the responsibilities of Head of State		
a) First position in warrant of precedence b) No standing in succession list for Head of State	a) 9,300 b) Availability of Senate staff, transport a) 33,900 b) Availability of House staff, transport	Appoint cttees and cttee chairman; maintain order in House and apply disciplinary sanctions; participate in vote.

Country and House(s)	9.1 Presiding Officer(s) or collective directing authority	9.2 Method of election or appointment	9.3 Term of office (years)
BELGIUM Senate	President and Bureau comprising President; 3 Vice-Presidents; 6 Secretaries; 5 Questors.	Elected by absolute majority of votes cast in secret ballot	One session
Chamber of Representatives	President and Bureau comprising President; 5 Vice-Presidents; 8 secretaries; 8 questors.		
BRAZIL Federal Senate	For each House: President; 2 Vice-Presidents; 4 Secretaries; 4 Delegates.	Elected by respective House	2 years
Chamber of Deputies			
BULGARIA National Assembly	President and Vice-Presidents of National Assembly	Elected by Parliament from among its Members, by majority vote of Members present.	Term of Parliament (5 years).
CAMEROON National Assembly	Bureau of Assembly comprising President; First Vice-President;3 Vice-Presidents; 7 Secretaries; 2 Questors; Secretary General; 2 Deputy Secretaries General.	Secret election by the Assembly. Secretary General and his deputies are ex-officio members.	One year, renewable.

9.4 Presiding Officer's position and status a) Precedence b) Succession list	9.5 Presiding Officer's a) Annual salary b) Allowances (US$ approx.)	9.6 Functions and powers
a) Immediately after the King and the Cardinal-Archbishop with precedence to the elder b) NA (see 8.6)	a) Same salary as other MPs plus 35,000, all taxable b) Residence; secretariat; car with chauffeur	Preside over proceedings according to SO; maintain order in House and apply disciplinary sanctions; must leave the Chair to participate in debates; may vote; represent respective House in external dealings.
a) Presidents of Houses after President and Vice-President of Republic b) For Head of State, after Vice-President of Republic, President of Chamber of Deputies, then President of Senate	a) 27,000 (same as other MPs) b) Residence; guard; staff; transport	Convene sessions; establish order of business; remove disqualifications of MPs; maintain order in House and apply disciplinary sanctions; no vote except if special decision taken by Presiding collegiate board; appointment of Secretary General and General Directors for administrative matters.
No provision	Same allowance as ordinary Members. Car provided.	Preside over Assembly proceedings; maintain order; submit draft sessional agenda; certify texts of Acts adopted; manage international relations of Assembly; may participate in debates but must surrender the chair; participate in vote.
a) 2nd b) 1st	a) 900 pm b) Representation: 800 pm. Mandate: 240 pm. Residence, guard, staff, official car	Maintain order in the House and apply disciplinary sanctions; may participate in debates, but must leave the chair; cannot vote; determine organisation of administration services in conjunction with the Bureau of the Assembly.

Country and House(s)	9.1 Presiding Officer(s) or collective directing authority	9.2 Method of election or appointment	9.3 Term of office (years)
CANADA Senate	Speaker of the Senate	Appointed from the Senators by the Governor-General on the advice of the Prime Minister	Normally appointed for one Parliament only.
House of Commons	Speaker of the House of Commons	Elected by the Members of Parliament from among themselves	Co-terminous with the current Parlt, but may be re-elected for the ensuing Parlt.
CAPE VERDE People's National Assembly	Permanent Bureau comprising President; 2 Vice-Presidents; 2 Secretaries.	Elected by Assembly during the first session of each Parliament	5 years

9.4 Presiding Officer's position and status a) Precedence b) Succession list	9.5 Presiding Officer's a) Annual salary b) Allowances (US$ approx.)	9.6 Functions and powers
a) 4th b) NA	a) 19,600 b) Sessional indemnity: 40,900 pa. Tax free allowances: expenses 6,700 pa; residence 2,500 pa; motor 800 pa. Executive assistant and 2 secretaries; use of chauffeured car	Preserve order and decorum in the House, but the House applies sanctions; may participate in debates by leaving the chair to sit among senators; may vote but not obliged to; member of the Cttee on Internal Economy (see 7.5); does not have power to convene sessions but may call meetings during recess "in the public interest".
a) 5th b) NA	a) 31,600 b) Sessional indemnity 40,900 pa. Tax free allowances: expenses 13,800 pa; residence: 2,500 pa or residence in Parlt; motor: 800 pa. Executive assistant; 5 special assistants; 5 secretaries; use of chauffeured car	Preserve order and decorum in the House but the House applies sanctions; by tradition does not participate in debate; has a casting vote; chairs the Board of Internal Economy (see 7.5); does not have power to convene sessions but may be authorised to cause the House to reassemble.
a) Highest representative of the Parliament b) Assures the Presidency in case of vacancy	a) 315 b) Residence; guard; transport; representation allowance	Convene sessions; propose order of business to Permanent Bureau; nominate Cttee chairmen and members; preside at meetings of cttee chairmen; propose removal of disqualifications; maintain order in Assembly; participate in debates (leaving the chair) and vote; exert administrative powers, including appointment of Secretary General and other staff; represent the Assembly and direct its international relations.

Country and House(s)	9.1 Presiding Officer(s) or collective directing authority	9.2 Method of election or appointment	9.3 Term of office (years)
CHINA National People's Congress (NPC)	NPC Standing Cttee (the permanent body of the NPC) comprising Chairman; Vice-Chairmen; Secretary-General and other members. Also a Presidium to conduct business.	Elected by the NPC from among the Members	Term of Parliament (5 years).
COMOROS Federal Assembly	President of Assembly; 3 Vice-Presidents.	Elected by House in secret ballot	Term of Parliament (5 years).
CONGO People's National Assembly (ANP)	ANP Bureau comprising President; 2 Vice-Presidents; 2 Secretaries.	Elected by secret vote of the Assembly	Term of Parlt (5 years).

9.4 Presiding Officer's position and status a) Precedence b) Succession list	9.5 Presiding Officer's a) Annual salary b) Allowances (US$ approx.)	9.6 Functions and powers
a) NPC Standing Cttee is permanent body of NPC b) When offices of both President and Vice-President fall vacant, the NPC Standing Cttee Chairman acts as temporary President until the NPC elects a new President	a) and b) Same as other Members (see 5.1 and 5.2)	Interpret the Const. and supervise its enforcement; enact and amend laws other than those in NPC competence (see 47.6); supervise the work of State Council, Central Military Commission, Supreme People's Court and Supreme People's Procuratorate; appoint and recall overseas representatives; ratify and abrogate treaties and foreign agreements; annul State Council's administrative rules, decisions, etc., contravening the Const., statutes or administrative rules and regulations; grant special pardons. Out of session: complete and partially amend laws enacted by NPC; examine and approve partial adjustments to economic and social plans and to State Budget; decide on choice of members of Central Govt (see 39.3), Auditor-General and Secretary General of State Council; decide on nomination by Chairman of Central Military Commission the choice of other personnel of the Commission; declare war and mobilisation; enforce martial law.
a) – b) First. Assures the Presidency in case of absence or vacancy	a) 14,750 b) –	Preside over Assembly proceedings; organise and direct all administrative and financial services; appoint the Secretary General of the Assembly; assure the security of the Assembly.
a) – b) Vacancy in office of Head of State temporarily filled by the President of the Assembly	a) – b) Guard; staff; official car	Preside over debates; monitor votes and announce results; transmit decisions and proceedings to the Head of State; maintain order and apply disciplinary sanctions; preside over meetings of the ANP Bureau and Presidents' Conference; manage Assembly staff and control its budget.

Country and House(s)	9.1 Presiding Officer(s) or collective directing authority	9.2 Method of election or appointment	9.3 Term of office (years)
COSTA RICA Legislative Assembly	President and a Directorate comprising: President; Vice-President; 2 Secretaries; and 2 Substitute Secretaries.	Elected from the Members by absolute majority of the Assembly in secret ballot	Term of Parlt (4 years).
CUBA National Assembly of People's Power	President of the National Assembly	By secret ballot requiring absolute majority of the Parlt	Term of Parlt (5 years).
CYPRUS House of Representatives	The President of the House	Elected by the House	Term of Parlt (5 years).
CZECHOSLOVAKIA Chamber of Nations Chamber of the People	Chairman of the Federal Assembly; Presidium of the Federal Assembly comprising 40 members (each Chamber has a Chairman and Presidium of 3-6 members).	Chairman elected from Presidium members by both Chambers. Each elects 20 Presidium members and its own Chairman and Presidium.	Term of Parlt (5 years).

9.4 Presiding Officer's position and status a) Precedence b) Succession list	9.5 Presiding Officer's a) Annual salary b) Allowances (US$ approx.)	9.6 Functions and powers
a) – b) Next in succession after Vice-President of the Republic	–	Preside over sessions and maintain order; nominate members of permanent cttees; confirm correctness of Acts and other legislation; grant leave of absence to Members; scrutinise the Assembly's administration and budget.
a) NA but attends Council of State meetings b) None	a) 5,400 b) Provision of staff and transport	Convene sessions; establish order of business; appoint cttees and cttee chairmen; maintain order and apply disciplinary sanctions; participate in vote; appoint administrative staff except the Secretary (a Member elected by the Parlt); authenticate for publication in the Gazette laws and resolutions adopted; organise the international relations of Parlt; lead and organise the work of parliamentary cttees; lead and organise external relations of Parlt.
a) Deputises for the Head of State during temporary absence or vacancy b) NA	a) 20,077 b) Representation 5,126 pa; cost of living 14,439 pa; guard; staff; car; medical care; postage; and telephone	Maintain order in the House; apply the Rules of Procedure; exercise supervision over House staff; authorise House expenditure; represent the House; participate in debate and vote.
a) – b) None	Determined by the Presidium	Preside over joint sittings; maintain liaison with the Govt and with the Czech and Slovak National Councils; coordinate business involving both Chambers; refer matters to cttees after consultation with chairmen of the Chambers; participate in vote.

Country and House(s)	9.1 Presiding Officer(s) or collective directing authority	9.2 Method of election or appointment	9.3 Term of office (years)
DEMOCRATIC YEMEN Supreme People's Council	Presidium of the Supreme People's Council comprising Chairmen, Vice-Chairmen, Secretary and 8 to 14 members.	Elected by the Council from among the Members.	Term of Parlt (5 years).
DENMARK Folketing	President and 4 Vice-Presidents who form the Presidium.	President elected by Folketing; 4 Vice-Presidents appointed by 4 parties having strongest representation other than President's party.	1 sessional year
EGYPT People's Assembly	Assembly Bureau comprising Speaker and two Deputy-Speakers.	Elected by an absolute majority of the Assembly in secret ballot	Parliamentary session and until day before new session starts.
FIJI Senate	President	Elected by the House in secret ballot	6 years
House of Representatives	Speaker		5 years

9.4 Presiding Officer's position and status a) Precedence b) Succession list	9.5 Presiding Officer's a) Annual salary b) Allowances (US$ approx.)	9.6 Functions and powers
Presidium Chairman is the President of Republic.	Provided with residence; guard; staff; and transport.	The Presidium Chairman administers the Presidium, chairs its meetings and signs its decrees and resolutions; represents the Republic in its foreign relations.
a) Equivalent to a Minister b) None	a) In addition to salary as a Member, President receives 29,995 pa b) President and First Vice-President have an apartment in the Folketing. President has a car with chauffeur	Convene sittings; establish order of business according to SO; chairman ex-officio of the Presidium and the SO Cttee; apply sanctions; take part in debates (but must leave the Chair); take part in votes; after consultation with the Vice-Presidents, manage the Folketing internal organisation.
Vacancy in office of President of Republic temporarily filled by the Speaker	a) Speaker's salary equals that of Vice-President of Republic; Deputy-Speakers receive Member's salary b) Equal to ministerial representation allowances	Convene sessions; establish order of business; nominate cttee members; act as head of Assembly Bureau and chairman of General Cttee; preside over proceedings of Assembly and maintain order; supervise General Secretariat and Assembly management; participate in debate and vote by leaving the chair.
a) 5th b) NA	a) 5,500 (taxable) b) 2,750 (not taxable) plus 40 a day during sittings	Convene meetings; appoint cttees; maintain order in the House; hold casting vote but for special legislation has original vote only; approve staff appointments and transfers.
a) 4th b) NA	a) 26,500 (taxable) b) 5,500 (not taxable)	

Country and House(s)	9.1 Presiding Officer(s) or collective directing authority	9.2 Method of election or appointment	9.3 Term of office (years)
FINLAND Eduskunta	Speaker; and Speaker's Conference comprising Speaker; 2 Deputy-Speakers; Chairmen of Cttees.	Speaker and Deputy-Speakers elected by Parlt; cttee chairmen elected by cttee members.	Speaker and Deputy-Speakers for one session, others for term of Parlt (4 years).
FRANCE Senate	President and Bureau comprising President; 4 Vice-Presidents; 3 Questors; 8 Secretaries.	President elected by an absolute majority of the respective House in secret ballot. Vice-Presidents and Questors elected as a House list reflecting relative strength of political groups.	3 years
National Assembly	President and Bureau comprising President; 6 Vice-Presidents; 3 Questors; 12 Secretaries.		President for term of Parlt; others for 1 year.
GABON National Assembly	Presidency comprising President and Vice-Presidents of the Assembly	Elected by Assembly in public vote, absolute majority on 1st ballot, then relative majority.	Term of Parlt (5 years).
GERMAN DEMOCRATIC REPUBLIC People's Chamber	Presidium of the People's Chamber comprising the President of the Chamber; the Vice-President and further Members.	Presidium is elected by the Chamber.	Until election of a new Presidium, following new general election.

9.4 Presiding Officer's position and status a) Precedence b) Succession list	9.5 Presiding Officer's a) Annual salary b) Allowances (US$ approx.)	9.6 Functions and powers
a) Speaker is second in the precedence list (after President of Republic and before Prime Minister) b) None	a) Speaker has the same salary as a Member plus 455 tax free per month during session b) Secretariat and car	Convene sessions; establish order of business; ex-officio Chairman of Speaker's Conference and Office's Cttee; maintain order in the House and apply disciplinary sanctions; represent Parlt in external dealings.
a) 3rd b) Exercises function of President of Republic should the office fall vacant pending elections for a new President	a) – b) Representatioin allowance; special allowance; office staff	Maintain order in the House and apply disciplinary sanctions; may participate in debates and vote, but usually does not; adminis- trative functions are exercised through the Bureau.
a) 4th b) None	Residence; guard; transport; secretariat.	
a) 4th in rank b) Member of the college which can fill temporary vacancy in office of Head of State	Staff and transport provided	Maintain order in House and apply disciplinary sanctions; participate in debates.
President of People's Chamber is Deputy Chairman of the Council of State.	See 5.1. The President of the Chamber also has a staff of advisers and aides.	Chairman of the Presidium; main- tain order in the Chamber; in concurrence with Presidium, es- tablish order of speakers and adjourn meetings when there are no further speakers; put matters to the vote and determine voting order; announce results of votes; draft the final copies of Laws and Chamber decisions for publication in the Law Gazette.

TABLE 9: PRESIDING OFFICERS OR COLLECTIVE DIRECTING
           AUTHORITY (continued)

Country and House(s)	9.1 Presiding Officer(s) or collective directing authority	9.2 Method of election or appointment	9.3 Term of office (years)
GERMANY Federal Council	President and Presidency comprising President and 3 Vice-Presidents (President is assisted by a Permanent Advisory Council comprising leaders of each State representation).	Elected by the Federal Council	1 year (office rotates among Heads of State Govts starting with the most populous).
Federal Diet	1. Presidium comprising President and 4 Vice-Presidents 2. Council of Elders, to assist in the conduct of business, comprising Presidium and 23 other Members	1. Elected by Bundestag (secret ballot) by an absolute majority 2. Nominated by political groups on the basis of proportional representation	Term of Parlt
GREECE Chamber of Deputies	Bureau comprising President; 3 Vice-Presidents; 3 Questors; 6 Secretaries.	Elected by the Chamber with separate ballots for President and 1st Vice-President.	President and Vice-Presidents for term of Parlt; others for one session.
HUNGARY National Assembly	President of the National Assembly	Elected by the Assembly	Term of Parlt (5 years).

9.4 Presiding Officer's position and status a) Precedence b) Succession list	9.5 Presiding Officer's a) Annual salary b) Allowances (US$ approx.)	9.6 Functions and powers
a) Second after the Federal President b) Exercises powers of Head of State in case of sudden vacancy	a) See 5.1 b) Monthly allowance: 833; sitting allowance: 32 pd; staff and official car	Convene extraordinary sessions; maintain order in House; participate in debates by leaving the Chair; vote (unusual); appoint House Director and senior officers.
a) Second after Head of State	a) 70,000 b) 8,300 pa; residence with personnel; House staff; official chauffeured car	Convene sessions; fix agenda only if empowered by the Diet; maintain order in House; participate in debates by leaving the Chair; vote; appoint and recruit staff; ex-officio member of the Council of Elders; Chairman of Federal Assembly (both Houses) and Chairman of Joint Cttee.
a) Immediately after the Prime Minister b) Fills any temporary vacancy in Presidency of the Republic	a) 140 % of MP's salary to include representation expenses b) Official car and guards	Establish order of business; appoint cttees; preside over debates; put matters to the vote and announce results; direct and supervise administrative services of Parlt; appoint parliamentary personnel responsible for security of the Chamber; represent the Chamber; control parliamentary expenditure.
a) - b) None	a) None b) 30 per month	Protect authority of Parlt; preside over deliberations; maintain order and apply sanctions; organise cttee activity; take part in debate by leaving chair; exercise a casting vote; represent Parlt externally; organise international relations of Parlt; hold overall responsibility for administration and staff; is not a member of the Presidential Council (see 8.5).

Country and House(s)	9.1 Presiding Officer(s) or collective directing authority	9.2 Method of election or appointment	9.3 Term of office (years)
INDIA Council of States	Chairman of the Council of States	Vice-President of India, elected by Parlt is ex-officio Chairman.	5 years
House of the People	Speaker	Elected by simple majority of the House	Term of the House (5 years). Eligible for re-election.
INDONESIA House of Representatives	House Leadership comprising Speaker and 4 Deputy-Speakers	Elected by House from the Members in secret ballot	Term of Parlt (5 years).
IRELAND Senate Dáil	Chairman of each House	Elected from MPs by a simple majority	Term of Parlt and until a successor is appointed.
ISRAEL The Knesset	The Knesset Presidium comprising the Chairman and Vice-Chairmen (popularly known as the Speaker and Deputy-Speakers).	Elected by the House on show of hands. Elections are prepared by a cttee representing all party groups.	Coterminous with the Knesset (4 years).

9.4 Presiding Officer's position and status a) Precedence b) Succession list	9.5 Presiding Officer's a) Annual salary b) Allowances (US$ approx.)	9.6 Functions and powers
a) Second b) First position	a) 190 per month b) 40 per month; residence; guard; staff; transport	Establish order of business; appoint cttees and chairmen; preside over sittings; maintain order and apply sanctions; ex-officio Chairman of certain cttees; participate in debate; exercise a casting vote; direct the Secretariat.
a) Sixth with the Chief Justice, ahead of all Ministers except the Prime Minister	a) 225 per month b) 50 per month; residence; guard; staff; transport	As above except that the Speaker does not participate in debate. The Speaker takes final decision on whether or not a Bill is a Money Bill.
a) Speaker is third in warrant of precedence b) –	Speaker receives salary; residence; guard; staff; transportation; housekeeper	Convene sessions; establish order of business; chair the Steering Cttee; maintain order and apply disciplinary sanctions; participate in vote.
a) Chairmen of Senate and Dáil are ex-officio members of Council of State advising the President b) When Presidency falls vacant, functions assured by a commission comprising Chief Justice and Chairmen of Senate and Dáil	a) 59,400 b) Official car a) 30,052 b) Official car and mileage allowance for private car	Jointly appoint Chairmen of the Joint Cttee on SO (Private Business); nominate a panel for temporary Chairman of the House or of Cttee of the Whole House; act as respective Chairman of Cttee on Procedure and Privileges of House; maintain order and apply disciplinary sanctions; summon special sessions; jointly appoint parliamentary staff; exercise casting vote; (chairmen do not participate in debate).
a) Ranks after the President of the State with equal precedence to Prime Minister b) Acts whenever the President of the State is abroad or otherwise unable to perform his duties	a) 18,000 b) Monthly allowance throughout the year: 129; residence; 4 staff members; car and chauffeur	Convene sessions; establish order of business; chair the Presidium and the Interpretation Cttee; maintain order in the House and apply disciplinary sanctions; participate in vote only to break a tie and on questions considered important; appoint Secretary General and staff; conduct sittings and determine results of votes and elections; represent the Knesset; preserve its dignity.

337

Country and House(s)	9.1 Presiding Officer(s) or collective directing authority	9.2 Method of election or appointment	9.3 Term of office (years)
ITALY Senate Chamber of Deputies	Respective Presiding Officer's Cttee, comprising for each House 4 Vice-Presidents, 3 Questors, 8 Secretaries. Groups must be represented in the Cttee.	Elected by ballot of the respective House (see 16.3).	Term of Parlt (5 years).
IVORY COAST National Assembly	Bureau of the Assembly comprising President; 8 Vice-Presidents; 16 Secretaries; 2 Questors.	Elected by the Assembly. Absolute majority in 1st 2 ballots then simple majority.	President 5 years; others 1 year year but may be re-elected.
JAPAN House of Councillors House of Representatives	Presiding Officer	Elected by respective House from the MPs	Coincides with term of office as Member (6 Councillors; 4 Representatives).
JORDAN Senate	President of the Senate	Appointed by the King	2 years
House of Deputies	Speaker of the House of Deputies	Elected by the House	1 year, but may be re-elected.

338

9.4 Presiding Officer's position and status a) Precedence b) Succession list	9.5 Presiding Officer's a) Annual salary b) Allowances (US$ approx.)	9.6 Functions and powers
a) House Presidents follow immediately the President of the Republic with precedence to the elder b) President of the Senate assures functions pending new elections	Supplementary allowance; residence; staff; car.	Represent the House; convene House and cttees; organise and supervise work of the House; supervise publication of records and documents; maintain order in the House and apply SO; establish order of the votes and proclaim results; does not vote or participate in debate. The President of the Chamber of Deputies presides over joint sittings.
a) President is 2nd b) No succession	–	Preside over plenary meetings, the Bureau and the Presidents' Conference; maintain order; put matters to the vote and announce the result. May participate in debate by leaving the chair. Direct the Assembly Administration.
a) None b) None	a) 78,670 b) Term-end: 31,140 pa; communication and traffic: 31,330 pa; daily miscellaneous: 18.1; official residence; 3 guards; 2 staff; official car	Determine order of the day; nominate cttee members; maintain order in House; participate in debate by leaving the chair; attend and speak in cttee meetings; exercise casting vote; refer matters to cttees; authorise some cttee functions; permit MPs' questions to the Cabinet; refer a disciplinary case to the relevant cttee; appoint House staff.
a) After the Head of State and the Prime Minister a) After the President of the Senate	a) 18,600 b) 1,350 monthly representation and transport	Preside over proceedings of the House; maintain order and discipline; represent the House; observe application of Const. and SO; exercise casting vote only; direct the House Secretariat.

Country and House(s)	9.1 Presiding Officer(s) or collective directing authority	9.2 Method of election or appointment	9.3 Term of office (years)
KENYA National Assembly	The Speaker and Deputy-Speaker	Elected in secret ballot by 2/3 majority among MPs or persons qualified to be MPs	5 years
KUWAIT National Assembly	Bureau of National Assembly comprising President; Deputy-President; Parliamentary Secretary; Comptroller; Chairmen of the Legislative and Legal Affairs Cttee and the Financial and Economic Affairs Cttee.	Absolute majority in ballot of those present. Chairmen elected by respective cttee.	President and Deputy President coterminous with Assembly (4 years). Others, one year.
LEBANON National Assembly	President of the National Assembly	Elected	1 year
LIECHTENSTEIN Diet	President of the Diet	Elected by the Diet. Absolute majority in 1st and 2nd ballots, then simple majority.	Term of session
LUXEMBOURG Chamber of Deputies	Business Cttee comprising the President of the Chamber and parliamentary group Leaders.	The President is elected by absolute majority in secret ballot.	Term of Parlt (5 years) subject to continued Chamber support.

9.4 Presiding Officer's position and status a) Precedence b) Succession list	9.5 Presiding Officer's a) Annual salary b) Allowances (US$ approx.)	9.6 Functions and powers
a) Equivalent to Cabinet Ministers	Salary 288 (same as other MPs); House allowance 590; House Responsibility allowance 870; residence, guard, staff and transport provided.	Preside over deliberations of the Assembly; maintain order; adjourn Assembly and fix sitting dates at Govt request; exercise casting vote.
a) In matters of protocol the President comes after the Head of State b) No position in succession	a) 83,500 b) Car with driver	Represent the Assembly; summon the Assembly and establish its agenda according to SO; preside over sessions and maintain order; may participate in debate by leaving the chair and vote; preside over Assembly Bureau and exercise casting vote; appoint Secretary General and senior Assembly staff; supervise the Secretariat.
a) Second in precedence b) None	a) – b) Guard and car provided by Assembly	Establish order of business; preside over Assembly proceedings; maintain order in House and apply sanctions; participate in debate and vote; appoint Secretary General and staff.
a) Immediately after the Prince b) None	a) and b) 2,400	Establish meeting dates and convene sessions; establish order of business; maintain order in House and apply measures; participate in debate and vote; direct Diet administration; appoint Secretary-General; sign Diet minutes and other documents.
a) 2nd b) None	a) 38,850 b) Representation allowance, official car.	Convene sittings; establish draft Order of the Day; chair the Bureau and the Business Cttee; preside over proceedings; maintain order and apply sanctions; participate in debate by leaving the chair; vote.

Country and House(s)	9.1 Presiding Officer(s) or collective directing authority	9.2 Method of election or appointment	9.3 Term of office (years)
MALAWI National Assembly	Speaker	Appointed by the President	Term of Parliament (5 years).
MALAYSIA Senate	President of the Senate	Elected by the House from among the Senators	Term of senatorial office
House of Representatives	Speaker	Elected by the House from persons qualified to be MPs. Becomes an ex-officio MP if not already one.	Term of Parlt (5 years).
MALI National Assembly	President's Conference comprising the President of the Assembly, 4 Vice-Presidents and cttee Chairmen.	Nominated by the National Leadership of the Party (see 19.2) and elected by the Assembly.	Term of Parlt (3 years).
MALTA House of Representatives	The Speaker	Elected by the House from among the Members or persons eligible for election to Parlt.	Term of Parlt (5 years).
MAURITIUS Legislative Assembly	The Speaker, in consultation with the Leader of the House (Prime Minister).	The Speaker is elected by the Assembly.	Term of Parlt (5 years).

9.4 Presiding Officer's position and status a) Precedence b) Succession list	9.5 Presiding Officer's a) Annual salary b) Allowances (US$ approx.)	9.6 Functions and powers
–	–	Summon Members to sessions; pre-side over deliberations; maintain order and apply sanctions; appoint cttee members; exercise a casting vote; direct the administration of the Assembly Secretariat.
a) 4th b) NA a) 5th b) NA	a) Presiding Officers receive allowance of 2,428 pm in addition to allowances in Table 5 b) Residence, guard, staff, car, etc. and enter-tainment allowance of 845 per month	Convene sessions; establish order of business; preside over sittings; maintain order and apply sanctions; Presiding Officers do not partici-pate in debates; if the Speaker is not an elected MP he may not exercise a casting vote; chair permanent cttees; direct the House administration and appoint staff.
a) – b) Temporarily acts as President of the Republic in case of need	Determined by law	Preside over deliberations of the Assembly; maintain order and apply sanctions; direct the activity of the Assembly.
a) After the Chief Justice and before Ministers b) No succession list but the Speaker has served as Acting President when the President was abroad	a) 6,900 (office not full time) b) Entertainment allowance not fixed; secretariat; car and driver	Convene urgent sittings; preside over proceedings; maintain order and apply sanctions; exercise a casting vote (does not participate in debate).
a) After Governor-General, Chief Justice and Prime Minister b) NA	a) 7,900 b) Residence; guard; chauffered car; entertain-ment allowance	Preside over proceedings; maintain order and apply cautions; vote and exercise a casting vote but not participate in debate; chair the Cttee of Selection and SO Cttee.

Country and House(s)	9.1 Presiding Officer(s) or collective directing authority	9.2 Method of election or appointment	9.3 Term of office (years)
MEXICO Chamber of Senators	President of the Great Cttee (comprising 1 Senator from each State and the Federal District)	Elected by the Members of the respective Great Cttee	3 years
Chamber of Deputies	President of the Great Cttee (comprising a representative of each regional district and each parliamentary group).		
MONACO National Council	President of the National Council; Bureau of the National Council comprising President, Vice-President, 2 secretaries.	Elected by an absolute majority of the National Council in secret ballot.	1 year
MONGOLIA Great People's Khural (GPKh)	GPKh Chairman and 4 Vice-Chairmen	Elected by the GPKh from among the Members	Term of Parlt (5 years).
NAURU Parliament	Speaker and Deputy Speaker	Elected by a majority vote. If votes equal or 3 or more candidates, by absolute majority ballot.	Term of Parlt (3 years).

9.4 Presiding Officer's position and status a) Precedence b) Succession list	9.5 Presiding Officer's a) Annual salary b) Allowances (US$ approx.)	9.6 Functions and powers
a) – b) None	a) 12,000 (same as other Members) b) None	Convene meetings of the Great Cttee; establish order of business in consultation with Members of Directorate; appoint cttees; advise the Great Cttee and the respective Chamber; maintain order in the Chamber; participate in debate and vote; exercise administrative powers.
a) – b) None	a) – b) –	Direct the organisation and functioning of the Secretariat; manage the Parliamentary Budget; preside over sittings; maintain order; apply sanctions. The Presiding Officer does not participate in debate, but may vote.
The Chairman of the GPKh is the Head of State.	a) Chairman and Vice-Chairmen continue to receive salary from their usual place of work b) The GPKh Presidium provides office services and transport	The Chairman presides over sittings of the GPKh.
a) Accorded due courtesies b) None	a) Speaker's allowance: 10,300 and MP's salary: 2,900 b) Entertainment allowance: 430 pa; secretary and state car	Convene sessions; preside over deliberations of Parlt and maintain order and apply sanctions; exercise a casting vote; certify Bills after passage; prorogue Parlt in accordance with advice of the President; dissolve Parlt in accordance with Const. (Art. 41); determine timing of a general election in accordance with advice of the President and issue writs for the election; appoint Clerk of the Parlt.

Country and House(s)	9.1 Presiding Officer(s) or collective directing authority	9.2 Method of election or appointment	9.3 Term of office (years)
NETHERLANDS First Chamber	President	Elected by the Chamber in secret ballot	Term of Parlt (4 years).
Second Chamber	Presidium comprising the Chairman and Vice-Chairmen of the Chamber which does not, however, determine business (see 11.1).		
NEW ZEALAND House of Representatives	Speaker	Elected by Parlt but in case of equality of vote, by secret ballot.	Term of Parlt (3 years).
NICARAGUA National Asembly	President of the National Assembly and the Directive Board	Elected by plenary sitting	3 years
NORWAY Storting	The Storting Presidium comprising the President and Vice-President respectively of the Storting, Odelsting and Lagting, and party group representatives.	Elected by the Storting, Odelsting and Lagting, respectively.	Storting term (4 years); others 1 year.
PHILIPPINES National Assembly	The Speaker	Elected by majority vote in roll call of the Assembly	Term of Parlt (6 years).

9.4 Presiding Officer's position and status a) Precedence b) Succession list	9.5 Presiding Officer's a) Annual salary b) Allowances (US$ approx.)	9.6 Functions and powers
a) 1st after the Monarch b) None	a) None b) As in Table 5 plus 8,000 and some administrative assistance	Convene sessions; maintain order in the Chamber and apply sanctions; participate in debate after leaving the Chair and vote; represent the Chambers. The President of the First Chamber also establishes the order of business, appoints cttees and chairmen and acts as ex-officio chairman of some cttees.
a) Personal adviser to the Monarch during govt formation b) None	a) None b) As in Table 5 plus a secretariat and transport	
a) 3rd, following Governor–General and Prime Minister b) None	a) 36,300 b) Residence at Parlt House, 3 personal staff; basic allowance; electorate allowance (abated by 1/3); and day allowance as for Members (see 5.2); official car	Preside over proceedings; maintain order in the House; recommend to Govt appointment of Clerk and officers; traditionally does not participate in debate; exercise casting vote.
a) NA b) NA	a) 33 per month b) Some allowances	Convene sessions; establish order of business; appoint cttees; maintain order in the Assembly; participate in debate and vote.
a) President of the Storting immediately after the King b) NA (hereditary monarchy)	a) 25,000 b) Same as other Members (see 5.2) plus annual expense allowance: 2,700 and car with driver	Determine dates of sessions; establish order of business; ex-officio chairman of Presidium and Election and Business Cttees; maintain order in the Storting and apply SO; participate in debate by vacating the chair; vote; exercise a casting vote; exercise administrative powers; advise the King on request; represent the Storting.
a) After the President and the Vice-President b) Acts as President in case of vacancy (Const. Art VIII, Sect. 9)	a) 6,300 b) Reimbursement of travel expenses; guard; staff; transport	Preside over proceedings; maintain order; apply disciplinary sanctions; participate in debate when not presiding; vote; appoint Secretary General and other staff; sign all Acts, regulations, etc.

347

Country and House(s)	9.1 Presiding Officer(s) or collective directing authority	9.2 Method of election or appointment	9.3 Term of office (years)
POLAND Diet	The Diet Bureau comprising Diet President and 4 Vice-Presidents	Elected by a majority vote, with at least 1/2 of Diet member-ship present at 1st sitting of a new Parlt	Term of Parlt (4 years).
PORTUGAL Assembly of the Republic	1. President of the Assembly 2. Assembly Bureau comprising the President; 4 Vice-Presidents; 4 secretaries and 2 vice-secretaries	Elected by absolute majority of the Assembly in secret ballot	One session (1 year).
REPUBLIC OF KOREA National Assembly	Speaker and 2 Deputy Speakers	Elected by absolute majority in secret vote	2 years
ROMANIA Grand National Assembly	Bureau of the Grand National Assembly comprising the Assembly President and 4 Vice-Presidents	Elected by and from the Assembly (see 16.3).	Term of Parlt (5 years).
RWANDA National Development Council (CND)	President of the CND	2 candidates are nominated from MPs by President of the MRND, 1 of which is elected by an absolute maj-ority of CND Members.	Term of Parlt (5 years).

9.4 Presiding Officer's position and status a) Precedence b) Succession list	9.5 Presiding Officer's a) Annual salary b) Allowances (US$ approx.)	9.6 Functions and powers
a) Diet Presidium is 2nd after the President of the State Council b) None	a) 68,000 zlotys pm b) Residence; guard; secretary; official car	Determine sitting dates and agenda in agreement with the Council of Sages (see 8.4); preside over sittings; maintain order and apply sanctions; participate in debates and vote; appoint the head of the Secretariat and provide overall direction of the Diet's administration.
a) Immediately after the President of the Republic b) Fills temporary vacancies in Presidency of the Republic	a) 1,000 pm b) Representation allowance: 350 pm; guards; staff of 5; car and driver	Convene sittings; establish order of business; preside over deliberations; maintain order and apply sanctions; participate in debate by leaving the chair; vote; direct the administrative services and appoint staff; represent the Assembly and authorise its formal documents.
a) Speaker immediately after the President of the Republic b) None	a) Speaker's salary: 12,900 pa b) Monthly allowance for legislative activities; 1,650; residence; guard; staff; transport	Convene sessions; establish order of business in consultation with House Steering Cttee; appoint cttee members on advice of party leaders; maintain order and apply sanctions; participate in debate and vote by leaving the Chair; ex-officio Chairman of Consultative Cttee on Parliamentary Overseas Activities; appoint Secretary General with approval of Parlt and Senior House staff.
No provisions	Special allowance for President	Bureau: propose convocation of Assembly; establish work programme proposed to Assembly. President: preside over sittings; determine time limits for speakers; participate in debate and vote; adjourn debates; appoint Assembly staff.
a) 3rd b) 3rd (after the Secretary General of the National Revolutionary Movement for Development (MRND), see 19.1)	a) 11,000 b) Daily sitting allowance: 22; daily allowance when overseas: 129; residence, guard, domestic staff, official car	Convene sessions; establish order of business; appoint cttees; preside over proceedings; maintain order and apply sanctions; participate in debate and vote; direct CND administrative services; represent the CND; authorise CND budget expenditure.

Country and House(s)	9.1 Presiding Officer(s) or collective directing authority	9.2 Method of election or appointment	9.3 Term of office (years)
ST VINCENT House of Assembly	Speaker	Elected by the House	Term of Parlt (5 years).
SENEGAL National Assembly	Assembly Bureau comprising the Assembly President, 9 Vice-Presidents, 7 Secretaries and 2 Questors.	Elected by absolute majority of the Assembly in secret ballot	1 year renewable
SOLOMON ISLANDS National Parliament	Speaker	Elected by Parlt from among persons qualified for election as a Member	Term of Parlt (4 years).
SOMALIA People's Assembly	President of the People's Assembly	Nominated by Central Cttee of the Somali Socialist Revolutionary Party and elected by Parlt	Term of Parlt (5 years).

9.4 Presiding Officer's position and status a) Precedence b) Succession list	9.5 Presiding Officer's a) Annual salary b) Allowances (US$ approx.)	9.6 Functions and powers
a) Just below Cabinet Ministers b) None, but may be called to deputise for the Head of State	a) 580 per month b) Travel: 230 per month; residence; guard	Establish order of business; preside over sittings of the House; maintain order; participate in vote if an elected Member; exercise administrative powers; recommend appointment of the Secretary General; sanction staff appointments.
a) 2nd b) 1st	a) 1,300 b) Representation allowance; residence; guard; domestic staff; official car	Convene sessions; chair Bureau meetings; preside over Assembly proceedings; maintain order and apply certain sanctions; participate in debate by leaving the chair but not vote except in election of Bureau members; direct the Assembly administration; maintain Assembly security.
a) – b) Performs interim functions on vacancy of office or absence of Governor-General	a) – b) Free transport in session	Preside over proceedings; advise Governor-General on appointment of Leader of Opposition; maintain order and apply sanctions; Speaker does not participate in debate nor exercise any kind of vote; a Deputy Speaker (other presiding officer) exercises a casting vote only.
a) – b) –	a) – b) –	Establish order of business; preside over proceedings; maintain order and apply sanctions; participate in debate.

Country and House(s)	9.1 Presiding Officer(s) or collective directing authority	9.2 Method of election or appointment	9.3 Term of office (years)
SOUTH AFRICA House of Assembly House of Representatives House of Delegates	Speaker of Parlt; Chairman of each House; Chairman of Committees and Deputy Chairman of Cttees of each House.	The Speaker is elected by an electoral college (see 39.1). Chairmen are elected at the 1st sitting of the respective Houses.	Term of Parlt (5 years).
SPAIN Senate Congress of Deputies	Presiding Body comprising House President, 4 Vice-Presidents (2 in the Senate); 4 Secretaries.	Presidents are elected by an absolute majority of Members (simple majority on 2nd ballot from the top 2 candidates), Vice-Presidents and Secretaries are elected by simple majority.	Term of Parlt (4 years).
SRI LANKA Parliament	Speaker	Elected by absolute majority of the Parlt in successive ballots if necessary	Term of Parlt (6 years).

9.4 Presiding Officer's position and status a) Precedence b) Succession list	9.5 Presiding Officer's a) Annual salary b) Allowances (US$ approx.)	9.6 Functions and powers
a) Speaker with Cabinet Ministers in Rubric 4 b) Only if Acting State President is not appointed	a) Speaker 18,250 b) 13 per day tax free; residence; secretary and chauffeur; free transport and telephone	The Speaker of Parlt presides at any House sitting whenever he deems it necessary or desirable but may only vote in the House of which he is a member. He maintains order and applies sanctions; appoints cttee chairmen; appoints staff other than the Secretary (see 10.1); exercises control over parliamentary records and accounts; interprets and safeguards the rights and privileges of the Parlt. Presides at meetings of cttees on Standing Rules and Orders. Chairmen of Houses preside in the respective Houses when Speaker is not in the Chair.
a) Senate President 3rd, Congress President 4th b) None	–	The respective House Presidents establish the plenary agenda in agreement with the Council of Spokesmen; preside over proceedings; maintain order; authorise payments; chair the Cttee on Rules of Procedure and the Permanent Cttee; exercise responsibility for security and administration of the House; convene meetings of the Council of Spokesmen (see 11.1).
a) 3rd b) None	a) 2,560 b) 1,600	Convene Parlt on Prime Minister's request; preside over proceedings; maintain order; does not participate in debate; exercise casting vote only; appoint members and chairmen of select cttees; responsible for management of buildings, security and general administration of Parlt.

Country and House(s)	9.1 Presiding Officer(s) or collective directing authority	9.2 Method of election or appointment	9.3 Term of office (years)
SWEDEN Riksdag	Speaker and 3 Deputy Speakers	Elected by the House	Term of Parlt (3 years).
SWITZERLAND States Council	The Bureau comprising Council President, Vice-President, 2 Tellers and a substitute Teller.	Vice-Presidents and Tellers are elected by absolute jority in secret ballot of the respective Council.	President and Vice-Presidents 1 year; Tellers 1 year; (4 years in National Council).
National Council	The Group Presidents' Conference comprising Council President, Vice-President and Group Chairmen. The Bureau comprising Council President, Vice-President and 8 Tellers.	Group Chairmen are designated by the respective groups.	
SYRIAN ARAB REPUBLIC People's Council	Bureau of the Council comprising Council President, 2 Secretaries, 2 Questors.	Elected by simple majority of the Council	1 year, renewable.
THAILAND Senate	Speaker of the Senate and President of the National Assembly	Elected	2 years
House of Representatives	Speaker of the House of Representatives and Vice-President of the National Assembly		4 years

9.4 Presiding Officer's position and status a) Precedence b) Succession list	9.5 Presiding Officer's a) Annual salary b) Allowances (US$ approx.)	9.6 Functions and powers
a) Speaker is 2nd b) Acts as temporary Regent if necessary	a) As the Prime Minister 32,700 b) Free accommodation in the Riksdag; secretary; same transport as other Members	Establish order of business; maintain order in the House and apply disciplinary sanctions; ex-officio Head of War Delegation, Board of Riksdag Administration and of Speaker's Conference.
a) 5th b) None	a) and b) 8,333	Preside over proceedings; maintain discipline; participate in debates by leaving the chair but not vote; exercise casting vote; represent the respective Council; ensure business is managed efficiently; supervise the Secretariat.
a) 4th b) None		
a) – b) None	a) 6,600 b) –	Convene sessions; establish order of business; appoint special cttees; maintain order in the Council; participate in debates; appoint the Secretary General and Council staff; represent the Council.
a) – b) None	a) 625 p.m. b) Entertainment: 830; guard; staff; transport	President of the National Assembly chairs the Constitutional Tribunal. The Speakers of the Houses convene sessions; establish order of business; maintain order in the House and apply disciplinary sanctions; participate in debate and vote.
a) – b) None	a) – b) As b) above	

TABLE 9: PRESIDING OFFICERS OR COLLECTIVE DIRECTING
          AUTHORITY (continued)

Country and House(s)	9.1 Presiding Officer(s) or collective directing authority	9.2 Method of election or appointment	9.3 Term of office (years)
TUNISIA Chamber of Deputies	Chamber Bureau comprising the President, 2 Vice-Presidents, cttee chairmen and rapporteurs.	Elected by the Chamber	1 year, renewable.
UGANDA National Assembly	Speaker	Elected by the Assembly from among the Members	Term of Parlt (5 years).
UNION OF SOVIET SOCIALIST REPUBLICS Soviet of Nationalities	Chairman of the Soviet of Nationalities and 4 Vice-Chairmen	Elected by a majority of the member-ship of the respective Soviet	Term of Parlt (5 years).
Soviet of the Union	Chairman of the Soviet of the Union and 4 Vice-Chairmen		
UNITED KINGDOM House of Lords	Lord Chancellor	Appointed by the Monarch on advice of the Prime Minister	Term of Parlt (5 years), at pleasure of the Prime Minister.
House of Commons	The Speaker	Elected by the House and approved by the Monarch	

9.4 Presiding Officer's position and status a) Precedence b) Succession list	9.5 Presiding Officer's a) Annual salary b) Allowances (US$ approx.)	9.6 Functions and powers
a) – b) 2nd provisionally after the Prime Minister; 1st provisionally when the President resigns following double motion of censure	a) – b) Subsistence: 250 p.m.; representation: 560 p.m.; duty: 430 p.m.	Convene sessions; chair meetings of the Bureau; preside over proceedings but not vote; maintain order and apply sanctions; direct the Chamber administrative services; chair certain cttees.
a) Ministerial status b) None	a) – b) Residence; guards; official transport; domestic servants	Convene ordinary sessions; approve order of business; appoint administrative cttees; maintain order and apply disciplinary sanctions; exercise no vote.
a) Heads of respective Soviets with no other status b) None	a) 828 p.m. b) Expenses: 276 p.m.; representation: 41,000 p.a.; office; transport; assistant and an aide	Preside over sittings and conduct affairs of the respective Soviet; preside alternately over joint sittings; participate in debate and vote; represent the Soviet in its external relations (President of the Presidium of the Supreme Soviet exercises administrative powers).
a) 5th on the Roll of Lords b) None	a) Small salary in respect of parliamentary duties b) None	Reconvene the House after adjournment; recommend appointments to the Joint Cttee on Consolidation Bills; preside over deliberations (except when House is in cttee); if a Peer (which is usual), participate in debate and vote as a Peer (has no casting vote); appoint Clerk Assistant and Reading Clerk.
a) 6th after the Royal Family b) None	a) 58,000 plus allowances for travel and entertainment and Member's allowances b) Residence; guard; office staff; transport	Convene sessions; appoint standing cttee chairmen; chair the House of Commons commission; preside over deliberations; maintain order and apply sanctions; does not participate in debate but may exercise a casting vote; exercise certain powers respecting staff and administration in conjunction with House of Commons Commission and Select Cttee on the House.

Country and House(s)	9.1 Presiding Officer(s) or collective directing authority	9.2 Method of election or appointment	9.3 Term of office (years)
UNITED REPUBLIC OF TANZANIA National Assembly	Speaker	Simple majority in secret ballot by the Assembly	Term of Parlt and until new Speaker elected
UNITED STATES OF AMERICA Senate	1. Vice-President of the USA (de jure) 2. President (pro tempore) 3. Majority Leader	1. Elected by the Electoral College at the same time as the President of the USA 2. Elected by the Senate following majority party nomination 3. Elected by the majority party	Term of Senate (6 years).
House of Representatives	Speaker	Elected by the House	Term of House (2 years).
VANUATU Parliament	Speaker	Elected by Parlt	Term of Parlt (4 years).

9.4 Presiding Officer's position and status a) Precedence b) Succession list	9.5 Presiding Officer's a) Annual salary b) Allowances (US$ approx.)	9.6 Functions and powers
a) 5th b) 3rd	a) 5,000 b) Entertainment: 800 p.a.; resi- dence; transport; domestic staff of 2 persons	May convene sessions earlier or later with approval of Leader of Govt business; may direct varia-tions in the order of business; preside over proceedings; maintain order; exercise a casting vote but not a deliberative vote (does not participate in debate); appoint standing cttees; ex-officio chairman of SO Cttee, Steering Cttee and cttees of the Whole House.
a) 1. 2nd 2. After foreign ambassadors, Supreme Court judges and Cabinet members b) 1. 1st 2. 3rd	a) 1. 85,000 2. 75,100 b) Residence; guard; staff; official transport	1. or 2. convenes Senate; presides over proceedings; maintains order. 1. does not participate in debate and has casting vote only. 2. may not participate when presiding but may vote. 3. has many adminis-trative powers.
a) 3rd b) 2nd	a) 94,200 b) Staff; allow-ances for official expenses; car and driver	Convene sessions; establish order of business; appoint select and conference cttee chairmen; preside over proceedings; maintain order and apply sanctions; may partici-pate in debate and vote; exercise administrative powers.
a) 2nd b) Acting President when necessary	a) 1,242 b) Housing and representation allowances	Preside over sittings; direct debates; maintain order; sign parliamentary documents.

Country and House(s)	9.1 Presiding Officer(s) or collective directing authority	9.2 Method of election or appointment	9.3 Term of office (years)
YUGOSLAVIA Assembly	President and Vice-President of the Assembly	Elected by both Chambers	1 year
Federal Chamber	President of the Federal Chamber	Elected by the Chamber	
Chamber of Republics and Provinces	President of the Chamber of Republics and Provinces	Elected by the Chamber	
ZAIRE Legislative Council	Bureau of the Legislative Council, comprising a President, 2 Vice-Presidents and 2 secretaries.	Elected by absolute majority of the Council in secret ballot	Term of Parlt (5 years) renewable on request of 2/3 MPs.
ZAMBIA National Assembly	Speaker	Elected by simple majority from persons qualified to be MPs but who are not MPs.	Term of Parlt (5 years).
ZIMBABWE Senate	President of the Senate	Elected by the respective House	Term of Parlt (5 years).
House of Assembly	Speaker		

9.4 Presiding Officer's position and status a) Precedence b) Succession list	9.5 Presiding Officer's a) Annual salary b) Allowances (US$ approx.)	9.6 Functions and powers
a) President of the Assembly is 2nd b) None	a) Income may not exceed 660 p.m. including allow- ances below b) Expenses: 100 p.m.; function: 45 p.m.; separ- ation: 115 p.m.; residence; car with driver; staff; guard	President of the Assembly convenes joint sittings of both Chambers; establishes their order of business; presides over joint sittings; signs decrees on the promulgation of laws adopted by the Assembly.
a) The Bureau President is 1st in the Council b) NA	a) Yes b) Residence; guard; staff; transport	Convene ordinary sessions; esta- blish order of the day; preside over proceedings; maintain order; participate in debate and vote; chair some cttees; nominate Sec- retary General and other staff.
a) 6th b) None	a) 5,105 b) Special allow- ance: 2,679 p.a.; residence; telephone; dom- estic servants and guards; official transport	Establish order of business; appoint all cttees; chairman of 4 cttees; maintain order and apply sanctions; exercise casting vote; exercise administrative powers; appoint Secretary General.
a) 5th b) Fills temporary vacancy pending new Presidential elections a) 6th b) None	a) 18,000 b) Entertainment: 2,800 p.a.; housing: 8,400 p.a.; telephone: 840 p.a.; guard; parliamentary staff; transport	Convene sessions at Govt request; appoint cttees and certain chairmen according to decision of Standing Rules and Orders Cttee which he chairs; also Chairman of Library and Parlt Buildings Cttees; preside over sittings; maintain order; does not participate in debate nor vote; appoint staff in consultation with other Presiding Officer and with House approval. The Speaker in addition to above controls parlia- mentary accounts, expenditures and appropriations in consultation with President of the Senate.

TABLE 10

SECRETARY GENERAL OF THE HOUSE

Every Parliament must have at its disposal a wide range of resources to enable it to carry out its work and exercise its powers. It is the function of the administrative services of Parliament to provide these resources under a head of staff who is responsible to the directing authority. Whatever his title happens to be, for example Secretary General, Clerk or Director General, this head of staff is responsible for a series of tasks the mere enumeration of which shows his importance:

He is the professional adviser to the directing authority and other Members, who continually draw on his experience and knowledge of the law, procedure, practice and privileges of Parliament. Especially during sittings of the House, that knowledge is at the disposal of the Chair. In addition, he is likely to provide similar assistance to the committees of Parliament and their Chairmen and Rapporteurs.

He is in control of the administrative and secretarial services of Parliament including library, staff, supplies, accommodation, accounts, etc. unless, as sometimes happens, this is in part or in title made the responsibility of a second high official such as a Sergeant-at-Arms.

The head of staff is responsible for planning the agenda and recording the proceedings of both Parliament and its subsidiary bodies.

This range of functions reveals that the task of the head of staff is to see that the Members and the directing authority of Parliament have at their disposal every facility to help them carry out their duties.

Appointment of Head of Staff

The abilities required for the performance of these tasks make it essential for special care to be exercised in making an appointment to this post. The way in which the head of staff is appointed is presented in Table 10A. In most countries the head of staff is appointed by the directing authority, the body to whom he is responsible on a day-to-day basis and which can best appreciate the requirements of Parliament and make a choice based on professional competence. In a number of countries including Belgium, the Federal Republic of Germany, Indonesia, Ivory Coast, Norway, Philippines and the Republic of Korea, although the directing authority chooses the Secretary General, this choice has to be approved by Parliament.

TABLE 10A. Appointment of Head of Staff

Appointment by	Number of Countries
Directing Authority	36
Appointed or Elected by Parlt	19
Head of State	16
Government	4
Public Service Commission	6
Total	81*

* Excludes Jordan and Solomon Islands for reasons of missing data.

The practice of allowing Parliament to choose its own head of staff is consistent with the nature of the office; nevertheless, this system of appointment, although democratic in conception, carries with it the risk of transforming what is in essence a professional and non-political office into a political one subject to the vagaries of successive majorities. Parliament appoints or elects the head of staff in eighteen countries among which are Argentina, Belgium, Finland, Japan, USSR and Yugoslavia. In China and Mongolia the head of staff is a Member of Parliament and is elected by the Parliament.

In sixteen countries, the head of staff is appointed by the Head of State. In Canada and Malaysia, for example, this appointment is made on the advice of the Prime Minister, and in Cape Verde, Congo, Rwanda, Thailand and Zaire, on the advice of the directing authorities of Parliament.

A further four countries entrust the appointment of the head of staff to the Government. This is the practice in, for example, Ireland (where the advice of the respective House Chairman and that of the Minister for the Public Service is sought), New Zealand (where the advice of the Speaker is sought), Malta (where the Prime Minister seeks the advice of the Public Service Commission) and Switzerland (where the Federal Council appoints the Secretary General of the Federal Assembly on the advice of the Presidents' Conference of the National Council and the Bureau of the Council of States). Six countries including Bahamas, Cyprus, Fiji and Monaco appoint the head of staff through the Public Service Commission, usually with advice from the directing authority.

Tenure of Head of Staff

In most countries the head of staff is appointed on a permanent basis or until retirement (Table 10B). This period of tenure ensures his independence from the Executive and from changes in the political composition of Parliament. There are, however, exceptions to this. In Argentina, Congo, Cuba, Democratic Yemen, Portugal, Somalia, Sweden, USSR and the United States House of Representatives, the head of staff is appointed for the life of the legislature, although he may be eligible for reappointment in the next legislature and usually is reappointed. In the United States the Clerk of the House (who is nominated by the majority

TABLE 10B. Term of Office of Head of Staff

Term of Office	Number of Countries
Until Retirement	44
Not Fixed	20
Life of the Legislature	9
Various Periods from 2 to 6 Years	5
Until Majority Party Changes	1
Provided by Collegiate Head of State	1
Total	80*

* Excludes Brazil, Mali and Mongolia, for reasons of missing data.

party and then elected by the House) and the Secretary of the Senate (who is selected by the majority party and approved by the Senate) continue in office until a new majority party is elected to either House. In Greece it is also a political appointment. In China two Secretary Generals are elected by and from the Members, one for a term of one session with sessional responsibilities, the other for five years with duties pertaining to the Standing Committee of the National People's Congress.

TABLE 10: SECRETARY GENERAL OF THE HOUSE

Country and House(s)	10.1 Title of the chief civil service officer of the House	10.2 Appointed by	10.3 Term of office/ age of retirement
ALGERIA National People's Assembly (APN)	Secretary General (secrétaire général).	APN President	Not fixed by regulation
ARGENTINA Senate Chamber of Deputies	Parliamentary Secretary and Administrative Secretary (non Members of House).	Elected by the House (absolute majority) against political criteria.	Term of office: one parliamentary year but may be re-elected.
AUSTRALIA Senate	Clerk of the Senate	Governor-General in Council	Term of office unspecified. Must retire at 65.
House of Representatives	Clerk of the House of Representatives		
AUSTRIA Federal Council National Council	Secretary General of the Parliament (Parlamentsdirektor).	President of National Council	Retirement at 65
BAHAMAS Senate House of Assembly	Chief Clerk	Public Service Commission, in consultation with Speaker.	Retirement at 60
BELGIUM Senate Chamber of Representatives	Secretary General or Clerk of the respective House (Secrétaire général ou greffier de la Chambre).	Proposed by the Bureau, elected by the respective House.	Senate: not fixed. Chamber: 72. In both cases at the pleasure of the respective House.
BRAZIL Federal Senate Chamber of Deputies	For each House and of equal rank: General Director (for administrative matters); Secretary General (for technical subjects).	President of each House, subject to approval of its Board from among House staff.	-

366

10.4
Functions and authority

10.5
Status vis-à-vis heads
of govt departments

Assist the APN President in management of the administrative services; provide Secretariat services for the APN Bureau and the President's Conference.	Collaborative relationship at the level of heads of govt departments
Described in the respective regulations	–
Provide advice to presiding officers, Ministers and MPs on procedure, practices and privileges; perform role of chief executive with respect to administration of their respective parliamentary departments.	Position and status comparable to Head of a govt department
Foremost adviser to the President on legal, financial, administrative, staff and procedural matters.	Rank with permanent secretaries
Final decision-maker on all matters	Equivalent to Head of a govt department
Responsible for the records of debates and decisions taken; assist the President of House during public sittings, private meetings and meetings of the Bureau; keep all records and files; maintain authority, on behalf of the Bureau, over all the services and staff of House.	Same status as Head of a govt department
Secretary General: supervise administrative support for the legislative functions according to SO; assist Presiding Officer in interpretation of SO. General Director: authorise expenditure; administer personnel.	Equivalent to Head of a govt department

Country and House(s)	10.1 Title of the chief civil service officer of the House	10.2 Appointed by	10.3 Term of office/ age of retirement
BULGARIA National Assembly	The State Council (see 39.1) provides parliamentary staff.	State Council (Head of State)	NA
CAMEROON National Assembly	Secretary General (secrétaire général)	Bureau of the Assembly	Not fixed. Up to normal retiring age.
CANADA Senate	Clerk of the Senate	The Governor-General on advice of the Govt	Serves "during pleasure" of the Governor-General.
House of Commons	Clerk of the House of Commons		
CAPE VERDE People's National Assembly	Secretary General (secrétaire général)	President, on advice of Permanent Bureau	2 years (renewable 4 times).
CHINA National People's Congress (NPC)	Secretary General for Session; Secretary General for NPC Standing Cttee.	Elected by the NPC from among the Members	1 session (for Secretary General for Session); 5 years (for Secretary General, NPC Standing Cttee).
COMOROS Federal Assembly	Secretary General (secrétaire général)	President of Assembly	Retirement at 55
CONGO People's National Assembly (ANP)	Secretary General (secrétaire général)	Presidential decree on advice of the ANP President	Term of Parlt (5 years). Retirement at 55.

10.4 Functions and authority	10.5 Status vis-à-vis heads of govt departments
NA	NA
Advise the President on legal and procedural matters; receive records of vote commissions; prepare draft budget of Assembly; responsible for staff management; keep the Assembly's archives; issue cards of access to plenary sessions of the Assembly; maintain order in Public Gallery.	Higher than head of a govt department
Ensure that Bills presented are correct in form; assume custody of legislation, records and documents; prepare budget of respective House; carry overall responsibility for House personnel and administration; act as chief procedural adviser to the Speaker; prepare and issue a daily Order Paper for each sitting; prepare the official record of the proceedings; administer Oath of Allegiance to new MPs; ensure that procedural aspects of divisions are correct.	Equivalent to Deputy Minister
Record laws, resolutions and motions of the Assembly, and the deliberations of the Permanent Bureau; prepare the Assembly's draft budget and financial statements; manage the Assembly's finances; assist the President, the Permanent Bureau and Chairmen of cttees; act as secretary to the Permanent Bureau; maintain liaison with State agencies.	Equivalent to Secretary General of the President of the Republic and the Prime Minister
Secretary General for the Session directs Secretariat of the Session. Secretary General for NPC Standing Cttee assists Chairman of Cttee and directs General Office of the Cttee.	Equivalent to the full status of Minister
Responsible for legal form of Bills submitted; presentation of Assembly business; verbatim records of plenary and cttee sessions; advice in legal matters; custody of Assembly records.	Equivalent to Secretary General of the Presidency or of govt departments
Head of the Assembly's administration, and responsible for parliamentary financial and personnel management.	Equivalent of deputy-head of a govt department.

Country and House(s)	10.1 Title of the chief civil service officer of the House	10.2 Appointed by	10.3 Term of office/ age of retirement
COSTA RICA Legislative Assembly	Administrative Director	Directorate of the Assembly	Not fixed
CUBA National Assembly of People's Power	Head of the Administrative Department (the Secretary is a Member elected by the Assembly).	The President of the National Assembly	Term of Parlt (5 years). Non-compulsory retirement at 60.
CYPRUS House of Representatives	Director-General	The Public Service Commission	Retirement at 60
CZECHOSLOVAKIA Chamber of Nations Chamber of the People	Head of the Office of the Federal Assembly	The Presidium of the Federal Assembly	No fixed term of office. Retirement at 60.
DEMOCRATIC YEMEN Supreme People's Council	Secretary General	Elected by the Council to the Presidium and by the Presidium to be Secretary.	Term of Parlt (5 years)
DENMARK Folketing	Secretary General (Head of the Administration office) and Clerk of the Folketing (Head of the Clerks Office).	The President, after consultation with the Vice-Presidents.	Life appointment, with retirement at 70 at latest.
EGYPT People's Assembly	Secretary General	Nominated by the Speaker and appointed by the Bureau.	Retirement at 60
FIJI Senate House of Representatives	Clerk of each House	The Public Service Commission on advice of presiding officer of respective House.	Retirement at 55

10.4 Functions and authority	10.5 Status vis-à-vis heads of govt departments
Direct all services and staff of the Assembly; assist Directorate in application of the law; liaise with the civil service.	-
Execute the approved budget; exercise financial and administrative supersision; assure provision of all parliamentary services to MPs.	No equivalent
Administer, co-ordinate and supervise House services; provide advice on procedural and legislative matters; control House expenditure.	Equivalent to Director-General of a ministry.
Administer the administrative, financial and legislative support services of the Federal Assembly.	NA
Draft Council budget; sign payment orders; administer staff; maintain Council buildings.	As a Presidium Member, is senior to heads of govt departments.
The Secretary General is secretary to the Presidium, supervises financial and administrative matters including personnel. The Clerk of the Folketing is secretary to the SO Cttee and assists the President in legislative matters and sessional planning.	Both have rank equal to ministerial permanent Under-Secretaries.
Supervise the activity of the General Secretariat; manage the Assembly's administrative, financial and technical business; administer and supervise the Secretariat staff.	Equivalent to a Minister
Keep all parliamentary records (including minutes, votes, order book, Hansard, messages). Administrative Head of respective House.	Equivalent to Head of department

Country and House(s)	10.1 Title of the chief civil service officer of the House	10.2 Appointed by	10.3 Term of office/ age of retirement
FINLAND Eduskunta	Secretary General	Elected by the Parlt. Must be qualified in Law.	Retirement at 63
FRANCE Senate	1. Secretary General of the Senate 2. Secretary General of the Questure	The Bureau of the Senate	1. and 2: retirement at 68 (extension to 70 possible).
National Assembly	1. Secretary General of the National Assembly and the Presidency 2. Secretary General of the Questure	The Bureau of the National Assembly	1. and 2. retirement at 65 (extension to 70 possible).
GABON National Assembly	Secretary General (secrétaire général).	President of the Republic	Retirement at 60
GERMAN DEMOCRATIC REPUBLIC People's Chamber	Director of the Secretariat of the People's Chamber	Presidium of People's Chamber	Retirement at 65
GERMANY Federal Council	Director of the Federal Council (Direktor des Bundesrates).	Appointed by the Council President with approval of the House	Retirement usually at 65
Federal Diet	Director of the Federal Diet (Direktor des Bundestags).	Appointed by the Diet President with approval of the Presidium	Retirement at 65

Assist the Speaker on legislative matters; keep a record of decisions of Parliament; keep the record of sittings; chief of the Central bureau in the office of the Parlt.	Not defined, but in practice comparable to Secretary General of a ministry.
1. Direct the legislative services and the services responsible for the records of the procceedings of the Senate; assist the Chair during sittings 2. Direct the administrative and financial services, and the library service	Not included in the State Administrative hierarchy as such
1. Direct all the legislative services, centred on the Presidency; assist the chair during sittings 2. Direct the administrative and financial services of the Questure, and supervise services of international relations and protocol	
Participate in preparation of Budget; maintain overall supervision of staff; administer the functioning of Parlt; provide legal advice on parliamentary procedures.	Awaiting full determination
On behalf of the Presidium, responsible for organisation and technical matters concerning plenary sessions and legislative proceedings; manage Secretariat personnel; inform Govt Ministers and officials of cttee projects and make relevant arrangements; prepare draft budget in agreement with Ministry of Finance, for submission to the Presidium; oversee budgetary spending; responsible for security in Parlt.	Comparable to Heads of govt agencies
Advise Council President and MPs on legislation and procedure; prepare a draft budget for Consultative Council examination; implement the approved budget; direct the House administration; supervise staff.	Comparable to Govt State Secretary
Advise the President on procedure; direct the Diet administration under the authority of the President	Equivalent to Secretary of State of a Ministry

Country and House(s)	10.1 Title of the chief civil service officer of the House	10.2 Appointed by	10.3 Term of office/ age of retirement
GREECE Chamber of Deputies	Secretary General of the Greek Chamber of Deputies	President of the Chamber	Political appointment with no fixed end of term
HUNGARY National Assembly	Head of Office of the Assembly	President of the Assembly	Not fixed
INDIA Council of States	Secretary General	Chairman of the Council	Retirement at 60
House of the People	Secretary General	Speaker	
INDONESIA House of Representatives	Secretary General	The President, upon the consideration of the House.	Not prescribed
IRELAND Senate	Clerk of the Senate	Prime Minister on recommendation of respective	Retirement at 65
Dáil	Clerk of the Dáil	Chairman and Minister for the Public Service	
ISRAEL The Knesset	Secretary General of the Knesset	The Chairman and Vice-Chairmen	Appointment can be discontinued at any time. Normal retirement at 65.
ITALY Senate	Secretary General of the House	The Presiding Officer's Cttee on proposal of the President	Retirement at 60
Chamber of Deputies			
IVORY COAST National Assembly	Secretary General (secrétaire général).	The Assembly on proposal of the Bureau	Retirement at 55
JAPAN House of Councillors	Secretary General of each House	Elected by each House	Not fixed
House of Representatives			

10.4
Functions and authority

10.5
Status vis-à-vis heads
of govt departments

Direct administrative and financial services under the supervision of the President; make available intellectual and physical resources needed to meet the Members' mandate.	Heads of govt departments are also political appointees.
Assist the work of the Assembly President; manage the Assembly's administrative services	–
Advise and assist the Presiding Officer in legislative and procedural matters; safeguard the records of the House; sanction expenditure within the House budget; administer the Secretariat under the overall direction of the Presiding Officer.	Equivalent to executive head of a ministry of the Govt of India
Administer House services; assist in preparation of House budget; meet legal obligations of House functions.	Has status as a "High State Institution Administration".
Management of staff, custody of records and documents, recording proceedings of House, etc.	Equivalent to Permanent Head of a govt department
Prepare and execute the Knesset's agenda in accordance with Presidium decisions; provide procedural advice; supervise expenditure authority; exercise responsibility for administrative matters; personnel appointment (but not discharge) and management.	Equivalent to Permanent Head of a ministry
Supervise preparation of parliamentary work; assist the President in legislative matters; prepare and keep records and other documents; direct the administration and staff; liaise with other constitutional bodies; receive proclamations of electoral results and challenges to them.	No institutional comparison possible
Executive Head of Assembly's legislative and administrative services. Assist the President and Bureau of the Assembly.	Status of a senior public servant
Under supervision of the Presiding Officer, administer the secretarial work of the House and sign official documents.	Special status, which is not comparable with heads of govt departments.

375

Country and House(s)	10.1 Title of the chief civil service officer of the House	10.2 Appointed by	10.3 Term of office/ age of retirement
JORDAN Senate House of Deputies	Secretary General of the National Assembly (both Houses).	According to civil service criteria	Retirement at 60
KENYA National Assembly	Clerk of the National Assembly	President	Retirement at 55
KUWAIT National Assembly	Secretary General	President of Assembly with approval of the Bureau	Permanent until retirement at 65
LEBANON National Assembly	Secretary General	President of Assembly	Retirement at 64
LIECHTENSTEIN Diet	Secretary of the Diet	The Diet President with Govt agreement	Not fixed
LUXEMBOURG Chamber of Deputies	Clerk of the Chamber of Deputies (greffier de la Chambre).	The Chamber	5 years, renewable. State pension from 60 to 65.
MALAWI National Assembly	Clerk of the National Assembly	Public Service Commission in consultation with the Speaker	Not fixed. Retirement at 60.
MALAYSIA Senate House of Representatives	Clerk of the Senate Secretary of Parlt/Clerk of the House of Rep.	The King, on recommendation of the Prime Minister.	Retirement at 60
MALI National Assembly	Secretary General (secrétaire général).	Bureau comprising the President, 4 Vice-Presidents, 4 Secretaries, 2 Questors elected by the Assembly.	–

10.4 Functions and authority	10.5 Status vis-à-vis heads of govt departments
Responsible to the Presiding Officer of both Houses; supervise Assembly staff; manage legislative, financial and administrative matters.	Same as heads of govt departments
Chief executive officer of the Assembly	Equivalent to a permanent secretary
Supervise General Secretariat and staff; assist at open meetings of the Assembly and with consent, closed meetings; assist at cttee meetings on request.	Equivalent to Under-Secretary of a ministry
Assist the President in management and operation of the Assembly. His authority in all matters derives from the President.	Equivalent to Director-General of a ministry
Administer the minutes and correspondence of the Diet.	-
Attend public sittings; prepare minutes and petition sheets; responsible for the Chamber's administration and financial management; supervise the staff; responsible for the Library and archives.	Independent of ministerial departments.
Attend all sittings; give effect to directions of the Speaker for management and administration of the Assembly; maintain custody of the records; responsible for preparation of the official report of proceedings.	-
Advise Presiding Officers and Members on parliamentary matters; administer staff, services and expenditure of both Houses; notify Members of sittings and provide associated documents; maintain records and papers; edit and verify Acts before publication.	Equivalent to Secretary General of a junior ministry.
Assist the President; manage and co-ordinate the Assembly services.	-

TABLE 10: SECRETARY GENERAL OF THE HOUSE (continued)

Country and House(s)	10.1 Title of the chief civil service officer of the House	10.2 Appointed by	10.3 Term of office/ age of retirement
MALTA House of Representatives	Clerk of the House of Representatives	The Prime Minister after consultation with the Public Service Commission	Public service post liable to transfer. Retirement at 60 (optionally 61).
MAURITIUS Legislative Assembly	Clerk of the Assembly	Public Service Commission, on recommendation of the Prime Minister who consults the Speaker.	Until retirement at 60
MEXICO Chamber of Senators Chamber of Deputies	Chief Official (Oficial Mayor)	The Chamber, on nomination of the Great Cttee (see 9.1).	6 years approximately
MONACO National Council	Secretary General	Appointed in the same way as other public servants in consultation with the President of the National Council	Not fixed
MONGOLIA Great People's Khural (GPKh)	Secretary of the GPKh Presidium	Is an MP and elected by the GPKh.	-
NAURU Parliament	Clerk of Parliament	The Speaker	Until retirement

10.4 Functions and authority	10.5 Status vis-à-vis heads of govt departments
Ensure accuracy of Bills before presentation and publication; manage the House administrative services and staff; keep all records of the House; ensure efficient support for House proceedings; issue warrants for witnesses and experts to attend the House.	One grade below permanent secretary of a govt department
Responsible for printing Bills and Acts; act as Chief Accounting Officer; manage the Assembly Office; secretary to cttees; carry out general administration.	Equivalent to Permanent Secretary of a govt department
Maintain parliamentary records; publish the Diary of Debates; coordinate administrative support for cttees; implement the budget; direct administrative matters and supervise staff.	Similar to Secretary General of a govt department
Manage the administrative services of the National Council.	–
Head of the GPKh staff	–
Administration of Parlt; issue Notice Paper; record votes and Proceedings; prepare approved Bills for certification by the Speaker; maintain control on parliamentary finance; act as secretary to various parliamentary cttees; maintain custody of parliamentary records and library; act as Chairman during election of the Speaker.	Exercises powers of a Head of a govt department but is ranked two grades lower.

Country and House(s)	10.1 Title of the chief civil service officer of the House	10.2 Appointed by	10.3 Term of office/ age of retirement
NETHERLANDS First Chamber	Clerk (Greffier)	The Chamber	Retirement at 65
Second Chamber			
NEW ZEALAND House of Representatives	Clerk	Govt, on the recommendation of the Speaker.	No fixed term. Usually retires at about 65.
NICARAGUA National Assembly	Secretary General	National Assembly in plenary sitting	3 years
NORWAY Storting	Secretary General (Stortingets kontorsjef)	Nominated by the Presidium and appointed by secret ballot of the Storting	Retirement at 70 but may resign at 67.
PHILIPPINES National Assembly	Secretary General	Speaker, with the concurrence of majority of Members.	No fixed term; office held until successor appointed.
POLAND Diet	Head of the Diet Chancellery	Diet Bureau	Term of office unspecified. Retirement at 65.
PORTUGAL Assembly of the Republic	Secretary General of the Assembly of the Republic	Appointed by the Assembly President on advice of the Assembly Bureau	Term of Parlt (4 years). Retirement at 70.

10.4	10.5
Functions and authority	Status vis-à-vis heads
	of govt departments

Functions and authority	Status vis-à-vis heads of govt departments
Assist in drafting reports and holding cttee and plenary meetings; prepare presidential decisions; supervise Chamber staff, services and expenditure	Equal in rank to the highest civil servant
Main adviser to the Chairman in the Chamber and the Presidium; head of Chamber staff; procedural duties. (Domestic and budgetary matters are handled by the Director of Services subordinate to the Clerk).	
Prepare Bills for submission to the Governor-General for Royal Assent, estimates of parliamentary expenditure and accounts for that expenditure; Head of the department servicing Parlt.	Equivalent to Head of govt department
Receive communications of the National Assembly and inform the President; verify quorum; prepare the record of resolutions and publications of the Assembly; prepare annual report; responsible for administrative and financial management; execute orders of the Assembly President.	Same as a Minister of State
Head constitutional services; plan work programmes; draft the agenda; advise Presidium and cttees; maintain international relations; liaise with the Palace; responsible for Presidium Budget, permanent cttees and international delegations. (Head of Administration is responsible for other administrative and financial matters.)	Same status as Head of a govt department
Assist the Speaker in the conduct of business; call the roll of Members; maintain record of proceedings; enforce House orders; maintain a library; certify all approved Acts and regulations; assist in all financial, budgetary and administrative matters; supervise staff.	Equivalent to a Cabinet Minister
Assist Ministers in drafting Bills; advise the Bureau and cttees on legal aspects of Bills; responsible for correctness of official texts of laws and resolutions adopted; responsible for preparation of cttee minutes; prepare Diet Budget, manage Diet administration and personnel; assist the Bureau on procedural matters.	Equivalent to Under-Secretary of State
Coordinate and manage the Assembly's administrative services under the President's overall direction; assume responsibility for the museum, security services, photocopying and microfilm.	No exact equivalent but similar to Secretary General of a ministerial department

Country and House(s)	10.1 Title of the chief civil service officer of the House	10.2 Appointed by	10.3 Term of office/ age of retirement
REPUBLIC OF KOREA National Assembly	Secretary General	The Speaker, with approval of Parlt.	No provisions
ROMANIA Grand National Assembly	Director General	Bureau of the Assembly	Not fixed. Retirement in principle at 62.
RWANDA National Development Council (CND)	Secretary General (Secrétaire général)	Nominated by the CND Bureau; appointed by the President of the Republic.	Retirement at 55
ST VINCENT House of Assembly	Clerk of Parlt	Public Service Commission on recommendation of the Speaker	Retirement at 55 or 60 as requested
SENEGAL National Assembly	Secretary General	Appointed by the Bureau on nomination of the Assembly President	Not fixed. Retirement conditions the same as for public servants.
SOLOMON ISLANDS National Parliament	Clerk of Parliament	–	Retirement at 50
SOMALIA People's Assembly	Secretary General	He is a Member nominated by the Central Cttee of the Somali Socialist Revolutionary Party and elected by Parlt.	Term of Parlt (5 years).
SOUTH AFRICA House of Assembly House of Representatives House of Delegates	Secretary	The House on recommendation of the Cttees on Standing Rules and Orders	Retirement at 65

Functions and authority	Status vis-à-vis heads of govt departments
Assist the Speaker in legislative work; direct financial and administrative services; control all staff.	Equivalent to Govt Ministers
Direct the Assembly Secretariat in accordance with regulations approved by the Assembly	No provisions
Prepare and organise the administrative aspects of meetings; supervise CND staff and allocate work.	Equivalent to Head of a govt department
Act as Secretary to Parlt; administer financial and legislative procedural matters; supervise staff.	Same status as Head of a govt department
Provide advice on legal and procedural matters; supervise the Assembly administration and personnel; assist the President in the Bureau's work; liaise between the Bureau and the Assembly President; maintain liaison between the Assembly and external bodies.	Same as the most senior category of public servant
–	–
Maintain record of proceedings; draft parliamentary resolutions; prepare the budget; exercise supervision over staff and administration.	Same status as a Minister
Supply copies of Bills to Members prior to debate; certify and transmit passed Bills for approval; responsible for records of debates; regulate all matters concerning the business of the House; keep all House records and papers; communicate resolutions of the House to the Prime Minister; supervise staff under the direction of the Chairman; exercise financial control and maintain accounts.	Equivalent to Head of a govt department

TABLE 10: SECRETARY GENERAL OF THE HOUSE (continued)

Country and House(s)	10.1 Title of the chief civil service officer of the House	10.2 Appointed by	10.3 Term of office/ age of retirement
SPAIN Senate Congress of Deputies	Secretary General	Presiding Body of the House (see 9.1).	Retirement at 70
SRI LANKA Parliament	Secretary General	President of the Republic	Retirement at 60
SWEDEN Riksdag	Clerk of the Chamber (Kammarsekreterare).	Elected by the Riksdag	Term of Parlt (3 years).
SWITZERLAND States Council National Council	Secretary General of the Federal Assembly (Secrétaire général de l'Assemblée fédérale).	Federal Council, on proposal of the National Council Presidents' Conference and the States Council Bureau.	4 years, renewable.
SYRIAN ARAB REPUBLIC People's Council	Secretary General	President of the People's Council	Retirement at 60
THAILAND Senate House of Representatives	Secretary General	The King on proposal of the respective Speaker	Retirement at 60
TUNISIA Chamber of Deputies	Secretary General	Chamber President	Retirement at 60
UGANDA National Assembly	Clerk to the National Assembly	Head of State	Permanent, pensionable post (public service conditions).

384

10.4 Functions and authority	10.5 Status vis-à-vis heads of govt departments
Advise the Presiding Body, particularly the President, on technical and legal matters, and draft relevant reports; prepare minutes of Presiding Body meetings and execute its decisions; supervise House administration as chief of staff.	Equivalent to Head of a govt department
Responsible for records and documents; advise the Speaker on procedure, practice and privileges of Parlt; manage administrative and financial matters.	Equivalent to Secretary of a govt department
Head of the Chamber Secretariat. Keep minutes of sittings; issue notification of Riksdag decisions; assist the Speaker with the business of the Riksdag. (A Managing Director of the Office of Administration is responsible for overall supervision of administration and personnel.)	Lower than Heads of govt departments
Represent Parlt's services externally and coordinate their activity; assure relations with the media; advise on legal and technical matters related to Parlt; supervise the work of Parlt's Secretariat; assist the Presidents.	-
Supervise Council staff; monitor the application of the administrative and financial decisions of the Council.	-
Organise respective House and cttee sittings; invite temporary chairmen to perform their duties; assist the Chairman in scrutiny of votes; supervise minutes; confirm resolutions of the House to interested parties; keep all House documents; control all activities in conformity with Speaker's regulations. In addition, the Secretary General of the House of Representatives prepares the Parliamentary Budget and administers the Parliamentary Secretariat.	Equivalent to permanent Secretary of State
Liaise with MPs; manage the administrative, legislative support and financial affairs of the Chamber.	Equivalent to Head of a govt department
Responsible for records of debates and decisions, and custody of all records and papers; ensures application of rules of public access; in charge of administrative and financial matters.	Permanent Secretary status

Country and House(s)	10.1 Title of the chief civil service officer of the House	10.2 Appointed by	10.3 Term of office/ age of retirement
UNION OF SOVIET SOCIALIST REPUBLICS Soviet of Nationalities Soviet of the Union	Supervision of the administrative service (the apparatus of the Presidium of the Supreme Soviet) is exercised by the President of this Presidium.	Elected by the Members at a joint sitting (see 8.5).	Term of Parlt (5 years).
UNITED KINGDOM House of Lords	Clerk of the Parliaments	The Crown	Retirement at 65
House of Commons	Clerk of the House		Life (retirement customary at about 65).
UNITED REPUBLIC OF TANZANIA National Assembly	Clerk of the National Assembly	The President of the Republic	Retirement at 55, optional at 50.
UNITED STATES OF AMERICA Senate	Secretary of the Senate	Elected by the Senate on nomination by the majority party	Not fixed. Serves at the pleasure of the Senate.
House of Representatives	Clerk of the House	Elected by the House	Term of Congress (2 years).
VANUATU Parliament	Clerk of Parlt	The President of the Republic	Not specified
YUGOSLAVIA Federal Chamber Chamber of Republics and Provinces	Secretary General of the Assembly	Both Chambers of the Assembly	Not specified

10.4 Functions and authority	10.5 Status vis-à-vis heads of govt departments
Provide legal, organisational and technical services required for the operation of the Supreme Soviet, including the Presidium and all cttees.	–
Endorse all Bills sent or returned to the House of Commons; pronounce Royal Assent to Bills; responsible for accuracy of texts of Acts of Parlt and Measures; appoint and supervise staff as Head of the Parlt Office; act as House accountant; advise on order and procedure; safeguard the records of both Houses; act as Registrar for House judicial business.	Equivalent to Head of a govt department
Advise the House and the Speaker on procedure, practice and privileges; responsible for House accounting.	
Overall administrative functions; custody of records and documents.	Same status as Head of a govt department
Assist in the legislative work; sign official documents; keep records and other documents; administer financial matters; direct the administrative services.	There are no comparable positions in govt departments.
As above; also preside over 1st sitting until Speaker elected.	
Provide general administration; submit Bills passed to the Presidency of the Socialist Federal Republic for assent; responsible for parliamentary records.	Equivalent to head of a govt department
Regulate the internal organisation of Assembly services; administer staff matters; procure office furniture, material, etc.	Same status as head of a federal administrative organ

TABLE 10: SECRETARY GENERAL OF THE HOUSE (continued)

Country and House(s)	10.1 Title of the chief civil service officer of the House	10.2 Appointed by	10.3 Term of office/ age of retirement
ZAIRE Legislative Council	Secretary General (Secrétaire Général)	The President of the Republic on proposal of the Council President	Term of office unspecified. Retirement at 55.
ZAMBIA National Assembly	Clerk	The Speaker, on resolution of the House.	Retirement at 55
ZIMBABWE Senate House of Assembly	Secretary to Parliament	The Speaker in consultation with President of the Senate and approval of House of Assembly	Retirement at 65, maximum (optional at 55).

Supervise the Council administrative staff and manage administrative matters.	Status of a senior public servant
Scrutinise and check all Bills during their passage; control parliamentary finances; discharge responsibility as administrative head.	Above level of Permanent Secretary
Oversee printing and processing of all legislation up to Act stage; responsible for accounting, administration and personnel.	Equal rank with heads of govt departments but with more secure tenure

TABLE 11

ORGANISATION OF BUSINESS

The organisation of business is of vital concern to the work of Parliament. The part played by the body which draws up the order of business is of fundamental importance, as are the provisions which govern it in its work, whether deriving from the Constitution, the rules of procedure, or practice, because they affect the control and the efficiency of parliamentary business. If the order of business is decided by the Government, awkward topics can easily be disposed of, and the Government may adopt a dictatorial attitude towards Parliament. Conversely, the order of business may be decided by Parliament itself, especially if the Government's representatives are not in the House. This may seem equally questionable if it is accepted that the work of legislation is valid only if it is directed by the Government or if it is considered that the Government should be able to decide when Parliament shall consider the measures it introduces. Though the scale of legislation in the modern world is an argument in its favour, such a prerogative is at variance with the old-established democratic principle that Parliament is the master of its own order of business. The difficulty is to find a compromise which will safeguard the independence of Parliament and, at the same time, provide the necessary powers to enable the Government to govern. Few systems appear to meet fully both of these conditions.

In theory, either the Government enjoys an almost absolute right to control the order of business, or Parliament has the right to choose what matters it will deal with. Between these extremes, some measure of consultation between the various parties and a disposition to compromise will have to be worked out, if serious crises in the relationship between the Legislature and the Executive are to be avoided. In practice, as Table 11A reveals, the order of business is settled by either the Government, if its representatives are in the House; by Parliament itself; by the directing authority of the House; by one of its official bodies; or by a special group. This group may comprise party leaders or the directing authority in consultation with other leaders such as committee chairmen. Sometimes certain guidelines for priorities are laid down in the standing orders. In Canada and the United Kingdom, among others, the powers of the Government are exercised through the Leader of the House and the Chief Whip, who arrange the order of business of the House after consultation with leaders of the opposition parties and other Members. In India, a similar system is found. The Speaker arranges the order of business in consultation with the Leader of the House. Ten countries (including Brazil, Italy, Kenya, Philippines and Somalia) set up a special committee or other body to establish the order of business.

While it is generally the practice to consult the Opposition, there is no formal obligation to do this, and the power of the Executive over the programme of parliamentary business is absolute, even though special

TABLE 11A. Establishment of Order of Business
(Popular House)

Order of Business Drawn up by	Number of Countries
Government	12
Parliament	12
Directing Authority	22
Directing Authority with Other Leaders	11
Presidents' Conference	9
Special Committee	10
Party Leaders	3
Secretariat	4
Total	83

provisions are made for both the Opposition and for individual Members to debate topics of their own choice on certain days. Although in theory a majority party or Government could take over all of the time set aside for debate, in practice this is never done. This system gives the Government considerable powers over the House, while at the same time provisions are made for the official Opposition and for individual Members to debate topics of their choice or bring up matters of current public important that might arise from time to time.

Role of Presidents' Conference and the Directing Authority

In most countries Parliament or one of its bodies determines its programme of work. In twelve countries (which include France, Senegal and Sweden) this task is entrusted to a Presidents' Conference, a body which usually consists of the chairmen of committees and leaders of the political groups. The role of the Presidents' Conference is to consider requests made by the Government and by committees and, on the basis of these, to work out the order of business for Parliament. In a majority of countries the arrangement of Parliament's business is placed in the hands of the directing authority. This arrangement contains a certain amount of flexibility, for, as the Speaker or President has to discharge his duties impartially, the management of business is treated as a technical rather than a political operation, and it is possible for him to take into account the requests of the Government and to ensure a priority for them which is not given by any written rule.

Role of Government

The influence of the Government in drawing up the order of business is difficult to evaluate, although examples of a number of practices can be noted:

- in Ireland, New Zealand and Vanuatu, the Government determines the parliamentary timetable and decides the order and timing in which it will bring its measures before the House;

- in a number of countries the Government's influence comes through membership of the Presidents' Conference, membership which usually provides it with a numerical majority so that it plays a very large part in determining the order of business;

- in Cameroon, Egypt and Somalia, although the Government does not draw up the order of business, its measures are given priority in the timetable when they are presented to Parliament;

- in the Federal Republic of Germany, Italy and Senegal, the Government may send a representative to the body which establishes the order of business; and

- in India, Monaco, Spain and Zambia, the Government is consulted when the order of business is prepared.

Role of Opposition Groups

It can be seen from the discussion so far that it is usual for the Government to play a major role in arranging parliamentary business. The role of opposition parties in this matter is, as would be expected, correspondingly smaller. In a number of countries, the Opposition's influence is limited to membership of the Presidents' Conference. The role of the individual Member in determining the order of business is even more limited, although in Australia, Belgium, Costa Rica, Ivory Coast, Romania and Somalia, for example, Members may propose formal motions to make changes in the agenda. In certain countries (for example Brazil, Canada, Fiji, Malta and the United Kingdom), special periods are set aside for individual Members to debate topics of their own choosing, and in several countries special days (Supply Days) are set aside for the official Opposition to decide what the House will debate.

Advance Timetabling

The purpose of preparing an order of business, whether it gives the Government the upper hand or confirms the traditional independence of Parliament, is to deal with one of the main obstacles to the working of Parliament today which is the shortage of time. The practice of settling the order of business for a fairly long period in advance makes it possible to organise the work of Parliament methodically and gives a certain stability and continuity to its proceedings. How far in advance a parliamentary timetable is set depends on the number and length of sessions. In the socialist countries the short length of the sessions makes it possible to determine the timetable for each session. In other countries the usual practice is for the timetable to be set about one week in advance. Often the timetable will refer to the details of debates and other matters, and the general legislative timetable will have been announced at the opening of the session.

Private Members' Business

In several Parliaments a special time is fixed for the discussion of Private Members' Business. Such provisions serve partially to redress the relationship between the Executive and Members of Parliament in the legislative process. In Australia, Canada, Lebanon, Mauritius,

Netherlands, South Africa, Sri Lanka and Switzerland, Members' Bills have precedence over Government legislation on certain hours or days of each week.   In India, two-and-a-half hours on Fridays are allotted for the consideration of Private Members' Bills.   In the United Kingdom, twenty Fridays and four other half days in each session are given over to their consideration.   In Canada, Fiji, New Zealand, Solomon Islands, Uganda, Zambia and Zimbabwe private Members' business is given priority one day per week.   In Ireland priority is granted for one and a half hours twice a week and in Malta on alternate Thursdays.

Standing Orders make provision for Private Members' Business in, for example, Brazil, Malawi, Sweden, and the United States of America, whilst in fifteen countries, including Austria, Costa Rica, Israel, Mongolia, Tunisia, Spain and USSR, Private Members' Business is taken into account when the parliamentary agenda is being drawn up.

TABLE 11: ORGANISATION OF BUSINESS

Country and House(s)	Work Programme	
	11.1 Proposed by	11.2 Form and timing
ALGERIA National People's Assembly (APN)	The APN Bureau (see 7.5), in consultation with the cttee chairmen and in agreement with the Govt, taking account of Govt priorities.	Posting on notice board and communication to Members and the Govt at least 15 days before the session opens.
ARGENTINA Senate	President	–
Chamber of Deputies	Cttee on Parliamentary Work	Meetings once a week
AUSTRALIA Senate House of Representatives	Determined under the SO.	Established in the course of a parliamentary sitting day, and placed in order on the Notice Paper.
AUSTRIA Federal Council National Council	Respective Presidents' Conference (see 9.1).	The business is proposed, and the priority settled by the respective Presidents' Conference, prior to a sitting.
BAHAMAS Senate House of Assembly	Government	Proposed by notices, at end of each meeting.

Order/priority of business		Order of the day
11.3 How settled and by whom	11.4 When or at what stage	11.5 a) Fixed requirements under the rules b) Opposition/Private MPs' business
See 11.1	See 11.2	a) - b) -
See 11.1 but priority order may be modified by House.	At any time during the sitting	a) Corrections, if needed, of the verbatim record; reading or mention of messages received from the Executive; other documents received; referral of documents to cttees; tributes proposed by MPs; consideration of order of the day; requests and proposals of MPs and agreement of revised order of the day b) No special provisions
While Govt business accorded some priority under the SO, order of priority is ultimately within the capacity of the relevant House to determine.	See 11.3	a) Detailed in SO, including petitions; notices; questions and Govt business b) SO specifiy times for considering opposition and private MPs' business
Respective Presidents' Conference	At any time during the sittings	a) Detailed in SO b) Agreed by the relevant Presidents' Conference as appropriate
Settled by Speaker, Leader of House and Opposition Leader.	According to need if no notice given	a) Notices of motion b) No specific provisions

TABLE 11: ORGANISATION OF BUSINESS (continued)

| | Work Programme | |
Country and House(s)	11.1 Proposed by	11.2 Form and timing
BELGIUM Senate	President, after consult-ation with the Parliament-ary Work Cttee. Programme may be modified later by plenary.	Houses usually agree the programme each Thursday for the following week.
Chamber of Representatives	President, after consultation with President's Conference (President and Vice-President, former Presidents, Leader and one member of each political group).	
BRAZIL Federal Senate Chamber of Deputies	Presiding Officer, assisted by Secretary General.	Published daily schedule
BULGARIA National Assembly	Assembly President in consultation with State Council and Council of Ministers	Sessional agenda approved by the Assembly at each session, within the framework of an annual parliamentary programme.
CAMEROON National Assembly	President's Conference comprising members of the Assembly Bureau (see 9.1) 5 cttee chairmen and Leaders of groups (parties).	Agenda (including Bills introduced) compiled as soon as sufficient business to hand to distribute to cttees.

Order/priority of business		Order of the day
11.3 How settled and by whom	11.4 When or at what stage	11.5 a) Fixed requirements under the rules b) Opposition/Private MPs' business
Parliamentary Work Cttee President's Conference	At the beginning of each sitting, plenary approves or modifies order of business.	a) No specific provisions, except for oral questions b) No specific provisions
House Boards by "first ready Bill" order, except on request under SO from party Leaders.	After report by cttees for most Bills. Exceptions concern priority requests from the Executive or Leader's request, subject to floor voting.	a) Questions, postponement of voting b) Agreement between party Leaders on allocation of time; SO provide for minorities
By Parliament	At session start	a) Determined by sessional agenda b) No special provisions
President's Conference taking into account Govt priorities	During first week of session	a) One sitting per week is devoted to oral questions at the initiative of the Presidents' Conference b) Incorporated in the business agenda

TABLE 11: ORGANISATION OF BUSINESS (continued)

	Work Programme	
Country and House(s)	11.1 Proposed by	11.2 Form and timing
CANADA Senate	The Govt in consultation with Opposition Leader within the framework of Rules concerning order of business	Broadly at the beginning of the session (Speech from the Throne). Detail provided in week-to-week planning.
House of Commons	Govt through the House Leader in cooperation with the Party Whip. Opposition leaders are consulted.	
CAPE VERDE People's National Assembly	Permanent Bureau (see 9.1).	–
CHINA National People's Congress (NPC)	The NPC Standing Committee	NPC preparatory plenary meeting
COMOROS Federal Assembly	President of Republic in a letter to the President of Assembly, covering draft Bills.	Presented as a Bill, during session.

Order/priority of business		Order of the day
11.3 How settled and by whom	11.4 When or at what stage	11.5 a) Fixed requirements under the rules b) Opposition/Private MPs' business
Rules of the Senate	Business for the coming week announced each Thursday	a) Detailed in SO including petitions; cttee reports; notices of motion; questions; Senate business b) No specific provisions, but private Members requirements always respected by mutual agreement
SO. Govt business decided by conference of party leaders.		a) Detailed in SO including cttee reports; notices of motion; Govt Bills; private Bills; ministerial statements; tabling of papers; questions b) SO also provide for the consideration of Opposition business. They also stipulate a period every Wednesday for private Members' business
Permanent Bureau	At the adoption of order of the day	a) – b) Any Member may advance topics for debate or propose motions
Presidium	Before the sessions opens	a) – b) NA
By Presidents' Conference comprising President of the ·Assembly and cttee chairmen	At beginning of session, after the opening sitting.	a) Members' Bills must be submitted to Govt scrutiny prior to cttee examination b) –

	Work Programme	
Country and House(s)	11.1 Proposed by	11.2 Form and timing
CONGO People's National Assembly (ANP)	Presidents' Conference	Form of an order of the day a week in advance
COSTA RICA Legislative Assembly	Secretariat of the Assembly	-
CUBA National Assembly of People's Power	President of the National Assembly	The President of the National Assembly distributes a draft for comment several months in advance
CYPRUS House of Representatives	President of the House	Time, date and agenda are announced at the end of the preceding session
CZECHOSLOVAKIA Chamber of Nations	The respective Presidium (see 9.1).	An annual plan of activity submitted 6 months in advance
Chamber of the People		
DEMOCRATIC YEMEN Supreme People's Council	Presidium Council (see 9.1).	Resolution of the Presidium at the start of each year
DENMARK Folketing	President	Announcement and/or distribution of printed order for the next session at the end of the preceding session

Order/priority of business		Order of the day
11.3 How settled and by whom	11.4 When or at what stage	11.5 a) Fixed requirements under the rules b) Opposition/Private MPs' business
Presidents' Conference	–	a) As under 11.2, except that Const. provides for MPs and Govt to request consideration or urgent matters; requests determined by simple majority of ANP b) –
2/3 majority of the Assembly	–	a) Exclusive prerogative of the Assembly b) All Members may influence the incorporation of business
By agreement of the National Assembly or the President in consultation with the Standing Cttees	A draft agenda is distributed at least 20 days before the session begins.	a) None b) No time limit for private business introduced by Members
President of the House	At the end of each meeting	a) Legislative work; introduction of Bills and documents; questions; matters entered into debate b) None
The respective Presidium	–	a) None b) –
By the Presidium	Before convening a session	a) At Council's discretion b) –
President usually after consultation with chairman of political group	Last sitting day of each week	a) Only first sitting of each sessional year or after a general election b) No specific provisions

Country and House(s)	Work Programme	
	11.1 Proposed by	11.2 Form and timing
EGYPT People's Assembly	Assembly Bureau (see 9.1).	Plan of action at the start of every ordinary session
FIJI Senate	Business Standing Cttee, without prejudice to powers of the President.	2 to 4 weeks in advance
House of Representatives	Business Cttee comprising Prime Minister, Leader of Opposition and 3 other Members, without prejudice to the powers of the President.	
FINLAND Eduskunta	Speaker's Conference (see 9.1).	The Speaker's Conference meets before every plenary sitting.
FRANCE Senate	The Presidents' Conference comprising President and Vice-Presidents of the respective House, cttee chairmen and group leaders, taking account of Govt priorities.	A Govt representative attends the Presidents' Conference, usually held weekly during sessions, to put forward a work programme for which he requests priority. The Presidents' Conference takes this into account when proposing the parliamentary work programme which is drawn up for the coming week or fortnight.
National Assembly		
GABON National Assembly	Govt and President of Assembly	After consideration by Council of Ministers, in form of Bills and Ordinances.

Order/priority of business		Order of the day
11.3 How settled and by whom	11.4 When or at what stage	11.5 a) Fixed requirements under the rules b) Opposition/Private MPs' business
By agreement on an agenda giving priority to Govt Bills and general and current issues	Prior to each sitting	a) Absences of Members; approval of previous minutes; messages to the Assembly; agenda items b) Special meeting at request of Speaker, a party representative or at least 20 MPs
At meetings and by collective agreement	Each day	a) Prayers; confirmation of minutes; petitions; papers and reports; questions; statements by Ministers; matters of privilege; reading of Bills; Govt motions; private Members' motions b) Takes precedence in the Senate on Wednesdays and in the House of Representatives on Fridays
The Speaker's Conference	Several days in advance of each session	a) Question hour for oral questions b) No special arrangements
Priorities fixed by the Govt cannot be modified except by the Govt, but other matters may be altered by cttee initiative or 30 Senators.	Two weeks before the first sitting of a session, subsequently one week in advance.	a) SO give priority to oral questions on Fridays or Tuesdays as decided by the Presidents' Conference. In principle, priority is given to cttee work on Wednesdays b) -
The Assembly takes note of Govt priorities and passes a resolution on complementary matters proposed by the Presidents' Conference.		a) SO; Wednesday or Friday afternoons for questions as determined by the Presidents' Conference. One morning each week is reserved for cttee activities b) -
In order of receipt of Bills and ordinances by the Secretary-General	At stage of considering cttee work schedule after consulting cttee	a) - b) -

| Country and House(s) | Work Programme | |
	11.1 Proposed by	11.2 Form and timing
GERMAN DEMOCRATIC REPUBLIC People's Chamber	Presidium (see 9.1).	List of agenda items in printed form
GERMANY Federal Council	Director establishes a draft order of the day	6 days before a sitting
Federal Diet	Council of Elders (attended by a Govt representative).	Orally in the Council of Elders, one week in advance.
GREECE Chamber of Deputies	President of the Chamber in consultation with the Govt, and assisted by the Bureau.	As an Order of Business for the week by Friday of the preceding week. It has 2 parts: legislative activity and parliamentary control.
HUNGARY National Assembly	-	-
INDIA Council of States House of the People	The Govt, coordinated by the Govt Department of Parliamentary Affairs.	Preliminary statement before session starts, then 2 to 3 days in advance for inclusion in List of Business.
INDONESIA House of Representatives	Steering Cttee comprising 66 Members (Factions: Armed Forces 11; Development Functional 37; Democratic Party 4; Development Unity 14).	Advance time-table at session start

Order/priority of business		Order of the day
11.3 How settled and by whom	11.4 When or at what stage	11.5 a) Fixed requirements under the rules b) Opposition/Private MPs' business
Proposed by Presidium and decided by the Chamber	At the preparatory stage	a) Obituaries are read before opening the agenda b) NA
By the Federal Council	Before debates open.	a) Questions from the States followed by Bills usually before other matters b) NA
By unanimous agreement of the Council of Elders	One week in advance	a) Weekly 3 hour question time included in agenda b) A parliamentary group or 26 MPs may request debate on any matter
See 11.1.	As Bills come forward they can be included in the Order of Business with priority determined by the President with Govt agreement, except for priorities fixed by SO	a) Priority for Bills approving legislation from the Executive; Bills returned by the President of the Republic for reconsideration; amdts to SO b) –
National Assembly on proposal of the President of the Assembly	Proposed before the start of each session	a) SO provide for Parlt to establish the date and agenda of individual meetings at each meeting b) –
The Govt		
The Speaker after consultation with the Leader of the House	At the last sitting of the week for the following week	a) Detailed in SO including messages from the President; questions; notice of motion; matters of urgent public importance b) Usually at least 2 1/2 hours on Fridays unless otherwise directed
Steering Cttee	When agenda fixed	a) None b) Time is provided in the agenda for Faction business

Country and House(s)	Work Programme	
	11.1 Proposed by	11.2 Form and timing
IRELAND Senate	Leader of the House	As and when proposed by Leader of the House
Dáil	Govt business proposed by the Prime Minister. MPs' business through SO and practice.	Govt business announced daily by the Prime Minister in the House. Private business determined by SO and practice.
ISRAEL The Knesset	By the Govt for 2 of 3 weekly sittings. For the 3rd sitting by the Chairman and Vice-Chairman acting collegially.	2 weekly sittings usually devoted to Govt business; remaining sitting is the "Members' Day". Bills must be submitted at least 2 days before 1st reading.
ITALY Senate Chamber of Deputies	Programme and calendar adopted by the Panel of Parliamentary Group Chairmen, comprising the Chairmen of Parliamentary Groups (see 19.1), chaired by the President of the Senate or the Chamber, and attended by a Govt representative.	When the Panel of Group Chairmen is unanimous, the programme is valid for not more than 3 months in the Chamber (2 months in the Senate), otherwise not more than 2 months. Final approval rests with Parlt which may debate and vote the programme when presented.
IVORY COAST National Assembly	Presidents' Conference comprising the President and 8 Vice-Presidents of the Assembly, group chairmen, cttee chairmen.	At the beginning of each session

Order/priority of business		Order of the day
11.3 How settled and by whom	11.4 When or at what stage	11.5 a) Fixed requirements under the rules b) Opposition/Private MPs' business
By the House	At the start of Public Business each sitting day	a) Decided each day at start of sitting against a printed order paper b) None, but Senators may raise matters on the daily adjournment motion
By Government in consultation with Opposition Whips		a) Questions; private business; cttee reports; Senate messages; Bills from the Senate; initiation of Bills; notices of motion; orders of the day b) 1 1/2 hours twice a week
By the Chairman on Govt days; by the Chairman and the Vice-Chairman collegially on Members' days.	In the early afternoon of Monday for sittings in the same week	a) Precedence for Govt statements, urgent Members' motions and con- sequent debate. No-confidence motions precede all but Govt sta- tements. A Govt statement may be made at any time, and may be debated 24 hours later on request of 30 Members b) The division between Govt and Members' days is flexible with the Chairman and Vice-Chairmen making accommodation as necessary
By unanimity of the Panel of Group Chairmen other- wise debated and approved by Parlt on proposal presented by the President.	Order of business covers a period not exceeding 2 weeks.	a) Declarations of urgent Bills; referral of Bills to cttees; ques- tions and interpellations; legislative matters b) Private Bills
The Assembly may modify the proposals of the Presidents' Conference.	At the beginning of each session	a) Order of the day is required for each sitting b) NA

	Work Programme	
Country and House(s)	11.1 Proposed by	11.2 Form and timing
JAPAN House of Councillors	-	-
House of Representatives		
JORDAN Senate	Presiding Officer in cooperation with the	Before each session
House of Deputies	Secretary-General	
KENYA National Assembly	Business Advisory Cttee	Weekly basis
KUWAIT National Assembly	President of the Assembly according to SO	Items arranged by subject according to SO
LEBANON National Assembly	Assembly President, who chairs the Assembly's Bureau.	At the beginning of each session
LIECHTENSTEIN Diet	Govt and Members through motions	In writing 3 to 4 weeks before session
LUXEMBOURG Chamber of Deputies	Chamber President in consultation with the Business Cttee (see 9.1)	Orders of the Day. The 1st is published at session start, then at 3 to 4 month intervals.

Order/priority of business		Order of the day
11.3 How settled and by whom	11.4 When or at what stage	11.5 a) Fixed requirements under the rules b) Opposition/Private MPs' business
Presiding Officer	The day before the sitting	a) Date and time of sitting; measures and matters for consideration and their order b) -
Presiding Officer and the Secretary- General	-	a) - . b) -
Sessional cttee of from 5 to 20 MPs	Daily basis	a) Oaths; communications from the chair; petitions; papers; notices of motion; questions; business as set down on order paper b) Maximum of 2 hours for a Member's Motion
President of the Assembly upon draft prepared by Secretary- General	At least 48 hours before sitting	a) Approval of minutes; petitions; messages and papers; questions; Bills; Members' motions; urgent matters b) NA
Assembly President and Bureau	-	a) Obituaries; special sitting for questions b) Special sitting devoted to Members' business
Calendar esta- blished by the President in consultation with political fractions; priorities deter- mined by the President.	Calendar fixed at the start of each session period and priorities after convening each sitting	a) Swearing new MPs; obituaries; and changes to the order of the day before debates b) Written motions must be pre- sented to the President before each convocation for inclusion in the order of the day
Chamber Presi- sident in consul- tation with the Business Cttee and the Clerk	See 11.2. Govt priorities are taken into account.	a) Obituaries; President's address and oaths; messages from the President and the Govt; questions, Bills b) Opportunity is provided by SO in the normal course of business

Country and House(s)	Work Programme	
	11.1 Proposed by	11.2 Form and timing
MALAWI National Assembly	-	-
MALAYSIA Senate House of Representatives	Clerk of the respective House in consultation with the Presiding Officer	At a meeting with the Cabinet before the sessions opens.
MALI National Assembly	Presidents' Conference (see 9.1).	Order of the day
MALTA House of Representatives	The Govt, through the Minister of Justice and Parliamentary Affairs, who is Leader of the House.	In the form of motions and Orders of the Day
MAURITIUS Legislative Assembly	The Govt for govt business and the Speaker for private Members' business	Pronounced by the Governor General at the start of each session and distributed to Members

Order/priority of business		Order of the day
11.3 How settled and by whom	11.4 When or at what stage	11.5 a) Fixed requirements under the rules b) Opposition/Private MPs' business
Clerk of the Assembly at the direction of the Speaker	Before each sitting	a) Oaths; messages from the President, from the Chair; presentation of petitions, papers; questions on notice; statements by Ministers; personal explanations; matters of urgent public importance; Govt business; private Members' business b) SO provide for private Members' business
By the Prime Minister and Cabinet at the meeting held in 11.2	Before the session starts.	a) Detailed in SO including: Royal messages; Speaker's announcements; petitions; questions; matters of urgent public importance; ministerial statements; personal explanations; Govt Bills; public business b) Considered after Govt business which has priority
Secretary General	Immediately after the Presidents' Conference	–
Minister of Justice and Parliamentary Affairs taking account of priorities in SO	Not later than adjournment of the previous sitting (items may be added given 3 days notice).	a) Prayers; minutes of the previous sitting; obituaries (customary); oaths; petitions; questions; presentation of papers and cttee reports; adjournment on a matter of definite, urgent, public importance; motions by Ministers, for cttee appointments and leave to introduce Bills; Orders of the Day and notices of motions b) SO provide for private Members' business to take precedence on alternate Thursdays
Speaker after consultation with the Leader of the House	At least 3 days before the sitting	a) Yes b) 2 or 3 sittings in a session of about 30 sittings

| | Work Programme | |
Country and House(s)	11.1 Proposed by	11.2 Form and timing
MEXICO Chamber of Senators	Bills and proposals received between sessions are scheduled for action by the Permanent Cttee.	Before the session starts.
Chamber of Deputies		
MONACO National Council	-	-
MONGOLIA Great People's Khural (GPKh)	GPKh Presidium comprising GPKh Presidium Chairman, Vice-Chairmen, Secretary and Members.	Long-term plan adopted at the beginning of each year
NAURU Parliament	President; Ministers; and Members.	As a list of matters for attention
NETHERLANDS First Chamber	The President of the Chamber with advice of the College of Senioren, comprising leaders of the political groups.	The President drafts an agenda sent to Members before the sitting.
Second Chamber	The Chair, or by individual Members supported by 4 other Members present.	Orally at the start of the 1st day of the weekly sitting, then usually every subsequent day after the lunch break.

Order/priority of business		Order of the day
11.3 How settled and by whom	11.4 When or at what stage	11.5 a) Fixed requirements under the rules b) Opposition/Private MPs' business
Determined under the SO	From one sitting to another	a) – b) –
National Council Bureau and Chairmen of per- manent cttees in consultation with the Minister of State	3 days in advance	At least every other sitting must be devoted to Bills submitted by the Prince. Questions must be shown in detail.
–	–	a) Statements; written questions b) There is a common order of business
According to SO with priority of govt business determined by Ministers	–	a) Yes b) No specific provisions
The President, unless otherwise decided by the Chamber.	At the meeting, where the Presi- dent informs the Chamber of his decision.	a) None b) None
The Chamber, if necessary, by simple majority.	When proposed, unless further consultations are desirable and the matter is not urgent.	a) The Chamber fixes at the start of each session the days and hours for oral questions b) Time is allocated proportional to respective group strength

TABLE 11: ORGANISATION OF BUSINESS (continued)

| | Work Programme | |
| | 11.1 | 11.2 |
Country and House(s)	Proposed by	Form and timing
NEW ZEALAND House of Representatives	General order of business specified in SO. Order of items in each category determined chronologically or, in the case of govt business, by the leader of the Govt in the House.	Published in an Order Paper
NICARAGUA National Assembly	National Assembly Directive Board	Each session
NORWAY Storting	Secretary General	Submitted every Thursday to the weekly Presidium meeting
PHILIPPINES National Assembly	Cttee on Rules (see 7.4).	Calender of Business distributed to Members with the Order of Business during sessions
POLAND Diet	Diet Bureau in agreement with the Council of Sages (see 8.4) and after consultation with the Govt.	Order of the Day in writing 1 week before the sitting
PORTUGAL Assembly of the Republic	President's Conference comprising the Assembly President, Group Chairmen, and representatives of parties not forming a group.	At meetings of the President's Conference

Order/priority of business		Order of the day
11.3 How settled and by whom	11.4 When or at what stage	11.5 a) Fixed requirements under the rules b) Opposition/Private MPs' business
Notified on the Order Paper in accordance with Leader of Govt's directions	Order Paper subject to revision up to 3 hours before a sitting	a) Prayers; private business; petitions; presentation of papers; notices of motion; unopposed motions for return; questions for oral answer; consideration of ministerial replies; leave to introduce Bills; cttee reports and associated debates; consideration of papers; other matters on the Order Paper b) Has priority on Wednesdays
The Directive Board	In a meeting before each sitting	a) National Hymn; day's agenda; last session's notes b) No specific provisions
The Presidium (see 9.1).	On Thursdays for the coming week, except Budget matters which require longer preparation.	a) Question time normally every Wednesday b) No specific provisions
By the Cttee on Rules through the Majority Floor Leader and approved by the Assembly	The sitting day prior to consideration of the business	a) As moved by the Majority Floor Leader and approved by the Assembly b) No specific provisions
Adopted by the Diet	Start of the sitting	a) None b) No special provisions
Priority is specified in SO but the Govt may request urgent consideration, in the national interest, of particular matters.	At the end of each sitting	a) Before the Order of the Day: messages; Members' statements on matters of political interest; congratulations; greetings; personal explanations. Order of the Day: legislative and other business specified in the Const. b) Each session, govt group, non-govt group and non-affiliated MP may prepare the Order of the Day for 4, 6 and 2 sittings respectively

TABLE 11: ORGANISATION OF BUSINESS (continued)

| | Work Programme | |
Country and House(s)	11.1 Proposed by	11.2 Form and timing
REPUBLIC OF KOREA National Assembly	The Speaker, in consultation with the Secretary General.	Proposals submitted for Assembly approval at least the day before or immediately after opening a session.
ROMANIA Grand National Assembly	Assembly Bureau (see 9.1).	Proposals submitted for Assembly's approval after consideration of priorities (see 11.3 and 11.4).
RWANDA National Development Council (CND)	CND Bureau comprising the CND President, Vice-President and Secretary.	At each session start as a submission to the CND
ST VINCENT House of Assembly	Government	According to need
SENEGAL National Assembly	Presidents' Conference comprising Assembly President and Vice-Presidents, cttee chairmen, General Rapporteur of Financial and Economic Affairs Cttee, group chairmen, the 2 general secretaries and a representative of the President of the Republic.	Before each session
SOLOMON ISLANDS National Parliament	The Speaker, with assistance of the Clerk of Parlt.	-
SOMALIA People's Assembly	The Standing Cttee	10 days before the session

Order/priority of business		Order of the day
11.3 How settled and by whom	11.4 When or at what stage	11.5 a) Fixed requirements under the rules b) Opposition/Private MPs' business
The Speaker, in consultation with the House Steering Cttee.	At the 1st plenary sitting	a) The Speaker must prepare and report agenda to the plenary session no later than the day preceding the date of opening the plenary session concerned b) No specific provisions
Priority proposals prepared by the Bureau and submitted to the Assembly for approval	At the 1st sitting of the session	a) Approval of previous summary minutes (except secret sittings); messages; questions; notice of interpellations; motions to alter priorities; business of the day b) No specific provisions
CND, on proposal of the President.	At the start of each sitting	a) An agenda is fixed for each sitting which may be rearranged by the CND b) –
Clerk of Parlt	The day before a sitting	a) The House should sit at least once a month b) Any matter of urgent importance may be raised by any Member to receive full debate
National Assembly on proposal of the Presidents' Conference	–	–
The Speaker, with assistance of the Clerk of Parlt.	–	a) – b) Every Friday during session
The Standing Cttee (see 8.4) on priorities from the Govt, given at the opening ceremony.	Debated by the Members and approved prior to adoption	a) – b) NA (see 19.1)

| | Work Programme | |
| | 11.1 | 11.2 |
Country and House(s)	Proposed by	Form and timing
SOUTH AFRICA House of Assembly House of Representatives House of Delegates	Govt and, to a lesser extent, the Members.	Order Paper which is arranged from day to day.
SPAIN Senate Congress of Deputies	Presiding Body (see 9.1), in consultation with the Council of Spokesmen, comprising spokesmen of the parliamentary groups.	-
SRI LANKA Parliament	Government, through Leader of the House who consults other parties as necessary.	One week in advance
SWEDEN Riksdag	Speaker's Conference, comprising Speaker, Deputy Speakers, representative of each party group, cttee chairmen, Vice-Chairman of Board of Administration of the Riksdag.	A preliminary programme is drawn up at session start in October and again in January after the Christmas recess.

Order/priority of business		Order of the day
11.3 How settled and by whom	11.4 When or at what stage	11.5 a) Fixed requirements under the rules b) Opposition/Private MPs' business
Chief Whip of Parlt in consultation with Leader of the House can arrange Govt business as he thinks fit.	Fixed from day to day by Chief Whip and Leader of the House with assistance from the various party Whips at a weekly meeting. Important debates announced at start of each week.	a) Motions concerning House privileges take precedence over other motions and orders of day b) Private Members' business has precedence at the times determined by the Leader of the House in consultation with the various party Whips
By the respective House President in agreement with the Council of Spokesmen (see 11.1) and considering Govt priorities.	–	a) – b) See 11.3, also 2 hours per week for questions, interpellations and opposition or private business
–	–	a) Oaths; messages from the President; Speaker's announcement; papers; reports; questions; condolences; leave of absence; ministerial statements; personal explanations; privilege; motions not requiring notice; motions requiring notice; public business b) Precedence on 1st Friday of each month
Speaker's Conference	The programme is revised during the session as required and the agenda distributed. Minor matters are agreed at the beginning or end of each sitting day.	a) Elections; Govt Bills and communications; proposals and reports from Riksdag organs other than cttees; private Members' Bills; cttee reports. Questions and interpellations on Mondays, Tuesdays, Thursdays and Fridays; Bills, amdts, etc., on Wednesdays and Thursdays (a new, somewhat modified agenda is being tried 1985/86) b) See a) above

	Work Programme	
Country and House(s)	11.1 Proposed by	11.2 Form and timing
SWITZERLAND States Council	Group Presidents' Conference (see 9.1), in consultation with the States Council Bureau (coordination conference).	Dates, probable duration of sessions and preliminary programme is established in May for the following civil year. The preliminary programme for each session is amended as work progresses.
National Council		
SYRIAN ARAB REPUBLIC People's Council	Bureau of the Council	At the start of each session
THAILAND Senate	Secretary General of the National Assembly with approval of the Speaker of each House for separate sittings, and of the President of the National Assembly for joint sittings.	Established when the House is in session as an agenda.
House of Representatives		
TUNISIA Chamber of Deputies	Chamber Bureau, comprising the President, 2 Vice-Presidents, cttee chairmen and rapporteurs.	Draft agenda once each week
UGANDA National Assembly	Government	Bills, motions, etc., presented at the start of, or during, a session.

Order/priority of business		Order of the day
11.3 How settled and by whom	11.4 When or at what stage	11.5 a) Fixed requirements under the rules b) Opposition/Private MPs' business
Coordination Conference (see 11.1).	Before each session and at the end of each sitting for the subsequent sitting	a) Obituaries; oaths; question time at the start of the 2nd and 3rd weeks b) The last day of session is reserved for private Members' business
–	Activities take place according to an agenda fixed in advance.	a) – b) –
Speaker of each House in accordance with Rules of Procedure	Not less than 3 days in advance unless considered urgent by the Speaker	a) Chairman's announcements; approval of minutes; questions to Ministers; matters examined by cttees; matters awaiting consideration; matters newly presented; any other matters b) No provisions
Chamber approves a draft prepared by the Bureau. Govt business and cttee reports may be added. The President of the Republic may request priority items.	Before each sitting	a) By agreement between the Chamber President and the Govt b) Members' business is submitted in writing to the Chamber Presi- dent who includes it in the agenda and/or refers it to cttees as appropriate
Govt in order of urgency or priority	Through the whips at the start of, or during, a session.	a) Detailed in SO including pet- itions; questions; papers and reports; public business b) Has priority on Fridays; also can move motions on adjournment (30-minute debates)

TABLE 11: ORGANISATION OF BUSINESS (continued)

| | Work Programme | |
Country and House(s)	11.1 Proposed by	11.2 Form and timing
UNION OF SOVIET SOCIALIST REPUBLICS Soviet of Nationalities Soviet of the Union	The Presidium following preliminary examination by the Council of Elders (see 7.4) and taking account of constitutional and other legal requirements.	At the 1st sitting of a session or a joint sitting the proposals are reported and Members may offer suggestions.
UNITED KINGDOM House of Lords	Govt after informal consultation with party leaders	Daily Order Paper showing the business for that day
House of Commons	The Government	As above, also an announcement each week, by the Leader of the House, of business proposed for the following week, made after consultation with the Opposition and other parties.
UNITED REPUBLIC OF TANZANIA National Assembly	The Government	Notice to the Clerk of the Assembly or publication of Govt Bills in the Gazette

Order/priority of business		Order of the day
11.3 How settled and by whom	11.4 When or at what stage	11.5 a) Fixed requirements under the rules b) Opposition/Private MPs' business
Discussed at the 1st separate or joint sitting and approved by separate vote of the members of each Soviet	See 11.3	a) No fixed requirements but the following are customary at session start: obituaries; report by Credentials Commission on new Members; approval of session agenda and order of the day; approval of decrees of the Presidium b) Each Soviet decides on priorities for consideration of matters raised by individual Members
Govt subject to SO and after informal consultation with party leaders	At least one day in advance	a) Prayers; starred (no debate) questions; statements on business; presentation of new Bills; private Bills; public Bills; measures; affirmative instruments and motions; unstarred questions b) Allocation of time is usually arranged by consultation with party representatives; also some time is allocated for debates, the motions being selected by ballot
Govt subject to SO and after consul- tation with the Opposition and other parties	Approximately one week in advance	a) Obituaries; unopposed private business; questions; statements; oaths; public business; petitions; adjournment motions b) 20 Fridays and 4 other 1/2 days for Private MPs' motions and Bills; 17 days for business selected by Leader of the Opposition with further time by arrangement; 3 days for business selected by Leader of 2nd largest opposition party; 3 hour debates on important matters subject to agreement of the Speaker and the House
Normally by the Speaker with approval of the Leader of govt business	As the business arises.	a) Detailed in SO including: petitions; questions; motions for the adjournment on matters of urgent public importance; public business b) NA (see 19.1)

Country and House(s)	Work Programme	
	11.1 Proposed by	11.2 Form and timing
UNITED STATES OF AMERICA Senate	Leadership of the majority party	There is no fixed timing. Schedule is often announced during a sitting. Assistant Leaders of both parties issue weekly notices.
House of Representatives	Speaker	Daily under standing rules
VANUATU Parliament	Clerk of Parlt	Agenda presented before a sitting
YUGOSLAVIA Federal Chamber	Presidents' Conference comprising President of the Chamber and chairmen of its working bodies	In the form of 3-month plans
Chamber of Republics and Provinces		
ZAIRE Legislative Council	Presidents' Conference comprising the Bureau and the cttee chairmen and vice-chairmen	Presented to the Council at the sitting following the formal opening of a session
ZAMBIA National Assembly	Government	Announced by Prime Minister every Friday during sittings
ZIMBABWE Senate	Secretary to Parliament in consultation with the Government	All items appear on the Order Paper at least 1 day in advance.
House of Assembly		

Order/priority of business		Order of the day
11.3 How settled and by whom	11.4 When or at what stage	11.5 a) Fixed requirements under the rules b) Opposition/Private MPs' business
Majority Leader	No fixed time	a) Detailed in SO including: Journal correction; presentation of communications; petitions and memorials; cttee reports; introduction and consideration of Bills and resolutions. Order may be changed by unanimous consent b) By unanimous agreement
Agreement among the leadership	On a weekly and daily basis	a) Detailed in SO including: prayers; Journal correction; Correction of reference of public Bills; matters referred to cttees; motions to go to Cttee of the Whole; Orders of the Day b) Formal arrangements under SO and informal by agreement
Government	After the Speaker reads the agenda	a) - b) Questions; motions; and Bills
Chamber	During establishment of the work programme	a) - b) NA
Bureau, on basis of work schedule for the session approved by the Council.	Adopted at the start of the session in plenary sitting	a) - b) -
Clerk, in consultation with the Prime Minister.	Every morning	a) Detailed in SO including: prayers; Speaker's announcements; private business; Ministers' statements; questions; motion on the adjournment; Govt Bills; other Bills; public business b) Takes precedence every Wednesday over Govt business
House Leader with Secretaries-at-the Table in conformity with the Rules	Immediately after daily adjournment of the House	a) b) Private Members' business 1 day per week. Also taken on Govt Business time by arrangement

TABLE 12

DEBATE IN THE HOUSE

Procedure for Calling Members to Speak

In all countries, the directing authority is responsible for calling on Members to speak in debates and giving them the floor of the House. Two main practices are followed. On the one hand, Members may (or must) register with the Presiding Officer in advance of a debate, as happens in thirty-eight countries. On the other hand, Members may apply to the Presiding Officer (or "catch his eye") to address the House during the course of a debate, as happens in thirty-three countries. In the remaining countries under consideration, Members can either register to speak in a debate in advance or apply to the Presiding Officer during a debate.

It is likely that, when the order of speakers is established in advance, a great deal of the spontaneity of a debate is lacking and the Presiding Officer has less authority than when he can choose speakers during a debate. He invariably has the power to recall speakers to the subject under debate, but as a rule is required to follow the order in which their requests to speak have been put down on a list drawn up before or during the debate. Where the Presiding Officer is free (within the usual boundaries of impartiality) to select the speakers, he is not hamstrung by a pre-determined list and has complete freedom to choose Members who are likely to make contributions of relevance to the proceedings. The House places its full confidence in the Speaker or President's sense of what is right and trusts him to see to it that speeches are relevant and not repetitious, and to ensure that as far as possible speakers debating either side of a matter are heard alternately.

Where Members Speak From

The quality of debate is affected by where Members speak from in the House, whether or not they are permitted to read their speeches, and whether it is possible for one Member to interrupt the speech of another. In thirty countries, Members speak from a rostrum at the front of the Chamber or a central aisle. In thirty-four countries, they speak from their seats in the House, and in sixteen countries, they speak from either their seats or a rostrum. In many countries where Members customarily speak from a rostrum, short statements may be made from their seats. The rostrum undoubtedly inspires the oratorical form of address and encourages set speeches which lack spontaneity. By contrast, where Members speak from their seats a more informal and participatory atmosphere is created. The seating arrangements of the chamber in part determine where Members speak from. Generally, where the seats are

429

arranged in rows on either side of the Chair, Members speak from their places, and where the seats are arranged in a semi-circle facing the Chair, they speak from a rostrum or a central aisle.

Speeches

As speeches are the lifeblood of Parliament, restrictions on them should, in theory, be as few as possible. In practice, however, Members' speeches do not lend themselves easily to self-discipline. In seven countries (Bahamas, Bulgaria, Finland, the German Democratic Republic, Liechtenstein, Mexico and St Vincent) there are no restrictions and any Member of the Government or Parliament can speak for as long as he pleases and can have the floor of the House as many times as he wishes in the course of the debate.

In the remaining countries, it has been found necessary to confine debates within reasonable limits. Two chief methods are used to save Parliament's time. The first is to limit the number and length of speeches by each Member, the second to limit the number and length of speeches by each party. Generally, these methods are not applied to members of the Government or the spokesmen of committees (the chairmen and the rapporteurs), who are granted special speaking privileges.

Restrictions on Members' Speeches

Several countries place limitations on the number of times a Member may speak in a debate. According to British practice a Member may, as a general rule, speak more than once in a debate only with the leave of the House. This rule is also observed in the Philippines, Poland and South Africa. Two speeches are allowed in, for example, Belgium, Kuwait, the Netherlands, Norway and the Republic of Korea, while in Costa Rica a Member may speak three times in a debate and four times when the Assembly grants permission.

The length of speeches in debates on Bills is restricted in several countries. In Denmark, Spain and Switzerland, for example, no Member may speak for more than 10 minutes, in Egypt, Kuwait, Luxembourg, Mongolia and Senegal, for more than 15 minutes, in Canada, Greece, New Zealand and the Republic of Korea for longer than 20 minutes, and in Belgium, Cameroon, Costa Rica, Philippines and Poland for more than 30 minutes. In Australia, Denmark, Italy, New Zealand, South Africa and Sweden, for example, the amount of time each Member can speak in a debate on a Bill is dependent upon the nature of the matter under consideration.

Where two speeches are permitted, the length of each may be specified. In Mongolia, for example, it is 15 minutes and 5 minutes, in Switzerland 10 minutes and 5 minutes, and in the USSR 15 and 5 minutes. Various other countries limit the time available to Members in certain other kinds of proceedings, such as Budget debates (as in the Republic of Korea or Tanzania), interpellations or oral questions with debate (France and USSR), motions of confidence (Italy and the United Kingdom) and on points of order (Costa Rica and Israel).

Where a particular time limit on speeches is not imposed by the rules, Parliament or the political groups may allocate the time available for its Members. In the Federal Republic of Germany the Council of Elders proposes the form and duration of debates. A similar practice is followed in India, where the Business Advisory Committee makes recommendations on the allocation of time. In Israel time is fixed by the Chairman.

Restrictions on Party Speeches

Limits are placed on the number and length of speeches by each party in nine countries. In the Federal Republic of Germany, France, India, Israel, Italy, Japan, the Netherlands and the Republic of Korea, speaking time is allocated to the parties proportional to their size in the House. In general discussions of the Budget in the Belgian House of Representatives, time is allocated to each of the political groups, and only one Member from each of them may speak in debates on the order of business, interlocutory questions, and orders on motions of closure. In the Federal Republic of Germany and France, similar restrictions apply to spokesmen of political parties in certain types of debates. An altogether different practice is found in Canada, Malta and South Africa, where the Leader of the official Opposition has, in most debates, the same speaking rights as the Prime Minister and other members of the Government.

How Members deliver their speeches also affects the quality of debates. Twenty-four countries do not permit Members to read their speeches although in many of these (for example Fiji, Greece, Mauritius and Spain) notes may be used to assist delivery and Members can read out technical material and quotations, but may not follow a prepared text word for word. In Cyprus reading is allowed under certain circumstances such as when introducing a private Bill or making a formal party statement, also in Egypt for reports, texts, proposals and amendments. The German Federal Diet allows statements to be read by leave of the President, and the United States House of Representatives allows speeches to be read by permission of the House. In Canada, although there is no rule, tradition opposes the reading of speeches and the practice is discouraged. In forty-nine countries Members are permitted to read their speeches and, once again, this has the effect of reducing the spontaneous nature of the debate.

In twenty-eight countries, no interruptions to a Member's speech are permitted. Once a Member has been granted the floor of the House, he can deliver his speech without fear of interruption. The remaining countries allow interruptions to speeches to be made, usually for points of order, or when the Presiding Officer permits them, or when the Member speaking yields the floor. When interruptions are permitted in moderation, the debate gains from exchanges of points of view between speakers. By contrast, debates suffer when no interruptions are permitted and when a series of set speeches are read out.

TABLE 12: DEBATE IN THE HOUSE

Country and House(s)	12.1 Procedure for calling Members to speak	12.2 Members speak from
ALGERIA National People's Assembly (APN)	Speakers must register with the APN Bureau (floor given in order of registration). The President may close the list of speakers.	The rostrum or their seats, as desired.
ARGENTINA Senate Chamber of Deputies	Members register with the Secretariat and are given the floor in order of registration.	Their seats
AUSTRALIA Senate House of Representatives	MPs are recognized by Presiding Officer, who calls on MP who, in his opinion, first rises. Presiding Officers usually provided with unofficial lists of MPs wishing to speak.	Their seats
AUSTRIA Federal Council National Council	Chronological order of registration with a Clerk at the Table	A rostrum usually; supplementaries during question time put from their seats.
BAHAMAS Senate House of Assembly	Obtain the attention of the Presiding Officer.	Their seats
BELGIUM Senate Chamber of Representatives	Members wishing to speak must register in advance or obtain permission of President.	Rostrum or their seats (for brief statements).

12.3 Rules governing Members' speeches	12.4 Reading of speeches	12.5 Interruption of speeches
The Bureau sets the speaking time for each debate according to the work programme. Precedence follows order of registration with the Bureau.	Yes	Only on points of order
Rapporteurs, movers and group leaders may speak for one hour. Other Members 30 minutes.	No (not respected in practice).	Only by the President of the House or with the Member's permission
No MP (other than mover of motion in reply) may speak more than once in plenary session. Senators may speak in plenary sessions for 30 minutes and Representatives for 20 minutes max. However, both Houses may vary speaking time depending on nature of their business.	Not permitted, although Senators may refer to notes. Yes	Only for quorums, points of order and privilege. To move that a MP be no longer heard and to draw attention to quorum, points of order or privilege.
No time limits except for procedural questions (theorically, provisions exist for limiting speaking time by vote and for closure of debate). Those in favour and those against the item under discussion take turns with the latter given precedence.	Yes	No
No time limits, but precedence applies.	No	Only on points of order
No Senator may speak more than twice on the same subject, without the President's authorisation, or longer than one hour.	Yes	Only on points of order or by the President
Principal speakers usually allowed 30 minutes. Other time limits are detailed in the respective SO. In both Houses, speakers alternate for and against a motion in registration and request order or on President's decision.		

Country and House(s)	12.1 Procedure for calling Members to speak	12.2 Members speak from
BRAZIL Federal Senate Chamber of Deputies	On basis of monthly registration list, including statements from Leaders, "short speeches" (maximum 5 minutes at session start). Daily register and urgent messages from leaders.	Rostrum
BULGARIA National Assembly	In order of request	Rostrum
CAMEROON National Assembly	Called in order of registration. A Member may cede his turn to a colleague.	Rostrum
CANADA Senate	Member wishing to speak rises to obtain recognition of the Speaker.	Their seats
House of Commons	Speaker's discretion is usually final but may be altered by motion.	
CAPE VERDE People's National Assembly	Members register with the Presidency	Rostrum
CHINA National People's Congress (NPC)	The leader of a delegation (see 19.1) or a Member elected by it speaks at a meeting of the Presidium or in plenary session.	Their seats or a rostrum
COMOROS Federal Assembly	Recognition by the President	Their seats

12.3 Rules governing Members' speeches	12.4 Reading of speeches	12.5 Interruption of speeches
Rules of Procedure, and agreement between party Leaders. (30 speakers for each party appointed daily by Leaders; time allotted proportional to number of seats.)	Yes	Only with agreement of the Member speaking
None	Yes	No
30 minute time limit, except for motion against closure of debate (5 minutes); President may recognise a Member at sitting end for private business.	Yes	Only on points of order
No time limit, but Senators may speak once only on a given matter. Leader of Govt and Leader of Opposition are given priority. The Speaker then recognises speakers to ensure a balanced representative debate.	No written rule, but reading of speeches is discouraged.	If Member speaking permits.
In general, Members are limited to 20 minutes, except the Prime Minister, Leader of Opposition, Minister moving a Govt order or Members replying to a Minister or Member on a motion of no confidence. Closure rule may also be moved at a previous sitting to limit debate on a given matter. Prime Minister and Leader of Opposition are given priority. Speaker then attempts to ensure a balanced, representative debate.	No written rule, but tradition opposes reading of speeches.	No. SO provide for a ten-minute exchange after each speech.
President may impose time limits depending on number of Members registered to speak.	Yes	Only on points of order
–	–	–
–	–	–

Country and House(s)	12.1 Procedure for calling Members to speak	12.2 Members speak from
CONGO People's National Assembly	In order of prior registration	Their seats or a rostrum
COSTA RICA Legislative Assembly	Authorisation must be sought from the President. Floor is given in order of requests to speak.	Their seats
CUBA National Assembly of People's Power	–	Their seats
CYPRUS House of Representatives	President gives the floor at request of Members. Parliamentary spokesmen have priority.	Rostrum, but from seats on points of order or procedure.
CZECHOSLOVAKIA Chamber of Nations Chamber of the People	Members register in advance or during debate and are given the floor in the order of their registration. Movers of amdts have priority.	Rostrum
DEMOCRATIC YEMEN Supreme People's Council	According to list of speakers	Rostrum
DENMARK Folketing	In the order requests are received, with spokesmen and movers given precedence.	Rostrum, or their seats at question time.

12.3 Rules governing Members' speeches	12.4 Reading of speeches	12.5 Interruption of speeches
Time limit 5 minutes	Yes	No
Time limit 30 minutes. May speak 3 times only on a given subject, but for motions of order, Assembly may grant an additional 30 minutes and a fourth speech.	No	Interruption may be conceded by the Speaker but not by the Member wishing to interrupt.
-	Yes	Only on points of order
May speak for a "reasonably sufficient time" and once only per subject (except by leave) unless: misinterpreted or criticised; is 'introducer' of a Bill, matter for debate, motion or substantial amdt; is a cttee rapporteur; expressing a new or opposing idea; or is answering a personal attack.	Allowed: when introducing a private Bill or matter for debate; making a Budget speech; making a formal party statement.	Only by leave to raise or clarify points of order.
Each Chamber may determine the maximum time limit, not shorter than 15 minutes. Each MP has the right to speak in his own tongue.	Yes	No
Priority awarded to Presidium members, Ministers, Council members inquiring about certain reports, in that order.	Yes	Only on points of order.
An annex to SO prescribes speaking limits for various items of business, and speakers (typically 10 minutes and 5 minutes for 1st and 2nd speech respectively. Ministers and spokesmen are granted more time, but President may grant latitude depending on topic).	Yes	No (expressions of approval or disapproval are considered disorderly).

Country and House(s)	12.1 Procedure for calling Members to speak	12.2 Members speak from
EGYPT People's Assembly	On Member's request with permission of the Speaker	Rostrum or their seats. Cttee rapporteurs usually speak from the rostrum.
FIJI Senate House of Representatives	Members are recognised by Presiding Officer who calls on the Member who in his opinion rises first.	Their seats
FINLAND Eduskunta	Members register in advance or during the debate with the Speaker. They are given the floor in order of registration.	Rostrum. Brief remarks made from their seats.
FRANCE Senate National Assembly	In organised debates, Members are chosen by their political groups within the time-limits allotted to each group by the Presidents' Conference. In other debates, Members register in advance with the respective President.	Rostrum, or for short statements, from various microphones available in the room.
GABON National Assembly	Speakers register in advance with the Assembly Bureau.	Their seats
GERMAN DEMOCRATIC REPUBLIC People's Chamber	Speakers must register in advance with the Presidium. The President determines the speaking order in consultation with the Presidium.	A rostrum, or from seats to move points of order or ask questions.

12.3 Rules governing Members' speeches	12.4 Reading of speeches	12.5 Interruption of speeches
Time limit of 15 minutes. No subject referred to twice. Chairmen and rapporteurs may intervene any time during debate on their items.	No, except reports, texts, proposals and amdts.	Only by the Speaker of the Assembly.
Speak in standing position and address the Chair; only one speech in any debate; no time limit, except when agreed to by resolution of the House; unlimited speaking rights during cttee stages.	Copious notes allowed	Only by Presiding Officer or on a point of order
None	Yes	Short interjections permitted
Speaking time is limited in organised debates in accordance with 12.1. For certain debates (e.g. on amdts, explanations of votes, etc.) SO generally impose a 5 minute limitation. In the Senate, oral questions with debate allow the author 20 minutes with a further 10 minutes after the Govt's answer. Other speakers 10 and 5 minutes, respectively. Oral questions without debate, allow 5 minutes. In the Assembly 10 to 20 minutes are allowed before the Govt's reply and 10 minutes after. Other speakers at President's discretion. Without debate, 2 minutes before Govt reply and 5 minutes after.	No	Only if the speaker permits, and by leave of the President.
Time limits are laid down in SO.	Yes	Only on point of order if speaker deviates from the subject.
Generally, no time limits.	Yes	Yes

Country and House(s)	12.1 Procedure for calling Members to speak	12.2 Members speak from
GERMANY Federal Council	In order of registration with the Council President	Rostrum
Federal Diet	Chosen by political fractions for organised debates and registered with the Secretary to the right of the President. In other debates Members are called by the President bearing in mind need for a balanced debate and relative group strengths.	Rostrum or floor microphones
GREECE Chamber of Deputies	The President calls speakers in order of registration. SO provide priority for certain speakers such as rapporteurs. Debate is not closed until all registered have spoken.	Rostrum, or for remarks of less than 5 minutes, from their seats.
HUNGARY National Assembly	Registration in advance with the President. Ministers, Under-Secretaries and cttee chairmen have priority.	Their seats
INDIA Council of States	Called by the Presiding Officer from a list of speakers prepared by the parties or groups.	Their seats
House of the People	The Speaker is guided, not bound, by the above list. Members may also register in advance with the Speaker or "catch his eye" during debate.	
INDONESIA House of Representatives	Speakers registered in advance in proportion to the strength of their faction	Rostrum
IRELAND Senate	Recognition by the chair	Their seats
Dáil		

440

12.3 Rules governing Members' speeches	12.4 Reading of speeches	12.5 Interruption of speeches
No time limits, but speeches are usually brief. Federal Govt members have priority.	Yes	Interruptions are permitted (infrequent in practice).
Generally, Council of Elders proposes form and duration of debates, otherwise 10 minute time limit applies to most speakers.	By leave of the President. Notes are allowed.	Only if the speaker consents.
SO specify maximum time limits, e.g. Members 20 minutes; rapporteurs or movers 30 minutes; Ministers and party leaders no limit.	No, but may refer to notes.	Only when the speaker permits, the President agrees and for 5 minutes maximum.
No time limits specified but President or Assembly may limit speeches.	Yes	May be allowed provided order of debate is not disturbed and the speaker permits.
Allocation of time is recommended by the Business Advisory Cttee and divided in proportion to party/group strength. SO detail rules prohibiting offensive remarks, personal charges, sub-judice matters, etc.	Only by leave of the Chairman. Notes are allowed.	No
No Member of the House of the People may speak more than once on the same motion except with the Speaker's permission or has the right of reply. The Speaker may limit speaking time on certain debates.	No	Points of order only or with Speaker's permission and consent of the Member speaking
Allocation of time to each Faction	Yes	Yes
MPs may speak only once on the same motion, except to close a debate, or in Cttee of the Whole House.	No, except for Ministers making statements of policy or fact.	Interruptions are out of order but occur.

Country and House(s)	12.1 Procedure for calling Members to speak	12.2 Members speak from
ISRAEL The Knesset	For debates on an individual basis, MPs register with the Secretary; for debates on a party group basis, MPs are given the floor as speakers for the party group.	Rostrum, except for supplementary questions, points of order or other special cases.
ITALY Senate Chamber of Deputies	SO require registration in advance, but practice allows registration during the sitting with permission of the President. For Bills, normally one speaker per group is registered, but open registration possible on request of 20 MPs, or one or more Group Chairmen, 24 hours in advance.	Their seats
IVORY COAST National Assembly	Called by the President in order of registration	Rostrum or their seats
JAPAN House of Councillors House of Representatives	Number of speakers and allocation to parties and groups usually determined by Proceedings Conference in House of Councillors and by Cttee on Rules and Administration in the House of Representatives. Names are given in advance to the President who then calls the speakers.	Rostrum or their seats if Presiding Officer grants permission.
JORDAN Senate House of Deputies	Registration with the Secretary-General; called by the Presiding Officer in order of registration.	Rostrum or their seats
KENYA National Assembly	Obtaining recognition by the Speaker	Their seats

12.3 Rules governing Members' speeches	12.4 Reading of speeches	12.5 Interruption of speeches
In debates on an individual basis, time is fixed by the Chairman. In party group debates it is fixed by the group (8 minutes minimum). Other time limits depend on the activity, e.g.: 1 minute maximum for points of order and 15 minutes maximum for agenda motions.	Yes	With consent of the Member speaking and Chairman's permission
Time limits vary from 5 to 45 minutes (exceptionnally 90) depending on subject. Unlimited for debates on motion of confidence. Speakers for and against alternate to the extent possible. Speakers absent when called cannot speak later.	Yes, but not exceeding 30 minutes.	Generally accepted, if very brief.
A speaker must have been given the floor by the President and his remarks must be relevant.	Yes, from the rostrum.	No
Presiding Officer allocates speaking time unless decided in advance by the House. MPs who have not given notice under 12.1 may speak after listed MPs by leave of the Presiding Officer. Leave is sought by standing and calling the Presiding Officer. Opposers and supporters speak alternately as far as possible. In the House of Representatives debaters appointed by a cttee may be allowed by the Presiding Officer to precede other speakers.	No, but brief notes allowed.	No
Cabinet members, Govt. representatives, cttee rapporteurs and chairmen are not bound by order of registration of speakers.	-	Only on points of order
SO provide detailed rules on relevance, priority and time limits. In general MPs may speak once only on a topic except in Cttee of the Whole and must remain in order.	No, but notes allowed.	No

TABLE 12: DEBATE IN THE HOUSE (continued)

Country and House(s)	12.1 Procedure for calling Members to speak	12.2 Members speak from
KUWAIT National Assembly	In order of registration with the Secretary–General except for Ministers and rapporteurs who have priority.	Rostrum or their seats
LEBANON National Assembly	Obtain recognition by the President	Rostrum or their seats
LIECHTENSTEIN Diet	Obtain recognition by the President	Their seats
LUXEMBOURG Chamber of Deputies	Called by the President after registration or requesting the floor. Speakers for and against alternate.	Rostrum or their seats
MALAWI National Assembly	Obtain recognition of the Speaker by rising.	Their seats
MALAYSIA Senate	Obtain recognition of the Presiding Officer by rising.	Their seats
House of Representatives		
MALI National Assembly	Registration in advance, called by the Presiding Officer.	Rostrum or their seats
MALTA House of Representatives	Members seek recognition of the Speaker by rising in their places.	Their seats
MAURITIUS Legislative Assembly	Obtain the attention of the Speaker	Their seats

444

12.3 Rules governing Members' speeches	12.4 Reading of speeches	12.5 Interruption of speeches
May not speak more than twice on the same subject or more than 15 minutes except by leave.	No	No, except for President drawing attention to SO.
-	Yes	No
None	Yes	No
SO detail speaking times. Usually in general debate 60 minutes for Group-mandated speakers, 15 minutes for others. In detailed discussion 15 minutes and 5 minutes respectively.	Yes	No
No Member may speak more than once in plenary except for certain replies or a Minister by assent. SO detail other values.	No, but notes may be used.	Only on points of order, attention to quorum or closure, unless the Member speaking consents.
No Member may speak more than once except in cttee, in reply or in explanation. Other rules are detailed in SO. The Presiding Officer sets time limits.	Yes	Only on points of order or to seek clarification
Ministers, Chairmen and rapporteurs have priority. Speech must be relevant and is limited to 15 minutes per Member.	-	No
In general Members may speak for up to 40 minutes which may be extended by 30 minutes on being proposed and seconded by other Members. Further extension is by leave of the House. Other time limits for various matters are detailed in SO.	No, but Members may refer to notes. The Speaker's rulings and ministerial statements are usually read.	On points of order and for personal explanations if the Member speaking gives way.
No specific rules but relevance is paramount.	No, but can refer to copious notes.	No

Country and House(s)	12.1 Procedure for calling Members to speak	12.2 Members speak from
MEXICO Chamber of Senators	Members register with the President of the Chamber.	Rostrum; points of order may be put from their seats.
Chamber of Deputies		
MONACO National Council	Members wishing to speak must "catch the President's eye" during a debate and are given the floor in the order of their requests.	Their seats
MONGOLIA Great People's Khural (GPKh)	Request to the Chairman	Rostrum
NAURU Parliament	Members are recognised by the Speaker who calls on the MP who in his opinion first rises. The Speaker's call may be challenged and determined by vote without debate.	Their seats
NETHERLANDS First Chamber	Members register with the Clerk (or the Clerk's office if the Chamber is not sitting). A speakers' list is prepared for every agenda item. Budget debates alternate between Govt and Opposition speakers.	Rostrum
Second Chamber		
NEW ZEALAND House of Representatives	Obtain the Speaker's attention	Their seats

12.3 Rules governing Members' speeches	12.4 Reading of speeches	12.5 Interruption of speeches
-	Yes	No
Speaking time is only limited in closure debates when the President of the Council determines the order and length of speeches.	Yes	Only with the permission of the President, or for points of order.
15 minutes for the 1st speech and 5 minutes for the 2nd. Points of order are not to exceed 5 minutes.	Yes	No
As provided by SO	Not prohibited by SO	Only on points of order, to call attention to want of quorum or presence of strangers, to move closure of debate or that business of the day be called on.
Members may speak twice only.	Yes	No
No Member may speak more than twice on the same subject without the permission of the Chamber except to propose an amdt or on a personal position or a motion of order. No limits on Govt members' speeches. The Chairman or 5 Members present can propose time limits to speeches.		At the Chairman's discretion
In general Members may speak for 20 minutes. Other time limits are prescribed by SO. An MP may speak only once on a matter except in cttee. The mover of a motion has the right to a 2nd speech in reply.	No, but notes may be used.	Only on points of order or to call attention to want of quorum or strangers in the House.

TABLE 12: DEBATE IN THE HOUSE (continued)

Country and House(s)	12.1 Procedure for calling Members to speak	12.2 Members speak from
NICARAGUA National Assembly	Members are given the floor in order of their requests to the Presiding Officer.	Their seats
NORWAY Storting	The President normally gives the floor in the order in which requests are made. For major debates the order of speaking is agreed beforehand between party group leaders and the President.	A rostrum
PHILIPPINES National Assembly	Members rise to obtain the floor on recognition by the Speaker.	Any one of a number of conveniently-placed microphones
POLAND Diet	Called by the President in order of prior registration with the Clerk. The Bureau, with advice of the Council of Sages, may establish a different order.	A rostrum, except at question time, when questions are posed from their seats.
PORTUGAL Assembly of the Republic	In order of registration with the Assembly Bureau	A rostrum, or their seats for brief statements.
REPUBLIC OF KOREA National Assembly	Advance notice, except motions for procedural matters, and Speaker's permission. Members not giving notification may be allowed to speak after those who have given notice.	The rostrum

12.3 Rules governing Members' speeches	12.4 Reading of speeches	12.5 Interruption of speeches
1st speech: 10 minutes; 2nd and 3rd speeches: 5 minutes.	Yes	Only by the Presiding Officer
Each Member may speak twice on a given matter. Cttee spokesmen, Ministers and party group leaders enjoy privileges respecting time and number of speeches.	Yes	No
No Member may speak more than once or longer than 30 minutes on a given matter without leave of the Assembly, except a cttee rapporteur who opens and closes a debate.	Yes	No
Speaking time in debates usually 30 minutes unless extended by the President or reduced on advice of the Council of Sages; 5 minutes for other matters; Members may speak once only on a given matter; State Council Members, President of the Supreme Audit Chamber, Ministers and the Attorney-General have priority.	Yes	Not prohibited by SO but rarely occurs.
The floor is given in order of registration except where a right of reply applies, taking account of time limitations.	Yes	Only if the Member speaking permits.
The Speaker may fix the number of speakers on a topic up to 3 for each political group; length of speeches may not normally exceed 20 minutes; 10 minutes for interpellations, budget matters and dismissal of Ministers. The Speaker may, however, permit party leaders up to 40 minutes; obstructive quotations (see 12.4) prohibited. Each speaker may not normally speak more than twice on a subject except to answer questions or explain Bills.	Yes, except reading newspapers, magazines, publications and other documents for the purpose of obstructing proceedings.	Only if points of order are accepted.

TABLE 12: DEBATE IN THE HOUSE (continued)

Country and House(s)	12.1 Procedure for calling Members to speak	12.2 Members speak from
ROMANIA Grand National Assembly	Members register in advance or, during the sitting, ask the President for the floor.	The rostrum
RWANDA National Development Council (CND)	Members register in advance and are called by the President in order of registration. They may also be recognised from the floor.	The rostrum or their seats
ST VINCENT House of Assembly	Order in which listed to speak, then by obtaining the Speaker's attention.	Their seats
SENEGAL National Assembly	Members wishing to speak register in advance. Registrations may be swapped or ceded to another Member.	Rostrum or their seats. The President may invite Members to the rostrum.
SOLOMON ISLANDS National Parliament	Varies according to the business of the day.	Their seats
SOMALIA People's Assembly	According to order of precedence	The rostrum or their seats
SOUTH AFRICA House of Assembly House of Representatives House of Delegates	Members are recognised by the Presiding Officer who calls on the MP who in his opinion first rises. The Presiding Officer has unfettered discretion but attempts to call speakers for and against alternately.	Their seats

450

12.3 Rules governing Members' speeches	12.4 Reading of speeches	12.5 Interruption of speeches
Ministers, proposers of Bills and cttee rapporteurs have priority even if they have not registered. Speeches must be relevant.	Yes	If the member speaking strays from the point.
Time limits are established by the CND President. Ministers, Secretaries of State, rapporteurs and authors of Bills are accorded priority.	Yes	Only on points of order
Speeches must not be repetitious. No time limits.	No, except for Ministers.	Only on points of order or if MP speaking permits.
Speaking time limited to 15 minutes in debate; 5 minutes for personal explanations and only at end of a sitting; 3 minutes for other matters.	Yes	Only with permission
–	–	–
Time limits and precedence laid down.	Yes	Only on points of order
Members must address the Chair, and normally speak once only on a given matter except in Cttee of the Whole House. Remarks must be relevant and not repetitious. Time limits are prescribed in SO and vary according to the topic, person speaking and legislative stage. Ministers and Leaders of the Opposition are not restricted, an MP in reply is limited to 1 hour, other MPs normally 30 minutes.	No, except for Member in charge of a Bill at the 2nd reading. Notes are allowed.	Only on points of order or privilege, absence of quorum, presence of strangers or to move closure of a debate.

Country and House(s)	12.1 Procedure for calling Members to speak	12.2 Members speak from
SPAIN Senate	Request the right to speak from the President	The rostrum or their seats
Congress of Deputies		
SRI LANKA Parliament	Members are recognised by the Speaker who calls on the MP who, in his opinion, first rises.	Their seats
SWEDEN Riksdag	A Member is usually given the floor on request to the Speaker. Preferably 1 day's notice is given of intention to speak. Orators are usually called in order of notification, but the Speaker's discretion prevails.	The rostrum or, usually for shorter speeches, their seats.
SWITZERLAND States Council	Members wishing to speak seek recognition of the President by raising the hand.	Their seats
National Council	Written request to the President	The rostrum
SYRIAN ARAB REPUBLIC People's Council	Members speak in order of registration.	Their seats
THAILAND Senate	According to SO rules of priority applied by the Speaker	Their seats
House of Representatives		

12.3 Rules governing Members' speeches	12.4 Reading of speeches	12.5 Interruption of speeches
Time limit of 10 minutes per speaker usually applies except principal speakers for and against who have 15 minutes; Ministers may request the floor at any time; a speaker whose arguments are contradicted by another has the right of reply, once, for 5 minutes; speakers claiming to have been misrepresented may be granted 3 minutes for a personal explanation.	No, but notes are allowed.	Only by the President on points of order
No Member (other than mover or with leave) may speak more than once.	No	With permission of the Chair and if the speaker is prepared to give way.
Certain time limits from 1 to 30 minutes are specified for questions and general debates. In other debates no time limits except for unnotified speeches (6 minutes). Rejoinders are restricted.	Yes	No
No time limits	Yes	No
Group spokesmen and movers of motions limited to 15 minutes. Others 10 minutes, or 5 minutes for a 2nd speech on the same subject. Council can determine total debate time and can extend or shorten speaking time.		
–	Yes	No
The Speaker may request an orator to discontinue his remarks when he considers he has spoken for sufficient time.	No, unless necessary.	Allowed

Country and House(s)	12.1 Procedure for calling Members to speak	12.2 Members speak from
TUNISIA Chamber of Deputies	SO prescribe priorities for various categories of speakers. Other speakers register in advance.	Rapporteurs use the rostrum, others speak from their seats.
UGANDA National Assembly	If 2 or more MPs rise simultaneously, he who first catches the Speaker's eye is called to speak.	Ministers and Shadow Ministers speak from the respective despatch boxes. Others from their seats.
UNION OF SOVIET SOCIALIST REPUBLICS Soviet of Nationalities Soviet of the Union	The Presiding Officer gives the floor on the basis of a List of Members registered in advance. The names of rapporteurs for various bodies are advised to the Presidium to be called as appropriate.	The rostrum
UNITED KINGDOM House of Lords	The right to speak is inherent in each Member's Writ of Summons	Members of Govt and Opposition front bench from the despatch box at the Table. Others from their seats.
House of Commons	When called by the Chair	
UNITED REPUBLIC OF TANZANIA National Assembly	Obtain the attention of the Presiding Officer	The nearest microphone

12.3 Rules governing Members' speeches	12.4 Reading of speeches	12.5 Interruption of speeches
Speaking order for Bills is govt representative, cttee rapporteur, Bill's author, MPs. The govt representative, cttee chairmen and rapporteurs may intervene on request at any time.	Yes	Only on points of order
Speaking time is determined by the Speaker. No Member (except in reply to a motion or in explanation) may speak more than once in plenary.	No, but notes may be used.	Only on points of order, to elucidate a matter, provided Member speaking gives way , or call attention to "strangers".
15 minutes for a 1st speech; 5 minutes for the 2nd, and for points of order, explanations and questions. The Presiding Officer can extend time. Debates are closed by the House.	Yes	Not practised
Members normally speak once only to a motion except in cttee. No time limits for individual speeches but Short Debates are limited to 2 1/2 hours.	No	Only if the Member speaking gives way. Ultimately, the House decides who should have the floor.
May not speak twice in the same debate except by leave of the House, but a proposer has right of reply. Some precedence is given to Privy Counsellors and party spokesmen. No time limits.	Speeches ought not to be read but some relaxation is allowed for Ministers' policy speeches, etc.	
MPs speak once except for right of reply. No time limit except 25 minutes during Budget sittings; no reference may be made to debates of the same or preceding sitting or to sub judice matters.	No, but notes may be used.	No

TABLE 12: DEBATE IN THE HOUSE (continued)

Country and House(s)	12.1 Procedure for calling Members to speak	12.2 Members speak from
UNITED STATES OF AMERICA Senate	Priority is: Majority Leader; Minority Leader; majority and minority floor managers for measure under consideration; then as recognised by the Presiding Officer.	Their seats
House of Representatives	Recognition by the Presiding Officer	The well of the House or leadership tables.
VANUATU Parliament	Hand raised to seek recognition by the Speaker	Their seats
YUGOSLAVIA Federal Chamber

Chamber of Republics and Provinces | Request and obtain leave to speak from the President | The rostrum |
| ZAIRE Legislative Council | Registration in advance and called by the Presiding Officer | The rostrum |
| ZAMBIA National Assembly | Members wishing to speak must catch the Speaker's eye. | Their seats |
| ZIMBABWE Senate

House of Assembly | MPs are recognised by the Presiding Officer who calls on the MP who in his opinion first rises (with some latitude at Presiding Officer's discretion). | Back benchers from their seats; Ministers from the table in the centre. |

12.3 Rules governing Members' speeches	12.4 Reading of speeches	12.5 Interruption of speeches
No time limits unless previously agreed or" cloture" invoked. 1 hour limit after cloture.	Yes	If the Senator speaking permits.
Governed by SO; precedents; prior resolution; agreement during debate; informal arrangement between MPs and floor managers of Bills.	With permission of the House	Certain interruptions permitted pursuant to SO
No MP may speak more than 3 times on a topic except for supplementary questions and answers.	Yes	No
None, but exceptionally the Chamber may decide to limit the duration of speeches.	Yes	Only by the President of the Chamber
No time limits. Speakers must not stray from the subject, engage in mutual dialogue nor make personal attacks.	Yes	Yes, if a Member infringes the rules in 12.3.
No MP may speak more than once on the same subject except the mover who has the right to reply.	No, but notes are permitted. Ministers may read Govt policy speeches.	Only on points of order or for clarification, with permission of the Chair.
Time limits are prescribed in SO.	No, except for Ministers speaking on behalf of Government.	For points of order, clarification, etc.

TABLE 13

ORDER IN THE HOUSE

Restrictions on the number and length of speeches which Members can make are designed to speed up the business of the House. In spite of them, however, Members can attempt to slow down the work of Parliament either by using the procedure of the House in legitimate ways which can eventually amount to obstruction or by resorting to deliberate disorder.

Legitimate Use of Procedures Amounting Eventually to Obstruction

Parliamentary procedure secures for every Member the right to speak in debates and submit amendments to legislation, but it also offers a whole range of opportunities which can be used in ways that are tantamount to obstruction. The nature of these opportunities varies from country to country, but they include motions for the adjournment, referring a Bill back to a committee, spurious points of order, requests for a fresh deliberation, calling for a count of the House to see if a quorum is present, requests for separate votes on each part of a Bill or a motion being debated, requests to suspend the sitting of the House, and so on. The abuse of these various procedures is what constitutes obstruction.

Among methods used in Parliaments to counter this kind of obstruction, four may be mentioned. First, motions to close the debate may be moved, though these are often subject to specific requirements, such as acceptance by the Chair or a stated number of Members to support the motion. Secondly, the right to call for a check on the quorum may either be removed altogether or restricted to the chairman of a party group. Thirdly, the directing authority may be empowered to refuse to accept a dilatory motion at variance with the spirit, if not the letter, of the rules. Fourthly, a motion to allocate time (or guillotine) may be passed by the House requiring one, several, or all stages of a Bill to be completed within a stated time.

Deliberate Disorder

The second possibility is obstruction of the business of the House which takes the form of deliberate disorder. This is a much more serious matter. Deliberate obstruction of this kind occurs when Members blatantly refuse to obey the rules of the House, and attempt through their words or actions to obstruct its business. Offences under this heading include speaking in debates without the directing authority's permission, refusing to discontinue a speech or come to order, disregarding the authority of the Chair, irrelevance or tedious repetition in a speech, the use of language or conduct designed to prejudice the dignity of the House, the use of violence or the threat of violence against Parliament, its members or its officers, and so on. The distinguishing characteristic of all these actions is that they are specifically outlawed by the rules of procedure.

Sanctions Applied against Members

The various sanctions which can be imposed by the House and by its directing authority on Members who indulge in deliberate disorder are presented in Table 13A. It can be seen that these sanctions range

TABLE 13A. Sanctions Applied to Members who Indulge in Deliberate Disorder

Type of Sanction	Number of Countries Sanction Applied by:	
	Directing Authority	House
Call to Order	40	0
Call to Order Noted in the Record	9	2
Removal of Words from the Record of Debates	3	0
Request to Withdraw Offending Words	6	0
Call to Order and Warning	12	5
Withdrawal of Right to Speak	39	5
Disconnection of Sound Facilities	1	0
Temporary Suspension (Usually for Remainder of the Sitting)	31	19
Censure or Naming	10	10
Suspension from more than One Sitting	8	24
Expulsion from Parliament	0	4
Other Disciplinary Action	1	8
Suspension or Adjournment of the Sitting of the House	12	0

considerably in their degree of severity, from a request from the directing authority to a Member to come to order or discontinue his speech, to a decision taken by the House itself to suspend or expel a Member. Generally, the less severe the sanction, the more likely it is to be applied by the directing authority ; the more severe the sanction, the more likely it is to be applied by the House. The less severe sanctions are those applied to offences which represent a minor infraction of the rules. As the directing authority is responsible for the conduct of debate, it is appropriate that he is the person to deal with these kinds of offences.

Where more serious offences are committed against the work of the House, more severe sanctions apply, and it is equally appropriate that they are taken by the House as a whole. In many countries the ultimate sanction is to suspend a Member from a number of sittings of the House. In Denmark, Finland or Kuwait, for example, a Member can be suspended for up to fourteen days, and in Jordan and the Netherlands for a period up to thirty days.

In the United Kingdom and a number of other countries, a Member who deliberately obstructs the business of the House can be "named" by the Speaker. This involves the Speaker referring to him by his name and not by the constituency which he represents. When a Member has been named in this way, the Leader of the House moves that the Member be suspended from the House, and the House immediately votes on the motion.

Expulsion from Parliament is used as a last resort in several countries including Cape Verde, Japan, Spain and the United States. Although nearly all countries (the exceptions include Bulgaria, China, the German Democratic Republic, Mexico, Mongolia, USSR, and the upper Houses in the Federal Republic of Germany and the United Kingdom) have some sanctions at their command to overcome deliberate disorder, the more severe ones are rarely used and, when so, they are used with considerable reluctance. Even though some Members may, on occasion, break the rules of procedure in debates, very few Members deliberately obstruct the business of Parliament by indulging in disorder to such an extent that severe sanctions need to be applied against them.

TABLE 13: ORDER IN THE HOUSE

Country and House(s)	13.1 Sanctions in increasing order of severity	13.2 Application of sanctions by
ALGERIA National People's Assembly (APN)	Call to order; warning; suspension.	President of the Assembly
ARGENTINA Senate Chamber of Deputies	Call to order; withdrawal of the right to speak; exclusion.	Presidents and respective House
AUSTRALIA Senate House of Representatives	Call to order; naming; suspension.	Presiding Officer, for call to order and naming; for suspension, the House.
AUSTRIA Federal Council National Council	Call to order; withdrawal of the right to speak.	Presiding Officer
BAHAMAS Senate House of Assembly	Temporary suspension by resolution of House	Respective House
BELGIUM Senate	1. Call to order 2. Call to order noted in record 3. Temporary suspension for remainder of the day's sitting 4. Suspension for 10 sittings	1. and 2. President; 3. and 4. decision of the Senate.
Chamber of Representatives	Call to order; withdrawal of the right to speak; call to order noted in record; temporary suspension for remainder of the day's sitting; suspension for 10 sittings.	President
BRAZIL Federal Senate Chamber of Deputies	Admonition; disconnection of sound facilities leading to non-publication of Member's speech.	Presiding Officer
BULGARIA National Assembly	No special provisions but the President may deny the floor to Members who indulge in personal attacks.	NA

462

Country and House(s)	13.1 Sanctions in increasing order of severity	13.2 Application of sanctions
CAMEROON National Assembly	1. Call to order 2. Call to order noted in record 3. Written warning recorded with censure 4. Admonition with suspension	1. and 2. by President; 3. and 4. by secret vote of the Assembly (simple majority) on President's proposal.
CANADA Senate	Member's conduct called to attention of House, then:	House
House of Commons	1. Member requested to discontinue speaking 2. Named if speaking continued 3. Suspension (following passage of a suspension motion)	1. Speaker or Chairman of Cttees; 2. Speaker (when in cttee the Chairman reports the offender to the House); 3. by the House, through a motion introduced by the Leader of the House.
CAPE VERDE People's National Assembly	1. Call to order 2. Withdrawal of right to speak 3. Expulsion	1. President; 2. President with support of Assembly; 3. Assembly.
CHINA National People's Congress (NPC)	None specified	NA
COMOROS Federal Assembly	Call to order; expulsion; adjournment of the sitting.	President of Assembly
CONGO People's National Assembly (ANP)	1. Withdrawal of the right to speak 2. Call to order 3. Call to order inserted in record 4. Simple admonition (entrains expulsion for 24 hours) 5. Admonition with expulsion for 5 days 6. Admonition with expulsion for 15 days (5 and 6 above result in loss of daily allowance)	1. to 4. by the ANP President; 5. and 6. by simple majority of the ANP in secret vote.
COSTA RICA Legislative Assembly	Call to order; withdrawal of right to speak.	President of the Assembly

Country and House(s)	13.1 Sanctions in increasing order of severity	13.2 Application of sanctions
CUBA National Assembly of People's Power	Call to order; withdrawal of right to speak.	President of the National Assembly
CYPRUS House of Representatives	Call to order; withdrawal of right to speak; deletion of words from the record; withdrawal of offending words.	The President of the House
CZECHOSLOVAKIA Chamber of Nations Chamber of the People	1. Call to order 2. Request to discontinue speech 3. Disciplinary measures	1. and 2. Chairman of the Chamber; 3. Presidium of the Chamber.
DEMOCRATIC YEMEN Supreme People's Council	Reprimand; warning; deletion from list of speakers; withdrawal of the right to participate in the current debate; suspension for remainder of the sitting.	Chairman
DENMARK Folketing	1. Request to discontinue speech 2. Call to order 3. Withdrawal of right to speak again in the same sitting 4. Suspension from the sittings for up to 14 sitting days	1., 2. and 3. the President; 4. the SO Cttee.
EGYPT People's Assembly	Withdrawal of right to speak; reprimand; suspension for 1 sitting; suspension for no more than 2 sittings; suspension for more than 5 sittings; referral to the Values Cttee, for urgent report, of the Member's violation.	The Assembly
FIJI Senate House of Representatives	1. Attention drawn to misconduct 2. Presiding officer orders withdrawal or discontinuation of remarks 3. After naming, MP may be suspended from House for a period of suspension (usually remainder of sitting) 4. If grave disorder, adjournment of the sitting	1., 2. and 4. by President in the Senate, or Speaker in the House of Representatives; 3. by the House.

Country and House(s)	13.1 Sanctions in increasing order of severity	13.2 Application of sanctions
FINLAND Eduskunta	Call to order; withdrawal of right to speak; warning; exclusion from Parliament for a specified period (not exceeding 2 weeks); trial by a Court.	Speaker and the Parlt by motion
FRANCE Senate National Assembly	1. Call to order 2. Call to order noted in record 3. Written warning with admonition 4. Admonition with temporary suspension	1. and 2. President; 3. and 4. House.
GABON National Assembly	Call to order; call to order noted in the record; admonition; admonition with temporary suspension.	President of Assembly
GERMAN DEMOCRATIC REPUBLIC People's Chamber	No sanctions prescribed	NA
GERMANY Federal Council	None	NA
Federal Diet	Call to order; request to discontinue speech; suspension for remainder of the sitting; suspension for up to 30 sittings. Adjourn the sitting in event of grave disorder.	The President
GREECE Chamber of Deputies	1. Call to order noted in the record 2. Withdrawal of right to speak until the debate ends 3. Publication of offence and call to order in the Official Journal, 3 daily newspapers of the capital and two of the offender's electorate, at the offender's expense 4. Suspension with loss of 1/2 salary and allowances for up to 20 days	1. President; 2., 3. and 4. President with approval of the Chamber.
HUNGARY National Assembly	Call to order; withdrawal of right to speak; suspension for remainder of sitting.	President of the Assembly

Country and House(s)	13.1 Sanctions in increasing order of severity	13.2 Application of sanctions
INDIA Council of States House of the People	1. Call to order 2. Request to discontinue speech 3. Order not to record remarks in the record of debates 4. Order to withdraw from the House 5. Naming, which may be followed by suspension not exceeding the remainder of the session 6. Adjournment of the sitting in case of great disorder	1., 2., 3., 4. and 6. Presiding Officer; 5. Named by the Presiding Officer with suspension on motion by the House.
INDONESIA House of Representatives	Call to order; withdrawal of right to speak; suspension from the sitting.	Chairman of the sitting
IRELAND Senate Dáil	1. Withdrawal of permission to speak 2. Suspension for the remainder of day's sitting 3. Suspension from service of the House till the 4th, 8th or 12th day for the 1st, 2nd and 3rd offence respectively 4. Adjournment of the House in case of grave disorder	1., 2. and 4. Chairman; 3. The House, following the naming of the Member by the Chairman.
ISRAEL The Knesset	1. Call to order 2. Withdrawal of right to speak 3. Withdrawal of the right to speak for remainder of sitting 4. Suspension for the sitting 5. Suspension for up to 5 sittings	1. to 4. Applied by the Chairman; 5. By the House Cttee.
ITALY Senate Chamber of Deputies	1. Call to order 2. Second call to order 3. Suspension for the rest of the sitting 4. Admonition with expulsion for a period of less than 10 sitting days in the Senate or from 2 to 15 sitting days in the Chamber	1., 2. and 3. The President with help of the Questors; 4. The President with help of the Questors on decision of relevant Presiding Officer's Cttee

Country and House(s)	13.1 Sanctions in increasing order of severity	13.2 Application of sanctions
IVORY COAST National Assembly	1. Call to order 2. Call to order recorded in the minutes 3. Admonition (entrains loss of half allowance for two weeks) 4. Censure with temporary suspension (entrains loss of half allowance for 1 month) 5. Suspension of the sitting for tumultuous disorder	1. and 5. President in the chair; 2. By show of hands on proposal of the President; 3. and 4. By a majority of those present in secret ballot on proposal of the President.
JAPAN House of Councillors House of Representatives	1. Admonition in an open sitting 2. Withdrawal of right to speak 3. Apology in an open sitting 4. Suspension from House for remainder of sitting 5. Suspension from the House for a certain period 6. Expulsion	1., 3., 5. and 6 are decided by the House, if necessary with assistance of the Cttee on Discipline. 5. Requires a 2/3 majority of Members present; 2. and 4. are taken by the Presiding Officer.
JORDAN Senate House of Deputies	Censure; withdrawal of right to speak for remainder of sitting; suspension for remainder of sitting; suspension for up to 1 month.	The respective House on proposal of the Presiding Officer
KENYA National Assembly	1. Warning 2. Withdrawal of right to speak 3. Suspension for remainder of the sitting 4. Naming (suspension for 3, 7 and 28 days for 1st, 2nd and 3rd offence respectively) 5. Removal for remainder of session (when Member refuses to withdraw voluntarily)	1. and 2. The Speaker; 3. to 5. The Assembly through the Speaker.
KUWAIT National Assembly	Warning; admonition; withdrawal of speaking rights; suspension from the sitting; suspension not exceeding 2 weeks.	National Assembly which may revoke sanction on submission of a written apology.
LEBANON National Assembly	Suspension from the sitting	President of the Assembly

Country and House(s)	13.1 Sanctions in increasing order of severity	13.2 Application of sanctions
LIECHTENSTEIN Diet	Call to order; withdrawal of the right to speak.	President of the Diet
LUXEMBOURG Chamber of Deputies	First and second call to order; withdrawal of the right to speak; admonition noted in the record; suspension for a sitting; suspension for 10 sittings	President of the Chamber
MALAWI National Assembly	1. Call to order 2. Withdrawal of the right to speak 3. Suspension for the remainder of the day's sitting 4. Naming, followed by suspension for 1, 2 or 4 weeks for the 1st, 2nd and subsequent offences respectively (suspension may be rescinded by the Assembly on receipt of written regrets) 5. Adjournment of the sitting in case of grave disorder	1., 2., 3. and 5. Speaker; 4. Assembly on Speaker's motion.
MALAYSIA Senate House of Representatives	Call to order; withdrawal of the right to speak; suspension for remainder of the day's sitting; naming; suspension for remainder of the session (in case of refusal to withdraw); adjournment of the House in case of grave disorder.	The Presiding Officer
MALI National Assembly	Call to order; call to order recorded in the minutes; admonition; admonition with temporary suspension.	President of the Assembly

468

Country and House(s)	13.1 Sanctions in increasing order of severity	13.2 Application of sanctions
MALTA House of Representatives	1. Call to order 2. Withdrawal of the right to speak (for irrelevance or repetition) or 3. A motion that the Member be no longer heard 4. Suspension for the remainder of the sitting 5. Naming, which involves suspension for 1, 2 or 4 weeks for the 1st, 2nd and 3rd occasion, respectively 6. Suspension for a longer period	1., 2. and 4. by the Speaker; 3., 5. and 6. by the House on initiative of the Speaker.
MAURITIUS Legislative Assembly	Immediate withdrawal from the Assembly; suspension from 1 to 20 sittings.	The Speaker
MEXICO Chamber of Senators	No provisions	NA
Chamber of Deputies		
MONACO National Council	Request to withdraw what has been said; order not to print what has been said in the verbatim record; call to order; call to order noted in the record.	Presiding Officer
MONGOLIA Great People's Khural (GPKh)	No sanctions are applied.	NA
NAURU Parliament	1. Named by the Chair (in plenary or cttee meetings) 2. Suspension from service (1st time in the year 1 day, 2nd time 7 days, 3rd and following times 28 days) 3. Order to withdraw immediately from House escorted by the Sergeant-at-Arms if necessary 4. Arrest by the Sergeant-at-Arms with subsequent disciplinary action by Parlt at the Bar of the House	1. Speaker; 2., and 3. Speaker on a motion of Parlt; 4. Parliament.

469

Country and House(s)	13.1 Sanctions in increasing order of severity	13.2 Application of sanctions
NETHERLANDS First Chamber	1. Warning 2. Order to resume seat for the duration of the debate 3. Suspension from remainder of the day's sitting 4. Suspension for a period not longer than the end of the parliamentary year	1., 2. and 3. The President; 4. The Chamber.
Second Chamber	1. Call to order or admonition 2. Withdrawal of the right to speak 3. Request to withdraw expressions and if so deletion from the verbatim report 4. Suspension for remainder of day's sitting 5. Suspension for up to 1 month	1., 2., 3. and 4. Chairman of the Chamber; 5. The Chamber.
NEW ZEALAND House of Representatives	1. Withdrawal of the right to speak 2. Suspension for remainder of the day's sitting 3. Naming and suspension from the service of the House (but not cttees) for 24 hours on the 1st occasion, 7 days for the 2nd, and 28 days for the 3rd 4. Adjournment of the House or suspension of the sitting in case of grave disorder	1., 2. and 4. Speaker or Chairman; 3. Speaker or Chairman and House on motion.
NICARAGUA National Assembly	Warning; withdrawal of the right to speak for the sitting; as above, for 3 consecutive sittings; suspension; withdrawal of the right to speak for an indeterminate number of sittings.	Directive Board
NORWAY Storting	Warning; withdrawal of the right to speak; suspension for remainder of the day's sitting.	Warning by the President; other sanctions by the Storting on the President's proposal.
PHILIPPINES National Assembly	Suspension not exceeding 60 days; expulsion.	The Assembly with the concurrence of 2/3 membership

Country and House(s)	13.1 Sanctions in increasing order of severity	13.2 Application of sanctions
POLAND Diet	Call to order; call to order noted in the record; call to order and warning of withdrawal of right to speak at the 3rd infraction; withdrawal of the right to speak; suspension from the sitting.	Diet Presidium (The Member disciplined has a right of appeal within 3 days to the Presidium which would seek advice from the Mandates and Rules Cttee).
PORTUGAL Assembly of the Republic	Call to order; withdrawal of the right to speak.	President of the Assembly
REPUBLIC OF KOREA National Assembly	Call to order; cut off microphone and stop recording; withdrawal of the right to speak; temporary suspension of speeches; order to delete portions of speeches from record.	Speaker or Presiding Officer
ROMANIA Grand National Assembly	Call to order; 2nd call to order; withdrawal of the right to speak.	President of the Assembly, supported by the Vice-Presidents and Secretaries.
RWANDA National Development Council (CND)	1. Call to order 2. Call to order noted in record 3. Suspension for the remainder of the day's sitting	1. and 2. President; 3. President on consulting the House.
ST VINCENT House of Assembly	Warning; naming; suspension for remainder of the sitting; fine by deduction from salary.	Speaker
SENEGAL National Assembly	1. Call to order 2. Call to order noted in record 3. Admonition 4. Suspension for up to 24 hours	1. Assembly President; 2., 3. and 4. Assembly on proposal of the President.
SOLOMON ISLANDS National Parliament	–	Speaker
SOMALIA People's Assembly	Call to order; suspension for the remainder of the sitting; suspension for 2 days.	President of the Assembly

Country and House(s)	13.1 Sanctions in increasing order of severity	13.2 Application of sanctions
SOUTH AFRICA House of Assembly House of Representatives House of Delegates	1. Warning 2. Withdrawal of right to speak 3. Suspension for remainder of the day's sitting 4. Naming, which entails suspension for 5, 10 or 20 sitting days on 1st, 2nd and subsequent occasions, respectively, with R40 deducted from salary for each day's suspension 5. Fine 6. Expulsion from the House 7. Suspension of the sitting in event of grave disorder	1., 2., 3. and 7. Presiding Officer; 4. Presiding Officer followed by motion of the Leader of the House or a Minister; 5. and 6. are sanctions available to the House by motion or on initiative of the Presiding Officer.
SPAIN Senate Congress of Deputies	1. Suspension for 1 or 2 sittings 2. Fine or loss of certain rights 3. Temporary removal of status as Member	1. House President; 2. Presiding Body; 3. Plenary of the House.
SRI LANKA Parliament	1. Call to order 2. Withdrawal of right to speak 3. Suspension for remainder of the day's sitting 4. Naming (entailing suspension for 1 week, 2 weeks or 1 month for 1st, 2nd and subsequent namings, respectively) 5. Suspension of the sitting for grave disorder	1., 2., 3., 5. and naming by the Speaker; suspension after naming by Parliament.
SWEDEN Riksdag	Admonition; withdrawal of right to speak.	Speaker
SWITZERLAND States Council	Call to order	Council President
National Council	Call to order; withdrawal of right to speak (if contested, put to the vote without debate, and if carried, entered in the record); suspension or adjournment of the Council in case of great disorder.	National Council President
SYRIAN ARAB REPUBLIC People's Council	Call to order; withdrawal of right to speak; suspension from the sitting.	President of the People's Council

Country and House(s)	13.1 Sanctions in increasing order of severity	13.2 Application of sanctions
THAILAND Senate House of Representatives	Warning; request to withdraw remarks; withdrawal of the right to speak; request for apology or temporary suspension with or without time limit.	Speaker of the House
TUNISIA Chamber of Deputies	Warning; call to order; suspension for remainder of the sitting. Other sanctions may be proposed by the Bureau depending on the nature of the case.	President of the Chamber of Deputies
UGANDA National Assembly	1. Reprimand 2. Withdrawal of the right to speak 3. Suspension for remainder of the day's sitting 4. Naming entailing suspension for 3, 7 or 28 sittings for the 1st, 2nd and subsequent offences respectively	1.,2. et 3. Speaker; 4. Speaker on motion moved by a Minister.
UNION OF SOVIET SOCIALIST REPUBLICS Soviet of Nationalities Soviet of the Union	None	Not governed by the rules of procedure
UNITED KINGDOM House of Lords	Motion that "The noble Lord be no longer heard " (very rare).	The House acting through the Leader of the House
House of Commons	Order for an MP to resume his seat (i.e. withdrawal of the right to speak); temporary suspension for remainder of the day's sitting; naming (entailing suspension for 5 or 20 sitting days or remainder of the session for the 1st, 2nd and 3rd offences respectively; if force required to make an MP withdraw, suspension is automatic for remainder of session); suspension of a sitting or adjournment of the House by the Speaker in case of grave disorder.	The Chair and the House with assistance if necessary of the Sergeant at Arms

473

Country and House(s)	13.1 Sanctions in increasing order of severity	13.2 Application of sanctions
UNITED REPUBLIC OF TANZANIA National Assembly	1. Order to resume one's seat (withdrawal of the right to speak) 2. Suspension for remainder of the sitting 3. Suspension for 5 or 20 days for 1st and 2nd offences respectively	1. and 2. Speaker; 3. The Assembly.
UNITED STATES OF AMERICA Senate	1. Call to order 2. Censure 3. Expulsion (see 3.3)	1. Presiding Officer; 2. and 3. The House.
House of Representatives	Sanctions include but are not limited to: call to order; reprimand; censure; fine; expulsion (see 3.3).	Speaker
VANUATU Parliament	1. Temporary suspension 2. Adjournment of Parlt in case of grave disorder	1. Parliament; 2. Speaker.
YUGOSLAVIA Federal Chamber	1. Warning 2. Withdrawal of the right to speak	1. and 2. President of the Chamber; 3. The Chamber.
Chamber of Republics and Provinces	3. Temporary suspension	
ZAIRE Legislative Council	Call to order; call to order by name; call to order noted in the record; temporary suspension.	Presiding Officer
ZAMBIA National Assembly	1. Call to order 2. Withdrawal of the right to speak 3. Suspension for remainder of the day's sitting 4. Naming which entails suspension for 1, 2 or 4 weeks for the 1st, 2nd and subsequent offences respectively 5. Adjournment of the House in case of grave disorder	1., 2., 3. and 5. Speaker; 4. The House.
ZIMBABWE Senate House of Assembly	Call to order; warning; withdrawal of unparliamentary language; temporary suspension; suspension for a period on resolution of the House.	Presiding Officer

TABLE 14

METHODS OF VOTING IN THE HOUSE

During the course of its proceedings, and especially when a debate comes to an end, Parliament has to take decisions, and usually does so by voting. From a vote, a majority emerges on the matter under discussion and, according to democratic principles, the opinion of the majority over-rides that of the minority and becomes binding on all citizens. Naturally enough, this crystallization of the will of the people is surrounded by special ceremony and is safeguarded by rules designed on the one hand to eliminate any possibility of error or fraud and, on the other hand, to ensure by publication of the vote that the electorate is informed of the actions of their representatives.

Public or Secret Voting

With few exceptions, decisions taken by Parliament are usually open and public, as can be seen from Table 14A. In most countries, voting is

TABLE 14A. Public or Secret Vote

Type of Vote	Number of Countries
Public, Except when SO or Parlt Requires Otherwise	20
Public	33
Public, Except for the Nomination or Election of Candidates for Office	28
Usually Secret	1
As decided by the Presidium	1
Total	83

public in the sense that it takes place in the presence of people who have come to attend the sitting and can see what line a Member is taking, or public in that the way a Member has voted can be ascertained because it is published in the official record of the debates. Publication of names is not always desirable and is generally avoided when the House functions as an electoral body and when it makes its own appointments either within the House itself or for the various bodies in which it is represented and for which it nominates members. Although voting is often public, when Parliament makes nominations or elections of candidates for office, the votes of its Members are not published.

475

Secret voting is not always confined to appointments and many Parliaments (for example, Algeria, Comoros, Cyprus, the Republic of Korea and Spain) have provisions for its use in certain circumstances such as checking the credentials of Members or unseating a Member. When a vote is secret, there is no way of knowing how any individual Member has voted. The most that can be done is to check the Members' names to ensure that they have voted only once. For a secret vote, ballot papers carrying the names of candidates (where appointments are being made) or the alternative proposals (where other matters are being decided) are inserted by each Member into unmarked envelopes which, in turn, are placed in a ballot box.

Although most of the votes taken by Parliament are public, the use of certain methods of voting designed to save the time of the House, give a certain measure of anonymity to the decisions taken and, because they are unrecorded, it is impossible to ascertain how each individual Member has voted. The various methods of voting employed, several of which may be used in any given Parliament, are presented in Table 14B. Four of these methods viz. voice, show of hands, standing and sitting and voting

TABLE 14B. Method of Voting

Method of Voting	Number of Countries
Voice	37
Show of Hands	43
Standing and Sitting	39
Division	20
Roll Call	46
Ballot Papers	40
Ballot Balls or Tokens	5
Electronic Voting Machines	15
Acclamation	2

papers or balls (unless bearing the Member's name), are all unrecorded. Four of them i.e. divisions, roll call, the use of electronic voting machines and voting papers bearing the Member's name, are recorded and enable the name of the Member and the way he has voted to be published. Each of these methods and the reason for its use will be discussed in turn.

Unrecorded Methods of Voting

First there is oral, or voice, voting where the Presiding Officer calls upon Members of the House to signify their views in turn by calling out "Aye" or "No". The opinion which is expressed most loudly is regarded as being the opinion of the majority. At times it may be difficult to say what is the outcome of an oral vote, as can be seen from the cautious wording used by the President or Speaker, "I think that..." and in the frequency with which these votes are challenged. The margin of error inherent in the system limits its use for practical purposes to votes in which there is virtually no dissent. It comes close to a vote by tacit consent in that the question from the Chair whether there are "any objections" usually leads to the adoption of a proposal. Voice votes are used in Japan, Kuwait, Malawi, Sweden, the United Kingdom, the United States, and a number of other countries.

Secondly, there is voting by show of hands. This method is more reliable than oral voting because it allows a rough count of those for and against a question and is used when a public ballot is not expressly required by the Constitution or by the rules of procedure. This is the usual method in many countries including Austria, Bulgaria, Cape Verde, Comoros, Democratic Yemen, Mongolia, USSR and Vanuatu.

The third form of anonymous voting is standing and sitting. This method resembles voting by show of hands but is more accurate, and is often used to check a vote by show of hands or voice voting. When the result of this method is difficult to decide, especially where the voting is close and the protagonists of each side of a question are scattered throughout the House, the accuracy of a vote by standing and sitting can be improved by the Presiding Officer asking Members to gather together according to opinion on one side of the Chamber or the other in order to facilitate the counting of the votes. Voting by standing and sitting is used in thirty-nine countries which include Brazil, Greece, Luxembourg and Portugal.

The fourth form of anonymous voting is by voting papers not bearing the name of the Member who casts his vote, or by balls or tokens differing in colour according to the way the Member wishes to vote. The voting papers are used for secret voting where the Member writes down his choice on the paper, folds it and either places it into urns that are passed around the benches, or deposits it into a single urn following a roll-call.

Recorded Methods of Voting

When any or all of these methods fail to give a result, or when it is necessary to record the vote given by each Member, a more precise form of ballot is held. This is more time-consuming and can provide an opportunity for obstruction, but it makes it possible for the names of the Members and an indication of how they have voted to be recorded in the official report or the minutes of proceedings of the House. Four main methods of voting are used to achieve these objectives.

Firstly, there is the division where Members gather on the side of the Chamber to the left or right of the Presiding Officer or walk through lobbies on either side of the Chamber, their names being noted by Clerks and their numbers counted by tellers as they emerge from these lobbies. This method is used in the United Kingdom and a number of other countries which follow the British practice.

The second kind of recorded vote, vote by roll call, is more widely used. As each name is called out, the Member replies "Aye" or "No", or "I abstain", the replies are ticked off as they are called, and the numbers in favour, against and abstaining give the result. Roll call votes are used in forty-six countries, often on request, in preference over simpler anonymous methods and are perhaps more suited to small Houses than to larger ones.

The third method of recorded voting is by electronic voting machine, which has the advantages of speed and precision as it saves time and avoids disputes. Votes are cast by pressing a series of buttons located on the desk of each Member, registered instantaneously and computed. The results are shown immediately on a lighted board on the wall of the Chamber and, simultaneously, all the particulars of the vote including the names of Members and the way in which they have voted, are printed or photographed so that the results can be published rapidly and completely. Electronic voting machines are used in fifteen countries, which include Belgium, Brazil, Egypt, India, Italy and Yugoslavia.

The final method of recorded voting is by using voting papers bearing the name of the Member who casts his vote by placing them into urns passed around the benches.

Although we have seen that there are several different methods of voting, one conclusion can be drawn which is that almost every Parliament uses at least one method of both unrecorded or recorded voting. Ordinarily, it uses methods of unrecorded voting which are rapid and informal but, if a result is in doubt, it can resort to methods of recorded voting which are slower but more accurate. In some Parliaments these latter methods are compulsory for certain matters such as motions of censure and final votes on Bills and money Bills. The British system is to rely on oral voting as the unrecorded method and voting by division as the recorded method, while on the European continent and in many other countries, voting by show of hands or by standing and sitting is the usual unrecorded method and voting by roll call the most widely used recorded method.

Voting by Proxy

Most of the voting methods already discussed require Members of Parliament to be present in the House in person. Voting by proxy is prohibited in all countries with the exception of Brazil, Cameroon, Comoros, France, Gabon, Ivory Coast, Luxembourg, Mali and Senegal. In the United Kingdom House of Commons a proxy is allowed for a Member incapacitated by illness, provided he is in the House precincts. The main objection to voting by proxy is that a Member cannot properly exercise his essential duty of voting if he is unaware, as he frequently must be if he is not present, of the precise issue on which his vote is to be cast. Proxy voting also encourages absenteeism, but it has the advantage of eliminating surprise votes especially when the balance between majority and minority is a fine one. To some extent the practice of "pairing" lightens the Members' burden of having to be present in order to vote. If a Member of Parliament intends to be absent from the House, he asks a Member in an opposite political group not to take part in votes during his absence, so leaving the balance between the majority and the minority unaffected. This system, based on personal agreements between Members is found, for example, in Australia, Canada, the United Kingdom and the United States of America.

TABLE 14: METHODS OF VOTING IN THE HOUSE

Country and House(s)	14.1 Methods of voting	14.2 Public or secret vote	14.3 Publication of names	14.4 Proxy voting
ALGERIA National People's Assembly	Show of hands or roll call	Public. Vote is secret: for elections; for disqualification of an MP; to waive an MP's immunity.	No	No
ARGENTINA Senate Chamber of Deputies	Show of hands; standing and sitting; electronic voting machines; roll call (for election of House authorities and cttee Members, also at the request of 1/5 of MPs present).	Public	Yes, for roll call.	No
AUSTRALIA Senate House of Representatives	Voice and division. Elections of Presiding Officers by ballot papers (provisions exist for ballot in other, rarely used, circumstances).	Public, except for ballots (see 14.1).	Only if division occurs.	No
AUSTRIA Federal Council National Council	Show of hands; roll call if requested by President or 5 Members. Standing and sitting; roll call if requested by President or 25 Members.	Secret ballot if demanded by President or 5 MPs in Federal Council or 25 MPs in National Council and approved by a vote.	Yes, in case of roll calls.	No
BAHAMAS Senate House of Assembly	Standing and sitting; divisions; roll call.	Public	Recorded in minutes, if requested.	No

Country and House(s)	14.1 Methods of voting	14.2 Public or secret vote	14.3 Public-ation of names	14.4 Proxy voting
BELGIUM Senate Chamber of Representatives	Standing and sitting; electronic voting machines; roll call; casting of ballot papers.	Public, except for appointments.	Yes, except for secret votes.	No
BRAZIL Federal Senate Chamber of Deputies	Leader votes for party. Standing and sitting (usually); voice vote and roll call (when requested by Members). Ballot (for election of Board). Electronic voting machines.	Public (except for secret sessions, election of Board or when requested and approved by House).	Only for roll call or electronic voting machine	Allowed when agreed beforehand or on sitting and standing voting
BULGARIA National Assembly	Show of hands; roll call if Assembly decides or ballot if Assembly decides on secret vote.	Usually public unless Assembly decides otherwise.	No	No
CAMEROON National Assembly	Ballot papers	Usually secret, but public for Const. amdts or if requested by 16 Members.	For public votes	Yes
CANADA Senate House of Commons	Voice or (at request of at least 5 MPs) roll call.	Public	Yes, for roll call	No
CAPE VERDE People's National Assembly	Show of hands (Bills, resolutions, motions); ballot paper (for elections).	Public, except for elections.	No	No
CHINA National People's Congress (NPC)	Show of hands; secret ballot; or otherwise, as decided by Presidium.	Public or private as decided by the Presidium	No	No

480

Country and House(s)	14.1 Methods of voting	14.2 Public or secret vote	14.3 Public-ation of names	14.4 Proxy voting
COMOROS Federal Assembly	Show of hands (usual); roll call; ballot papers.	Ballot is secret. Roll call is decision of President of Assembly, at request of Govt, or the cttee concerned, or when the col-lective respon-sibility of Govt is at issue.	For roll call	Yes, but must be legally authentic-ated for motion of censure or con-fidence or elec-tion of Assembly Presi-dent.
CONGO People's National Assembly (ANP)	Show of hands (usually); standing and sitting; ballot papers.	Both	No	No
COSTA RICA Legislative Assembly	Standing and sitting; roll call; casting of black (no) and white (yes) balls.	Public	No	No
CUBA National Assembly of People's Power	Show of hands; roll call; ballot papers.	Both. Secret ballot for elections.	When voting by roll call	No
CYPRUS House of Representatives	Show of hands	Public, except for impeachment of the President or Vice-President of the Republic.	No	No
CZECHOSLOVAKIA Chamber of Nations Chamber of the People	Usually by show of hands unless Chamber decides otherwise; by ballot papers for a motion of confidence.	Both. Secret for election of President of Republic; Presidium, Chairman, and Vice-Chairman of the Assembly and the Cham-bers; and cttee chairmen.	No	No

481

TABLE 14: METHODS OF VOTING IN THE HOUSE (continued)

Country and House(s)	14.1 Methods of voting	14.2 Public or secret vote	14.3 Public-ation of names	14.4 Proxy voting
DEMOCRATIC YEMEN Supreme People's Council	Show of hands	Public	No	No
DENMARK Folketing	Electronic voting (usual); standing and sitting; roll call, if requested in writing by 17 Members or if President decides.	Public	Only for roll call	No
EGYPT People's Assembly	Electronic voting (may be opposed by 30 Members in writing); show of hands; standing and sitting ; roll call (for special majority, on request of Speaker, Prime Minister or 30 Members, or uncertainty from other methods.)	Public	For roll call	No
FIJI Senate House of Representatives	Voice vote or by division on request of a Member	Public	Yes	No
FINLAND Eduskunta	Electronic voting (most common); standing and sitting; ballot papers (when machine vote tied and for elections).	Public, except for elections.	Generally yes	No

Country and House(s)	14.1 Methods of voting	14.2 Public or secret vote	14.3 Public-ation of names	14.4 Proxy voting
FRANCE Senate National Assembly	Show of hands (usually, except for elections); standing and sitting (when show of hands leads to doubt); electronic voting machines only in the Assembly (or ballot in case of machine failure); ballot papers (in National Assembly, only for elections).	Public, except for elections.	For public vote	Yes
GABON National Assembly	Show of hands; standing and sitting; public ballot papers; acclamation.	Public	No	If MP is unavoid-ably absent through sickness.
GERMAN DEMOCRATIC REPUBLIC People's Chamber	Show of hands; standing and sitting.	Public	No	No
GERMANY Federal Council	Show of hands; roll call if requested by a State and for election of Council Presi-dent.	Public	Only in case of roll call	Votes may be cast by MPs present or their substi-tutes.
Federal Diet	Show of hands; standing and sitting; voting cards bearing MP's name (if requested by a group or 26 MPs); secret ballot (for certain elec-tions); division.	Usually public. Secret for election of President and Federal Chancellor.	After a vote by voting cards	No

483

Country and House(s)	14.1 Methods of voting	14.2 Public or secret vote	14.3 Public-ation of names	14.4 Proxy voting
GREECE Chamber of Deputies	Standing and sitting (usual); roll call; secret ballot papers.	Public, except for ballot.	Yes, in case of roll call.	No
HUNGARY National Assembly	Show of hands; roll call (by Assembly decision or written request of 30 Members).	Public	Yes	No
INDIA Council of States

House of the People | Voice vote; standing and sitting; electronic voting machines; "Aye/No" slips; division into lobbies (which includes roll call). | Public | Yes | No |
| INDONESIA House of Representatives | Voice vote; show of hands; standing and sitting; ballot papers. | Both. Secret for matters concerning persons or when decided by the House. | No | No |
| IRELAND Senate

Dáil | Division, by walking through lobbies. | Public | Yes | No |
| ISRAEL The Knesset | Show of hands; roll call if requested by at least 20 MPs; ballot papers for elections and withdrawal of immunity. | All public, except for ballot. | Roll call: names and votes. Ballot: only of those voting. | No |
| ITALY Senate

Chamber of Deputies | Show of hands; division; electronic voting machines; roll call; ballot by balls (obsolescent); ballot papers. | Both | Roll call: names and vote. Secret ballot: names only. | No |

484

Country and House(s)	14.1 Methods of voting	14.2 Public or secret vote	14.3 Public- ation of names	14.4 Proxy voting
IVORY COAST National Assembly	Show of hands (usually); standing and sitting (in case of doubt); public ballot; secret ballot.	Both	No	If absent for sickness or offi- cial duty
JAPAN House of Councillors House of Representatives	Voice vote; standing and sitting (when voice opposed); casting white or blue named ballots (when 1/5 MPs re- quest).	Public	Yes (in case of an open ballot).	No
JORDAN Senate House of Deputies	Show of hands (usual); secret ballot papers; roll call (for constitutional matters or vote of confidence).	Usually public, but secret for election of the Presiding Officers and cttees.	Yes, except secret ballot.	No
KENYA National Assembly	Voice vote; division if the Speaker consi- ders doubt exists, or if 20 Members rise to support division motion, or for Const. Bills.	Public	Yes	No
KUWAIT National Assembly	Voice vote; show of hands; roll call (Bills, decrees, treat- ies, for special majorities or when requested by Govt, Presi- dent or 10 MPs). Ballot papers (for elections).	Public (secret when Assembly sits in camera).	For roll call vote	No

Country and House(s)	14.1 Methods of voting	14.2 Public or secret vote	14.3 Public-ation of names	14.4 Proxy voting
LEBANON National Assembly	Voice vote (for Bills); roll call (in case of doubt); ballot papers (for elections).	Secret for elections	Yes	No
LIECHTENSTEIN Diet	Voice vote; show of hands (votes and public elections); ballot papers (secret elections).	Public including election of Diet Officers, the National Cttee and Diet cttees. Other elections are secret unless decided otherwise.	No	No
LUXEMBOURG Chamber of Deputies	Standing and sitting (usual); roll call for final vote on Bills and if requested by 5 Members.	Public except for secret sessions	Yes	Limited to 1 proxy per Member
MALAWI National Assembly	Voice vote (usual); division (at discretion of Speaker or requested by 4 Members); ballot papers (for elections).	Public	When divisions occur.	No
MALAYSIA Senate House of Representatives	Voice vote; division (if supported by at least 15 Members).	Public	For divisions	No
MALI National Assembly	Voice vote; show of hands; sitting and standing.	Usually public, secret for appointments.	–	Yes
MALTA House of Representatives	Voice vote; roll call.	Public (SO provide for a closed sitting but this has never occurred since 1947).	Yes, un-less the House orders other-wise.	No

Country and House(s)	14.1 Methods of voting	14.2 Public or secret vote	14.3 Public- ation of names	14.4 Proxy voting
MAURITIUS Legislative Assembly	Voice vote (usual); stand- ing (where a Member's re- quest for div- ision is viewed as unnecessary by the Speak- er); division by roll call.	Public, except for election of Speaker and Deputy Speaker.	Yes	No
MEXICO Chamber of Senators Chamber of Deputies	Voice vote; show of hands; stand- ing and sitting; roll call to aprove laws for decrees; ballot papers for elec- tion of govern- ing body.	Public, except for election of governing body.	No	–
MONACO National Council	Show of hands; roll call; ballot papers.	Public, except for elections and office nomina- tions, or if the National Council decides other- wise.	Yes	No
MONGOLIA Great People's Khural (GPKh)	Show of hands	Public	Not necess- arily	No
NAURU Parliament	Voice vote; division (if voice vote is chal- lenged by more than 1 Member); ballot papers (for elections and when Parlt so decides).	Public, except for ballots.	For divisions	No

Country and House(s)	14.1 Methods of voting	14.2 Public or secret vote	14.3 Public- ation of names	14.4 Proxy voting
NETHERLANDS First Chamber	Roll call; standing and sitting; ballot papers (for votes on persons).	Public, except for votes on persons.	Yes, for roll call but not for standing and sitting.	No
Second Chamber	Show of hands; standing and sitting; roll call; ballot papers (for votes on persons).	Public, unless the Chamber is sitting in camera or for votes concerning persons.	Yes for roll call.	
NEW ZEALAND House of Representatives	Voice vote; division if voice vote contested.	Public	Yes	No
NICARAGUA National Assembly	Show of hands	Public	No	No
NORWAY Storting	Electronic voting is usual but standing and sitting used when agreed by all Members; roll call for Const. amdts and no-confi- dence motions; ballot papers for elections and appointments.	Public, except for ballots.	Names appear in the pro- ceedings for a roll call. They are available from an electronic vote on request.	No
PHILIPPINES National Assembly	Voice vote; standing and sitting in case of doubt or a division is called (with tellers if doubt persists); roll call if requested by 1/5 Members.	Public	Yes, for nominal voting (roll call) on 3rd read- ing of a Bill.	No

TABLE 14: METHODS OF VOTING IN THE HOUSE (continued)

Country and House(s)	14.1 Methods of voting	14.2 Public or secret vote	14.3 Public-ation of names	14.4 Proxy voting
POLAND Diet	Show of hands (usual); roll call (at request of President or 30 Members but not used in the last 30 years).	Public	No, except for roll call.	No
PORTUGAL Assembly of the Republic	Sitting and standing (usual); secret ballot using black and white balls; roll call if requested by 25 Members and for certain matters in SO.	Public, except for elections, appointments, certain matters specified in SO and if Assembly so resolves on request of 25 Members.	No. Distribu-tion of votes by parties is usually announced.	No
REPUBLIC OF KOREA National Assembly	Voice vote; standing and sitting; ballot papers. Show of hands used in cttees.	Public, except on a request of Speaker or deci-sion of plenary; for Bills vetoed by President; elections in National Assem-bly; motions for dismissal of Min-isters; impeach-ments; discipli-nary measures.	Yes, except secret vote or decision by Assembly.	No
ROMANIA Grand National Assembly	Show of hands; secret ballot papers for elections or balls for other votes.	Both, but secret if so resolved by the Assembly on Bureau propo-sal.	No	No
RWANDA National Development Council	Voice vote; standing and sit-ting; roll call; division; ballot papers.	Secret for elections and when SO specify.	No	No
ST VINCENT House of Assembly	Voice vote (usual); division by roll call; casting of ballot papers.	Public, unless otherwise de-cided by the House.	When division occurs.	No

489

Country and House(s)	14.1 Methods of voting	14.2 Public or secret vote	14.3 Public- ation of names	14.4 Proxy voting
SENEGAL National Assembly	Show of hands (usual); stand- ing and sitting (if show of hands indeter- minate); public ballot papers with names (if doubt persists); secret ballot without names.	The vote is always published even when the ballot itself is secret.	For public votes by ballot	Only when absence of MP is officially authorised.
SOLOMON ISLANDS National Parliament	Voice vote; division if called for.	Public	-	-
SOMALIA People's Assembly	Show of hands	Public	No	No
SOUTH AFRICA House of Assembly House of Representatives House of Delegates	Voice vote; division if requested by any Member, supported by 3 others.	Public	Yes	No
SPAIN Senate Congress of Deputies	By assent (no objection raised to proposal put by the Presi- dent); standing and sitting or electronic voting machines (at the discretion of the President); roll call (when requested by SO, or on request of 2 groups or 1/5 MPs); secret ballot (papers or balls).	Public, except when required by SO or requested by 2 groups or 1/5 Members. Voting on legislative matters must be public.	-	No

Country and House(s)	14.1 Methods of voting	14.2 Public or secret vote	14.3 Public- ation of names	14.4 Proxy voting
SRI LANKA Parliament	Voice vote; division by recording names separately (if voice vote challenged).	Public	Public	No
SWEDEN Riksdag	Voice vote (usual); stand- ing and sitting; electronic voting machines if requested by any MP. Elec- tions are usually by voice vote but secret ballot may be used on request.	Public, except for secret ballot.	Yes	No
SWITZERLAND States Council	Show of hands; roll call if requested by 10 Members.	Public, except for elections by secret ballot.	Yes, for roll call.	No
National Council	Standing and sitting; roll call if requested by 30 Members.			
SYRIAN ARAB REPUBLIC People's Council	Show of hands; standing and sitting; roll call.	Public, except for cases stipu- lated in the Const. or SO.	–	No
THAILAND Senate House of Representatives	Show of hands or voting machine is usual as determined by the Chairman; standing or sitting; roll call; other method, as the sitting considers ap- propriate, is used on request of the Council of Ministers of for a recount.	Secret only if Council of Min- isters or 30 MPs (20 in House of Representatives) so request, unless opposed by not less than 1/3 MPs pre- sent.	Names published (but not the vote) only from a roll call.	No

TABLE 14: METHODS OF VOTING IN THE HOUSE (continued)

Country and House(s)	14.1 Methods of voting	14.2 Public or secret vote	14.3 Public-ation of names	14.4 Proxy voting
TUNISIA Chamber of Deputies	Voice vote; show of hands; roll call if requested by the President or an MP; secret ballot for nominations.	Public, except for ballots.	Yes	No
UGANDA National Assembly	Voice vote; division by passing through 2 lobbies (on request sup-ported by 5 Members).	Public (can be secret for certain elections).	For divisions	No
UNION OF SOVIET SOCIALIST REPUBLICS Soviet of Nationalities	Show of hands	Public	No	No
Soviet of the Union				
UNITED KINGDOM House of Lords	Voice vote; division (if both sides persist in expressing oral opinion).	Public	Yes	No
House of Commons	Voice vote; division (if voice vote challen-ged); standing and sitting (if Chair considers division un-necessarily claimed – rare).			Yes, if Member is in the House precincts but incapaci-tated by illness.
UNITED REPUBLIC OF TANZANIA National Assembly	Voice vote; division if Speaker consi-ders voice vote doubtful or it is challenged by at least 10 MPs.	Public, except for election of Speaker, Deputy Speaker and MPs elected by Parliament.	No	No

TABLE 14: METHODS OF VOTING IN THE HOUSE (continued)

Country and House(s)	14.1 Methods of voting	14.2 Public or secret vote	14.3 Public-ation of names	14.4 Proxy voting
UNITED STATES OF AMERICA Senate House of Representatives	Voice vote; standing and sitting (known as a division); roll call; electronic voting machine (House of Representatives only).	Public	Yes	No
VANUATU Parliament	Show of hands; roll call (if requested on motion).	Public, except for election of the President of the Republic	Yes	No
YUGOSLAVIA Federal Chamber Chamber of Republics and Provinces	Show of hands (usual); electronic voting machines; roll call if requested by at least 10 Members.	Usually public but the Chamber may decide on a secret vote.	No	No
ZAIRE Legislative Council	Voice vote; show of hands; standing and sitting; roll call; ballot papers; acclamation; as determined by the Presiding Officer.	Public, except for elections.	No	No
ZAMBIA National Assembly	Voice vote; division (if voice vote challenged by at least 8 Members).	Public	Yes	No
ZIMBABWE Senate House of Assembly	Voice vote (when non controversial); division (to left and right of the table).	Public	Only in the Journal of the House	No

TABLE 15

QUORUM REQUIREMENTS

Whatever method of voting is used in Parliament, decisions are taken by a certain defined majority of the votes cast. As, with rare exceptions, voting by proxy is prohibited (see 14.4), the size of the majority is dependent upon the number of Members present in the House, and this has its drawbacks. In theory, it is possible for a Bill to be passed in the name of an entire nation by an extremely small number of Members and, as a safeguard against it, most Parliaments require the presence of a minimum number of Members (a quorum). The size of the quorum varies from country to country, as indicated in Table 15A. Most countries require a

TABLE 15A. Quorum Requirements, Popular or only Chamber

Ordinary Quorum	Number of Countries
2/3 Membership	4
Majority of 1/2 or More	48
1/3 Membership	11
1/4 Membership	6
Less than 1/4 Membership	8
Other	3
None	2
Total	82*

* Finland excluded for reasons of missing data.

quorum of at least half the membership. Costa Rica, Jordan, Liechtenstein and Vanuatu require a quorum of two-thirds membership. No quorum is required for deliberations in the United Kingdom (although the House can be "counted out" if the quorum is challenged), and for deliberations and voting in Israel and Sweden. In twenty-three countries (for example, Austria, Bahamas, Congo, Kuwait and Poland) the quorum need not be achieved for debate to continue.

In practice, the question of a quorum rarely arises. The quorum may only arise automatically when a sitting cannot be opened unless there is a quorum or when a form of voting that gives an exact count of Members (i.e. roll call, division, voting papers, electronic voting machines) is being used (even then, if it is not challenged before the vote, it is usually considered to be attained), and it does not arise in unrecorded votes which are the most common kind.

TABLE 15: QUORUM REQUIREMENTS

Country and House(s)	15.1 Quorum	15.2 If required for deliberations	15.3 If required for voting
ALGERIA National People's Assembly (APN)	Absolute majority of Members	Yes, in principle, but see 15.3.	Yes. If quorum not attained President postpones vote to following meeting. Vote is then valid, regardless of number of MPs present.
ARGENTINA Senate	Absolute majority of Members	Yes	Yes
Chamber of Deputies			
AUSTRALIA Senate	1/3 of Members for each House	Yes	Yes
House of Representatives			
AUSTRIA Federal Council	1/3 of membership	No	Yes
National Council			
BAHAMAS Senate	6 Members	No, unless its lack drawn to Speaker's attention.	Yes
House of Assembly	10 Members		

496

15.4 If quorum assumed unless questioned	15.5 Special quorum requirements
No, see 15.3.	None
Yes	3/4 majority of Members for scrutiny of Presidential election or for possible election of President and/or Vice-President.
Yes, once Presiding Officer takes chair, or unless want of quorum is indicated by teller's report at a division.	Absolute majority of Members of each House for proposals to submit a constitutional amendment to referendum and for suspension of SO without notice.
No	For revision of Const. regarding certain aspects of federal structure, quorum is 1/3 with presence of delegated MPs of at least 4 provinces. Raised to 1/2 for amdts to Const. restricting Lander (provincial) competences in the field of legislation and execution also for amdts to Rules of Procedure and for authorising Federal President to dissolve a provincial legislature. Quorum raised to 1/2 for amdts to Const., adoption of constitutional provisions embodied in a "simple" law, state-treaties amending or supplementing constitutional law, laws and state-treaties changing certain aspects of educational system, amdts of Rules of Procedure, overriding of a Federal Council veto, and impeachment proceedings.
Yes	Yes, 2/3 or 3/4 of Members for Const. amdts (see 16.2).

TABLE 15: QUORUM REQUIREMENTS (continued)

Country and House(s)	15.1 Quorum	15.2 If required for deliberations	15.3 If required for voting
BELGIUM Senate	Majority of Membership	No	Yes
Chamber of Representatives			
BRAZIL Federal Senate	Varies according to type of Bill, but usually an absolute majority of Members.	Yes	Yes
Chamber of Deputies			
BULGARIA National Assembly	More than half of all national representatives	Yes	Yes
CAMEROON National Assembly	Majority of all elected Members	Yes	Yes
CANADA Senate	15 Members, including Speaker.	Yes	Yes
House of Commons	20 Members, including Speaker.		
CAPE VERDE People's National Assembly	Simple majority of the Members	No	Yes
CHINA National People's Congress (NPC)	Majority of all Members	Yes	Yes
COMOROS Federal Assembly	Absolute majority	Yes, but see 15.5.	Yes, but see 15.5.
CONGO People's National Assembly	Absolute majority of Members	No	No
COSTA RICA Legislative Assembly	2/3 of Members (38).	Yes	Yes

498

15.4 If quorum assumed unless questioned	15.5 Special quorum requirements
Yes, but vote is valid only if quorum is present.	2/3 of Membership of each House required for constitutional amdts (see also 16.7).
Yes	2/3 of MPs for constitutional amdts or to overcome Presidential veto; simple majority for elections; absolute majority for Complementary Laws and Bills to create new posts in the Legislative or Judiciary.
Formally verified by the Presiding Officer	More than half of all Members for voting. 2/3 of all Members for const. amdts.
No, President must ensure quorum is maintained.	Absolute majority of all elected Members for const. amdts; 2/3 majority if President of Republic requests reconsideration of a Bill.
Rules require action "when it appears... that no quorum is present".	None
Yes, except at the start of each sitting or after a break.	
–	2/3 for election of President of the Republic, const. amdts; greater than 1/2 the Members for election of President and members of the Permanent Bureau, and appointment of the Prime Minister, also for deliberations on various matters of major national importance.
–	Constitutional amdts require a majority vote of more than 2/3 of all Members.
–	If quorum is lacking, deliberations are postponed to the following day when they are valid regardless of numbers.
Yes	–
–	If, after an emergency Presidential decree Assembly lacks quorum to ratify (see 44.3) it may meet following day and ratify by vote of not less than 2/3 of those present.

Country and House(s)	15.1 Quorum	15.2 If required for deliberations	15.3 If required for voting
CUBA National Assembly of People's Power	Half plus one	Yes	Yes
CYPRUS House of Representatives	1/3 of all Members	Yes	Yes
CZECHOSLOVAKIA Chamber of Nations	Absolute majority of Members from the Czech and Slovak Socialist Republics respectively	Yes	Yes
Chamber of the People	Absolute majority		
DEMOCRATIC YEMEN Supreme People's Council	Majority of Members	Yes	Yes
DENMARK Folketing	More than half the Members	No	Yes
EGYPT People's Assembly	Absolute majority of Members	No	Yes
FIJI Senate	7, excluding Presiding Officer.	Yes	Yes
House of Representatives	17, excluding Presiding Officer.		
FINLAND Eduskunta	–	No	No
FRANCE Senate	Absolute majority of Members	No	No (except on request of parlia- mentary group leader).
National Assembly			
GABON National Assembly	More than half the MPs	Yes	Yes
GERMAN DEMOCRATIC REPUBLIC People's Chamber	More than half the MPs	Yes	Yes

15.4 If quorum assumed unless questioned	15.5 Special quorum requirements
Yes	More than 2/3 MPs for constitutional amendments
Yes	-
No	Const. amdts, election of the President of Republic and decisions declaring war, require a 3/5 majority of Members of the Chamber of the People and 3/5 majority in the Chamber of Nations elected in the Czech and in the Slovak Socialist Republics respectively.
Quorum announced by the Chairman at the start of the sitting	2/3 MPs for constitutional amendments
President ensures observance of quorum rules.	None
Yes	No
Yes	-
-	-
No	None
Yes	-
Yes. Motions to ascertain quorum only admissible before a vote.	At least 2/3 for constitutional amdts and for premature dissolution of the Chamber

Country and House(s)	15.1 Quorum	15.2 If required for deliberations	15.3 If required for voting
GERMANY Federal Council	Majority of votes (see 1.6).	No	Yes
Federal Diet	Absolute majority of MPs		
GREECE Chamber of Deputies	Not required for debate. Required (see 15.3) for roll call vote on written request.	No (see 15.1).	1/4 Members in plenary; 2/5 in "Holiday Section" (see 8.5).
HUNGARY National Assembly	More than 1/2 the MPs	Yes	Yes
INDIA Council of States	1/10 of total House membership	Yes	Yes
House of the People			
INDONESIA House of Representatives	Absolute majority of MPs with more than one Faction	Yes	Yes
IRELAND Senate	12	Yes, for business to start. No, for adjournment debates or Dáil debates in Private MPs' time.	Yes
Dáil	20		
ISRAEL The Knesset	None	NA	NA
ITALY Senate	Absolute majority of Members (Members absent on duty are considered present for quorum purposes).	Yes	Yes (not for the vote itself, but for its validity).
Chamber of Deputies			
IVORY COAST National Assembly	Number not specified. The Assembly is always in sufficient number to deliberate, agree the order of the day and adopt the minutes.	See 15.1	1/2 plus 1 of all MPs but if not present vote deferred to next sitting

15.4 If quorum assumed unless questioned	15.5 Special quorum requirements
Yes	None
See 15.1. Considered by the President of the Chamber at moment of voting.	Constitutional amdts (see 16.2); votes of no confidence (see 40.3); censure (see 16.5).
Verified by the President	–
Yes	None
Yes	2/3 Members for constitutional amendments
Yes	None
NA	3/4 Members for removal of the State President from office
No, but may be verified on request of 20 Members when about to vote by show of hands.	–
Yes	3/4 of all Members for constitutional amendments

503

Country and House(s)	15.1 Quorum	15.2 If required for deliberations	15.3 If required for voting
JAPAN House of Councillors	1/3 of membership	Yes	Yes
House of Representatives			
JORDAN Senate House of Deputies	Const. requires 2/3 Membership to constitute absolute majority for continuance.	Yes	Yes
KENYA National Assembly	30 Members	Yes	Yes
KUWAIT National Assembly	More than 1/2 Members	No	Yes
LEBANON National Assembly	Absolute majority of Members	Yes	Yes
LIECHTENSTEIN Diet	2/3 of membership	Yes	Yes
LUXEMBOURG Chamber of Deputies	Majority of Members	No (see 15.4).	Yes
MALAWI National Assembly	1/4 of all Members	Yes	Yes
MALAYSIA Senate	10, excluding the Presiding Officer.	Yes	Yes
House of Representatives	26, excluding the Presiding Officer.		
MALI National Assembly	SO provide that the Assembly is always in sufficient number to deliberate and to agree its agenda.	See 15.1	Absolute majority of all Members
MALTA House of Representatives	15 Members and the Presiding Officer	Yes	Yes

15.4 If quorum assumed unless questioned	15.5 Special quorum requirements
No. (Determined by Presiding Officer).	Constitutional amdts require initiation by at least 2/3 members of each House.
Yes	None
Yes	2/3 membership for vote on constitutional amendments
Ascertained at start of sitting	2/3 all Members for constitutional amendments
No, it is verified by Assembly staff.	2/3 for constitutional amendments, election of President of Republic and to approve Bills returned by President of Republic for reconsideration.
Verified by the President	None
Roll call for quorum cannot be repeated for a sitting except for a vote.	3/4 membership to debate and 2/3 to adopt a constitutional amdt; 2/3 Members present to reduce the clear day interval between 1st and 2nd vote.
Yes	–
Yes	2/3 of all Members of each House for constitutional amendments
Yes	4/5 membership for constitutional amendments
Yes	2/3 majority of Members for certain const. amdts and to remove the incumbents of certain posts (see 47.4).

505

TABLE 15: QUORUM REQUIREMENTS (continued)

Country and House(s)	15.1 Quorum	15.2 If required for deliberations	15.3 If required for voting
MAURITIUS Legislative Assembly	17 Members plus the Speaker	Yes	Yes
MEXICO Chamber of Senators	2/3 membership	Yes	Yes
Chamber of Deputies	1/2 membership plus 1		
MONACO National Council	Absolute majority of Members but after 3 successive convocations at 3 days interval, proceedings are valid regardless of numbers.	Yes	Yes
MONGOLIA Great People's Khural (GPKh)	Absolute majority of Members	Yes	Yes
NAURU Parliament	Absolute majority of Members	Yes	Yes
NETHERLANDS First Chamber	Absolute majority of membership	Yes	Yes
Second Chamber			
NEW ZEALAND House of Representatives	20 Members including the Speaker (or other Member in the Chair).	Yes	Yes
NICARAGUA National Assembly	Absolute majority of Members	Yes	Yes
NORWAY Storting	1/2 membership	No, except to open a sitting.	Yes
PHILIPPINES National Assembly	Majority of membership	Yes	Yes

15.4 If quorum assumed unless questioned	15.5 Special quorum requirements
Yes	2/3 on 3/4 majority vote for amdt to entrenched sections of the Const. on fundamental rights and for 2/3 majority vote to remove the Speaker.
No. Sittings start with a roll call.	2/3 for constitutional amendments
–	2/3 Members for constitutional amendments and to decide on a secret sitting
No	2/3 Members for constitutional amendments
Quorum must be present for the start of each sitting. Proceedings then continue unless a Member requests verification.	None
No	None
Yes	None
No, the quorum is confirmed at the start of each sitting.	None (a special quorum is expected to be required to approve the Constitution).
No. The President has a duty to ensure sufficient Members are present.	2/3 membership for constitutional amdts and transfer of powers to international organisations
Yes	None

TABLE 15: QUORUM REQUIREMENTS (continued)

Country and House(s)	15.1 Quorum	15.2 If required for deliberations	15.3 If required for voting
POLAND Diet	Varies depending upon the matter under consideration but in general requires at least 1/3 membership.	No	Yes
PORTUGAL Assembly of the Republic	For the Assembly to function more than 1/4 for matters Before the Order of the Day; more than 1/3 for matters in the Order of the Day (see 11.5).	More than 1/2 effective membership except for routine procedural matters and notices	See 15.2.
REPUBLIC OF KOREA National Assembly	1/3 membership	Yes, 1/3 membership.	Yes, 1/2 membership.
ROMANIA Grand National Assembly	Absolute majority of Members	Yes	Yes
RWANDA National Development Council (CND)	Absolute majority of Members	Yes	Yes
ST VINCENT House of Assembly	8 Members	No	Yes
SENEGAL National Assembly	Absolute majority of Members. If a quorum is not present, the sitting is postponed 3 days, after which the quorum is not required.	Yes	Yes
SOLOMON ISLANDS National Parliament	1/2 membership	No, unless objection taken that a quorum is not present.	-
SOMALIA People's Assembly	Simple majority of membership	No	Yes

508

15.4 If quorum assumed unless questioned	15.5 Special quorum requirements
Yes	1/2 Members to amend the Const., to waive immunities, recall a Member, for elections and appointments.
Yes	None
Yes	2/3 membership for constitutional amdts, decision on qualification of Members and impeachment of the President; 1/2 for other impeachments, motions of censure and elections, requests for lifting martial law or presidential emergency measures.
Yes, but the Assembly President confirms presence of a quorum at the start of each sitting.	2/3 Members for constitutional amendments and to elect the President of the Republic
Yes, but the CND President confirms presence of a quorum at the start of each sitting.	2/3 majority to vote on laws pertaining to the CND; 3/4 majority for const. amdts, to impeach the President of the Republic or the Govt, or to waive a Member's immunity from arrest; 4/5 majority to charge the President with violation of the Const.
Yes, except to open a sitting.	2/3 majority of elected Members for constitutional matters
No	None
Yes	3/4 membership for amdts to the Const.
Yes	–

TABLE 15: QUORUM REQUIREMENTS (continued)

Country and House(s)	15.1 Quorum	15.2 If required for deliberations	15.3 If required for voting
SOUTH AFRICA House of Assembly	50	Yes	Yes
House of Representatives	25		
House of Delegates	13		
SPAIN Senate	Majority of Members	No	Yes
Congress of Deputies			
SRI LANKA Parliament	20 Members, including the person presiding.	Yes	Yes
SWEDEN Riksdag	None prescribed	None prescribed	None prescribed
SWITZERLAND States Council	Absolute majority	Yes	Yes
National Council			
SYRIAN ARAB REPUBLIC People's Council	Majority of Members	–	–
THAILAND Senate	More than 1/2 the membership of a House	Yes	Yes
House of Representatives			
TUNISIA Chamber of Deputies	Absolute majority of Members	Yes	Yes
UGANDA National Assembly	36 MPs excluding the Speaker	Yes	Yes

510

15.4 If quorum assumed unless questioned	15.5 Special quorum requirements
Yes	2/ 3 Members for certain constitutional amdts
Yes	For constitutional amdts (see 16.2).
Yes	2/3 Members for amdts to the Const.
NA	3/4 Members to transfer the right to decision to an international organisation; 1/2 Members for Amdts to the Riksdag Act on a single decision (see also 16.2); 1/2 Members for vote of confidence (if more than 1/2 Members vote against proposal for a new Prime Minister the proposal is rejected − see 39.3).
Yes	None
−	2/3 of all Members for amdts to the Constitution.
No	None
No	2/3 MPs for Bills returned by the President of the Republic, for Bills pertaining to Parlt, for constitutional Bills, and for motions of censure.
Yes	2/3 membership for amdt of certain constitutional provisions

511

TABLE 15: QUORUM REQUIREMENTS (continued)

Country and House(s)	15.1 Quorum	15.2 If required for deliberations	15.3 If required for voting
UNION OF SOVIET SOCIALIST REPUBLICS Soviet of Nationalities	Majority of membership	Yes	Yes
Soviet of the Union			
UNITED KINGDOM House of Lords	3, including the Lord Chancellor or Deputy Speaker	Yes	Quorum for division on a Bill is 30.
House of Commons	40	No	Yes, on a division.
UNITED REPUBLIC OF TANZANIA National Assembly	1/2 of membership	Yes	Yes
UNITED STATES OF AMERICA Senate	Absolute majority of Members	Yes	Yes
House of Representatives			
VANUATU Parliament	2/3 of membership	Yes	Yes
YUGOSLAVIA Federal Chamber	Majority of Members	Yes	Yes
Chamber of Republics and Provinces	Representation of all delegations and majority of delegates		
ZAIRE Legislative Council	1/2 of membership	2/3 MPs present	2/3 MPs present
ZAMBIA National Assembly	1/3 of membership	Yes	Yes
ZIMBABWE Senate	14	Only if an MP draws attention to lack of quorum.	See 15.2 except for certain constitutional provisions
House of Assembly	25		

15.4 If quorum assumed unless questioned	15.5 Special quorum requirements
Each sitting is preceded by a registration of Members attending.	None
Yes, but there is no provision for questioning the quorum.	None
	Closure motion "That the Question be now put" requires 100 voting in the majority.
Yes	2/3 membership for amdts to the Const.
Yes	Senators from 2/3 States for election of Vice-President 100 for Cttee of the Whole
No	3/4 Members for amdts to the Const., special sitting or dissolution.
No, it is verified by the President of the Chamber.	2/3 Members of the Federal Chamber for amdts to the Const. (see also 16.2).
No	2/3 Members for amdts to the Const., elections and motions.
No	2/3 for amdts to the Constitution
Yes	For constitutional amdts see 16.2

TABLE 16

VOTING MAJORITY REQUIREMENTS

Ordinary Motions

Many parliamentary decisions which do not require an exact tally of the number of votes, are taken "on the voices". However, an exact count of the votes is always essential where a specific majority (that is, a given proportion of either the votes cast, of Members present, or of the total number of Members of the House) is necessary to pass a Bill or agree to a motion. But this is an exceptional requirement for ordinary motions where, subject to a rule governing the quorum, all decisions are taken by a simple majority of the votes cast.

In seventeen countries (which include Bulgaria, China, Costa Rica, Egypt, Luxembourg, Mexico and Rwanda) this requirement is raised to an absolute majority of either the total number of votes cast including abstentions, or the total number of Members present in the House. In Zaire an absolute majority is required with two-thirds of the Members being present.

Special Majorities

Besides different majorities for constitutional amendments (which we consider below), special majorities are required in various countries for certain categories of legislation, some examples of which are as follows:

- motions to change the rules of procedure require an absolute majority in Argentina, Egypt, the Federal Republic of Germany, Hungary, Italy, Mexico, the Republic of Korea, Romania, Rwanda, Spain, Tunisia and Zaire, a two-thirds majority in Austria, Costa Rica and Philippines, and a three-quarters majority of votes cast in Denmark;
- decisions to hold private sittings must be taken by a two-thirds majority of Members present in the Federal Republic of Germany, Ireland and Japan;
- in Argentina, Japan, Philippines, Romania and the United States, a two-thirds majority is required to expel a Member; three-quarters of the Members are required in Thailand;
- in Belgium, certain provisions must be passed by a two-thirds majority of votes cast in both Houses, provided that a majority of members of each linguistic group have voted;
- in the Yugoslav Chamber of Republics and Provinces, decisions must be taken by a general agreement of all the delegations of the Republics and autonomous Provinces;

515

- elections of senior governmental and parliamentary authorities require various majorities ranging from two-thirds to elect the President of the Chamber in Italy and Romania, to a simple majority for elections in many other countries;

- motions to impeach or remove senior governmental and judicial officers require a simple or absolute majority in most countries but a two-thirds majority is required in Argentina, Costa Rica, the Federal Republic of Germany, India, Ireland, Jordan, Mali, Philippines, Sri Lanka, Uganda and the United States of America, three-quarters in Cyprus, Finland and Rwanda, and three-fifths in Senegal.

Given that, ordinarily, decisions are taken by a majority of the votes cast, what happens on those statistically rare occasions when there is no majority, that is, when there is a tie in the voting? In most countries, when this happens, the question put to the vote is not carried; but in twenty-five countries (see Table 9) the directing authority has a casting vote when there is a tie.

Majorities for Constitutional Amendments

Both in theory and practice, the principle that the Constitution overrides ordinary law is unchallenged today. In most of the countries which have a written Constitution, the actual supremacy of that Constitution is reinforced by a formal supremacy. Its essential feature is that all Bills to revise the Constitution are subject to extremely stringent rules.

The methods devised by Constitution makers to safeguard their work are many and varied. They include restrictions on the right to introduce a revising Bill; time limits and special majorities required to pass amendments; ratification of the amending legislation by the States in federal systems before presentation for assent; joint sittings of both Houses or the setting up of a Constituent Assembly; and appeals to the country by general election or referendum. All of these methods, either singly or in combination, make the path of the constitutional reformer difficult.

It is usually the case that Parliament is the sole authority to amend the Constitution, and it is customary to require a special parliamentary majority to support an amendment in order to preserve the supremacy of the Constitution. Although a few countries allow Parliament to amend the Constitution by a simple or an absolute majority, most of the countries under consideration increase this to at least two-thirds. In certain countries, different majorities are required. For example, in Algeria a majority of two-thirds is increased to three-quarters if the amendment concerns the procedure to change the Constitution. Different majorities are also required in the Bahamas, Fiji, and the Solomon Islands (either two-thirds or three-quarters) and in Greece, Malta and South Africa (either an absolute or a two-thirds majority), depending on the amending procedure used and the portion of the Constitution being amended.

TABLE 16: VOTING MAJORITY REQUIREMENTS

Country and House(s)	16.1 Ordinary motions	16.2 Constitutional amendments	16.3 Elections
ALGERIA National People's Assembly (APN)	Simple majority	2/3 of MPs, but 3/4 of MPs if the amdt concerns changes to arrangements for amending the Const. (except for Art. 195 which cannot be changed).	–
ARGENTINA Senate Chamber of Deputies	Absolute majority	Congress cannot amend Const. Decision on need for amdts requires 2/3 majority.	Election of House authorities: absolute majority in Senate, simple majority in Chamber; absolute majority for election of President.
AUSTRALIA Senate House of Representatives	Simple majority	Absolute majority of members of each House before submission to referendum	Simple majority
AUSTRIA Federal Council	Absolute majority	Can only veto or agree with a bill passed by the National Council, except 2/3 majority when legislative and executive competences of Lander affected.	Absolute majority; second and third ballots if necessary.
National Council		2/3 majority	

16.4 Approval of appointments	16.5 Censures/ impeachments	16.6 Procedural changes	16.7 Other requirements
–	–	–	2/3 of MPs to adopt a law returned by the President of the Republic for reconsideration.
Simple majority	2/3 majority of Members present for impeachment	Absolute majority	For each House insisting on its approval of a project; sanction or expulsion of MPs or overcoming Presidential veto: 2/3 majority.
Simple majority	Simple majority	Simple majority	Absolute majority of members of relevant House required to suspend SO without notice.
NA	NA	2/3	–
	Absolute majority for vote of no-confidence or impeachment of a member of the Govt; 2/3 for impeachment of the Federal President.		

Country and House(s)	16.1 Ordinary motions	16.2 Constitutional amendments	16.3 Elections
BAHAMAS Senate House of Assembly	Simple majority	2/3 majority to amend certain articles, 3/4 for others.	Simple majority
BELGIUM Senate Chamber of Representatives	Majority of votes cast. Equality of votes results in rejection.	2/3 majority of votes cast by at least 2/3 membership of each House	Absolute majority of votes cast. At 2nd scrutiny in the Senate and 3rd scrutiny in the Chamber a simple majority suffices. With a tie the older is appointed.
BRAZIL Federal Senate Chamber of Deputies	Simple majority	2/3 majority	Simple majority
BULGARIA National Assembly	Absolute majority	2/3 of all Members	State Council Elections: absolute majority of all Members.

16.4 Approval of appointments	16.5 Censures/ impeachments	16.6 Procedural changes	16.7 Other requirements
NA	Simple majority	Simple majority	Simple majority
See 16.3	No special provisions	Majority of votes cast. Equality of votes results in rejection.	2/3 MPs casting 2/3 majority of votes to approve successor chosen by the King in absence of a male descendant, or to authorise the King to be Head of an additional state. 2/3 majority to create new categories of elegibility to the Senate. Absolute majority of MPs of each linguistic community with corresponding absolute majority of votes cast representing together 2/3 of the total vote to carry matters concerning regional divisions.
Absolute majority	Absolute majority	Simple majority	–
NA			
No provisions	No provisions	No provisions	No provisions

Country and House(s)	16.1 Ordinary motions	16.2 Constitutional amendments	16.3 Elections
CAMEROON National Assembly	Simple majority	Majority of all Members of the Assembly for amdts initiated by MPs or President of Republic; 2/3 majority of all MPs if the President of the Republic requests reconsideration of a Bill amending the Const.	Majority of votes cast
CANADA Senate	Simple majority	Simple majority	Simple majority
House of Commons			
CAPE VERDE People's National Assembly	Simple majority	2/3 membership	2/3 MPs to elect President of Republic; 1/2 MPs to elect Permanent Bureau and Prime Minister.
CHINA People's National Congress (NPC)	Simple majority	See 15.5	Simple majority
COMOROS Federal Assembly	Majority of Members present	2/3 majority of MPs then by majority referendum and in at least 3 islands	Absolute majority on the first 2 ballots

16.4 Approval of appointments	16.5 Censures/ impeachments	16.6 Procedural changes	16.7 Other requirements
Simple majority	N A	Simple majority	None
Simple majority	Simple majority	Unanimity to suspend Rules Unanimity to suspend SO or withdraw a motion (except motion to continue a sitting which requires 25 Members or urgency motion which requires 10 Members).	2/3 to rescind an order, resolution or other decision.
–	–	–	–
Simple majority	N A	Simple majority	None
Majority of MPs present	2/3 majority for censures. 2/5 of representatives of each island for impeachment.	At least 1/4 of the represent-atives of every island	–

Country and House(s)	16.1 Ordinary motions	16.2 Constitutional amendments	16.3 Elections
CONGO People's National Assembly (ANP)	Simple majority	NA	Election of ANP President 1st round: absolute majority; 2nd round and other elections: simple majority.
COSTA RICA Legislative Assembly	Absolute majority of votes cast	2/3 of all Members	–
CUBA National Assembly of People's Power	Simple majority	2/3 of all Members	Simple majority
CYPRUS House of Representatives	Simple majority of those present	2/3 majority of all Members	Simple majority of those present
CZECHOSLOVAKIA Chamber of Nations	Simple majority of the Members elected in the Czech and the Slovak Socialist Republics respectively.	3/5 majority as in 15.5	As 16.2
Chamber of the People	Simple majority	–	
DEMOCRATIC YEMEN Supreme People's Council	Simple majority	2/3 majority	Simple majority

524

16.4 Approval of appointments	16.5 Censures/ impeachments	16.6 Procedural changes	16.7 Other requirements
-	-	-	-
-	2/3 of all Members for impeachment; 2/3 of those present for censures.	2/3 of all Members	2/3 majority for treaties and conventions involving territorial integrity or political organisation
Majority of all Members	NA	Simple majority	None
Simple majority of those present	3/4 of all Members for prosecution of President or Vice-President of the Republic for high treason	Simple majority of all Members	2/3 majority to close the debate; absolute majority of MPs to dissolve the House; 3/4 majority of all MPs to hold a secret session.
As 16.1	As 16.1	As 16.1	In all cases under the Constitutional Act where a majority of representatives of one republic over another is prohibited requirement is as 16.1 for the Chamber of Nations.
-	-	-	Simple majority to reconstitute the Presidium on request of 1/3 Members

TABLE 16: VOTING MAJORITY REQUIREMENTS (continued)

Country and House(s)	16.1 Ordinary motions	16.2 Constitutional amendments	16.3 Elections
DENMARK Folketing	Simple majority	Simple majority (but passing of a Bill entails new elections and a plebiscite).	More than half votes cast in 1 to 3 ballots
EGYPT People's Assembly	Absolute majority	2/3 majority	Absolute majority
FIJI Senate House of Representatives	Majority	3/4 or 2/3 of all Members depending on the section of the Const.	Simple majority
FINLAND Eduskunta	Simple majority of votes cast	Simple majority of votes cast at the 3rd reading and 2/3 majority at the 1st ordinary session after the subsequent elections	Simple majority
FRANCE Senate National Assembly	Simple majority	Simple majority in each House but 3/5 majority in joint sitting (see 8.6).	Absolute majority of MPs for election to the High Court of Justice; absolute majority of votes cast for 1st 2 ballots for election of each Chamber's President; otherwise absolute majority of votes cast.
GABON National Assembly	Simple majority	Simple majority	Simple majority

16.4 Approval of appointments	16.5 Censures/ impeachments	16.6 Procedural changes	16.7 Other requirements
Simple majority	Simple majority	3/4 of the Members voting	5/6 of Members for Bills delegating powers to international authorities. If this majority not obtained, but a simple majority achieved, a referendum is called.
Absolute majority	Absolute majority	Absolute majority	Absolute majority for approval of resolutions of General Cttee, Values Cttee and permanent cttees.
–	–	–	–
NA	3/4 to arraign the President for treason	Simple majority	2/3 majority of votes cast for Bills increasing taxes for a period exceeding 1 year. Qualified majority for certain other matters.
NA	Absolute majority of members of the Assembly for a censure motion	Simple majority	Absolute majority of votes in the Assembly to approve Govt programme. Absolute majority of members of the Assembly for final reading of laws concerning Parlt when the two Houses fail to agree.
Simple majority	Simple majority	Simple majority	Simple majority

TABLE 16: VOTING MAJORITY REQUIREMENTS (continued)

Country and House(s)	16.1 Ordinary motions	16.2 Constitutional amendments	16.3 Elections
GERMAN DEMOCRATIC REPUBLIC People's Chamber	Majority	2/3 of all Members	Majority
GERMANY Federal Council	Absolute majority. State votes may be cast only as a bloc.	2/3 majority	Absolute majority
Federal Diet	Majority of votes cast	2/3 majority of membership	Absolute majority of membership
GREECE Chamber of Deputies	Absolute majority of Members present and not less than 1/4 membership	3/5 of Members present for a proposal, followed by absolute majority of membership to approve. If proposal approved by absolute majority of membership, 3/5 membership must then approve the amdt.	Absolute majority of Members present and not less than 2/5 membership
HUNGARY National Assembly	Absolute majority of all Members	2/3 of all Members	Absolute majority of all Members
INDIA Council of States House of the People	Simple majority	Majority of House membership and 2/3 majority of votes cast	Simple majority, except election where provided, to cttees and bodies with parliamentary representation which is by proportional representation or single transferable vote.

16.4 Approval of appointments	16.5 Censures/ impeachments	16.6 Procedural changes	16.7 Other requirements
Majority	NA	Majority	–
Absolute majority NA	2/3 majority in both Houses to impeach Federal President before the Federal Contitutional Court for wilful violation of a Federal Law. Absolute majority of Diet member· ship for a vote of confidence.	Absolute majority of Members for amdt; unanimity for a specific derogation. Absolute majority of Members for amdt; 2/3 majority of votes for a specific derogation.	Absolute majority of Members to reject Federal Council objections to a Bill; 2/3 majority to reject objections passed by 2/3 majority of the Federal Council, to exclude public from a meeting and to determine a state of defence.
–	Proposed by at least 50 Members against the President, and motions of censure by 1/6. Vote requires an absolute majority.	–	–
Absolute majority of all Members NA	Absolute majority of all Members Censure: simple majority; impeachment of President: 2/3 House membership and 2/3 votes cast.	Absolute majority of all Members Simple majority	– Majority of House membership and 2/3 votes cast to approve a proclamation of emergency for war, external aggression or armed rebellion.

Country and House(s)	16.1 Ordinary motions	16.2 Constitutional amendments	16.3 Elections
INDONESIA House of Representatives	More than 1/2 membership and seconded by more than 1 Faction	As 16.1	As 16.1
IRELAND Senate	Simple majority of those present and voting	Simple majority of those present and voting	Simple majority of those present and voting
Dáil			
ISRAEL The Knesset	Majority of votes cast	Basic Laws require simple majority vote except for certain sections which require a special majority.	Majority of votes to elect Chairman, Vice-Chairman and representatives to the Judges Appointment Cttees. Absolute majority in the 1st and 2nd ballots for election of State President. Majority of votes for a later ballot.
ITALY Senate Chamber of Deputies	Majority of Members present (abstainers are counted for calculation in the Senate, but not in the Chamber where they are considered present for the sitting but not for the vote).	Absolute majority	Absolute majority of MPs to elect President of the Senate at first 2 ballots, then absolute majority of those present, then if necessary simple majority of the 2 candidates with most votes; 2/3 total membership to elect President of the Chamber at first 3 ballots. Then absolute majority.

530

16.4 Approval of appointments	16.5 Censures/ impeachments	16.6 Procedural changes	16.7 Other requirements
As 16.1	NA	As 16.1	As 16.1
Simple majority of those present and voting	2/3 total membership of House to adopt proposal to prefer a charge against the President and to sustain such a charge	Simple majority of those present and voting	2/3 of Members present for a private sitting of House in case of special emergency
–	3/4 Members for removal of State President; 2/3 of votes for removal of the State Comptroller.	Majority of votes cast	–
–	Absolute majority of all Members in a joint sitting to impeach the President of the Republic	Absolute majority of Members for SO amdts; 3/4 majority to amend the Order of the Day.	–

Country and House(s)	16.1 Ordinary motions	16.2 Constitutional amendments	16.3 Elections
IVORY COAST National Assembly	Simple majority	Majority of 3/4 of all MPs followed by a referendum, but if 4/5 of all MPs are in favour, no referendum is required.	Absolute majority
JAPAN House of Councillors House of Representatives	Simple majority	2/3 members of each House before submission to referendum	Absolute majority to elect one person. In order of number of votes received for more than one, but in House of Representatives a person must also secure at least 1/4 votes divided by number of persons to be elected.
JORDAN Senate House of Deputies	Simple majority	2/3 majority	Simple majority
KENYA National Assembly	Simple majority	2/3 majority	NA
KUWAIT National Assembly	Simple majority of Members present	2/3 majority of all Members	Simple majority of Members present
LEBANON National Assembly	1/2 of quorum	2/3 membership	Absolute majority except 2/3 membership for election of the President of the Republic
LIECHTENSTEIN Diet	Absolute majority of Members present	Unanimity of Members present or 3/4 majority in 2 consecutive sittings	Absolute majority in 1st and 2nd ballots, simple majority in 3rd.
LUXEMBOURG Chamber of Deputies	Absolute majority	2/3 majority	Relative majority

16.4 Approval of appointments	16.5 Censures/ impeachments	16.6 Procedural changes	16.7 Other requirements
NA	NA	NA	–
Simple majority	Simple majority	Simple majority	2/3 of Members present for decision on disqualification or expulsion, to hold a secret meeting or to pass a bill for the second time in the House of Representatives.
NA	2/3 majority	Simple majority	2/3 majority to carry vote of confidence in the Govt
NA	Absolute majority	Simple majority	NA
Simple majority of Members present	Simple majority of Members present	Simple majority of Members present	–
–	–	1/2 of quorum	–
–	–	Absolute majority of Members present	–
Absolute majority	Absolute majority	Absolute majority	–

Country and House(s)	16.1 Ordinary motions	16.2 Constitutional amendments	16.3 Elections
MALAWI National Assembly	Majority of those present and voting	2/3 of all Members of the Assembly on 2nd and 3rd readings	For Deputy Speaker, absolute majority through as many ballots as necessary.
MALAYSIA Senate House of Representatives	Simple majority	2/3 majority in 2nd and 3rd readings	Simple majority. Speaker requires more votes than aggregate of other candidates in ballot.
MALI National Assembly	Simple majority	To approve proposals 3/4 membership; to approve text 4/5 membership.	Absolute majority for 1st 2 ballots, simple majority on 3rd.
MALTA House of Representatives	Simple majority	2/3 majority of all Members for certain Const. amdts	Simple majority
MAURITIUS Legislative Assembly	Simple majority	See 15.5	Simple majority
MEXICO Chamber of Senators Chamber of Deputies	Absolute majority	2/3 majority	Absolute majority
MONACO National Council	Simple majority	2/3 majority	Absolute majority of Members
MONGOLIA Great People's Khural (GPKh)	Simple majority	2/3 majority of Members	Simple majority
NAURU Parliament	Majority of Members present and voting.	Not less than 2/3 membership	For Speaker: majority of votes of Members present; otherwise Members having the most votes.

534

16.4 Approval of appointments	16.5 Censures/ impeachments	16.6 Procedural changes	16.7 Other requirements
–	–	Majority of those present and voting	–
Simple majority	Simple majority	Simple majority	None
Absolute majority for 1st 2 ballots, simple majority on 3rd.	2/3 Members to establish permanent disability of the President.	Simple majority	–
NA	See 47.4	Simple majority	None
Simple majority	Simple majority	Simple majority	See 15.5
Absolute majority	Absolute majority	Absolute majority	–
NA	NA	Simple majority	–
Simple majority	NA	Simple majority	–
–	–	–	Majority of Members present and voting to approve a declaration of emergency

Country and House(s)	16.1 Ordinary motions	16.2 Constitutional amendments	16.3 Elections
NETHERLANDS First Chamber	Simple majority	2/3 majority	Simple majority
Second Chamber			
NEW ZEALAND House of Representatives	Simple majority	NA	Simple majority
NICARAGUA National Assembly	Simple majority	NA (pending establishment of the Const.)	Simple majority
NORWAY Storting	Simple majority	2/3 majority	Relative majority (but see 16.7).
PHILIPPINES National Assembly	Simple majority (2/3 majority to pass measures for which SO have been suspended).	3/4 majority of all Members	Simple majority
POLAND Diet	Simple majority	2/3 majority	Relative or absolute majority

16.4 Approval of appointments	16.5 Censures/ impeachments	16.6 Procedural changes	16.7 Other requirements
Simple majority	Simple majority	Simple majority	2/3 majority for ratification of treaties deviating from the Const., legislation on Members' financial positions, legislation concerning succession to the Throne and the Royal household's financial position. See also 32.2.
Simple majority	Simple majority	Simple majority	3/4 MPs for certain important changes to electoral law (terms of Parlt, voting age, etc.).
Simple majority	Simple majority	Simple majority	60 % quorum to approve each art. of the Const.
NA	Simple majority	Simple majority	More than 1/2 votes cast to appoint the President, Secretary General and Head of Administration.
NA	2/3 majority of all Members	2/3 majority	2/3 majority to override a presidential veto, suspend or expel a Member.
NA (see 47.3).	NA (see 47.4).	Simple majority	2/3 majority to waive immunities or recall a Member

Country and House(s)	16.1 Ordinary motions	16.2 Constitutional amendments	16.3 Elections
PORTUGAL Assembly of the Republic	Simple majority	2/3 effective membership; 4/5 for a major revision.	2/3 of those present provided this constitutes an absolute majority of effective membership.
REPUBLIC OF KOREA National Assembly	Absolute majority	2/3 membership	Absolute majority of membership
ROMANIA Grand National Assembly	Attendance of an absolute majority of membership and concurrence of majority present	2/3 majority of Members	2/3 majority of Members to elect the President of the Republic, Speaker and Vice-Speakers. Absolute majority of at least 1/2 membership to elect cttee chairmen.
RWANDA National Development Council (CND)	Absolute majority of Members present	3/4 majority of membership	Relative majority
ST VINCENT House of Assembly	Simple majority	2/3 majority of elected Members	Simple majority
SENEGAL National Assembly	Simple majority	3/5 of all Members	Majority of all Members plus 1
SOLOMON ISLANDS National Parliament	Simple majority	3/4 membership for some provisions, 2/3 membership for others.	Absolute majority for Prime Minister, in successive ballots, if necessary.

16.4 Approval of appointments	16.5 Censures/ impeachments	16.6 Procedural changes	16.7 Other requirements
Majority of valid votes	Absolute majority of effective membership for censure; 2/3 to proceed against the President of the Republic.	Simple majority	Absolute majority of effective membership to reject the Govt's programme.
Absolute majority	Absolute majority of membership; 2/3 membership to impeach the President.	Absolute majority	Absolute majority of membership to lift emergency or martial law; 2/3 majority of membership to expel a Member.
Attendance of at least 1/2 membership and concurrence of absolute majority of those present	Majority of Members to revoke Council of Ministers (see 40.4).	Attendance of at least 1/2 membership and concurrence of absolute majority of those present	–
NA	3/4 majority for motion of censure; 4/5 majority to declare the President of the Republic unworthy of office.	Absolute majority of Members present	–
NA	Simple majority	Simple majority	None
NA	3/5 of all Members to impeach the President of the Republic	–	–
–	Absolute majority for vote of no-confidence	–	–

Country and House(s)	16.1 Ordinary motions	16.2 Constitutional amendments	16.3 Elections
SOMALIA People's Assembly	Simple majority	2/3 majority	Simple majority
SOUTH AFRICA House of Assembly House of Representatives House of Delegates	Simple majority	2/3 majority of all Members in every House for Section 89 concerning official languages and for 99 entrenching 89 and itself. Certain other Sections require a majority of all Members in every House.	Simple majority
SPAIN Senate Congress of Deputies	Simple majority. A tied vote, after 2 periods for reflection, passes in the negative. Absolute majority is required to reject a Bill.	3/5 membership for partial amdt. 2/3 membership for total amdt or to titles I and II.	President of the House: absolute majority. Other members of Presiding Body: simple majority.
SRI LANKA Parliament	Simple majority	2/3 of all Members	Simple majority
SWEDEN Riksdag	Simple majority	Simple majority on 2 decisions for identical wording, with an intervening general election or (also for Riksdag Act) 1 decision with 3/4 majority of at least 1/2 membership.	Simple majority
SWITZERLAND States Council National Council	Simple majority	Simple majority	Absolute majority of valid votes
SYRIAN ARAB REPUBLIC People's Council	Majority	2/3 majority of all Members	-

16.4 Approval of appointments	16.5 Censures/ impeachments	16.6 Procedural changes	16.7 Other requirements
Simple majority	Simple majority	Simple majority	–
Simple majority	Simple majority	Simple majority	Simple majority
3/5 majority	Absolute majority	Absolute majority	–
Simple majority	2/3 membership to remove President (see 47.4).	Simple majority	–
For appointment of Prime Minister, see 39.3.	5/6 majority to give consent to bring an action against a present or former Member for his statements or acts as an MP.	If amdt to Const., see 16.2; simple majority if amdt to an Act.	–
NA	NA	Simple majority	Absolute majority of all Members for urgency
–	Majority of mem- bership for a vote of no-confidence	–	–

Country and House(s)	16.1 Ordinary motions	16.2 Constitutional amendments	16.3 Elections
THAILAND Senate House of Representatives	Simple majority	1st and 3rd readings roll call vote of 1/2 of all members of both Houses. Simple majority in 2nd reading.	Simple majority
TUNISIA Chamber of Deputies	Absolute majority	2/3 majority at 2 readings separated by at least 3 months	Absolute majority
UGANDA National Asembly	Simple majority	Simple majority except 2/3 membership for certain provisions	Simple majority
UNION OF SOVIET SOCIALIST REPUBLICS Soviet of Nationalities Soviet of the Union	Majority of membership	2/3 majority of all Members	Majority of membership
UNITED KINGDOM House of Lords House of Commons	Simple majority	NA	NA
UNITED REPUBLIC OF TANZANIA National Assembly	Simple majority	2/3 membership for ordinary amdts (but see also 16.7).	Simple majority for Speaker and Deputy Speaker. Absolute majority for MPs elected by Parliament.

16.4 Approval of appointments	16.5 Censures/ impeachments	16.6 Procedural changes	16.7 Other requirements
Simple majority	Majority of members of House of Representatives for vote of no-confidence on individual Minister or Council of Ministers as a whole.	Simple majority	3/4 members of the House to expel a Member (see 3.3).
Absolute majority	2/3 majority	Absolute majority	2/3 majority for Bills pertaining to Parlt and for Bills returned by the President of the Republic
NA	2/3 membership	Simple majority	None
Majority of membership	NA	See 7.3	None
NA	Simple majority	Simple majority	None See 15.5
NA	NA	Simple majority	2/3 majority of all Zanzibar MPs and all Mainland MPs to amend funda-mental constitu-tional issues

TABLE 16: VOTING MAJORITY REQUIREMENTS (continued)

Country and House(s)	16.1 Ordinary motions	16.2 Constitutional amendments	16.3 Elections
UNITED STATES OF AMERICA Senate	Simple majority	2/3 majority	Simple majority except when election of Vice- President devolves on the Senate (see 15.5).
House of Representatives			
VANUATU Parliament	Simple majority	2/3 majority	2/3 electoral college (see 39.1) to elect the President.
YUGOSLAVIA Federal Chamber	Simple majority	2/3 majority in the Federal Chamber (agreement of Assemblies of all Republics and Autonomous Provinces also required).	Simple majority
Chamber of Republics and Provinces			
ZAIRE Legislative Council	Absolute major- ity, 2/3 Members being present.	2/3 of all Members	Absolute major- ity, 2/3 Members being present
ZAMBIA National Assembly	Simple majority	2/3 of all Members	Absolute majority
ZIMBABWE Senate	Simple majority	2/3 of membership	Simple majority
House of Assembly		Fundamental rights: all Members; others:7/10.	

16.4 Approval of appointments	16.5 Censures/ impeachments	16.6 Procedural changes	16.7 Other requirements
Simple majority NA	Simple majority for censure; 2/3 majority for impeachment.	Usually simple majority; 2/3 majority to suspend the rules.	2/3 majority for expulsions and to override Presi- dential veto. 3/5 majority to invoke cloture in the Senate except 2/3 to close debate on questions of amending SO; 2/3 majority in the House for various procedures.
–	Absolute majority	2/3 majority to suspend SO	–
Simple majority	Simple majority	Simple majority	–
NA	NA	Absolute major- ity, 2/3 Members being present	None
NA	2/3 of membership (see 47.4).	Simple majority	None
Simple majority	2/3 membership of both Houses sitting jointly	Simple majority	None

PART IV

PROCEEDINGS AND DEBATES

TABLE 17

PUBLICATION OF DEBATES

Records of debates of plenary sessions of Parliament are published and made available to the public. The records are considered as authentic, and as such express the will of the House and can influence subsequent legal decisions even though their contents may not be considered definitive in law. In a number of countries the corrected version of the record of decisions is formally signed by either the directing authority or the senior administrative officer and placed in the parliamentary archives.

Records of the House

In almost all countries the records of debates comprise a verbatim account of everything that was said by Members. In nine countries, however, the records are published only in a summary format. The task of preparing the records is usually the responsibility of the senior administrative officer of the House, although it may be delegated to the head of a specially created legislative service such as the Department of Records in Kuwait, or the Editor of Debates in Malta. The preparation of the records necessarily takes time, and practices differ as to how quickly they are made available to Members, the press and the public. A number of countries (for example, France and Israel) begin issuing their records while their sittings are in progress. In some cases there are summary reports, in others a full account of debate in the House, and in yet others both a summary and a full account.

The purpose of such published records is to supply rapid information to the media and to Members as to what has happened in the House. Where such early reports are published they are later supplemented by a more correct version of the records. The full record is usually published the day after the sitting (as in, for example, Canada, the Federal Republic of Germany, Sri Lanka and the United Kingdom), or a few days later (as in Ireland, Malta and Spain), although in countries such as Jordan, Liechtenstein and Sweden, publication occurs some weeks after the sitting. In the Philippines, Switzerland, USSR and Zambia, the records are published at the end of each legislative session.

Deletion of Material from the Record

The record of debates is essentially a verbatim account of what was said by Members in the House, and a record of its decisions. Two things follow from this. Firstly, everything that is spoken by a Member should appear in the records and, secondly, what is not spoken by a Member should not appear. There are exceptions to both of these rules. In

549

thirty countries, the directing authority of Parliament has the power to order that speeches, or parts of them, which have been delivered in the House may be omitted from the record of debates. The reasons for such action include speaking without leave, refusal to come to order, using unparliamentary language or expressions, repetitious speeches, deviating from the subject, and the reading of speeches. It is rare that a Speaker or President will order words to be deleted from the record, but this is a power considered necessary to maintain the dignity of Parliament.

In at least twenty-five countries (for example, Fiji, Hungary, Malaysia, Rwanda, USSR and the United Kingdom), the records of the debates may be edited by Members (or by the administrative service responsible for the production of the report) so as to omit repetitions, improve grammar and to correct obvious errors. The general rule applied in these instances is to maintain the accuracy and reliability of the record, and nothing is permitted to be inserted or omitted which would tend to change the meaning of what was said in the House.

Addition of Material to the Records

The conditions or circumstances under which material not spoken in Parliament can be included in the record of its proceedings are somewhat less restrictive, as can be seen from the following examples. In Canada, Greece, Italy, the Netherlands, Sri Lanka, the United Kingdom and a number of other countries, tables, technical documents, and lengthy reports can, with the consent of Parliament, be incorporated into the records. This rule is applied because the nature of the material involved is often unsuitable to be delivered in an oral debate. In these countries, questions may be put down for written answer, and an answer to an oral question which involves technical or statistical material, or which is unduly lengthy, may be added to the records. Also, all papers laid on the table of the House are added to the records. In Czechoslovakia, the unfinished portion of a Member's speech may be inserted in the record when he has been unable to deliver it because of time limitations. In the United States, wide latitude is shown in the way in which unspoken material is incorporated into the "Congressional Record". A Member may be permitted by the House to extend his remarks to any length in a separate section of the "Record" ("Extension of Remarks") and to include extraneous matter quite unconnected with the debate in progress.

TABLE 17: PUBLICATION OF DEBATES

Country and House(s)	17.1 Title and nature of records	17.2 Publication authority
ALGERIA National People's Assembly (APN)	Summary and verbatim	Secretary General
ARGENTINA Senate Chamber of Deputies	Journal of Sessions (Diario de Sesiones) verbatim record.	Secretary of the respective House
AUSTRALIA Senate House of Representatives	Parliamentary Debates "Hansard" verbatim.	Presiding Officer of each House
AUSTRIA Federal Council National Council	Verbatim "Stenographische Protokolle des Bundes-rates" or 'Nationalrates', respectively. Also "Par-laments-Korrespondenz", summary.	Secretary General under the overall responsibility of the respective President
BAHAMAS Senate House of Assembly	Hansard and Votes of House;verbatim. Summary	Presiding Officer

17.3 Publication time and limits	17.4 Amendments and deletions	17.5 Addition of material
Draft summary distributed to MPs for comment within 48 hours of end of meeting. Corrected version is then published in the official journal.	MPs must make comments within 24 hours of receiving the draft. Deletions allowed if agreed by the President and announced in the House.	Committee reports, written questions and Government answers
No time limit prescribed (usually 20 days).	Deletion of non-allowed interruptions and insults on decision of the Secretaries or the Presidents of the Houses	On Members' request and when related to the subject debated.
Proof copy of parliamentary debates in each House usually available by 9.00 a.m. following adjournment of House. MPs have one week to request minor editorial corrections. Corrected weekly Hansard available 5 to 6 weeks after debates.	Deletion of material by relevant Presiding Officer possible on grounds that matter is objectionable, questions are irregular, or offensive words have been withdrawn at direction of Presiding Officer.	By leave of relevant House and subject to appropriateness for reproduction in Hansard
Summary reports of both Councils usually issued on the day of the sitting. Verbatim records take from 4 to 6 weeks; no time limits prescribed.	Interruptions, even unparliamentary language, not expunged. MPs may propose stylistic alterations to the transcripts of their speeches. The President decides admissibility.	No
No set pattern or time	Yes, by decision of Speaker.	No

Country and House(s)	17.1 Title and nature of records	17.2 Publication authority
BELGIUM Senate Chamber of Representatives	1. Summary minutes (Compte-Rendu Analytique/Beknopt Verslag) 2. Parliamentary Annals, verbatim (Annales Parlementaires/Parlementaire Handelingen) 3. Bulletin of Questions and Answers (Bulletin des Questions et des Réponses /Bulletin van Vragen en Antwoorden)	The director of the respective service
BRAZIL Federal Senate Chamber of Deputies	Congress Diary ("Diario do Congresso") verbatim and summary records.	Secretary General under supervision of Presiding Officer
BULGARIA National Assembly	Verbatim shorthand minutes (Stenographski Dnevnits).	National Assembly President
CAMEROON National Assembly	Official Gazette of the Debates of the National Assembly (Journal officiel des débats de l'Assemblée Nationale) verbatim.	Secretary General, through the Sessional and Cttee Service (Service des séances et des commissions).

17.3 Publication time and limits	17.4 Amendments and deletions	17.5 Addition of material
1. The day of the sitting; 2. Within 15 days; 3. Weekly.	President may authorise deletion of words contrary to public order, or pronounced by a Member not entitled to speak, or who exceeds time-limits or who twice strays from the topic.	No
Normally 3 days	For "lack of decorum" on decision of Presiding Officer. Const. prohibits publication of statements involving offence against national institutions; war propaganda; subversion of political or social order; religious, race or class prejudices; crime against honour or incitement to crime.	Yes, relevant material such as letters, telegrams or news articles.
No prescribed time-limit, but measures taken for earliest possible publication of records.	No	No
Record of a sitting is available before the subsequent sitting. Formal printed version available 2 months after session, but no time-limit is prescribed.	No	No

Country and House(s)	17.1 Title and nature of records	17.2 Publication authority
CANADA Senate	Debates of the Senate "Hansard" (Débats du Sénat) verbatim. Minutes of the Proceedings of the Senate (Procès-verbaux du Sénat) record decisions. They are published at session end as "Journals of the Senate".	Clerk of Senate
House of Commons	House of Commons Debates "Hansard" or (Débats de la Chambre des Communes) verbatim. Votes and Proceedings (Procès-verbaux) which record decisions are published at session end as "Journals of the House of Commons".	"Debates": Administrator; "Journal": Clerk of the House.
CAPE VERDE People's National Assembly	Minutes of Sessions (Acta das Sessões) verbatim.	Secretary General.
CHINA National People's Congress (NPC)	Bulletin of the Standing Cttee of the NPC of the People's Republic of China	General Office of the NPC Standing Cttee
COMOROS Federal Assembly	Verbatim report	Secretary General
CONGO People's National Assembly (ANP)	Journal of Debates (Journal des Débats) verbatim.	Secretary General
COSTA RICA Legislative Assembly	Proceedings of the Sessions (Actas de las sesiones) verbatim.	Assembly Secretariat
CUBA National Assembly of People's Power	Record (Acta). More than a summary but not verbatim.	The Secretary of the National Assembly

17.3 Publication time and limits	17.4 Amendments and deletions	17.5 Addition of material
Unedited Debates within an hour, edited version: the following day.	Minor alterations to clarify but not change meaning are allowed. Major changes require explanation to and approval from the House.	Material tabled but not spoken may be incorporated. Some voluminous texts may require unanimous consent.
Publication is hindered by lack of equipment and funds but proceedings are recorded electronically.	No	Not found necessary
Five volumes per year	Yes, but meaning must not be changed.	No
–	–	–
No time limits specified but ready before the following session, in which they are approved.	Only those adopted by the plenary before approval of the Journal	No
One hour before the start of the next sitting	No	No
60 days	Amdts are determined by majority vote of the Assembly.	No

Country and House(s)	17.1 Title and nature of records	17.2 Publication authority
CYPRUS House of Representatives	Minutes of the proceedings of the House of Representatives (Practica Voulis Antiprosopon) verbatim.	Director-General
CZECHOSLOVAKIA Chamber of Nations	Report on meetings of the Chamber, verbatim.	Office of Federal Assembly
Chamber of the People		
DEMOCRATIC YEMEN Supreme People's Council	Minutes	Secretariat
DENMARK Folketing	Verbatim Folketings-tidende (Proceedings of the Folketing), contain summarised decisions and supplements showing proposed, passed and finance Bills, and cttee reports.	Clerk of the Folketing under Presidential supervision
EGYPT People's Assembly	Minutes recording proceedings, debates and decisions.	Assembly General Secretariat
FIJI Senate	"Hansard", verbatim.	Clerk of the House
House of Representatives		
FINLAND Eduskunta	Pöytäkirja, verbatim. Minutes and record of decisions.	Secretary General

17.3 Publication time and limits	17.4 Amendments and deletions	17.5 Addition of material
No prescribed time limit but unedited record published in 2 to 3 months.	The President, with House consent, may order removal of material which is irrelevant, out of order, or offensive with respect to the President of the Republic or other high officials.	Permitted
8 days	No, only for purely editing reasons.	The Chamber may approve incorporation of speeches which were not delivered for lack of time.
Minutes deemed approved if no change proposed in writing within 15 days	No	No
Proofs available 2-3 days after the sitting. Final bound edition later.	Only for pure editing reasons	Written material announced in the Folketing such as replies to questions and ministerial statements.
Within 10 days of the sitting	Deletion, ordered by the Speaker, of matter contravening the rules, subject to agreement of the Assembly.	No
Unedited record daily; edited record within 8 to 10 weeks.	If correctness of unedited record disputed within 14 days the Presiding Officer rules on correctness.	No
2 months after sitting	Only when agreed by Parlt and provided no parliamentary decision rests on the passage.	No

TABLE 17: PUBLICATION OF DEBATES (continued)

Country and House(s)	17.1 Title and nature of records	17.2 Publication authority
FRANCE Senate National Assembly	1. Official Journal of Debates (Journal officiel des débats) verbatim report of each House 2. Synopsis of Sittings of each House 3. Summary Report or Bulletin of Sittings	Director of the appropriate Parliamentary Service
GABON National Assembly	Bulletin de liaison de l'Assemblée Nationale. Summary record.	President of Assembly
GERMAN DEMOCRATIC REPUBLIC People's Chamber	People's Chamber of the German Democratic Republic (Volskammer der Deutschen Democratischen Republik) verbatim.	Presidium of the Chamber
GERMANY Federal Council	Reports of Proceedings of the Bundesrat (Verhandlungen des Bundesrates Stenographische Berichte) verbatim.	Shorthand service, under the responsibility of the Director of the Council.
Federal Diet	Reports of Proceedings of the Bundestag (Verhandlungen des Deutschen Bundestages, Stenographische Berichte) verbatim.	The Diet President
GREECE Chamber of Deputies	Minutes of the Chamber of Deputies (Praktika tis Voulis) verbatim.	Official Minutes Service
HUNGARY National Assembly	Proceedings of Debates, verbatim.	Clerk in charge of the Records Service

17.3 Publication time and limits	17.4 Amendments and deletions	17.5 Addition of material
1. 1 day after sitting; 2. A few hours after sitting; 3. As convenient during a sitting	Only should the President decide if a Member speaks without authorisation or reads his speech.	In the Assembly the Bureau can authorise publication of certain reports in an annexe. Instead of oral presentation of a report, the Assembly may authorise its publication in the Official Journal.
One month	Yes, where the summary is not a true record on decision of Assembly President and cttee Rapporteur.	No
Draft submitted on request for examination within 3 days. If no written request for correction received within a further 3 days it is deemed to be approved.	No	If submitted as written "motions" or "printed matter" related to the topic under consideration.
2 days after sitting	No	When speech is foregone in favour of a written text but only personally and during the sitting
1 day after sitting	Interruptions may be deleted with consent of the President and parties concerned	Occasional written explanations of voting are incorporated in the record.
First draft 1 to 1 1/2 hours after debate. Corrected copy within 48 hours.	Amdts not changing the sense are allowed. Deletions on President's decision where Members speak out of order.	Statistics and technical documents with the President's permission
21 days after the sitting	Mistaken and improper material with consent of the Assembly	No

Country and House(s)	17.1 Title and nature of records	17.2 Publication authority
INDIA Council of States	Parliamentary Debates Rajya Sabha Official Report or Sansadiya Vad-Vivad Rajya Sabha Adhikariya Prativedan (Hindi Sanskaran) verbatim. Also Synopsis of Debates or Vad-Vivad Ka Saransh, summary.	Secretary General under overall direction of the Chairman
House of the People	1. Lok Sabha Debates or Lok Sahba Vad-Vivad, verbatim 2. Lok Sabha Synopsis of Debates or Lok Sabha Vad-Vivad Ka Saransh, summary 3. Lok Sabha Bulletin Part I or Lok Sabha Samachar Bhag I, brief record 4. Lok Sabha Journal, résumé of proceedings and record of business	Secretary General
INDONESIA House of Representatives	Risalah Rapat, verbatim.	Secretary General
IRELAND Senate Dáil	1. Journal of the Proceedings (record of decisions taken) 2. Official Report of the Debates, verbatim	1. Clerk of each House; 2. Editor of Debates.
ISRAEL The Knesset	The Knesset Record (Divrei Haknesset) verbatim.	Chairman of the Knesset

17.3 Publication time and limits	17.4 Amendments and deletions	17.5 Addition of material
No time limit prescribed but unedited and uncorrected copies available overnight. Final printed edition in English within 30 days and in Hindi within 45 days.	Minor corrections allowed. Chairman may order deletion of defamatory, indecent, undignified or unparliamentary words. Deleted words are indicated by asterisks.	No
1. Uncorrected copies available overnight. Final printed edition in English in 6 to 8 weeks, and in Hindi in 8 to 10 weeks; 2. and 3. overnight circulation; 4. as early as possible after sitting ends.	The Speaker may remove unparliamentary or defamatory words and parts of a speech of a Member not recognised by the Chair.	Presidential address and Ministerial Statements which are tabled but not read and written questions and answers are incorporated.
Draft provided as soon as possible	Corrections may be made within 4 days of availability of draft, on authority of Chairman of sitting.	Yes by leave of the Chairman
No prescribed time limits. Journal published daily and subsequently indexed and published in bound form. Unrevised but edited report of Dáil debates is available within 2 days.	No	Written replies to questions in Dáil and oral replies to questions which are lengthy or statistical may be incorporated in Official Report.
Not prescribed but about 2 hours for unedited record, several months for edited.	On decision of the Presiding Officer on grounds of national security.	The Chairman may occasionally permit a Minister to incorporate voluminous material, also questions in absence of questioner or answers on request of the questioner.

TABLE 17: PUBLICATION OF DEBATES (continued)

Country and House(s)	17.1 Title and nature of records	17.2 Publication authority
ITALY Senate Chamber of Deputies	Summary record (Resoconto sommario) summary; shorthand record (Resoconto stenografico) verbatim.	Chief Counsellor of the Parliamentary Record Service and the Editor of the record
IVORY COAST National Assembly	Official Journal (Journal Officiel) comprising Summary Records (Procès-verbaux sommaires); Verbatim Records (Comptes-rendus intégraux).	Central Bureau of the Legislative Services Commission
JAPAN House of Councillors House of Representatives	Minutes of the House of Councillors (Sangiin-Kaigiroku). Minutes of the House of Representatives (Shugiin-Kaigiroku) both verbatim.	Presiding Officer
JORDAN Senate House of Deputies	Debates of the House of Senate (Muthakarat Majles Al-ayan); debates of the House of Deputies (Muthakarat Majles al-Nuwab) both verbatim.	Secretary General
KENYA National Assembly	National Assembly Official Report (Baraza la Taifa, Taarifa Rasmi) verbatim.	Secretary General
KUWAIT National Assembly	Minutes of the sitting (Madbatat Al-Jalsah) verbatim.	Department of Records under the Parliamentary Secretary
LEBANON National Assembly	Record of Parliamentary Debates (Comptes-rendus des débats parlementaires) verbatim.	Secretary General

17.3 Publication time and limits	17.4 Amendments and deletions	17.5 Addition of material
Summary record and "immediate" Chamber verbatim available 8.30 a.m. the day after sitting. Two hours after a speech allowed to submit corrections. Final verbatim published within a few weeks.	Formal corrections to verbatim record permitted which do not alter the sense. Deletion of obvious repetition is allowed but arises rarely.	Tables, lists, technical material with permission of Presiding Officer.
Before the beginning of the following sitting	Yes, if the record is contested.	On decision of the Assembly
One week after the sitting	Presiding Officer can order deletion of improper remarks.	On decision of Presiding Officer
2 weeks	Proposed by Presiding Officer and approved by the House	Yes
Unedited record is ready in 6 hours. Record is edited the day of the sitting.	Members may correct but not alter substance. Secret or purely domestic matters are transferred to a non-public record on Speaker's decision.	Written answers to questions
Digest within one week. Full edited and printed edition within 2 weeks.	President may expunge material which violates SO but Assembly may oppose without debate.	No, except supplementary documents related to minutes.
None specified	No	No

Country and House(s)	17.1 Title and nature of records	17.2 Publication authority
LIECHTENSTEIN Diet	Minutes of the Diet (Landtagsprotokoll) verbatim.	President
LUXEMBOURG Chamber of Deputies	Chamber of Deputies Report of Public Sittings (Chambre des députés Compte rendu des séances publiques) verbatim.	Chamber Bureau (In practice the responsibility of the President and Clerk).
MALAWI National Assembly	Official Verbatim Reports of the Debates (Hansard)	Clerk to the National Assembly
MALAYSIA Senate	Official Report, Senate (Penyata Rasmi Dewan Negara) verbatim.	Preparation supervised by the Secretary General under the direction of the respective Presiding Officer.
House of Representatives	Official Report, House of Representatives (Penyata Rasmi Dewan Rakyat) verbatim.	
MALI National Assembly	The Official Journal (Journal officiel).	Administrative Service
MALTA House of Representatives	Debates of the House of Representatives – Official Unrevised Report (Debates tal-Kamra tad-Deputati – Rapport Uffiċjali mhux Rivedut) verbatim.	Editor of Debates under the overall responsibility of the Clerk of the House
MAURITIUS Legislative Assembly	Mauritius Legislative Assembly Debates or "Hansard", verbatim.	The Speaker
MEXICO Chamber of Senators	Diary of the Debates (Diario de los Debates) verbatim record.	Secretary General
Chamber of Deputies		

17.3 Publication time and limits	17.4 Amendments and deletions	17.5 Addition of material
Available at the next sitting (3 to 8 weeks).	No	No
10 days after the sitting (distributed free to the household of every elector).	The President may delete matter "out of order".	Written questions and answers; general activities of Parlt; cttee work; parliamentary visits, etc. (printed on green paper).
1 day after the sitting	No	No
No time limit prescribed. Unedited version available in one day; edited version between 6 and 12 months.	May be requested by Members and ruled upon by the Presiding Officer.	Answers to oral questions which are not delivered for lack of time.
No time limit prescribed	No	No
No time specified but usually published within a week	Matter contrary to SO or House practice may be deleted by the Speaker. Members' revisions, if accepted, appear in a separate annual publication.	No
Unedited: 2 days maximum. Edited: 15 days approximately.	Unparliamentary expressions may be deleted by the Speaker.	Yes, but the practice is discouraged.
–	Yes, by erratum notice after publication.	No

TABLE 17: PUBLICATION OF DEBATES (continued)

Country and House(s)	17.1 Title and nature of records	17.2 Publication authority
MONACO National Council	Record of Proceedings (Débats) verbatim; Minutes of the Sittings of the Cttee of the Whole House (Summary).	Secretary General
MONGOLIA Great People's Khural (GPKh)	"The Session ... of the Great People's Khural of ... Convention", minutes of debate with record of decisions appended.	Office of the GPKh Presidium
NAURU Parliament	Votes and Proceedings of the House, summary. A verbatim record has not been published since independence.	Clerk of Parliament
NETHERLANDS First Chamber Second Chamber	Verbatim Reports of the Plenary Sittings of both Chambers (Handelingen van de Staten-Generaal) and of the debates in extended cttee meetings of the Second Chamber (see 23.2).	Director of the Stenographic Service, under the control and supervision of the Joint Cttee of both Chambers for this service.
NEW ZEALAND House of Representatives	Parliamentary Debates (Hansard) verbatim.	Clerk of the House
NICARAGUA National Assembly	Journal of Debates (Diario de Debates) verbatim; quarterly magazine "Monexico".	Secretary General
NORWAY Storting	The Storting Record (Stortingstidende) verbatim.	Presidium (see 9.1).
PHILIPPINES National Assembly	Record of the Batasang Pambansa, verbatim.	Secretary General

17.3 Publication time and limits	17.4 Amendments and deletions	17.5 Addition of material
5 weeks after the sitting	The President may delete words spoken by a Member after he has been called to order. Members may request corrections which, if contested, are decided by the Council.	No
No time limit for publication of minutes, but laws and resolutions of the Presidium are published within a week in the central newspapers.	No	No
Circulated to Members at the following sitting	NA	NA
No time limit prescribed but editions appear weekly on Wednesday of the following week. Enlarged cttee reports appear in about 6 days. No time limit for publication.	The Chairman or President may delete offensive, unparliamentary expressions or violations of secrets, incitement to unlawful action, etc.	Relevant material unsuitable for oral presentation, written replies to questions posed during debates, if provided before the debate ends.
Unedited (for Members) in 1 1/2 hours; edited in 10 days.	No	No
The following week	No	Yes
No time limit prescribed but official edition usually available in 2 weeks (unedited record on request shortly after the end of each sitting).	Deletions not permitted	No
Unedited record not published; edited: printed and distributed within 2 months of session's end.	Presiding Officer may delete unparliamentary words, subject to Assembly approval.	With the approval of the Assembly

TABLE 17: PUBLICATION OF DEBATES (continued)

Country and House(s)	17.1 Title and nature of records	17.2 Publication authority
POLAND Diet	Record of Proceedings of the Plenary Sittings, verbatim. Minutes of the Plenary Sittings, summary.	Diet President
PORTUGAL Assembly of the Republic	Journal of the Assembly of the Republic (Diaro da Assembleia da República) verbatim.	President and Secretaries of the Assembly Bureau
REPUBLIC OF KOREA National Assembly	National Assembly Records, verbatim.	Speaker of the National Assembly
ROMANIA Grand National Assembly	Proceedings of the Grand National Assembly (Lucrările Marii Adunări Naționale) verbatim.	Assembly Bureau
RWANDA National Development Council (CND)	Record of Debates (Procès-verbal or Inyandiko mvugo) verbatim, and Report of Debates (compte rendu or Inyandiko ivunaguye) summary.	CND President
ST VINCENT House of Assembly	Minutes (Hansard) verbatim.	Clerk of Parliament
SENEGAL National Assembly	Report of Debates (Compte rendu in extenso des débats) verbatim.	Legislative Secretary under supervision of the Secretary General
SOLOMON ISLANDS National Parliament	Hansard Report, verbatim.	Clerk of Parliament

17.3 Publication time and limits	17.4 Amendments and deletions	17.5 Addition of material
7 days after the sitting in the daily journal "The Republic" (Rzeczpospolita). Official Record 1 1/2 to 2 months after the sitting.	The President may delete material attacking the dignity of Parlt, which is contrary to the parliamentary oath or to duty towards the Republic. Appeal may be made to the Bureau, which takes advice from the Mandates and Rules Cttee.	No
None specified, but in practice 2 to 5 weeks after a sitting.	No	Written personal declarations of vote submitted before the end of the relevant sitting
Unedited National Assembly Records the day after the sitting. Edited within 6 months.	Matters which the National Assembly or the Speaker decided to be kept secret are deleted from the temporary record.	Yes, with the Speaker's permission.
None specified, but the record is prepared immediately after each sitting.	Drafting changes may be made.	See 17.4.
No specified time limits	On request of a Member, with agreement of the Bureau and the CND.	No
No limits specified. Publication time depends on length of sitting and staff available.	No, unless the tape recording confirms absence of material challenged.	No, unless the tape recording confirms presence of material claimed for addition.
15 days	Corrections may be made.	No
–	–	–

TABLE 17: PUBLICATION OF DEBATES (continued)

Country and House(s)	17.1 Title and nature of records	17.2 Publication authority
SOMALIA People's Assembly	Record of Debates, verbatim.	President of the Assembly and Secretary General
SOUTH AFRICA House of Assembly	Official Report of the Debates of the House (name of House)	Speaker
House of Representatives	(Amptelike Verstag van die Debatte van die (name of House) referred to as	
House of Delegates	Hansard, verbatim.	
SPAIN Senate	Journal of Sessions of the Plenary Assembly of the House, of the Permanent	Presiding Body
Congress of Deputies	Cttee and of the Cttees (Diario de Sesiones del Pleno de la Cámera, de la Diputación Permanente y de las Comisiones) verbatim.	
SRI LANKA Parliament	Official Report of Parliamentary Debates (Hansard), verbatim. Minutes of Parliament.	Secretary General
SWEDEN Riksdag	Minutes of the Riksdag (Riksdagens protokoll) verbatim, including questions and interpellations. Govt. Bills, Private Bills, cttee and other reports, are supplements to the Minutes.	Clerk of the Chamber
SWITZERLAND States Council	1. Official Bulletin of the Federal Assembly (Bulletin officiel de l'Assemblée fédérale; Amtliches Bulletin der Bundesversammlung) verbatim	1. Minutes Service; 2. Secretary General.
National Council	2. Abstract of Debates (Résumé des délibérations)	

17.3 Publication time and limits	17.4 Amendments and deletions	17.5 Addition of material
–	No	No
Unedited in 3 hours; weekly edition at the end of the following week.	The Speaker may delete only remarks which derogate from the dignity of the House or are of a personal and insulting nature. Other changes require consent of the Member concerned.	No, except replies to certain parliamentary questions.
Within 1 week	No	No
1 day after the sitting	By decision of the Speaker	Answers to written questions and oral answers with associated lengthy technical material may be incorporated.
Preliminary minutes of sittings ending before 6 pm are normally published before 11 am the next day; sittings after 6 pm later in the day. A final edition appears in a month.	No	No
4 editions per year, about 6 weeks after each session.	No	Written personal contributions to debate and questions; cttee reports.

Country and House(s)	17.1 Title and nature of records	17.2 Publication authority
SYRIAN ARAB REPUBLIC People's Council	Minutes (Mahdar el Jalssé)	–
THAILAND Senate House of Representatives	Minutes of the sitting, one verbatim, the other concise.	Secretary General
TUNISIA Chamber of Deputies	Official Journal of Debates, verbatim.	Chamber President
UGANDA National Assembly	Parliamentary Debates, verbatim; Minutes, summary.	Clerk in consultation with the Speaker
UNION OF SOVIET SOCIALIST REPUBLICS Soviet of Nationalities Soviet of the Union	Stenographic report of the Session of the Supreme Soviet, verbatim.	Secretary of the Presidium of the Supreme Soviet
UNITED KINGDOM House of Lords	House of Lords Official Report (Hansard) verbatim.	Editor under direction of Clerk of the Parliaments
House of Commons	Official Report of Debates (Hansard) verbatim.	Editor of the Official Report
UNITED REPUBLIC OF TANZANIA National Assembly	Proceedings of the National Assembly (Hansard) Official Report; (Majadiliano ya Bunge – Hansard – Taarifa Rasmi) verbatim.	Clerk of the National Assembly

17.3 Publication time and limits	17.4 Amendments and deletions	17.5 Addition of material
30 days	–	–
No time-limit	MPs have 3 days to submit proposed corrections, first to the relevant chairman and if refused, to the House for approval.	No
None prescribed, but usually 1 month.	Chamber President may authorise amdt to text contested by an MP.	No
None prescribed, but as soon as possible.	On the Speaker's decision	No
Bulletins with stenographic record 10 to 12 hours after each sitting. Report of the Session within 1 month of session closure.	A Member retains the right to edit his speech	Only material considered during sittings is included.
The morning after the debate	None	Written answers to questions and (rarely) a document incorporated by a Minister.
Normally overnight		Written answers to questions and material (e.g. tables) supplementing oral answers.
About 3 months	No provision	Written questions and answers

TABLE 17: PUBLICATION OF DEBATES (continued)

Country and House(s)	17.1 Title and nature of records	17.2 Publication authority
UNITED STATES OF AMERICA Senate	Congressional Record, verbatim; Senate Journal containing minutes of actions and decisions.	Senate Journal Clerk under direction of Secretary of the Senate
House of Representatives	Congressional Record, substantially verbatim.	Cttee on House Administration
VANUATU Parliament	Summarised proceedings	Clerk
YUGOSLAVIA Federal Chamber	Verbatim records of the Chamber sessions	Secretary General for verbatim record of joint sessions and respective Secretary for each Chamber
Chamber of Republics and Provinces		
ZAIRE Legislative Council	Minutes (procès-verbaux) summary; report (compte rendu analytique); Parliamentary Annals (Annales parlementaires) verbatim.	President of the Legislative Council
ZAMBIA National Assembly	Daily Parliamentary Debates	Clerk
ZIMBABWE Senate	Parliamentary Debates, verbatim.	Secretary to Parliament
House of Assembly		

17.3 Publication time and limits	17.4 Amendments and deletions	17.5 Addition of material
Congressional Record is issued daily, then in permanent edition 3 years after session end. Senate Journal is issued a few months after session end.	Deletions by unanimous consent on motion by leadership. Senators may correct their own remarks subject to rules prohibiting changes or additions to correct material.	Yes, with symbols indicating it was not spoken.
	At discretion of the House	By permission of the House
No time limit	When summary proceedings conflict with the tape recording.	No
–	No	No
Indeterminate	The President may delete material considered detrimental to public order and morals.	Yes
Unedited version appears daily and edited record is published at each sessional year end.	Yes, by decision of the Speaker.	No
Unrevised in 24 hours Unrevised produced overnight for delivery at 8.00 a.m.	Only unparliamentary terms which the Presiding Officer has ruled out.	No, except for written answers to questions.

TABLE 18

OFFICIAL LANGUAGES OF PARLIAMENT

The problem of language arises in thirty-two of the countries under consideration. In twenty-two of these, Members may speak in either of two languages, and in Congo, Fiji, Sri Lanka, Switzerland, Vanuatu and Zimbabwe, in any of three languages. Members may use any of four languages in Zaire, and in China, USSR and Yugoslavia, more than four languages are in use.

Two associated problems where more than one language is spoken in Parliament are, firstly, the problem of simultaneous interpretation and, secondly, the language or languages in which the official papers of the House are to be published. Simultaneous interpretation is provided in eighteen of the above countries. A further seven provide interpretation on special occasions or when visitors are present.

Practices concerning the publication of the official papers and other documents of Parliament differ from country to country. In seven countries with more than one working language they are published in one language only. In others they are published in both or all of the languages used. Reports of the sittings are frequently published in the language in which speeches were delivered. Several countries which have only one official language, produce documents in other languages for the benefit of minorities.

TABLE 18A. Languages of Parliament

	For Debates	For Documents
One Language	51	57
Two Languages	22	19
Three Languages	6	3
More than Three Languages	4	4
Total	83	82*

* Excludes Comoros for reasons of missing data.

Country	18.1 Official language	18.2 Simultaneous interpretation	18.3 Languages of official documents
ALGERIA	Arabic	Only on special occasions involving heads of states and the diplomatic corps	Arabic, but also French for summaries of debates.
ARGENTINA	Spanish	NA	Spanish
AUSTRALIA	English	NA	English
AUSTRIA	German	NA	German
BAHAMAS	English	NA	English
BELGIUM	Dutch, French and occasional short statements in German.	Yes	Dutch and French
BRAZIL	Portuguese	Special occasions, e.g. Head of State visit.	Portuguese
BULGARIA	Bulgarian	NA	Bulgarian
CAMEROON	French and English	Yes	French and English
CANADA	French and English	Yes (Houses and cttee meetings).	French and English
CAPE VERDE	Portuguese and Creole	Not necessary	Portuguese only (official written language).
CHINA	Major language: Han; 6 minority nationality languages: Inner Mongolian; Tibetan; Uygur; Kazak; Korean and Yi.	Provided for all 7 languages	Documents and other written material published in all 7 languages
COMOROS	French and Arabic	–	–
CONGO	French; Lingala; Munukutuba.	No	French only
COSTA RICA	Spanish	NA	Spanish

Country	18.1 Official language	18.2 Simultaneous interpretation	18.3 Languages of official documents
CUBA	Spanish	NA	Spanish
CYPRUS	Greek	No (Const. provides for translation but see 18.3)	The Const. provides for documents to be drawn up in the official languages of Greek and Turkish. At the time of compiling this compendium the seats in the House of Representatives allocated to Representatives elected by the Turkish Community were vacant; accordingly documents in Greek only were provided.
CZECHOSLOVAKIA	Czech and Slovak	No	Czech and Slovak
DEMOCRATIC YEMEN	Arabic	NA	Arabic
DENMARK	Danish	NA	Danish
EGYPT	Arabic	Only when President of Republic opens sessions and when foreign delegations attend.	Arabic
FIJI	English, Fijian and Hindi.	Provisions made, but not in use.	English
FINLAND	Finnish and Swedish	No. (But consecutive translation is possible).	Official documents published in both languages. Minutes are published in Finnish with summary in Swedish.
FRANCE	French	NA	French
GABON	French	NA	French

Country	18.1 Official language	18.2 Simultaneous interpretation	18.3 Languages of official documents
GERMAN DEMOCRATIC REPUBLIC	German	Provided for foreign govts in Russian, English French and Spanish.	German
GERMANY	German	NA	German
GREECE	Greek	NA	Greek
HUNGARY	Hungarian	Possible when required	Hungarian
INDIA	English and Hindi (Members may use other languages with the Presiding Officer's permission).	English into Hindi and vice versa; into English and Hindi from Assamese, Bengali, Gujara- ti, Kannada, Malayalam, Marathi, Oriya, Punjabi, Tamil and Telugu.	English and Hindi
INDONESIA	Bahasa Indonesia	NA	Bahasa Indonesia
IRELAND	Irish, the first official language, and English.	Senate: No. Dáil: from Irish into English.	Irish and English. Records of debates are produced in the language used in debate.
ISRAEL	Hebrew and Arabic	From Hebrew into Arabic	Record of de- bates is in Hebrew only but laws are in Hebrew and Arabic.
ITALY	Italian	NA	Italian
IVORY COAST	French	NA	French
JAPAN	Japanese	NA	Japanese
JORDAN	Arabic	NA	Arabic
KENYA	English and Kiswahili	No	English and Kiswahili

Country	18.1 Official language	18.2 Simultaneous interpretation	18.3 Languages of official documents
KUWAIT	Arabic	NA	Arabic
LEBANON	Arabic	NA	Arabic
LIECHTENSTEIN	German	NA	German
LUXEMBOURG	Luxembourg and French	No. All citizens know both languages.	The verbatim report reproduces the language used in Parlt. Other documents in French.
MALAWI	English	NA	English
MALAYSIA	Bahasa Malaysia	Bahasa Malaysia into English	Bahasa Malaysia
MALI	French	NA	French
MALTA	The official language is Maltese but English may also be used.	No	Records of debates appear in the language used in the House. Other documents are published in Maltese.
MAURITIUS	The official language is English but French is permitted.	Not required as Mauritius is bilingual.	Debates are produced in the language used but other official documents are in English.
MEXICO	Spanish	NA	Spanish
MONACO	French	NA	French
MONGOLIA	Mongolian	For foreign guests, translation into Russian.	Mongolian
NAURU	English and Nauruan	No	English
NETHERLANDS	Dutch	NA	Dutch
NEW ZEALAND	English	NA	English

Country	18.1 Official language	18.2 Simultaneous interpretation	18.3 Languages of official documents
NICARAGUA	Spanish	NA	Spanish
NORWAY	Norwegian	NA	Norwegian
PHILIPPINES	English and Filipino	No	English
POLAND	Polish	No	Polish
PORTUGAL	Portuguese	NA	Portuguese
REPUBLIC OF KOREA	Korean	NA	Korean
ROMANIA	Romanian	For diplomatic corps and foreign visitors	Romanian and other languages for national minorities
RWANDA	French and Kinyarwanda	No	French and Kinyarwanda
ST VINCENT	English	NA	English
SENEGAL	French and English (with establishment of confederative Parliament).	Yes	French and English (with establishment of confederative Parliament).
SOLOMON ISLANDS	English	No	English and Pidgin English
SOMALIA	Somali and Arabic	Yes	Somali and Arabic
SOUTH AFRICA	English and Afrikaans	Only for major speeches delivered in Afrikaans	English and Afrikaans
SPAIN	Spanish	NA	Spanish
SRI LANKA	Sinhala, but Tamil or English may be used.	Yes	Speeches recorded in Hansard in language of delivery. Order Paper in Sinhala, Tamil and English.
SWEDEN	Swedish	NA	Swedish

TABLE 18: OFFICIAL LANGUAGE(S) OF PARLIAMENT

Country	18.1 Official language	18.2 Simultaneous interpretation	18.3 Languages of official documents
SWITZERLAND	German, French and Italian	In the National Council, planned for the States Council.	Office records reproduce proceedings in the language in which they were conducted.
SYRIAN ARAB REPUBLIC	Arabic	NA	Arabic
THAILAND	Thai	NA	Thai
TUNISIA	Arabic	For international conferences	Arabic
UGANDA	English	NA	English
UNION OF SOVIET SOCIALIST REPUBLICS	There is no official language in the USSR but Russian is commonly used in the work of the Supreme Soviet. MPs speak in their native languages.	Into Russian and languages of the Union Republics when necessary	Languages of the Union Republics including Russian
UNITED KINGDOM	English	NA	English
UNITED REPUBLIC OF TANZANIA	Swahili and English	No	Proceedings are reproduced in the language used in debate.
UNITED STATES OF AMERICA	English	NA	English
VANUATU	Bislama, English and French.	Yes	English and French
YUGOSLAVIA	The languages of the Yugoslav nations and of the nationalities (principal languages are Serbo-Croatian, Slovenian and Macedonian).	Yes	As agreed by the delegates, members of the Chambers.

TABLE 18: OFFICIAL LANGUAGE(S) OF PARLIAMENT (continued)

Country	18.1 Official language	18.2 Simultaneous interpretation	18.3 Languages of official documents
ZAIRE	French is the customary language, but any of the 4 national languages may be used.	Into French from another national language when requested	French
ZAMBIA	English	NA	English
ZIMBABWE Senate	English, Shona and Ndebele.	Yes	Debates printed in English only
House of Assembly	English		Debates printed in English, Shona and Ndebele; other documents in English only.

PART V

PARLIAMENTARY GROUPINGS

TABLE 19

PARLIAMENTARY PARTIES AND GROUPS

Within representative forms of government, political parties have become instruments for the expression of the people's will. In liberal democracies, the most easily observable aspect of their activity is the effort of each to send as many representatives as possible to Parliament. The struggle between the parties gives meaning to elections, but it is not confined to them. The contest is carried on inside Parliament through political groupings, which appear in the form of clubs, fractions, groups, depending on the country, and which bring together Members who belong to the same party, hold similar views, and so on.

For a long time official recognition of political parties lagged considerably behind the important contributions they made to public affairs. Today in many countries this is still the position. Only in recent years have parties been accorded any constitutional status, and this has been for their part in elections rather than for their activities in Parliament. According to certain theorists, the representative system has no room for political groups because each Member represents the whole nation, not a political, socio-economic, or geographical part of it. Thus if he is to contribute to the nation's will he can do so only as an individual, and his speeches and votes ought to be guided solely by his conscience and not by any other considerations. Even so, political groups have gradually become an inseparable part of modern parliamentary practice, although often ignored by Constitutions, statutes, and even the rules of procedure of Parliaments.

The idea of the group or party derives in the first instance from man's natural tendency to consort with those who hold the same views as himself. It has gained ground for historical reasons because political groups have often played a major role in various movements which have brought about constitutional changes and the emergence of new States. Acceptance of the role played by political parties has profited from theoretical arguments which have led many countries to adopt proportional representation which is a system favourable to the formation and growth of political groups. It also reflects a psychological feature of modern life, namely the predilection for collective activity and the sense of discipline that goes with it.

Official Recognition of Political Parties and Groups

The previously discussed reasons explain why the position of political groups within Parliament, even in the classical democracies, is marked by a great diversity as Table 19A reveals. In nine countries, including the Bahamas, Jordan, Monaco, Nauru and Tunisia, political groups are not recognised in Parliament, and in 17 countries there are

**TABLE 19A. Official Recognition of Political Groupings
within Parliament**

Recognition of Political Groupings	Number of Countries
In the Constitution	15
In Rules of Procedure	15
Explicit or Implied in Legislation	15
Exist but not Formally Recognised	11
Only One Party Exists	17
No Parties Recognised in Parliament	9
Total	82*

* Excludes the Syrian Arab Republic for reasons of missing
data.

single party-systems. In the remaining countries the development and
functioning of parliamentary democracy is closely bound up with political
parties and groups. Their existence is usually recognised in the Constitution, the parliamentary rules of procedure, a law relating to parties
or elections, or by official registration. This recognition is frequently
granted if the parties and groups have a minimum size of membership, a
condition which reduces the harm thought to be done to parliamentary
business by excessive fragmentation of parties and groups.

The minimum number of Members a group must have to be recognised
varies from country to country. It may be as few as one in Norway, two
in Japan, three in Argentina and Israel, five in the popular Houses of
Austria and Switzerland, seven in Ireland, ten in the Ivory Coast,
twenty in the Republic of Korea and the Italian Chamber of Deputies, and
as many as thirty in France or India. Some countries such as Brazil,
Costa Rica and Spain have requirements for recognition which depend on
the amount of electoral support gained and various other factors. The
official recognition of groups (which is usually granted by the directing
authority) often gives rise to various rights and facilities. These can
include membership of the more important parliamentary bodies which
arrange the business of the House, representation on committees and
allocation of speaking time in debates in proportion to their numbers,
priority to their leaders in debates, offices and secretarial assistance
within the parliamentary building, and so on.

Given the importance of political parties in the work of Parliament, it
is interesting to note that a number of countries (for example, Australia,
Finland and Norway) refrain from according official recognition to them
in the rules of procedure, or merely allude to their presence (as in Costa
Rica, Japan and the United States) without making any direct
acknowledgement of their parliamentary existence. Whether or not
political parties or groups are granted formal recognition, they
undoubtedly perform important functions such as examining in their own
committees Government or individual Members' Bills before they come up
for debate in the House or in committee, and in deciding which of their
Members shall speak in debate on behalf of the whole group.

Recognition of an Official Opposition

In a number of countries the most important distinction between the parties in the House is that between the Government and the official Opposition. This system of majority and minority (found in twenty-nine countries including Australia, Brazil, Egypt, Fiji, Ireland, Italy, Luxembourg, Malta, Philippines, the Republic of Korea, Senegal, South Africa and Thailand) combines efficiency with a high degree of flexibility by compelling all sections of parliamentary opinion to concentrate behind one side or the other. Under this system the Opposition of today, which may become the Government of tomorrow, has official standing in the machinery of Government and, above all, in Parliament. The function of the Leader of the Opposition is essential to the working of Parliament. The post corresponds to that of the Prime Minister, involving consultation when the Government prepares the order of business of the House (see Table 11). He or she frequently has the same speaking rights in debates as the Prime Minister and other Members of the Government (see Table 12), and often, like the Prime Minister, draws an official salary.

TABLE 19: PARLIAMENTARY PARTIES/GROUPS

Country and House(s)	19.1 Recognition of groups and name	19.2 Legal basis for recognition	19.3 Conditions for recognition
ALGERIA National People's Assembly (APN)	All MPs belong to the National Liberation Front (FLN).	NA	NA
ARGENTINA Senate	Parliamentary blocs	By customary practice in the Senate	Chamber of Deputies SO indicate at least 3 Members.
Chamber of Deputies		By SO in the Chamber of Deputies	
AUSTRALIA Senate	Parties	No formal basis	None
House of Representatives			
AUSTRIA Federal Council	"Fraktionen" which in practice are included in the "Klub" within the framework of the National Council.	Federal Council SO (section 14).	At least 5 Members elected on the same electoral list notify the President.
National Council	Yes, "Klubs".	Section 7 of the Act on the Rules of Procedure of the National Council	

19.4 Recognising authority	19.5 Official recognition of opposition	19.6 Rights and facilities of groups and opposition	19.7 Rights of unattached Members
NA	NA	NA	NA
Presidents of Houses on formal request	No	Bloc presidents are ex-officio members of the Parliamentary Work Cttee and participate in the preparation of order of the day. Blocs are proportionally represented in cttees, offices are provided. Proposals for bloc staff may be made to the respective Presidents.	Same as other Members
NA	Yes, the second largest grouping in the House. Leader of Opposition receives special priority in debates.	Opposition consulted unofficially on order of business. Opposition nominates some members of all parliamentary cttees. Certain Opposition office-holders receive special allowances. Opposition party rooms are provided at Parlt House and special status is accorded Opposition office-holders.	Same as other Members
The President	No	Representation at the Presidents' Conference of the respective Council; participation in establishing order of business; proportional representation for election to cttees; subsidies from public funds, to facilitate their parliamentary activities; offices in the Parliament premises; a certain number of parliamentary employees.	Same rights as party men except provision of office-space in the Parliament premises. They do not serve on any cttee; and have no access to services provided by parliamentary groups.

TABLE 19: PARLIAMENTARY PARTIES/GROUPS (continued)

Country and House(s)	19.1 Recognition of groups and name	19.2 Legal basis for recognition	19.3 Conditions for recognition
BAHAMAS Senate	Not recognised	NA	NA
House of Assembly			
BELGIUM Senate	Political groups	SO of both Houses	2 MPs, but at least 8 to be granted group facilities.
Chamber of Representatives			3 MPs, but at least 12 to be granted group facilities.
BRAZIL Federal Senate	Parties	Constitution and regulations re-lating to Parties and Electoral Laws	Const. requires: affiliation by 10 % of MPs or 5 % electoral support in Chamber of Deputies distri-buted over at least 9 states; continuing program appro-ved by Superior Electoral Court; party discipline; financial control.
Chamber of Deputies			
BULGARIA National Assembly	Parliamentary Groups	Rules of Proce-dure of the National Assembly	None

19.4 Recognising authority	19.5 Official recognition of opposition	19.6 Rights and facilities of groups and opposition	19.7 Rights of unattached Members
NA	Opposition constituted as group of MPs in House not supporting the Govt. Acknowledged by Governor-General and in communications to Speaker.	Establishment of order of business	Table notices of motion; introduce Bills; take part in debates.
Bureau President	No, but groups not represented in Govt form an ipso facto opposition.	Proportional representation in cttees, including Parliamentary Work Cttees and President's Conference which determine programme and priorities for each House. Subsidies for each member per year(US$ 13,000); premises and offices; group spokesmen have priority in some debates such as the Budget debate.	As other Members
Presiding Officer	Rights of opposition provided in SO cover positions, speech time, cttee chairmanship and members, composition of presiding collegiates, etc.	Participation in order of business and on cttees proportional to seats held. All MPs have similar office facilities and same privileges.	NA
NA	NA	Parliamentary groups make proposals regarding: order/priority of business; drafting and approval of annual Assembly program and sessional agenda; appointment of cttees; election of the Assembly President; appointment of Govt.	Same as those of members of the parliamentary groups

595

Country and House(s)	19.1 Recognition of groups and name	19.2 Legal basis for recognition	19.3 Conditions for recognition
CAMEROON National Assembly	Groups	Constitution	Must be created and operate according to law; must respect principles of democracy, sovereignty and national unity.
CANADA Senate House of Commons	Political parties	None	Parties with 12 or more elected MPs receive certain benefits, but smaller ones are also recognised in the House.
CAPE VERDE People's National Assembly	There is only one party but non-party members may be elected to the Assembly (see 1.6).	-	-
CHINA National People's Congress (NPC)	Deputies from the same electoral unit are grouped into one delegation, named after the unit e.g. Hebei Province Delegation.	Organisational Law of NPC	Election from the same electoral unit
COMOROS Federal Assembly	Only one party	NA	NA
CONGO People's National Assembly (ANP)	No	Under Art. 15 of the Electoral Law, the final lists of parliamentary candidates are established by the Central Cttee of the Congolese Labour Party.	NA

19.4 Recognising authority	19.5 Official recognition of opposition	19.6 Rights and facilities of groups and opposition	19.7 Rights of unattached Members
Minister for Territorial Administration	None existing at present	Proportional representation in Bureau, President's Conference and cttees.	All Members must belong to a party.
The House, with Speaker interpreting its will.	Leader of opposition receives priority in debates.	Consulted in drafting the order of business; proportional representation in House cttees; parties with at least 12 MPs receive research funds; party leader enjoys higher salary.	Same as other Members
NA	NA	NA	–
NA	NA	Discuss the preparatory items proposed by NPC Standing Cttee before the sessions and discuss NPC Bills during session	NA
NA	NA	NA	NA
NA	No	NA	NA

Country and House(s)	19.1 Recognition of groups and name	19.2 Legal basis for recognition	19.3 Conditions for recognition
COSTA RICA Legislative Assembly	Parties	Inscription in the Register of Parties of the Civil Register	Notary certificate; and 3,000 members for national parties or 1 % of electors in province for regional parties.
CUBA National Assembly of People's Power	No	NA	NA
CYPRUS House of Representatives	Political Party Groups	Representation by at least 12 % of House membership is entitled to recognition under the Const. as a political party group.	At least 6 Members (see 19.2).
CZECHOSLOVAKIA Chamber of Nations Chamber of the People	Clubs of Members, according to political parties.	Under the Constitution	-
DEMOCRATIC YEMEN Supreme People's Council	Yemeni Socialist Party	One Party recognised by the Const.	Some MPs, but not all, are party members.
DENMARK Folketing	"Party groups" or 'Folketing groups'	None, but existence is acknowledged in SO and electoral Acts.	None as such, but financial and other support normally depends on representation in the Folketing at the previous general election (see also 19.4).
EGYPT People's Assembly	Parties	Law No 40 of 1977 on system of political parties.	Conformity of party principles and goals with various points and conditions

19.4 Recognising authority	19.5 Official recognition of opposition	19.6 Rights and facilities of groups and opposition	19.7 Rights of unattached Members
Supreme Tribunal of Elections	No	Parties provided with offices and secretarial staff	–
NA	NA	NA	NA
The President of the House	No	Cttee representation; political party group spokesman entitled to priority; office in Parlt.	Same as other Members
–	–	–	All MPs have the same rights.
Constitution Art. 2	–	–	–
Even without 19.3, the President may grant financial support.	No	Parties may appoint 1 or 2 substitutes for members on a cttee. Financial support and office facilities.	See 19.4.
Cttee on Political Parties Affairs	Yes, criteria is number of seats in As- sembly. Same rights as ma- jority party.	All Members have equal rights.	–

Country and House(s)	19.1 Recognition of groups and name	19.2 Legal basis for recognition	19.3 Conditions for recognition
FIJI Senate House of Representatives	Parties	Parties are mentioned in the Const. Their registration is not legally required but they must register as an association under the Trusts Act.	–
FINLAND Eduskunta	Groups	None	None
FRANCE Senate	Groups	SO	At least 15 Senators
National Assembly			At least 30 Members, without counting "Députés apparentés"(non-full Members).
GABON National Assembly	All MPs are members of the Gabon Democratic Party.	NA	NA
GERMAN DEMOCRATIC REPUBLIC People's Chamber	Fractions	SO	Written advice of the fraction formation with list of names and officers.

19.4 Recognising authority	19.5 Official recognition of opposition	19.6 Rights and facilities of groups and opposition	19.7 Rights of unattached Members
–	Const. provides for appointment by Governor-General of Leader of the Opposition.	–	–
None	None	Nomination of cttee members; entitlement to subsidies (see 6.1); provision of offices.	Same as other Members
The Bureau The President	No	Political configuration represented in the Bureau. Groups are also represented in the Presidents' Conference which establishes order of business; representation in cttees according to relative strength; allowances and offices for secretariat; group leaders register speakers and may request adjournment of debate, public vote, quorum check or creation of cttee.	Speaking time proportional to their number; cttee seats left vacant following proportional distribution to groups. Their delegate in the Senate has the same rights as a group leader to make nominations for cttees and the Bureau.
NA	NA	NA	NA
The relevant party or mass organisation	NA	Representation in the Presidium; on request, floor leaders may be invited to participate in Presidium meetings; nomination of speakers for debates and to make statements; introduction of Bills; presentation of questions, motions and amdts.	NA

Country and House(s)	19.1 Recognition of groups and name	19.2 Legal basis for recognition	19.3 Conditions for recognition
GERMANY Federal Council	No	NA	NA
Federal Diet	Fractions	Rules of Procedure	5 % of total Diet membership but smaller groups may be recognised.
GREECE Chamber of Deputies	Parliamentary party groups	SO	At least 1/20 of membership; at least 1/10 of popular vote.
HUNGARY National Assembly	One party, the Hungarian Socialist Workers Party.	Constitution	Not specified. Not all Members are party members.
INDIA Council of States	Party or group depending on their strength in the House	Chairman's Directions	Distinct ideology and common electoral programme of parliamentary work; organisation in and out of the House; at least 1/10 of the Council membership (25) for a party or 15 Members for a group in the Council of States and 55 and 30 Members respectively in the House of the People.
House of the People		Directions by the Speaker of the Lok Sabha	
INDONESIA House of Representatives	Factions	Law 3/1975	Determined by Law

19.4 Recognising authority	19.5 Official recognition of opposition	19.6 Rights and facilities of groups and opposition	19.7 Rights of unattached Members
NA	NA	NA	NA
In exceptional cases the Diet	No	Representation on Council of Elders; nomination of cttee members; provision of offices and subsidies.	–
Parliament	–	Representation on parliamentary bodies (cttees, sections, etc.) in proportion to their number. Party offices and staff.	Unattached members comprise a single group with same rights as party groups in certain cases.
–	–	–	–
The Chairman The Speaker	Yes	Law provides for special salary and other privileges for Opposition Leader. Parties and groups in the House of the People where necessary are consulted on business of the House, nomination to cttees, allotment of seats, etc.	No special provisions
Law 3/1975	No	Nominate respective cttee members; office and subsidies.	All Members required to belong to a Faction.

TABLE 19: PARLIAMENTARY PARTIES/GROUPS (continued)

Country and House(s)	19.1 Recognition of groups and name	19.2 Legal basis for recognition	19.3 Conditions for recognition
IRELAND Senate	Parties	Electoral Act	At least 7 members
Dáil			
ISRAEL The Knesset	Party groups	Members from the same candidates list constitute a group. The Knesset Elections Law applies this principle generally and requires that new groups be confirmed by the House Cttee.	One member from a candidates list constitutes a group but the Law Financing requires a new group formed by a split to have at least 3 Members unless the majority agrees to the split.
ITALY Senate	Parliamentary groups	Constitution and SO	At least 10 members (5 if they belong to the same party, presented candidates in at least 15 regions, and had Senators elected in at least 3 of them).
Chamber of Deputies			At least 20 members (fewer in certain conditions).

19.4 Recognising authority	19.5 Official recognition of opposition	19.6 Rights and facilities of groups and opposition	19.7 Rights of unattached Members
Chairman of the Dáil. Parties do not formally exist in the Senate.	Yes. Secretarial Staff are provided for each party. The leader of any party not in Govt receives a secretarial assistance grant.	Consultation on order of business; participation in nomination of cttee members; leaders of opposition parties receive secretarial assistance grants.	Unattached members of the Dáil being not less than 7 in number, form a group which can present Bills or move motions. Any Dail member may seek leave to introduce a Bill.
The House Cttee	No official opposition but in a party basis debate the largest opposition group provides the first speaker.	Large groups are represented in the Presidium; cttees composition is proportional to group strength. Monthly subsidy of US$ 96 plus US$ 107 for each group member; premises in the Knesset.	A Member who leaves a group is entitled to speak in debates and to a quota of motions and Bills.
Presiding Officer's Cttee	No specific statute exists but opposition may use all parliamentary instruments of Members and groups.	Representation in the Panel of Parliamentary Group Chairmen (see 11.1); nomination of members of cttees; parliamentary subsidies proportional to size; offices and facilities.	Same as other groups as members of the "Mixed" group
Bureau of the Presidency			

Country and House(s)	19.1 Recognition of groups and name	19.2 Legal basis for recognition	19.3 Conditions for recognition
IVORY COAST National Assembly	Groups	SO	Publication in the Official Journal of a list of at least 10 members
JAPAN House of Councillors	Parties or groups	No specific provision in SO but some aspects of Diet Law are premised on their existence.	2 or more members
House of Representatives			
JORDAN Senate	No parties or groups recognised	NA	NA
House of Deputies			
KENYA National Assembly	All Members belong to the Kenya Africa National Union	Constitution	–
KUWAIT National Assembly	No	NA	NA
LEBANON National Assembly	Groups, blocs and parties.	Established practice	No specific provisions
LIECHTENSTEIN Diet	Fractions	SO	At least 3 members
LUXEMBOURG Chamber of Deputies	Political groups	SO	At least 5 members

19.4 Recognising authority	19.5 Official recognition of opposition	19.6 Rights and facilities of groups and opposition	19.7 Rights of unattached Members
National Assembly	NA	Represented by their Chairman at the President's Conference	Members may be allied to a group without belonging and are counted with it for recognition purposes.
Executive Officer of a group is required to report its formation to the Presiding Officer.	No	Membership of cttees; designation of speakers for plenary debates; subsidies for studies and research; group offices in Diet.	-
NA	No official opposition	NA	-
-	NA	NA	NA
NA	No	NA	NA
-	-	-	-
The Diet	-	Representation in cttees	-
Chamber of Deputies	Yes (comprises all non-govt groups).	Same as govt groups, e.g. representation on Business Cttee (see 9.1); nomination of cttee members; offices, facilities, grants.	In principle the same as group members, but lack advantages listed in 19.6 and may have difficulty advancing motions and amdts requiring support of 5 MPs.

Country and House(s)	19.1 Recognition of groups and name	19.2 Legal basis for recognition	19.3 Conditions for recognition
MALAWI National Assembly	Only one National Party, the Malawi Congress Party, is recognised.	Constitution	–
MALAYSIA Senate House of Representatives	Parties	Constitution (Art. 10).	Registration with the Registrar of Societies
MALI National Assembly	The Party	Const. (Art. 5) provides for one party, the "Union démocratique du peuple malien" (UDPM).	–
MALTA House of Representatives	Govt Members Group and Opposition Members Group	None	None
MAURITIUS Legislative Assembly	Parties	Registration for electoral purposes	None
MEXICO Chamber of Senators Chamber of Deputies	Parliamentary groups	Const. (Art. 41); Federal Law of Political Organisations and Electoral Processes; Organic Law of the Federal Congress.	None
MONACO National Council	No	NA	NA
MONGOLIA Great People's Khural (GPKh)	One party system with no parliamentary groups	NA	NA
NAURU Parliament	There are no political parties.	NA	NA

19.4 Recognising authority	19.5 Official recognition of opposition	19.6 Rights and facilities of groups and opposition	19.7 Rights of unattached Members
-	No	NA	NA
Registrar of Societies	Yes	Parties nominate representatives to cttees. Special allowance for Opposition Leader.	Same as other Members
-	-	NA	-
None	Yes (Const. Art. 91).	Opposition Leader has a secretariat assistance allowance.	Same as other Members
Electoral Commissioner	Yes, the Party, after the Govt, with the most Members.	Office for Chairman of the Public Accounts Cttee. Requests in relation to order of business can be made to the Speaker or Prime Minister.	Same as other Members
See 19.2.	No	-	Same as other Members
NA	NA	NA	NA
NA	NA	NA	NA
NA	NA	NA	NA

Country and House(s)	19.1 Recognition of groups and name	19.2 Legal basis for recognition	19.3 Conditions for recognition
NETHERLANDS First Chamber Second Chamber	Fracties meaning groups or fractions	SO	Members from the same electoral list are considered a fraction from the start of the new session, unless or until the Speaker is informed otherwise.
NEW ZEALAND House of Representatives	Parties	None (organisation is voluntary).	None
NICARAGUA National Assembly	Parties and organisations	Political Parties Law of 1983	None
NORWAY Storting	Parliamentary groups	No legal basis	None. 1 member is sufficient.
PHILIPPINES National Assembly	Parties	National Act No. (Butas Pambansa Blg.) 697 with the 1978 Election Code as supplementary rule.	None

19.4 Recognising authority	19.5 Official recognition of opposition	19.6 Rights and facilities of groups and opposition	19.7 Rights of unattached Members
Chairman/President of the relevant Chamber	No official opposition.	Consulted on appointments to cttees, delegations etc.; fraction leaders receive allowances; First Chamber fraction leaders participate in the Bureau which advises the President. The Speaker and 2 Vice-Presidents are elected from among the 3 largest fractions; Second Chamber fractions receive an annual govt subsidy for staff and office expenditure. They have space in Parlt proportional to their size. Fraction staff can be appointed and dismissed by the Presidium, thus giving them formal civil service status.	NA (a single member can constitute a group).
NA	Recognised in practice	Separate party staffs including secretaries and researchers	Similar to other Members
National Council of Political Parties	Yes	Office facilities	None specified
–	No	Party Groups are represented in the Presidium in proportion to relative strength. They nominate cttee members, receive subsidies and office accommodation.	Decided on basis of individual cases
None	The Party gaining at least 10 % of votes at the previous presidential election, otherwise accreditation by Electoral Commission under law.	Representation in the Cttee on Rules (see 7.4 and 11.1); proportional representation on all cttees; offices and staff.	–

Country and House(s)	19.1 Recognition of groups and name	19.2 Legal basis for recognition	19.3 Conditions for recognition
POLAND Diet	Groups	SO (Arts. 13 and 14).	None
PORTUGAL Assembly of the Republic	Parliamentary Groups or Parties	Constitution (Art. 183).	According to SO at least 2 members, or for groups of independent MPs at least 25 members.
REPUBLIC OF OF KOREA National Assembly	Political Groups	National Assembly Act (Art. 35).	At least 20 members
ROMANIA Grand National Assembly	The Romanian Communist Party is recognised as the political force guiding the community.	Constitution (Art. 3).	–
RWANDA National Development Council (CND)	The sole political formation recognised is the National Revolutionary Movement for Development (MRND).	Constitution (Art. 7).	Every citizen is a member of the MRND by right.

19.4 Recognising authority	19.5 Official recognition of opposition	19.6 Rights and facilities of groups and opposition	19.7 Rights of unattached Members
Not specified	No	Participation of Group Leaders in the Council of Sages, and representation on cttees.	Same as other Members
President of the Assembly	There is no official opposition.	Participate in the President's Conference which fixes the Order of the Day; nominate cttee members; receive subsidies and allocation of parliamentary premises and staff; obtain rights in presentation of motions and proposals; request creation of an inquiry cttee.	A group of independents or a lone representative of a party has the same right as in 19.6 except for presentation of motions and proposals.
Speaker	Yes	Offices for group leaders; group leaders are members of the House Steering Cttee (see 11.3); nominate cttee members; nominate speakers in plenary sitting; distribute Chamber seats; membership of the Council for Diplomatic Activities of Members of the National Assembly.	20 or more independent members may establish a political group whose leader participates in the House Steering Cttee.
None	No	NA	–
Constitution	NA	NA	NA

Country and House(s)	19.1 Recognition of groups and name	19.2 Legal basis for recognition	19.3 Conditions for recognition
ST VINCENT House of Assembly	Parties	Const. (Arts 10 and 11) guarantees freedom of expression and association.	It suffices to hold 1 seat in Parlt.
SENEGAL National Assembly	Groups	Constitution	At least 1/10 Assembly membership
SOLOMON ISLANDS National Parliament	Parties	Constitution (Art. 13).	–
SOMALIA People's Assembly	The Somali Revolutionary Socialist Party is the only legal political grouping.	Constitution (Art. 7).	–
SOUTH AFRICA House of Assembly House of Representatives House of Delegates	Parties	Registration as political parties with the Chief Electoral Officer	Deed of foundation signed by at least 50 voters and aimed at promoting candidates for election to Parlt
SPAIN Senate Congress of Deputies	Parliamentary Groups	Const. (Art. 6) and SO.	At least 10 MPs in Senate or 15 MPs in Congress, or 5 seats and 15 % party vote in their constituencies, or 5 % of the national vote.
SRI LANKA Parliament	Parties	Implied	No formal provision

19.4 Recognising authority	19.5 Official recognition of opposition	19.6 Rights and facilities of groups and opposition	19.7 Rights of unattached Members
Parliament	Const. (Art. 59.1).	Proportional representation in cttees; nomination of 2 Senators.	Same as other Members
Assembly Bureau, on receipt of a programme of group political action.	Enjoys the same rights as the majority groups.	Group chairmen are members of the Presidents' Conference (see 11.1). They nominate cttee members; they have an office and secretariat.	Same as other Members but do not constitute a group. They may serve on cttees.
–	Yes	Leader of the Opposition appointed by the Governor-General	–
–	No	NA	–
Chief Electoral Officer	Opposition party with most representatives in House is recognised as the official opposition.	All Members have the same rights and facilities.	Same as other Members
Presiding Body	No	Participation in Council of Spokesmen (see 11.1); may request reconsideration of order of business; nomination of cttee members, premises, equipment and subsidies.	NA. All unattached Members belong to a Mixed Group.
Commissioner of Elections	Yes	Join in agreeing order of business; offices and staff provided; Opposition Leader receives ministerial salary.	Same as other Members

Country and House(s)	19.1 Recognition of groups and name	19.2 Legal basis for recognition	19.3 Conditions for recognition
SWEDEN Riksdag	Party Groups	Constitution (Chapter 3, Art. 7).	Elected Members of a political party form a group.
SWITZERLAND States Council	Groups (Groupes, Fraktionen, Gruppi).	Law on relations between the Councils; SO of the National Council.	No formal basis
National Council			At least 5 Members
SYRIAN ARAB REPUBLIC People's Council	Parties	–	–
THAILAND House of Representatives (Senators may not be members of any political party).	Political parties	Political party Act B.E. 2524	5000 Thai members
TUNISIA Chamber of Deputies	No	None	NA
UGANDA National Assembly	Party parliamentary groups	Customary practice	None

19.4 Recognising authority	19.5 Official recognition of opposition	19.6 Rights and facilities of groups and opposition	19.7 Rights of unattached Members
The Speaker	No	Representation in the Speaker's Conference (see 11.1); proposal of cttee members; receipt of certain subsidies.	Non-Members do not enjoy the facilities made available in 19.6.
NA	No	Proposals to the Bureau for nomination of cttee members; subsidies and premises.	Non-group Members do not enjoy the facilities
Group Const. announced to the Federal Assembly Secretariat		Representation in the Group Presidents' Conference (see 11.1); subsidies and premises.	made available in 19.6, except premises.
-	-	-	Same as other Members
Registrar, Ministry of Interior.	Leader of the Opposition (largest non-govt party) appointed by the King, provided party has not less than 1/5 members of House of Representatives.	Parties can nominate cttee members and are provided with office accommodation and facilities.	-
NA	No	NA	NA
Custom	Members not belonging to govt party can constitute an official Opposition.	Nominate cttee members (proportional representation); party whips assist establishment of daily order of business.	NA (inexistent).

TABLE 19: PARLIAMENTARY PARTIES/GROUPS (continued)

Country and House(s)	19.1 Recognition of groups and name	19.2 Legal basis for recognition	19.3 Conditions for recognition
UNION OF SOVIET SOCIALIST REPUBLICS Soviet of Nationalities Soviet of the Union	The Communist Party of the Soviet Union is the only political party in the USSR.	Constitution (Art. 6).	–
UNITED KINGDOM House of Lords House of Commons	Parties	Implicit in Ministerial and other Salaries Act 1975 making financial provision for Leader of the Opposition and Opposition Chief Whip.	None
UNITED REPUBLIC OF TANZANIA National Assembly	All MPs belong to the Party of the Revolution.	NA	NA
UNITED STATES OF AMERICA Senate	Parties	None	None
House of Representatives			
VANUATU Parliament	Parties	Constitution (Art. 4.3).	Registration as a party
YUGOSLAVIA Federal Chamber	None recognised	None	NA
Chamber of Republics and Provinces			

618

19.4 Recognising authority	19.5 Official recognition of opposition	19.6 Rights and facilities of groups and opposition	19.7 Rights of unattached Members
–	No	The Party group gives preliminary consideration to agenda items and submits proposals to the Supreme Soviet.	The 425 non-party MPs have the same privileges as the 1,075 Communist Party Members.
NA	Yes (the party in opposition to the Govt having greatest strength in the House of Commons).	Consultation in order of business (see Table 11); consideration in cttee nominations; some financial assistance; party offices. Leader of Opposition and Chief Whip are salaried.	Same as other Members
NA	No	NA	NA
None	Yes, but no official criteria for recognition.	Priority recognition by Chair of Majority and Minority Leaders; equal time in consideration of conference reports; minority can appoint 1/3 cttee staff positions. Majority party establishes order of business. Minority has rights of recognition sequences; time allotments; personnel appointments. Both parties have rights regarding cttee nominations, subsidies, offices, etc.	None
Registrar General	Yes	Provision of an office	–
NA	No	NA	NA

Country and House(s)	19.1 Recognition of groups and name	19.2 Legal basis for recognition	19.3 Conditions for recognition
ZAIRE Legislative Council	Regional groups (region = province),	Parliamentary convention	NA
ZAMBIA National Assembly	No, the United National Independence Party is the only legal party.	Constitution (Art. 4).	NA
ZIMBABWE Senate House of Assembly	Parties or groups	Constitution (Art. 21).	None

19.4 Recognising authority	19.5 Official recognition of opposition	19.6 Rights and facilities of groups and opposition	19.7 Rights of unattached Members
Legislative Council	No	NA	NA
NA	No	NA	NA
NA	Yes, second largest party.	Consulted in establishment of order of business; decide order of votes in Cttee of Supply; participation in Standing Rules and Orders Cttee on cttee nominations.	Same as other Members

PART VI

PARLIAMENTARY COMMITTEES

TABLE 20

COMMITTEES

Committees are recognised as an important structural element in the rules of procedure of all Parliaments. Committees exist to meet a practical need. The House as a whole is too unwieldy a body to make full inquiries into matters of interest to it or to consider matters in detail. Pressure of circumstances, and in particular the increasing range of subjects with which Parliament is concerned, has led to the steady development of committees. Today they are essential to the efficient despatch of parliamentary business. Nevertheless the division of labour, the principle underlying specialisation, should not be used by a committee as a pretext for taking upon itself powers which properly belong to the House. A committee is given existence as an extension of, and assistance to, Parliament, not as a substitute for it.

In most Parliaments committees can be divided into two distinct categories: permanent (sometimes called standing) and ad hoc or special committees. In the countries following the British system those two categories are not so distinctly separated and the different types of committees may be defined more on the basis of their composition and terms of reference than the duration of their mandate. In this system, therefore, committees may be said to fall into the following two main categories: select committees and the Committee of the Whole House. The British Parliament has in addition to those two types, certain ad hoc committees confusingly called standing committees. We shall describe all these different conceptions of committees later in this chapter.

We will not discuss here distinctions between the committees that have purely legislative functions as opposed to those concerned with the functioning of the House, or such committees that are strictly committees of investigation or inquiry to which we refer in Table 23.

Permanent Committees

The first type of committees, permanent committees, are, as a general rule, specialised. Each is concerned with one particular branch of activity, such as finance, foreign affairs, education, social affairs or national defence, and is entrusted with the study of all Bills or other matters relating to that particular field. The degree of specialisation differs from country to country, and seems to be particularly affected by the size of Parliament and the length of its sessions. The number of committees appointed for at least the length of a typical session differs from country to country as Table 20A shows, from one in St Vincent and

625

the Grenadines, and two in Vanuatu, to fifty-two in each Chamber of the Mexican Parliament.

TABLE 20A. Number of Permanent Committees

Number of Committees	Number of Countries	
	Federal or Upper Chamber	Popular (or Only) Chamber
0	0	2
1- 5	4	23
6-10	6	18
11-15	6	16
16-20	6	14
21-25	3	3
More than 25	2	7
Total	27*	83

* Excludes South Africa for reasons of missing data.

Permanent committees are usually appointed for the duration of the session or of the Parliament. The long and guaranteed term of office of a committee gives its members an opportunity to acquire real knowledge and specialisation on their subject, but at the same time there is a danger of increasing its powers unduly to the detriment of the House itself.

In practice, there is little or no difference between a committee lasting for the session and lasting for the term of the Parliament, because re-appointment at the beginning of each session does not usually mean that many changes are made in the composition of the committees although it does, however, provide an opportunity to make changes which may not be possible in the course of a session.

Ad Hoc Committees

Ad hoc committees are established to deal with a particular matter and cease to exist as soon as they have made a report to the House. The brief existence of these committees makes it difficult for them to infringe the powers of the House. Their terms of reference make it impossible for them to consider subjects not of direct relevance to the matter they are established to deal with. Ad hoc or special committees are found alongside permanent committees in most countries, of which France is an example. Bills introduced by the Government or by an individual Member are referred to an ad hoc committee if the Government or the National Assembly so request. In the absence of such a request, a Bill is automatically referred to one of the six permanent committees.

Select Committees

The term select committee is used in the British Parliament and in countries following British practice, to describe any committee consisting of a small number of members in contrast to the Committee of the Whole House. As a general rule they are appointed to inquire into a particular subject, and they make recommendations to the House. They rarely consider Bills at the committee stage in the course of a typical legislative process.

In some instances their terms of reference may be extended for the duration of a session. They may then be called sessional select committees and they deal with various matters falling into the same category so that they tend to resemble permanent committees, more especially because the same members tend to be reappointed automatically at the beginning of every session.

The Committee of the Whole House

The Committee of the Whole House, found in the United Kingdom and, in one form or another, in several countries which have been influenced by the British type of Parliament, is a working body which comprises all the Members of the House presided over by a Chairman instead of by the Speaker, which enables the more stringent rules of debate of the House to be laid aside and more informal procedure applied. The only surviving use of the Committee of the Whole House is for the committee stage of a few Bills in each session (such as the more important clauses of the Finance Bill, Bills with special constitutional significance, etc.), for which this treatment is prescribed by the Standing Orders or specifically ordered by the House.

In other legislatures following the British pattern the Committee of the Whole House meets to consider matters relating to expenditure and taxation (see Table 38). For these purposes it may be called the Committee of Supply or the Committee of Ways and Means.

Standing Committees in the British Parliament

Standing committees in the United Kingdom are, despite the implication of permanence in their title, ad hoc committees in that they are appointed to consider a specific Bill. Their terms of reference are not specialised, that is to say they have no exclusive field of legislation to work in; they are simply designated by letters of the alphabet - A, B, C, D, and so on. There is no limit to the number of these committees that may be established, and in a session of normal length six or seven may be appointed. Each committee considers any Bill allocated to it by the Speaker after a second reading debate if it is not referred by the House to the Committee of the Whole House, a select committee, or a joint committee of both Houses.

Specialisation of Committees

As far as the work of Parliament is concerned, a convenient basis for a system of permanent committees is where their terms of reference correspond in varying degrees to the responsibility of the various ministerial departments. This is the position in forty-eight countries, which include Canada, Japan, the Netherlands, Spain and the United States. In the remaining countries, the link between the specialisation of a committee and that of a ministerial department is less exact and the terms of reference of a permanent committee may relate to a particular subject involving Government responsibility, such as public corporations, the economy, or science and technology.

Committees Meeting Together

In a number of countries, two or more committees may be empowered to meet together to study particular problems of interest to them. The use of this procedure is limited, however, because of the practice of referring the substance of a matter to one committee and of requesting an opinion on it from one or more additional committees. Furthermore, the system of referring complex problems to ad hoc committees, especially in countries where this is the usual practice, has the merit of avoiding procedural complications which may arise where committees sitting together are not able to take decisions.

Bicameral Parliaments frequently establish joint committees of both Houses in order to consider questions of common interest. The joint committees, as any other committee, can be formed on a permanent or ad hoc basis. The joint committees with the task to supervise the administrative services of the Parliament are most often set up for the duration of one session at least. We postpone to later sections (see Tables 30 and 38) the role that joint committees play in the legislative and budgetary processes.

Appointment of Members to Committees

The determination of the membership of the various types of committees we have been examining is an important consideration. Appointment to committees is frequently based on the special qualifications, knowledge, ability, personal preferences and seniority of individual Members who are employed in the committee work of the House where their services can best be utilised. As Table 20B reveals, there are three broad methods of appointing Members to serve on committees: firstly by the directing authority of Parliament, secondly by a committee especially established for the purpose, or thirdly by Parliament itself.

In practice, whichever of these methods is used, the most important influence in most countries are the political parties or groups, at least wherever their existence is implicitly or explicitly recognised. In Brazil, Italy, the Republic of Korea and Switzerland, for example, the directing authority appoints Members to committees on the recommendation of the parties, taking into account their relative sizes and importance.

TABLE 20B. Appointment of Members to Committees

Appointment to Committees by	Number of Countries
Directing Authority	19
Special Committee of Selection	10
Parliament	52
Total	81*

* Excludes Solomon Islands and Somalia for reasons of missing data.

In some Parliaments the appointment of Members to committees is the duty of a committee of selection set up for this purpose. For example, the Committee of Selection in Cyprus, Ireland, Malaysia and Mauritius, the Elections Committee in Norway and the Council of Sages in Poland. Generally speaking, such appointments are made by the House itself, which as a rule does no more than ratify the choice made by the political groups.

In many countries - which include Czechoslovakia, Denmark, France and Liechtenstein - the composition of committees is based on the proportional representation of political parties and groups in the House. The seats in each committee are allocated to the parties and groups in proportion to their numbers in the House either by agreement between the party leaders or Whips, or as a result of an arithmetical calculation. This rule has the effect of making each committee a microcosm of the House, to the extent that the political balance of the committee by-and-large reflects that of the House itself.

Limitations on Membership of Committees

In many countries an obligation is laid upon Members of Parliament either by law, by custom, or by the rules of procedure, to take part in the work of committees. In practice, distinctions between the sources of the obligations are not of importance because membership of committees is generally regarded as a valuable experience. In this respect the problem is to limit the number of committees to which any Member may belong at the same time. In seventeen countries, Members may not belong to more than one permanent committee, and in thirteen to no more than two permanent committees. In many other countries, although no rules exist, it is customary for Members to serve on no more than one or two committees. In these countries it is not considered desirable to disperse the special knowledge and ability of a Member over too many different legislative fields. An additional consideration here is the fact that as the meetings of committees are frequently held simultaneously it can be physically impossible for a Member to participate in more than one or two.

TABLE 20: COMMITTEES

Country and House(s)	20.1 Types of committees	20.2 Number of permanent committees
ALGERIA National People's Assembly (APN)	Standing; temporary ad hoc; coordination; inquiry and inspection; limited term.	5
ARGENTINA Senate	Permanent; special (ad hoc); inquiry; bicameral.	29
Chamber of Deputies		28
		Bicameral: 2
AUSTRALIA Senate	Cttee of Whole House; standing (term of Parlt); select (until report); joint (Standing or Select).	23
House of Representatives		10
		Joint: 7
AUSTRIA Federal Council	Permanent and joint (term of Parlt); ad hoc (until report).	10
National Council		25
		Joint: 1
BAHAMAS Senate	Permanent "Select Committees" (term of Parliament).	6 in each House. (In principle, number and size of cttees decided by the House; some provided in the Constitution).
House of Assembly		
BELGIUM Senate	Permanent; special ad hoc; internal inquiry cttees.	14
Chamber of Representatives		15
BRAZIL Federal Senate	Standing cttees (term of Parlt); joint cttees; temporary, special or inquiry cttees with limited ambit and fixed term (180 days for inquiry cttees).	18
Chamber of Deputies		20
BULGARIA National Assembly	Standing cttees (term of Parlt); ad hoc cttees (for specific tasks; are dissolved on completion).	7

630

20.3 Correspondence with ministerial departments or subject-based	20.4 Appointment of committee members	20.5 Restrictions on multiple membership
The standing cttees cover the ambit of the ministerial departments.	Elected by the Assembly following proposals from the Bureau.	A MP may serve on one standing cttee only.
Most are subject-based, but not necessarily corresponding with ministerial departments.	Generally, the Houses delegate power to appoint cttee members to their President. Appointments follow consultation with parliamentary blocs and are based on proportional bloc representation.	No
Subject-based, but having broad correspondence with ministerial departments.	By each House, on basis of nominations by party leaders and respecting the proportional representation of political groups.	No
General correspondence with ministerial departments	Appointed by each Council following proportional representation principle and on basis of names submitted by each group to Presiding Officer	No
Correspond with ministerial departments.	In proportion to representation of political groups	No
Broad correspondence with ministerial departments	Elected by the respective House	No
Cttees are subject-based without exact correspondence with ministries.	By each House President after consulting party leaders	Unlimited in Senate, limited in Chamber of Deputies.
Subject-based but not corresponding to departments	By Parliament	No, but it is exceptional.

TABLE 20: COMMITTEES (continued)

Country and House(s)	20.1 Types of committees	20.2 Number of permanent committees
CAMEROON National Assembly	General (permanent cttees elected for 1 year); ad hoc SO cttee formed at start of Parlt; special cttees for a specific task; inquiry cttees.	5
CANADA Senate	Permanent or "Standing Cttees" (term of Parlt); ad hoc or 'Special Cttees' with limited life; joint cttees (comprising Members of both Houses, may be Standing or Special).	10
House of Commons		20
		Joint: 4
CAPE VERDE People's National Assembly	Standing (term of Parlt); ad hoc (for period of their given mandate).	4
CHINA National People's Congress (NPC)	Special permanent (5 year term); inquiry as necessary.	6, plus other cttees as necessary.
COMOROS Federal Assembly	Standing cttees (term of Parlt).	5
CONGO People's National Assembly (ANP)	Standing; inquiry (see 3.1).	4
COSTA RICA Legislative Assembly	Permanent; special ad hoc.	6
CUBA National Assembly of People's Power	Permanent; ad hoc; temporary (to examine particular problems).	16
CYPRUS House of Representatives	Permanent; temporary; ad hoc; and special.	15

20.3 Correspondence with ministerial departments or subject-based	20.4 Appointment of committee members	20.5 Restrictions on multiple membership
Each General cttee covers activities of several ministries.	Allocated proportional to group representation. Nomination lists are posted, then ratified by Assembly after 24 hours, unless 14 MPs oppose, when Assembly votes on lists.	Two, maximum.
Standing Cttees generally correspond with ministerial departments.	By Cttee of Selection (9 Members appointed at beginning of session). For Standing Cttees: on adoption of report of the Striking Cttee; for Special Cttees: by House.	No
All subject-based, but with larger ambit than any corresponding ministerial department.	Elected	No
Special cttees are subject-based. General Office of NPC Standing Cttee corresponds with organs corresponding generally to ministerial departments.	Nominated by Presidium and approved by NPC plenary or when out of session nominated by executive meetings of NPC Standing Cttee and approved by Cttee.	No
Subject-based.	By Assembly, through simple majority vote.	Each MP must belong to at least one cttee.
Subject-based corresponding broadly to ministerial departments	A list of candidates established by the ANP Bureau is submitted to the Assembly for acceptance or rejection.	No
Subject-based	Permanent: appointed by President taking account of proportional representation of parties. Special: elected by Assembly.	One permanent cttee only
Subject based but collectively covering whole of the Administration	Proposed by the President and ratified by the Assembly	No
Both	By the Committee of Selection	No

Country and House(s)	20.1 Types of committees	20.2 Number of permanent committees
CZECHOSLOVAKIA Chamber of Nations	Permanent	9 in each Chamber
Chamber of the People		
DEMOCRATIC YEMEN Supreme People's Council	Permanent; ad hoc	4
DENMARK Folketing	Permanent; ad hoc	23
EGYPT People's Assembly	Permanent (according to SO); ad hoc (until report debated); joint (for topics within competence of several cttees. Life continues until report debated.)	20 (18 standing)
FIJI Senate	Standing; ad hoc; Cttee of the Whole.	5 in each House
House of Representatives		
FINLAND Eduskunta	Permanent (term of Parlt). There are no investigation cttees. Grand Cttee.	14
FRANCE Senate	Permanent; special; ad hoc; joint.	6 in each House
National Assembly		
GABON National Assembly	Permanent; ad hoc.	6

20.3 Correspondence with ministerial departments or subject-based	20.4 Appointment of committee members	20.5 Restrictions on multiple membership
Subject-based and wider than coverage of ministries	The respective Chamber	No
Subject-based	Elected by the Council	–
Cttees are subject-based. An approximate correspondence also exists between most cttees and ministerial departments.	Elected by the Folketing through a system ensuring proportional group representation	No
Standing cttees are subject-based.	Appointed by the Assembly on the basis of the members' candidatures and the nominations coordinated by the Bureau	One cttee only except with Bureau approval. Ministers may not serve on cttees.
Most standing cttees are concerned with matters pertaining to the House such as business, petitions, privileges, etc. Two House of Representatives cttees are subject-based: Public Accounts and Sugar.	By President or Speaker, as appropriate.	No
All, except the Grand Cttee, are subject-based. (The Grand Cttee, of at least 45 members, considers Bills after preliminary cttee examination.)	By Parlt if unanimous; otherwise, election by 45 parliamentary electors, on basis of proportional representation of Groups. Grand Cttee is elected by Parlt.	No, but Ministers may not serve on cttees.
Subject-based but not necessarily corresponding with ministerial departments.	Election by each House, on the basis of proportional representation of groups	Not more than one permanent cttee
Cttees' areas of competence correspond with those of ministerial departments.	Appointed by Asssembly following criteria of provincial origin, qualifications and experience.	No

TABLE 20: COMMITTEES (continued)

Country and House(s)	20.1 Types of committees	20.2 Number of permanent committees
GERMAN DEMOCRATIC REPUBLIC People's Chamber	Permanent; ad hoc.	15
GERMANY Federal Council	Permanent; ad hoc.	14
Federal Diet	Permanent (legislative); ad hoc; joint; cttees of investigation (which include outside experts).	20
GREECE Chamber of Deputies	Parliamentary (for one session); permanent (term of Parlt); special inquiry cttees.	19 to consider Bills; 5 to consider internal parliamentary matters.
HUNGARY National Assembly	Permanent; ad hoc.	11
INDIA Council of States	Standing (for 1 year or until new cttee elected or nominated); joint or select ad hoc (until report submitted).	18 (including 10 cttees for mainly domestic parliamentary matters).
House of the People		17
INDONESIA House of Representatives	Permanent; ad hoc; joint; inquiry.	13
IRELAND Senate Dáil	Cttee of the whole House; permanent (term of Parlt); select (sessional or ad hoc); joint (permanent or ad hoc).	Select cttees : Senate 2, Dáil 3; joint cttees : 6.
ISRAEL The Knesset	Permanent (term of Parlt); ad hoc; joint cttees (Membership from 2 or more permanent cttees).	10
ITALY Senate	Permanent (2 years); ad hoc (until task complete); mixed (term of Parlt or end of their inquiry).	12
Chamber of Deputies		14

20.3 Correspondence with ministerial departments or subject-based	20.4 Appointment of committee members	20.5 Restrictions on multiple membership
Subject-based	Nominated by the Fractions and elected by the Chamber	One cttee only
Subject-based and correspond broadly with ministerial departments.	Nominated by each State. Each State is represented with 1 vote on every cttee.	No
Correspond with ministerial departments.	Nominated by groups in proportion to their strength	
Parliamentary cttees correspond with ministerial departments. They consider Bills referred to them.	Parliamentary cttees have 20 to 30 members appointed by the President taking account of relative strength of groups in Parlt.	Yes
Broad correspondence with ministerial departments	Designated by National Assembly	No
No (proposals are under consideration).	Appointed or elected by the House on a motion made, or nominated by the Presiding Officer under the rules.	No
Correspondence with ministerial departments	By the respective Faction	Limited to one cttee per MP
Select and joint cttees are subject-based.	By the Cttee of Selection of the House, taking account of the strength of parties and non-party groups.	No
Subject-based	Elected by the Knesset to reflect party/group balance.	No
All are subject-based but correspond with ministerial departments.	Parliamentary groups nominate same number of representatives for each cttee. The President then appoints nominees proportionally to group strength.	1 cttee per MP, except to replace Govt members and for groups with fewer members than cttees.

637

Country and House(s)	20.1 Types of committees	20.2 Number of permanent committees
IVORY COAST National Assembly	Permanent; special.	4
JAPAN House of Councillors	Standing cttees (term of Parlt); special cttees (until matter referred is decided).	16
House of Representatives		18
JORDAN Senate	Permanent; ad hoc.	4
House of Deputies		
KENYA National Assembly	Select (general purpose); Cttee of the Whole.	8
KUWAIT National Assembly	Permanent; ad hoc (for a particular task); joint.	8
LEBANON National Assembly	Permanent; special.	13
LIECHTENSTEIN Diet	Permanent; ad hoc.	3
LUXEMBOURG Chamber of Deputies	Permanent; special ad hoc; reglementary (Business, Petitions, Accounts).	17
MALAWI National Assembly	Select (permanent for each session).	3

20.3 Correspondence with ministerial departments or subject-based	20.4 Appointment of committee members	20.5 Restrictions on multiple membership
Reflect the major directions of Govt.	List drawn up by the Bureau for Assembly ratification (special cttees nominated by the Presidents' Conference).	One cttee only
Most correspond with Govt agencies.	Places are allocated by the Presiding Officer according to relative group strength.	Limited to 2 standing cttees.
		At least 1 standing cttee (but those holding other office may refuse). Special cttees unrestricted.
Subject-based with some correspondence	Elected by secret ballot	Not more than 2
2 subject-based. Others correspond with ministerial departments.	Sessional cttee (5 to 20 members nominated by Assembly).	No
Each cttee covers activities of several ministerial departments.	Elected by simple majority of Assembly	Limited to 2 cttees
Both, depending of circumstances.	Elected by Assembly	Limited to 1 cttee
Subject-based	Elected by the Diet	Yes
Most correspond with ministerial departments.	Appointed by the Chamber on proposal of the groups in proportion to their relative strength.	No
Subject-based	Appointed by the Speaker	Yes

TABLE 20: COMMITTEES (continued)

Country and House(s)	20.1 Types of committees	20.2 Number of permanent committees
MALAYSIA		
Senate	Permanent (Senate-1 session, House-term of Parlt); ad hoc	4
House of Representatives	(until report); joint (as necessary); Cttee of the Whole.	5
MALI		
National Assembly	Permanent; ad hoc.	5
MALTA		
House of Representatives	Cttee of the Whole House; select cttees (infrequently appointed).	0
MAURITIUS		
Legislative Assembly	Permanent; ad hoc.	4
MEXICO		
Chamber of Senators	Ordinary or permanent (3 years); special or ad hoc (1 year); mixed or joint (duration of task); in-	52 in each Chamber
Chamber of Deputies	quiry (for investigation see 42.3).	
MONACO		
National Council	Permanent (1 year); special (ad hoc).	4
MONGOLIA		
Great People's Khural (GPKh)	Permanent (5 years); ad hoc.	14
NAURU		
Parliament	Permanent; select; Cttee of the Whole.	4
NETHERLANDS		
First Chamber	Permanent (for the session); ad hoc (until task completed); joint	19
Second Chamber	(for the session).	30
NEW ZEALAND		
House of Representatives	Permanent; ad hoc (both gener- ally for duration of Parlt); Cttee of the Whole.	17
NICARAGUA		
National Assembly	Permanent; ad hoc.	12

20.3 Correspondence with ministerial departments or subject-based	20.4 Appointment of committee members	20.5 Restrictions on multiple membership
Ad hoc and joint cttees have some correspondence with ministerial departments.	Appointed by the permanent Cttee of Selection	No
Correspond with ministerial departments.	Appointed by the Assembly	Limited to 2
Correspond with ministerial departments or subject-based.	By motion of the House	No
Public Accounts Cttee concerned with ministerial departments. Select cttees are subject-based.	By the Cttee of Selection chaired by the Speaker	No
Correspond with ministerial departments with some over-lapping.	Elected by the respective Chamber on proposal of the Great Cttee (see 9.1).	No
Subject-based	Elected by the National Council	No
One cttee usually embraces the ambit of several ministries.	Elected by the GPKh	No restriction but in prac-tice only one cttee.
Permanent cttees are con-cerned with domestic House matters. Select cttees are subject-based.	Elected by the House	No
Correspond with ministerial departments.	By the Chairman of each Chamber after consultation with fractions and propor-tional to fraction strength	No
Most are subject-based, not necessarily corresponding to departments.	By motion in the House	No
Correspond with ministerial departments and social organisations	Appointed by the President of the Assembly	No

TABLE 20: COMMITTEES (continued)

Country and House(s)	20.1 Types of committees	20.2 Number of permanent committees
NORWAY Storting	Permanent	13
PHILIPPINES National Assembly	Permanent Standing (term of Parlt); ad hoc (until report).	30
POLAND Diet	Permanent (term of Parlt); special ad hoc; inquiry (authorised under the Const.).	20
PORTUGAL Assembly of the Republic	Permanent (for 1 session); ad hoc.	19
REPUBLIC OF KOREA National Assembly	Standing (permanent) (2 years); special; ad hoc.	13
ROMANIA Grand National Assembly	Permanent; temporary; special.	9
RWANDA National Development Council (CND)	Permanent; special.	6
ST VINCENT House of Assembly	Permanent (for 1 session); ad hoc or select (until report); Cttee of the Whole House.	1

20.3 Correspondence with ministerial departments or subject-based	20.4 Appointment of committee members	20.5 Restrictions on multiple membership
All correspond with ministerial departments except the Control Cttee which scrutinises all of them.	Elected by the Election Cttee on proposals of the party groups	All Members are members of 1 cttee. Some are also members of the Control Cttee.
There is a cttee for every department as well as other permanent cttees.	Elected by the Assembly on the Steering Cttee's recommendations	Limited to 5 permanent cttees
Cttees collectively cover the whole national administration without necessarily corresponding exactly to ministerial departments.	Elected by the Diet on proposals of the Council of Sages	None. In practice most Members serve on 2 cttees.
Subject-based but having general correspondence with ministerial departments	By deliberation of the Assembly on proposals of the President following consultation with groups and non-group Members	Restricted to 2 permanent cttees, or 3, if a group is too small to be represented on all cttees.
Most cttees correspond with ministerial departments. Others are subject-based.	By the Speaker on advice of each intra-parliamentary group	Limited to 1 standing cttee except the House Steering Cttee
8 permanent cttees are subject-based.	Elected by and from the Assembly. The Cttee on Constitutional and Legal Affairs may have up to 1/3 membership drawn from outside experts.	Limited to 2 permanent cttees
5 are subject-based but having broad correspondence with ministerial departments.	Nominated by the CND Presidium	Limited to 2 except for members of the CND Bureau (see 11.1).
–	Elected by the House	No

TABLE 20: COMMITTEES (continued)

Country and House(s)	20.1 Types of committees	20.2 Number of permanent committees
SENEGAL National Assembly	Permanent; special; inquiry (until report or 4 months maximum).	11
SOLOMON ISLANDS National Parliament	Select	4
SOMALIA People's Assembly	Permanent (term of Parlt); ad hoc and joint (occasional).	6
SOUTH AFRICA House of Assembly House of Representatives House of Delegates	Select (for duration of session to consider a specific matter); standing select (for term of House to act as component of a standing cttee); joint (for duration of session consisting of 3 select cttees, 1 from each House); standing (for term of Parlt consisting of 3 standing select cttees, 1 from each House); Cttee of the Whole House.	Standing: 26
SPAIN Senate	General; legislative; non-legislative permanent; investigating or special.	13
Congress of Deputies	Permanent; ad hoc; joint.	14
SRI LANKA Parliament	Select (to hear evidence); consultative (to consider matters referred – each chaired by a Minister); standing (to consider Bills); Special Purpose (mainly for domestic parliamentary matters); Cttee of the Whole Parlt.	Standing: 2

20.3 Correspondence with ministerial departments or subject-based	20.4 Appointment of committee members	20.5 Restrictions on multiple membership
Correspond with ministerial departments	Appointed by the Assembly following proposals from the group chairmen	Limited to 3 cttees. Bureau members may not serve on parliamentary cttees.
2 subject-based; 2 correspond with ministerial departments.	–	–
Subject-based	–	Limited to 1 cttee (except for Standing Cttee).
17 standing cttees correspond with ministerial portfolios. Others cover House domestic matters.	Speaker appoints the Cttees on Standing Rules and Orders which in turn appoint select cttee members proportional to their respective party strengths.	None
Senate has 2 subject-based special cttees. Cttees correspond with ministerial departments.	By the respective Presiding Body after consultation with the Council of Spokesmen, in proportion to relative group strengths.	None. Every MP has a right to serve on at least 1 cttee.
No (except consultative cttees).	Appointed by the Speaker	Limited to 1 standing cttee

Country and House(s)	20.1 Types of committees	20.2 Number of permanent committees
SWEDEN Riksdag	Cttees are usually permanent (term of Parlt) but ad hoc cttees and joint meetings of cttees are allowed under the Constitution.	16
SWITZERLAND States Council	Permanent; ad hoc; joint.	10
National Council		11
SYRIAN ARAB REPUBLIC People's Council	Permanent; ad hoc (1 year).	10
THAILAND Senate	Permanent (term of Parlt); ad hoc and joint (until report); Cttee of the Whole House (on request of Council of Ministers or 30 Senators or 20 Members).	13
House of Representatives		15
TUNISIA Chamber of Deputies	Permanent (1 year); ad hoc (for specific tasks); Budget and Development Planning (indeterminate term); Parliamentary Immunity (1 year).	6
UGANDA National Assembly	Sessional (term of session); ad hoc (until report); Cttee of the Whole.	3 (sessional).
UNION OF SOVIET SOCIALIST REPUBLICS Soviet of Nationalities	Standing (term of Parlt); joint; inquiry and audit; ad hoc.	17 in each Soviet
Soviet of the Union		

20.3 Correspondence with ministerial departments or subject-based	20.4 Appointment of committee members	20.5 Restrictions on multiple membership
Subject-based but broadly corresponding with ministerial departments	Elected by the Riksdag	No
Correspondence with ministerial departments in some cases	Permanent cttees elected by the States Council, others by the Bureau (see also 19.6).	Limited to 2 permanent cttees
	Nominated by the Bureau on group proposals. Members of ad hoc and joint cttees are nominated by the respective Bureau.	
–	Nominated by the Bureau of the Council	Limited to 2 cttees
Mainly correspond with ministerial departments.	Elected by the House in proportion to relative party strength	Limited to 1 cttee
		Limited to 2 cttees
Subject-based	Elected by the Chamber	Limited to 1 cttee
Subject-based	By the Assembly following consultation between the party whips	–
The standing cttees embrace the various spheres of state administration.	Elected by the respective Soviet	No restrictions but usually a Member serves 1 cttee only.

TABLE 20: COMMITTEES (continued)

Country and House(s)	20.1 Types of committees	20.2 Number of permanent committees
UNITED KINGDOM House of Lords	Permanent (reappointed each session); ad hoc (until report); joint (with the other House); Ecclesiastical Cttee (considers legislation from the Church of England); Cttee of the Whole.	14 (with 17 permanent sub-cttees).
House of Commons	Most select cttees are permanent but some are ad hoc; standing cttees (nominated ad hoc for individual Bills); joint (with the other House); cttees on private Bills; Cttee of the Whole.	30
UNITED REPUBLIC OF TANZANIA National Assembly	Permanent (1 year); ad hoc (until report).	8
UNITED STATES OF AMERICA Senate	Cttee of the Whole (only to consider treaties); standing (duration not fixed); select or special (ad hoc duration not fixed); joint (permanent or ad hoc).	Standing: 16 Select cttees: 3 Special cttee: 1
House of Representatives	Cttee of the Whole; standing (permanent); select permanent; select or special (ad hoc); joint (permanent or ad hoc).	Standing: 22 Select permanent: 2 Joint: 4
VANUATU Parliament	Standing; ad hoc; Cttee of the Whole.	2
YUGOSLAVIA Federal Chamber Chamber of Republics and Provinces	Permanent; ad hoc; joint (with representatives of socio-political organisations and including scientific, professional and public workers).	28 (18 cttees and 10 commissions).

20.3 Correspondence with ministerial departments or subject-based	20.4 Appointment of committee members	20.5 Restrictions on multiple membership
No correspondence with ministerial departments. One (Science and Technology) is subject-based.	On recommendation of the the Cttee of Selection except Ecclesiastical Cttee and Joint Cttee on Consolidation Bills whose members are recommended by the Lord Chancellor.	None
14 examine activities of ministerial departments.	Cttee of Selection nominates standing cttees and proposes members of 14 select departmental cttees for appointment by the House. Other select cttees are appointed by the House on motion of Govt Whip after discussions between the parties.	
6 are subject-based.	By the Speaker taking account of Member's preferences	In practice 1 numerically large cttee and 1 specialised cttee
Correspond with ministerial departments.	Election by each House on the basis of proposals of parties	Limited to 1 or 2 cttees depending on the cttees; same limits for sub-cttees.
Generally correspond with ministerial departments but with exceptions and certain duplications.		Certain limitations are effected by party rules.
-	Proportional to party strength in Parlt	No
Each cttee deals with specific issues.	Elected by the Chambers and delegated by socio-political organisations according to SO.	No

TABLE 20: COMMITTEES (continued)

Country and House(s)	20.1 Types of committees	20.2 Number of permanent committees
ZAIRE Legislative Council	Permanent (term of Parlt); ad hoc special (until report). A Cttee of Control functions as an audit office (Cour des Comptes – see 47.6).	4
ZAMBIA National Assembly	Sessional; ad hoc; Cttee of the Whole.	13
ZIMBABWE Senate House of Assembly	Permanent (term of Parlt); ad hoc (until report); sessional; Cttee of the Whole House.	1 (Senate Legal Cttee – see also 35.2 – which examines conformity with the Declaration of Rights).

20.3 Correspondence with ministerial departments or subject-based	20.4 Appointment of committee members	20.5 Restrictions on multiple membership
Cttees, with their sub-cttees, correspond with ministerial departments.	MPs select their preferred cttee guided by the Council President to ensure each cttee comprises 1/3 of all Members.	1 permanent cttee only
3 correspond broadly with ministerial departments; 4 are subject-based.	By the Speaker	No
3 subject-based; 4 for domestic matters of Parlt.	Appointed by the respective Standing Rules and Orders Cttee (see 7.4).	No

TABLE 21

CHAIRMEN AND STAFF OF COMMITTEES

Every committee requires a chairman to direct the conduct of its work. The powers of the chairmen are more or less the same in all Parliaments, and for the handling of debates they correspond mutatis mutandis to those of the directing authority of the House. The three methods by which committee chairmen are elected or appointed are shown in Table 21A. In most countries the committee, like the House itself, elects

TABLE 21A. Designation of Committee Chairmen

Method of Designation	Number of Countries
Elected by Committee	52
Elected by Parliament	16
Appointed by Directing Authority	12
Appointed by Special Committee	2
Ex-Officio	1
Total	83

its own chairman from among its members. In sixteen countries Parliament has the responsibility for electing the chairmen of committees. In twelve countries Parliaments find it preferable to give the directing authority a free hand in nominating persons to direct the work of the committees. In Cyprus and Kenya a special committee appoints the chairman, whilst in Malaysia the Presiding Officers are ex-officio chairmen of all committees, except the Public Accounts Committee.

Allocation of Posts of Committee Chairmen

The allocation of committee chairmen among the majority and minority groups in Parliament is a matter of importance. The main ways in which the chairmen are distributed between parliamentary groups is shown in Table 21B. The practice in twenty Parliaments is for the chairmen of committees to be distributed between the parliamentary groups, generally in proportion to their relative strength within the Parliament. In seventeen all or nearly all chairmen are drawn from the majority (or Government) group(s), whilst in a further two most are members of the majority with the chairmanship of only a few committees being offered to minority group members. In nine countries the distribution is decided by

653

TABLE 21B. Distribution of Chairmen between Parliamentary Groups

Distribution of Chairmen	Number of Countries
Proportional to Relative Group Strength	20
Majority Group(s) Only	17
Most to Majority Group but some to Minorities	2
As Agreed between Groups or Decided by the Committee	9
No Groups Recognised or Only One Party	28
Total	76*

* Excludes Costa Rica, Czechoslovakia, Lebanon, Solomon Islands, Syrian Arab Republic, Uganda and Vanuatu for reasons of missing data.

agreement between the groups or is the result of the elections held by each individual committee. In twenty-eight countries there is either only one party or parties and groups are not recognised.

In some countries it is usual for certain chairmanships to be held by members of the minority or Opposition party. For example, in Canada, Fiji and India, the chair of the Public Accounts Committee (the function of which is to ensure that the parliamentary grants for each financial year have been applied to the objects which Parliament prescribed) is not held by a member of the Government party. In the United Kingdom, this is also the position for the European Legislation Committee.

Staff of Committees

Like the Assembly to which they belong, committees have a chairman to direct the conduct of their work and can call on the administrative services of the House. Parliaments most usually provide their committees with staff drawn from a special committee secretariat or from the administrative services of the House. In four countries, Congo, Ivory Coast, Romania and Senegal, committees elect a secretary and other officers from among their members. The range of services provided to a committee by its staff can include:

- advice to the chairman on procedure;
- responsibility for the minutes of proceedings and calling witnesses;
- arrangement for the committee's use of facilities;
- preparation of correspondence on behalf of the committee;
- travel arrangements where necessary; and
- assistance in the drafting of reports.

The staff of permanent committees may prepare factual, statistical and other data on the matter under consideration. They may also prepare summary and preliminary analyses for the committee, provide organisational, technical and legal services for meetings and undertake surveys and provide other material to assist the committee in its work. Research and counselling staff from the research branch of the parliamentary library may also be available to committees when required.

Expert Advisers and Committees

Although the staff assigned to a committee provide invaluable administrative, technical and legal assistance, this is supplemented in many countries by the use of expert advisers. "Expert" in this context refers to an individual who has acquired a high degree of specialisation, usually of a scientific or technical nature, in the subject of interest to the committee. It is unusual for a Parliament to engage such specialists on a permanent basis. The common practice is for a parliamentary committee to recruit them for a specific purpose. They are always subject to the authority of the chairman of the committee, and their function is to undertake research, provide advice, attend hearings, prepare reports, and assist the committee and its rapporteurs in preparing their reports which will eventually be submitted to the House. Expert advisers are recruited from many fields, such as universities and research organisations, commerce and industry, trade unions, scientific and cultural organisations, Government departments, and so on, on the basis of the special contribution they can make to assist a committee in its work.

TABLE 21: CHAIRMEN AND STAFF OF COMMITTEES

Country and House(s)	21.1 Appointment of chairmen	21.2 Distribution of chairmen among parties
ALGERIA National People's Assembly	Elected by each cttee	NA (see 19.1).
ARGENTINA Senate Chamber of Deputies	Elected by each cttee	No provisions, but usually distribution is proportional to their parliamentary strength.
AUSTRALIA Senate House of Representatives	Most cttees elect their own Chairman.	Cttee chairmen are usually members of the Govt Party.
AUSTRIA Federal Council National Council	Elected by cttee members after consultations in the respective Presidents' Conference	Most to the majority party but with a sizeable share to opposition parties
BAHAMAS Senate House of Assembly	By Speaker, based on knowledge of subject.	See 21.1
BELGIUM Senate	Elected by each cttee. The President is ex-officio chairman of certain cttees.	Proportionally to their strength in respective House
Chamber of Representatives	Elected by each cttee except for 1 permanent cttee chaired by President. President and Vice-Presidents are ex-officio chairmen of certain cttees.	
BRAZIL Federal Senate Chamber of Deputies	Elected by Members	By agreement between parties, as nearly as possible proportional to seats held.

21.3 Committee secretariat	21.4 Secretariat functions: a) Administrative b) Research c) Document preparation	21.5 Expert advisers
Provided from the administrative staff	a) Preparation of minutes b) All aspects of research c) Yes	Standing cttees may call upon part-time expert advice.
Appointed by House President	a) Yes b) Yes c) Drafting of memoranda and reports	Permanent appointment by House President and included in cttee secretariat
Cttee secretariat is drawn from staff of each House.	a) Organise meetings, advise Chairman and members b) Yes c) Prepare draft reports for consideration by Chairman and Cttee	With approval of the relevant Presiding Officer, cttees have access to experts, who are usually appointed, either full-time or part-time, for a single inquiry.
No permanent staff but a clerk is assigned part-time to every cttee.	a) Preparation of meetings b) No c) Under supervision of the relevant rapporteur.	Part-time experts (provided by the Minister concerned or summoned by the cttee).
No additional personnel provided other than House staff	a) Yes b) Yes c) Yes	Part-time
8 secretaries for permanent cttees; drawn from Sessional Staff for other cttees. Cttee Secretariat with a staff of 13	a) Yes b) No c) Yes	Yes
Secretary and auxiliary personnel	a) Secretarial and administrative b) Yes c) Yes 657	Part-time experts can be requested. Occasionally provided full-time.

Country and House(s)	21.1 Appointment of chairmen	21.2 Distribution of chairmen among parties
BULGARIA National Assembly	Elected by Parlt	No special provisions but usually party members
CAMEROON National Assembly	Elected by each cttee	According to party strength
CANADA Senate House of Commons	Elected by each cttee	Chairmen usually from govt party, except Chairman of Standing cttee on Public Accounts (Official Opposition). Some Joint Cttees with Joint Chairmen have one each from Govt and Opposition.
CAPE VERDE People's National Assembly	Elected by Assembly on advice of Permanent Bureau	NA (see 19.1).
CHINA National People's Congress (NPC)	Nominated by Presidium and approved by NPC plenary	NA (see 19.1).
COMOROS Federal Assembly	Elected by each cttee	NA (see 19.1).
CONGO People's National Assembly (ANP)	Elected by each ctteee	NA (see 19.2).
COSTA RICA Legislative Assembly	Appointed by President	None
CUBA National Assembly of People's Power	By the Assembly on proposals of the President	NA
CYPRUS House of Representatives	Appointed by the Cttee of Selection	In proportion to their numerical strength

21.3 Committee secretariat	21.4 Secretariat functions: a) Administrative b) Research c) Document preparation	21.5 Expert advisers
1 to 3 councillors for each standing cttee	a) and b) Yes c) -	As required on a voluntary basis
Drawn from the staff of the Assembly's legislative division.	a) No b) and c) Yes	No
Cttee clerk, with support from wide range of services.	a) Yes b) No c) Yes	Few cttees have full-time experts but most have part-time expert assistance.
Consists of a Secretary elected from cttee members with assistance from staff of the Assembly.	a) Yes b) No c) Yes	As required
An office and staff for each special cttee	a) Yes b) Yes c) Yes	Special cttees may have expert advisers appointed by the NPC Standing Cttee.
-	-	Yes
Drawn from the cttee members	a) Attendance record b) No c) Minute taking and draft reports	As required
Secretariat drawn from Assembly administrative staff	a) Yes b) Yes c) Yes	Yes
A group of specialised officers	a) Yes b) Yes c) Yes	Group of experts for each cttee providing services when required
No individual cttee staff	a) Yes b) No c) Yes, including preparation of draft reports	No

Country and House(s)	21.1 Appointment of chairmen	21.2 Distribution of chairmen among parties
CZECHOSLOVAKIA Chamber of Nations	Elected by the respective Chamber	Adequately
Chamber of the People		
DEMOCRATIC YEMEN Supreme People's Council	Elected by the Council	NA (see 19.2).
DENMARK Folketing	Elected by each cttee	According to party strength and agreement between parties
EGYPT People's Assembly	Elected by each cttee from among its candidated members.	NA
FIJI Senate	Chairman either stipulated in SO or elected by each select cttee	From Govt party except for House of Representatives Public Accounts Cttee who is no nominated by Leader of the Opposition.
House of Representatives		
FINLAND Eduskunta	Elected by each cttee	According to their respective strengths.
FRANCE Senate	Elected by each cttee	Concerted attempt to distribute between the political groups
National Assembly		Distributed among the groups forming the parliamentary majority
GABON National Assembly	Chosen by the cttee according to regional balance within Assembly	NA (see 19.1).
GERMAN DEMOCRATIC REPUBLIC People's Chamber	Elected by each cttee	As agreed between Fractions

21.3 Committee secretariat	21.4 Secretariat functions: a) Administrative b) Research c) Document preparation	21.5 Expert advisers
A secretary and secretariat	a) Yes b) Yes c) Yes	Experts as required
Technical and administrative officials, clerks, typists, etc.	a) Yes b) Yes c) Yes	Some are permanently attached, others consulted as necessary.
One secretary with university degree	a) Yes b) Yes c) Yes	No
Technical, administrative and secretarial staff.	a) Yes b) Yes c) Yes	Permanent and part-time experts
Secretary and shortand writers (3 minimum per sitting).	a) Yes b) Yes c) Verbatim recording	Co-opted if necessary
Secretary and office personnel	a) and c) Yes b) No	Experts can be called by cttees.
Permanent secretariat of several people for each cttee	a) Yes b) Yes c) Yes	No, except for Cttees of National Defence and Finance which have civil servants from the central administrative services permanently attached.
Provided by administrative staff of Assembly	a) and b) – c) Prepare Bills and Ordinances for cttee examination	None currently
One secretary per cttee	a) Yes b) No c) Yes	Permanently attached to Constitutional and Legal Cttee and Cttee on Labour and Social Policy. Other cttees invite advisers as required.

Country and House(s)	21.1 Appointment of chairmen	21.2 Distribution of chairmen among parties
GERMANY Federal Council	Elected by House from among cttee members	Distributed between States
Federal Diet	Elected by each cttee in accordance with arrangements of the Council of Elders	Proportional to party strength
GREECE Chamber of Deputies	Elected by each cttee	All from Govt party
HUNGARY National Assembly	Elected by each cttee	NA (see 19.1).
INDIA Council of States	Appointed from among the cttee members by the respective Presiding Officer. The Presiding Officer is ex-officio Chairman of some cttees.	Appointments attempt to accommodate the maximum number of parties and groups.
House of the People		Usually but not invariably from the Govt party. (By recent convention, Chairman of Cttee on Public Accounts appointed from major opposition groups in rotation.)
INDONESIA House of Representatives	Elected by each cttee	According to relative Faction strength
IRELAND Senate Dáil	Elected by each cttee except for Joint Cttee on a Private Bill where chairman is jointly appointed by Chairmen of each House.	By agreement in the cttee or by majority decision
ISRAEL The Knesset	Elected by each cttee on recommendation of the House cttee with prior understanding between groups	Distributed between coalition and opposition groups but coalition assures chairmanship of the most important cttees.

662

21.3 Committee secretariat	21.4 Secretariat functions: a) Administrative b) Research c) Document preparation	21.5 Expert advisers
6 secretaries for 14 cttees. Each cttee has 1 or 2 academically qualified asssistants and 1 or 2 other assistants.	a) Yes b) No c) Yes	No
Each cttee usually has 1 or 2 clerks, 1 or 2 professional grade assistants and 1 or 2 secretaries.	a) Yes b) Yes c) Yes	Yes
Provided by the parliamentary administration	a) Yes b) No c) Yes	Provided rarely and then via the relevant Minister
–	–	Yes
Provided according to the requirements of each cttee	a) Yes b) No c) Yes	Expert advice may be called and comment sought from Govt bodies with specialised knowledge.
The House Secretary is secretary to all cttees but is assisted by joint secretaries and the secretariat		No, except cttees on Public Accounts and Public Undertakings assisted by the Comptroller and Auditor General.
From 5 to 9 persons	a) and c) Yes b) No	May be attached part-time to ad hoc cttees.
Provided from parliamentary staff	a) Yes b) No c) Yes	Yes, some cttees empowered to engage specialist services.
Usually a secretary and a clerical and typing assistant. (See also 21.5).	a) Yes b) Yes c) Yes	Advisers in various fields are from the Knesset staff. Other advisers may be contracted as required.

TABLE 21: CHAIRMEN AND STAFF OF COMMITTEES (continued)

Country and House(s)	21.1 Appointment of chairmen	21.2 Distribution of chairmen among parties
ITALY Senate	Elected in the same way as President of the Senate (see 9.2).	By agreement between groups supporting the Govt
Chamber of Deputies	Elected by absolute majority in 1st ballot, 2nd ballot between the 1st 2 candidates, then the most senior or the elder.	
IVORY COAST National Assembly	Elected by each cttee	NA
JAPAN House of Councillors	Elected by House from cttee members or House may delegate nomination to	According to relative group strength
House of Representatives	Presiding Officer for standing cttees. Special cttees elect their chairman.	Practice allocates to the ruling party.
JORDAN Senate	Elected by each cttee	NA (see 19.1).
House of Deputies		
KENYA National Assembly	Appointed by the Sessional Cttee unless nominated by Assembly	NA (see 19.1)
KUWAIT National Assembly	Elected by each cttee	NA
LEBANON National Assembly	Elected by each cttee	-
LIECHTENSTEIN Diet	Elected by the Diet	Chairmen belong to majority party
LUXEMBOURG Chamber of Deputies	Elected by each cttee (Vice-Chairman and Secretary also elected).	Proportional to relative group strength in Parlt.
MALAWI National Assembly	Elected by each cttee unless otherwise ordered	NA (see 19.1).

664

21.3 Committee secretariat	21.4 Secretariat functions: a) Administrative b) Research c) Document preparation	21.5 Expert advisers
1 or 2 staff with other assistants	a) Yes b) No c) Yes	Cttees draw on expertise of House staff and occasionally from outside.
2 members of the cttee are elected secretaries	a) and c) Yes b) No	Yes
Each cttee has a professional advisor and researchers and can draw on parliamentary staff.	a) Yes b) Yes c) Yes	Full-time adviser for each standing cttee
One secretary for each cttee	a) No b) Yes c) Yes	Ad hoc from the relevant ministry/department
Drawn from Assembly Secretariat	a) Yes b) Yes c) Yes	Full-time and part-time experts
Staff ranging 2 to 12	a) Yes b) Yes c) Yes	Full-time experts and researchers. Govt experts also available on request.
2 secretaries	-	Yes
Provided by national administration civil servants	a) Yes b) No c) No	Part-time experts
Staff with secondary and tertiary qualifications	a) Assist Chairman and rapporteurs b) No c) Prepare minutes	No (but see Table 23).
-	-	-

TABLE 21: CHAIRMEN AND STAFF OF COMMITTEES (continued)

Country and House(s)	21.1 Appointment of chairmen	21.2 Distribution of chairmen among parties
MALAYSIA Senate House of Representatives	Presiding Officers chair permanent cttees except Public Accounts Cttee, the Chairman of which is appointed by the House. See also 21.2.	Subject to the order of the House, each ad hoc cttee elects its own chairman (see also 21.1).
MALI National Assembly	Elected by the Assembly	NA (see 19.2).
MALTA House of Representatives	Usually elected by the Select Cttee. Chairman of the Whole House elected by the House.	Usually a govt member
MAURITIUS Legislative Assembly	Appointed by each cttee except Chairman of the Public Accounts Cttee appointed by the Speaker.	Govt members except Chairman of Public Accounts Cttee
MEXICO Chamber of Senators Chamber of Deputies	Nominated by the respective Great Cttee (see 9.1), appointed by the Chamber.	Only one party represented Proportional to party strength
MONACO National Council	Elected by each cttee	NA
MONGOLIA Great People's Khural (GPKh)	Elected by the GPKh from the cttee members	NA (see 19.1).
NAURU Parliament	Elected by each cttee. When the Speaker is a Member, he is ex-officio Chairman.	NA

21.3 Committee secretariat	21.4 Secretariat functions: a) Administrative b) Research c) Document preparation	21.5 Expert advisers
Comprises a secretary, stenographers, clerical assistants and typists.	a) Yes b) Yes c) Yes	Part-time
-	c) Preparation of minutes	-
Secretary, assistant secretary, typists and report editors provided from the House staff.	a) Yes b) Yes (limited) c) Yes	Expert advice may be sought as required.
Secretary, reporting and supporting staff, from the Assembly Office or relevant ministry.	a) Yes b) Yes c) Yes	Yes
Some advisers; secretariat staff; administrative support.	a) Yes b) Yes c) Yes	Some cttees have part- time experts as required.
Drawn from the administrative services of the National Council	a) Yes b) - c) Yes	Yes
Provided by the Office of the GPKh Presidium	Any necessary services provided by the GPKh Presidium Office	Cttees have non-staff specialist assistants as well as assistance from State officials, co- operatives, public organisations and scientists.
No special staff	a), b) and c) As assigned by the Chairman	No

Country and House(s)	21.1 Appointment of chairmen	21.2 Distribution of chairmen among parties
NETHERLANDS First Chamber	Appointed by the President from among cttee members	Distributed proportionally among the larger fractions
Second Chamber	Elected by each cttee	Distributed among fractions on the basis of agreement between their leaders
NEW ZEALAND House of Representatives	Elected by each cttee	Usually members of the govt party
NICARAGUA National Assembly	Selected by each cttee	Distributed proportionally among the parties.
NORWAY Storting	Elected by each cttee (following agreement between party groups).	Proportional to their strength and depending partly upon tradition and partly upon agreement between party groups
PHILIPPINES National Assembly	Nominated by the cttee members from among themselves and elected by Assembly majority vote on recommendation of the Steering Cttee	Majority party only
POLAND Diet	Elected by each cttee	Correspond roughly to the political structure of the Diet. Unattached Members may chair cttees.
PORTUGAL Assembly of the Republic	Elected by each cttee	Proportional to their strength in the Assembly

21.3 Committee secretariat	21.4 Secretariat functions: a) Administrative b) Research c) Document preparation	21.5 Expert advisers
A secretary for each cttee	a) Yes b) No c) Yes	No
Full-time secretariat comprising 1 or more deputy clerks, some-times a clerk assistant. Assistance also avail-able from Library and Documentation Service.	a) Yes b) Yes c) Yes	Available for some cttees
Cttee secretary and occasionally an advisory officer	a) Yes b) Yes c) Yes	Occasionally full-time but ad hoc experts on a contract basis
Cttee secretary but no special staff	a) Yes b) Yes c) Yes	Advisers and ad hoc lawyers for each cttee
Each cttee has a staff member.	a) Yes b) To some extent c) Yes	The staff member can sometimes provide expert advice. Advice may also be sought from govt departments and occasionally from the party group secretariat or elsewhere.
Provided by the Assembly	a) Yes b) Yes c) Yes	Technical research and counsel from the Legislative Assembly Reference Service and ministry experts
Cttee secretaries are drawn from the Diet Chancellory	a) Yes b) Yes c) Yes	Part-time experts may be invited. A group of parliamentary experts was also formed in 1981 to assist on request.
Provided by the As-sembly Cttee Service	a) Yes b) No c) No	May be sought through Assembly President.

TABLE 21: CHAIRMEN AND STAFF OF COMMITTEES (continued)

Country and House(s)	21.1 Appointment of chairmen	21.2 Distribution of chairmen among parties
REPUBLIC OF KOREA National Assembly	Elected by the plenary from among cttee members	It is the practice for chairmen to be govt party members.
ROMANIA Grand National Assembly	Elected by each cttee	NA (see 19.1).
R W ANDA National Development Council (CND)	Permanent cttee chairmen nominated by the CND Bureau. Special cttee chairmen elected by the CND.	NA (see 19.1).
ST VINCENT House of Assembly	Appointed by the House	Proportional to relative party strength
SENEGAL National Assembly	Elected by each cttee	Proportionally to their strength in the Assembly
SOLOMON ISLANDS National Parliament	Nominated by the Speaker	–
SOMALIA People's Assembly	Appointed on the basis of special competence or knowledge	NA (see 19.1).
SOUTH AFRICA House of Assembly House of Representatives House of Delegates	The Speaker appoints chairmen of standing cttees. Other cttees elect their chairmen.	Usually from majority party

21.3 Committee secretariat	21.4 Secretariat functions: a) Administrative b) Research c) Document preparation	21.5 Expert advisers
Each cttee has a Staff Director, 1 or 2 Legislative Counsellors, 2 or 4 Legislative Researchers and 5 Administrative Secretaries.	a) Yes b) Yes c) Yes	The Staff Director provides expert assistance.
Cttee secretaries are elected from the members.	a) No b) No c) Yes	Specialists are available from the Assembly staff.
Cttee secretariat is that of the CND. Cttees do not have individual secretariats.	a) No b) No c) Yes	Cttees may seek advice, notably that of the Legal Service.
Provided by the House staff. No specific secretariat for each cttee.	a) No b) Yes c) Yes	Full-time and part-time advisers as requested by the cttee
A Member is elected Secretary. The Financial and Economic Affairs Cttee also appoints a General Rapporteur.	a) Yes b) No c) Yes	No experts as such, but cttees may consult as required.
Provided by Parlt Office	a) – b) – c) –	If required
An executive and a secretary	a) Yes b) Yes c) Yes	Full-time
Each cttee has a cttee clerk from the Legislation and Cttee Section.	a) Yes, also advises on procedure b) By departmental officials c) By departmental officials in conjunction with cttee clerk	Departmental officials or other persons whose assistance is considered necessary.

Country and House(s)	21.1 Appointment of chairmen	21.2 Distribution of chairmen among parties
SPAIN Senate	Elected by each cttee	No specific rules. In practice they are distributed according to strength of the 2 main parties.
Congress of Deputies		
SRI LANKA Parliament	Standing Cttee Chairman appointed by the Speaker	Usually members of the Govt party
SWEDEN Riksdag	Elected by each cttee	Usually according to party representation in Parlt
SWITZERLAND States Council	Nominated by the respective Bureau	The groups propose candidates in turn to chair a permanent cttee for 2 years.
National Council		
SYRIAN ARAB REPUBLIC People's Council	Elected by each cttee	–
THAILAND Senate	Elected by each cttee	Members of govt party
House of Representatives		
TUNISIA Chamber of Deputies	Elected by each cttee	NA
UGANDA National Assembly	By Speaker in consultation with party whips	–
UNION OF SOVIET SOCIALIST REPUBLICS Soviet of Nationalities	Elected by the respective Soviet	NA
Soviet of the Union		

21.3 Committee secretariat	21.4 Secretariat functions: a) Administrative b) Research c) Document preparation	21.5 Expert advisers
Professional parliamentary advisers and staff	a) Yes b) Yes c) Yes	Full-time permanently attached expert. Additional ad hoc expertise may be sought.
The Clerk of the Parliament is secretary to all cttees. Secretariat is drawn from Assembly staff.	a) Yes b) Yes c) Yes	Yes
A Principal Secretary, 1 to 4 subordinate secretaries and 2 to 3 clerks.	a) Yes b) Yes c) Yes	May be requested
Comprises 9 secretaries and includes minute-takers, typists, process-servers.	a) Yes b) Yes c) Yes	Expert advice may be sought.
Drawn from the Council's administrative staff	a) - b) - c) -	Provided on an ad hoc basis
A secretary and other staff provided by Parlt	a) Yes b) Yes c) Yes	No
Each cttee has a secretary.	a) Preparation of minutes b) No c) No	Each cttee has a full-time expert. Cttees may also consult other persons as required.
Drawn from the National Assembly staff	a), b) and c) Yes	No
Provided by the staff of the Presidium	a) Yes b) Yes c) Yes	Expert assistance may be sought from ministries; state cttees; state and public bodies; research centres; specialists; scientists.

TABLE 21: CHAIRMEN AND STAFF OF COMMITTEES (continued)

Country and House(s)	21.1 Appointment of chairmen	21.2 Distribution of chairmen among parties
UNITED KINGDOM House of Lords	Selected by the House, or in default, by the cttee.	No party distribution
House of Commons	Elected by each cttee	Varies, some are allotted on a party basis by convention.
UNITED REPUBLIC OF TANZANIA National Assembly	Elected by each cttee (except see 9.6).	NA (see 19.1).
UNITED STATES OF AMERICA Senate	Traditionally cttee members nominate the longest-serving member. The nomination is ratified in full party caucus before election by Senate resolution.	All chairmen are members of the majority party.
House of Representatives	Elected by the House	
VANUATU Parliament	Elected by each cttee	–
YUGOSLAVIA Federal Chamber Chamber of Republics and Provinces	Elected by Chambers on the proposal of Assembly Commission for Elections and Appointments	NA (see 19.1).
ZAIRE Legislative Council	Elected by each cttee	NA (see 19.1).
ZAMBIA National Assembly	Elected by each cttee	NA (see 19.1).
ZIMBABWE Senate House of Assembly	Elected by each cttee except Public Accounts and Estimates Cttees appointed by Standing Rules and Orders Cttee	NA: appointed on basis of seniority and experience.

21.3 Committee secretariat	21.4 Secretariat functions: a) Administrative b) Research c) Document preparation	21.5 Expert advisers
A clerk and one or more specialist advisers as suitable	a) Yes b) To a limited extent c) Yes	Part-time (European Communities Cttee has 2 full-time legal advisers).
A clerk, one or more assistants, a secretary and part-time specialist advisers.	a) Yes b) Yes c) Yes	Temporary full-time and/or part-time expert advisers
1 to 3 cttee clerks	a) Yes b) No c) Yes	Part-time
Standing cttee staff ranges from 22 to 153.	a) Yes b) Yes c) Yes	Full-time and part-time, permanent and ad hoc experts.
Staff varies from 30 to 140 with an average of about 70 per cttee.		
Provided by the Clerk's office	a) and b) – c) Yes	Provided on an ad hoc basis
–	a) Yes b) Yes c) Yes	Full-time experts
Drawn from the Council administration	a) Yes b) No c) Yes	Assistance from the Council Research Section
Clerks drawn from the parliamentary staff	a), b) and c) Yes	No
Parliamentary cttee secretaries	a) Yes b) No c) Yes	–

TABLE 22

MEETINGS OF COMMITTEES

An important question concerning the conduct of business in committees is whether or not they are bound by the rules of procedure which apply to the sittings of Parliament as a whole. In several countries the same procedure is used for both plenary meetings of the House and committee meetings, but there are exceptions. While the House as a whole finds it necessary to adopt somewhat rigid rules of procedure (particularly those which affect the number and length of speeches) because of the number of Members involved and the demands which are made on the limited amount of time available for debate, those rules become unnecessarily inflexible in the context of committee meetings. In the majority of countries the rules followed by committees are founded on the rules governing debates in the House itself, but are much less formal. This informality manifests itself in a number of ways, and results from the small number of Members participating in the work of a committee and the more intimate atmosphere of its meetings.

Debate in Committees

We have already considered (Table 12) the restrictions which Parliaments in most countries find necessary to place on speeches made in the House. The different circumstances under which committees undertake their work make it unnecessary for these restrictions to be applied to them. In a number of countries there are no limitations on the number of times a Member can speak. As long as he has the permission of the Chair to speak, he can do so in committee as many times as he wishes. While the House places time limitations on speeches, committees can usually conduct their proceedings without these same limitations. The possibility of the filibuster may still arise in committees, but the probability of its arising is reduced by the small size of the committee, the more informal atmosphere in which it works, and the fact that, in a committee, there is little or no chance of talking out the matter under consideration. The informality of committee proceedings is further promoted in a number of countries by relaxing the requirement of plenary sittings that Members must register in advance to speak in debates. Where only a small number of Members are involved in the work of the committee, this requirement becomes superfluous. Although rules of procedure for committees are laid down in most countries, it is sometimes the case that each committee can decide its own rules of procedure. This is the logical extension of the principle that the committee is master of its own proceedings.

Public and Private Committee Meetings

An important question concerning the meetings of committees (whether executive sittings or deliberations) is should they be held in public or in private? Those who argue in favour of public meetings believe that no aspect of parliamentary activity should be withheld from public knowledge. On this reasoning, the public are usually admitted to meetings of committees in at least twenty-one countries. Twelve others may hold either public or private meetings depending on the topic and the decision of the House or the committee. In forty-nine countries, committees usually meet in private.

TABLE 22A. Public or Private Meetings of Committees

Meetings of Committees	Number of Countries
Private or Usually Private	49
Either Public or Private	12
Public or Usually Public	21
Total	82*

* Excludes Malawi for reasons of missing data.

Those who are against committees meeting in public argue that the work of a committee is provisional in character, and should not commit any of the Members taking part in it. They conclude that it is for the House as a whole to take the final decisions and to do so publicly. Furthermore, it is argued, the way in which an individual behaves in private is not the same as it is in public. Frankness and mutual trust are affected by the presence of an audience, and there is no doubt that off-the-record discussions tend to prevent playing to the gallery, encourage a spirit of compromise and make for quicker and more satisfactory results.

Meetings of Committees

In most countries committees meet when Parliament itself is not sitting. The advantage of this is that it spreads the work demanded of committee members over a longer period, lightens their burden, and makes it possible to study problems more thoroughly in an atmosphere free from the immediate demands of the plenary debates.

However, the work-load of committees can be eased by permitting them to meet while the House itself is sitting, as occurs in eighteen countries and may be permitted in thirty-one more. A major disadvantage of this practice is that attendance in the House is likely to suffer if too many committee meetings are held during a sitting. The committee meetings are also likely to be disrupted by the necessity to attend votes and divisions of the House.

Meetings outside Parliament

Should committees be permitted to meet outside the precincts of Parliament? The way in which this important question has been answered is shown in Table 22B. The right of committees to meet outside Parliament is

TABLE 22B. Committee Meetings outside Parliament

Meetings outside Parliament	Number of Countries
Yes	50
Yes, with Permission	7
No	22
Total	79*

* Excludes Comoros, Costa Rica, Mali and Syrian Arab Republic, for reasons of missing data.

granted in fifty countries, which include Australia, China, Czechoslovakia, Liechtenstein, Sweden, Thailand and Zambia. Supporters of this position argue that the efficiency of parliamentary committees can be significantly increased when they are allowed to carry out fact-finding tours and on-the-spot investigations. Generally, committees of inquiry and investigation are permitted to meet outside Parliament. The same right exists in seven other countries, where committees can also meet outside Parliament, but each request to do so must be granted by either the House or by its directing authority. The fact that a committee must receive permission to meet outside Parliament reflects the belief that committees can carry out their function satisfactorily within the precincts unless a special case can be made for going outside the precincts.

Voting and Deliberation Quorums

In general, decisions are taken by a majority of the votes cast in committees. In most countries the voting quorum for committees is a simple majority or an absolute majority of the Members (in Finland and Norway it is raised to a two-thirds majority and a three-fifths majority, respectively), but a lower figure is specified in many Parliaments. This raises the possibility that a handful of Members could take important decisions and make major changes in legislation. In practice, this is unlikely, as Members will be responsible in their attendance of the committee, and is mitigated by the fact that the House inevitably has the opportunity at a later stage to reverse any decision taken by a committee.

The general informality of committee proceedings extends to matters of voting in many countries. For example, votes may only be put formally or may be in meetings of joint and select committees by show of hands; in some countries, proxy votes may be cast in committees; and so on. Also many committees seek to arrive at decisions by consensus rather than formal vote. The quorum for deliberation in most countries is a simple majority or an absolute majority of the members of a committee, and in seventeen countries (including Israel, the Netherlands, Poland and Senegal) no quorum is specified for a committee to hold meetings.

TABLE 22: MEETINGS OF COMMITTEES

Country and House(s)	22.1 Public or private meetings	22.2 Meetings during sittings of the House
ALGERIA National People's Assembly	Private, but Govt members, and APN President and Vice-Presidents have access to the work of cttees.	No meetings may be held while House is sitting, except for immediate examination of matters raised by the Assembly.
ARGENTINA Senate	Usually private	No
Chamber of Deputies		
AUSTRALIA Senate	On decision of cttee	Senate and Joint Cttees do not meet when Senate is sitting, unless authorized by Senate to do so.
House of Representatives		Cttees may meet both when House is sitting and when not.
AUSTRIA Federal Council National Council	Private but not confidential unless otherwise decided	No
BAHAMAS Senate House of Assembly	Private	No, unless specially authorised.

22.3 Meetings outside Parliament	22.4 Quorum for deliberations	22.5 Quorum for voting/ taking decisions
No	Absolute majority	Reports of permanent cttees are usually adopted by consensus but may be voted on if the chairman considers necessary.
Meetings must be held in Congress premises.	Standing cttees: 3 or 4 members; special cttees: absolute majority.	Absolute majority (possibility of minority reports).
No provisions	Absolute majority and, after 30 minutes, 1/3 of membership (Budget and Finance Cttee 1/4). At the subsequent meeting, members may draft a minority report even when quorum is not present.	
Most cttees have power to meet outside parliamentary premises.	At least half the cttee members (most cttees have 6 or 7 members, and the quorum is usually 3 or 4).	Same quorum as for deliberations
No, but some visits of inspection may be made.	None	Absolute majority, presence of more than half the members.
Yes	Absolute majority	Absolute majority

Country and House(s)	22.1 Public or private meetings	22.2 Meetings during sittings of the House
BELGIUM Senate	Private	No, except when author- ised by the Senate President.
Chamber of Representatives	Usually private, but public when designated by the Chamber on proposal of the Presidents' Con- ference for examination of budgets transmitted by the Senate or for cttees hearing interpellations.	Not prohibited
BRAZIL Federal Senate	Public	No
Chamber of Deputies		Occasionally, except during Order of the Day hours.
BULGARIA National Assembly	Generally public, but private if cttee decides.	Both when sitting and when not
CAMEROON National Assembly	Private	Only when sitting
CANADA Senate	Both	
House of Commons		Both when sitting and when not
CAPE VERDE People's National Assembly	Private	Only when House is not in session.
CHINA National People's Congress (NPC)	Public except when neces- sary as decided by Pres- idium and meeting of delegation heads	Yes
COMOROS Federal Assembly	Private	Cttees meet during session and between sessions.

22.3 Meetings outside Parliament	22.4 Quorum for deliberations	22.5 Quorum for voting/ taking decisions
No	Not required	Majority of members
No	Majority	Majority
Yes	Majority of members	Majority of members
No	Not required	Absolute majority of members
Yes	4 Majority of members (except when authorised to hear witnesses without a quorum).	Majority of members for most cttees; Senate Standing Cttees 4; Special Cttees 1/3 of members; Joint Cttees agree quorum between Houses.
Yes	Majority of cttee members	Majority of cttee members
Yes	Majority of cttee membership	Majority of cttee membership
—	Not specified	Majority of members, but if no quorum present, vote may be taken at next meeting regardless of number provided it is held not less than 3 hours later.

TABLE 22: MEETINGS OF COMMITTEES (continued)

Country and House(s)	22.1 Public or private meetings	22.2 Meetings during sittings of the House
CONGO People's National Assembly (ANP)	Private	Only during sessions (except inquiry cttees).
COSTA RICA Legislative Assembly	Public unless otherwise decided by cttee	No
CUBA National Assembly of People's Power	Public unless cttee decides otherwise.	Both when the House is sitting and when not.
CYPRUS House of Representatives	Private	Both when the House is sitting and when not.
CZECHOSLOVAKIA Chamber of Nations	Usually public, except for meetings of the Mandate and Immunities Cttees, which are always private.	Both when the Chamber is sitting and when not.
Chamber of the People		
DEMOCRATIC YEMEN Supreme People's Council	Public unless the Chairman decides otherwise.	Both when the Council is sitting and when not.
DENMARK Folketing	Private	Both when the House is sitting and when not.
EGYPT People's Assembly	Private	Both when the Assembly is sitting and when not.
FIJI Senate	Normally private	No
House of Representatives		
FINLAND Eduskunta	Private	Only when the House is sitting, except Foreign Affairs and Finance cttees.
FRANCE Senate	Private	Both, but when House is sitting, only when required by order of the day.
National Assembly		

684

22.3 Meetings outside Parliament	22.4 Quorum for deliberations	22.5 Quorum for voting/ taking decisions
Yes	Absolute majority of members	Absolute majority of members
–	2 to 7 depending on size. Majority for ad hoc cttee.	See 22.4.
Yes	Majority	Majority
Yes	1/2 the membership	1/2 the membership
Yes	Absolute majority	Absolute majority of those present
Yes	Majority of members	Majority of members
Yes	None	More than 1/2 members present
Usually inside parliamentary premises	1/3 cttee members	Absolute majority, but if majority not obtained, 1/5 cttee members suffices at the subsequent meeting.
Yes	Half plus one	Half plus one
Only in the capital city	2/3 members	2/3 members
No	Majority on duty, except if meeting held between sessions at Govt request.	Majority on duty, if requested by 1/3 of members

TABLE 22: MEETINGS OF COMMITTEES (continued)

Country and House(s)	22.1 Public or private meetings	22.2 Meetings during sittings of the House
GABON National Assembly	Usually private, but persons with particular interest occasionally admitted.	No, except on request of the Assembly.
GERMAN DEMOCRATIC REPUBLIC People's Chamber	Public, unless the cttee decides otherwise.	Generally not during plenary sittings
GERMANY Federal Council	Private	No
Federal Diet	Generally private	Usually when the House is not sitting, except by leave of the President.
GREECE Chamber of Deputies	Private	3 permanent (legislative) cttees meet during the Holiday Section sittings.
HUNGARY National Assembly	Public	Both when the Assembly is sitting and when not.
INDIA Council of States	Private	Usually when the House is not sitting.
House of the People		When House is sitting and when not, but not after a sitting starts and before 15.00 hours without the Speaker's permission.
INDONESIA House of Representatives	Usually public; private on cttee decision.	Only when sitting, except on request of Steering Cttee.
IRELAND Senate	At discretion of the cttee	Both when the House is sitting and when not.
Dáil		
ISRAEL The Knesset	Private, except when cttee decides otherwise.	No, except with permission of Knesset Chairman
ITALY Senate	Both but usually public	No, except with permission of the President Officer.
Chamber of Deputies		

22.3 Meetings outside Parliament	22.4 Quorum for deliberations	22.5 Quorum for voting/ taking decisions
No	More than half the members	More than half the members
Yes	Majority of membership	Majority of members present
Only by leave of the Council President	Absolute majority of States represented	Absolute majority of States represented
By leave of the Diet President	None	Majority of members
No	–	Absolute majority of members present and not less than 1/3 membership.
Yes	1/2 membership	1/2 membership
With Presiding Officer's permission	1/3 membership	1/3 membership
Yes	1/2 membership and not less than 2 Factions	1/2 membership and not less than 2 Factions
Possible, but not frequent.	As specified in cttee's terms of reference	As specified in cttee's terms of reference
Yes, with permission of the Knesset Chairman.	No requirement	No requirement
No	1/3 membership 1/4 membership (ma- jority of members when cttee approves a Bill).	Simple majority

TABLE 22: MEETINGS OF COMMITTEES (continued)

Country and House(s)	22.1 Public or private meetings	22.2 Meetings during sittings of the House
IVORY COAST National Assembly	Private	No, except for urgent matters.
JAPAN House of Councillors House of Representatives	Private, but visitors including journalists may be admitted with permission of the chairman.	No, except with permission of the Presiding Officer.
JORDAN Senate House of Deputies	Both	Only when the House is sitting.
KENYA National Assembly	Private	Both when the House is sitting and when not.
KUWAIT National Assembly	Private	Usually when sitting, may meet during recess.
LEBANON National Assembly	Private	No specific provisions
LIECHTENSTEIN Diet	Private	Both when the House is sitting and when not.
LUXEMBOURG Chamber of Deputies	Private	Cttes may meet at any time during sessions (see also 8.1).
MALAWI National Assembly	–	No, except by order of the Assembly.
MALAYSIA Senate House of Representatives	Both	No
MALI National Assembly	Private	–

688

22.3 Meetings outside Parliament	22.4 Quorum for deliberations	22.5 Quorum for voting/ taking decisions
With consent of the President of the Assembly	Cttees are always in sufficient number to deliberate	Absolute majority of members if requested by 1/3 present. If quorum not present meeting adjourned 1 hour when vote is valid regardless of numbers.
No	1/2 membership	1/2 membership
No	–	More than 1/2 membership
Yes	Chairman and 2 members	Chairman and 2 members
No	Absolute majority	Absolute majority
No	1/2 membership	1/2 membership
Yes	Absolute majority of members	Absolute majority of members
Yes	Chairman may decide whether or not to open a meeting.	Majority of members. If not present, votes at a subsequent meeting, convened for voting, are valid regardless of numbers.
No	Usually 4 or 5 members and the Chairman	Same as 22.4
Yes	3 members including the Chairman	3 members including the Chairman
–	Not required	Majority of members but failing quorum, vote of those present valid after 1 hour suspension.

TABLE 22: MEETINGS OF COMMITTEES (continued)

Country and House(s)	22.1 Public or private meetings	22.2 Meetings during sittings of the House
MALTA House of Representatives	Select cttees are private.	No, except by order of the House.
MAURITIUS Legislative Assembly	Private	Both when the House is sitting and in recess.
MEXICO Chamber of Senators	Private except for public hearings	Both when the House is sitting and when not.
Chamber of Deputies		
MONACO National Council	Private	No
MONGOLIA Great People's Khural (GPKh)	Public	Both when the House is sitting and when not.
NAURU Parliament	Permanent: private; select: public when examining witnesses.	Both
NETHERLANDS First Chamber	Private, except for public hearings.	Yes
Second Chamber	Public, except when Chamber decides otherwise, to discuss procedural matters or if requested by a Member or a Minister.	Yes, with certain exceptions concerning extended cttee meetings (see 23.2).
NEW ZEALAND House of Representatives	Both	On days when Parlt is meeting but not actually sitting.
NICARAGUA National Assembly	Private, but occasionally public.	No
NORWAY Storting	Private	Cttees may meet both when Parlt is sitting and when not.
PHILIPPINES National Assembly	Public, except executive cttee meetings.	Yes

690

22.3 Meetings outside Parliament	22.4 Quorum for deliberations	22.5 Quorum for voting/ taking decisions
Yes	3 members	3 members
No	3 members	3 members
Infrequently	Simple majority	Simple majority
No	Majority	Majority
Yes	More than 1/2 membership	Absolute majority (decisions taken by simple majority).
Yes, if so ordered.	3, unless otherwise ordered.	3, unless otherwise ordered.
Yes	None	None
Yes, particularly for public hearings on problems of a particular region.		More than 1/2 members for the Cttee on Pet- itions or an extended cttee meeting
Yes	3 members	3 members
No	Majority of members	Majority of members
Yes	None	3/5 members
Yes, when authorised by the Speaker.	1/2 plus 1 of cttee membership	1/2 plus 1 of cttee membership (decision by majority vote).

TABLE 22: MEETINGS OF COMMITTEES (continued)

Country and House(s)	22.1 Public or private meetings	22.2 Meetings during sittings of the House
POLAND Diet	Private, but the media may attend with the chairman's permission.	Both when the House is sitting and when not.
PORTUGAL Assembly of the Republic	Private, unless otherwise decided by the cttee.	Both when the House is sitting and when not.
REPUBLIC OF KOREA National Assembly	Usually public, but private if the cttee so decides.	No, except by decision of the plenary session or with Speaker's permission.
ROMANIA Grand National Assembly	Public	Both when the House is meeting and when not.
RWANDA National Development Council (CND)	Both	Both when the House is sitting and when not.
ST VINCENT House of Assembly	Both	No
SENEGAL National Assembly	Private	In session only, except during a state of emergency
SOLOMON ISLANDS National Parliament	Private	–
SOMALIA People's Assembly	Public	Yes
SOUTH AFRICA House of Assembly	Private	Yes, but meet mostly when Houses are not sitting.
House of Representatives		
House of Delegates		

692

22.3 Meetings outside Parliament	22.4 Quorum for deliberations	22.5 Quorum for voting/ taking decisions
Yes, but this occurs rarely.	None	1/2 cttee membership
Exceptionally	Majority	Majority
Yes	1/3 membership	1/2 membership/ absolute majority of members present.
Yes	1/2 plus 1	1/2 plus 1
Yes	None specified	Absolute majority
Yes, always.	Simple majority	Simple majority
No	None specified	Majority of members but if not present, cttee may vote if 8 members are present after 1 hour's suspension.
Yes	–	–
Yes, except the Standing Cttee.	Simple majority	Simple majority
Yes	The quorum of a standing select cttee is 3 for a membership of 9 or fewer, 5 for 10 or more. Quorum of a standing cttee is the separate quorums of its 3 constituent cttees.	Same quorum as for deliberations (see 22.4).

TABLE 22: MEETINGS OF COMMITTEES (continued)

Country and House(s)	22.1 Public or private meetings	22.2 Meetings during sittings of the House
SPAIN Senate	Private, but media representatives may attend, except when secret.	No
Congress of Deputies		
SRI LANKA Parliament	Private	Yes
SWEDEN Riksdag	Private	Not allowed, but exceptions may be made.
SWITZERLAND States Council	Private	Cttees usually meet between sessions.
National Council		
SYRIAN ARAB REPUBLIC People's Council	Private	Yes
THAILAND Senate	Both	No
House of Representatives		
TUNISIA Chamber of Deputies	Usually private, but the Chamber President may authorise a public meeting.	No
UGANDA National Assembly	Both	When the House is sitting and when not.
UNION OF SOVIET SOCIALIST REPUBLICS Soviet of Nationalities	Usually public but a cttee may resolve to meet in private.	Yes
Soviet of the Union		

22.3 Meetings outside Parliament	22.4 Quorum for deliberations	22.5 Quorum for voting/ taking decisions
No	Not required	Absolute majority
Yes	3 members	Majority of members
Yes	None specified	Simple majority
Yes, frequently, except during sessions.	Absolute majority	Absolute majority
–	–	–
Yes	Majority	Majority
No	Absolute majority	Majority
Yes	Differs from cttee to cttee, usually about 1/2 membership.	See 22.4 (e.g. 6 in 13. 4 or 6 in 10, 3 in 5, etc.).
Yes	Majority of members	Simple majority

TABLE 22: MEETINGS OF COMMITTEES (continued)

Country and House(s)	22.1 Public or private meetings	22.2 Meetings during sittings of the House
UNITED KINGDOM House of Lords	Both	When the House is sitting and when not.
House of Commons		
UNITED REPUBLIC OF TANZANIA National Assembly	Private	Yes
UNITED STATES OF AMERICA Senate	Usually public unless cttee decides otherwise.	Only during the first 2 hours of a sitting and before 2 pm otherwise Senate permission required
House of Representatives		No cttee of the House (except the Cttees on Appropriations, Budget, Rules, Standards of Official Conduct, and Ways and Means) may sit, without special leave, while the House is reading a measure for amdt under the five-minute rule.
VANUATU Parliament	Private	No
YUGOSLAVIA Federal Chamber	Usually public	Yes
Chamber of Republics and Provinces		
ZAIRE Legislative Council	Private	No
ZAMBIA National Assembly	Private	No
ZIMBABWE Senate	Private	Rarely
House of Assembly		

22.3 Meetings outside Parliament	22.4 Quorum for deliberations	22.5 Quorum for voting/ taking decisions
Select cttees may be given power to sit outside parliamentary premises.	Fixed by the House for each select cttee. 17 or 1/3 members, whichever is less, for standing cttees.	See 22.4
If authorised by the House	Usually 3	Usually 3
Yes	1/2 membership	1/2 membership
Yes	Set by each cttee but not less than 1/3 membership except a lesser number may constitute a quorum to take testimony and receive evidence.	See 22.4 except majority vote required to report a measure to the House.
Yes	2/3 members	2/3 members
Yes	Majority of members	Majority of members
Yes	1/2 cttee members	2/3 cttee members
Yes	4 members	Majority of members
Yes	3/7 or 5/8	Same quorum as for deliberations

TABLE 23

ATTENDANCE AT COMMITTEE MEETINGS

It is exceptional for Government officials to sit on parliamentary committees, a practice found only in eleven countries, and in five of these (Bulgaria, China, Indonesia, Mongolia and USSR) only when they are also elected Members of Parliament.

Committees in most countries have the power to call Ministers before them, although this power is usually limited to matters concerning the respective portfolio or the committee's ambit of legitimate interest. Sometimes the power is exercised through the Parliament. In four countries (Algeria, Costa Rica, India and Monaco) this power does not exist and in a further ten, Ministers can be called but are not obliged to appear. However, refusal could entail questions being posed elsewhere. In seven countries Ministers have a right to be heard by committees to give explanations or defend a Bill. The situation is summarised in Table 23A.

TABLE 23A. Calling of Ministers before a Committee

	Number of Countries
Ministers Cannot be Called	4
May be Invited but no Obligation to Respond	10
Can be Called (Usually only Concerning the Portfolio)	59
Ministers have a Right to be Heard	7
Total	80*

* Excludes Gabon, Malawi and Solomon Islands, for reasons of missing data.

Non-Committee Members attending Committee Meetings

We have already examined (Table 22) the public or private nature of committee meetings. A question which naturally arises is should the privacy of these meetings extend to Members of Parliament who are not members of a committee? Whether or not Members can attend and take part in the discussions of committees to which they do not belong is considered in Table 23B.

699

ATTENDANCE AT COMMITTEE MEETINGS

TABLE 23B. Non-Committee Members Attending and Speaking at Committee Meetings

Attendance	Number of Countries	Speaking	Number of Countries
Yes	52	Yes	34
Yes, with Permission or Invitation	12	Yes, with Permission or if Invited	14
Yes, if Proposer of a Bill or other Initiative	5	Yes, if Proposer of a Motion or other Initiative	6
No	14	No	29
Total	83	Total	83

In twelve countries including Cameroon, Costa Rica, Israel, Japan, Poland and the Republic of Korea, leave may be given for non-committee members to attend by a special decision of the committee in question. In Denmark, France, the Federal Republic of Germany, Switzerland and Thailand, a Member may attend a committee meeting if he is the proposer of a Bill or other initiative being debated, and in France the rapporteur of another committee which is considering the same Bill may attend a committee meeting. In fifty-two other Parliaments, Members are entitled to attend meetings of committees of which they are not members, even though these meetings may be closed to the public. They may attend in either an observer or consultative capacity, but are frequently required to withdraw when decisions are being taken. In many countries the presence of non-committee members does not entitle them to participate in the deliberations of the committee without the permission of the committee or when they are movers of a motion or amendment being considered, but in thirty-four countries such Members are permitted to take part in a committee's discussions, though not in its decisions.

Powers to Summon Witnesses and Request Documents

The work of committees of inquiry and investigation is facilitated by the granting to them of certain powers which it is convenient for the House to delegate. These powers are summarised in Table 23 C. In seventy-two countries, committees of Parliament can require papers, documents, books, tapes, etc. to be produced before them. In seventy-three countries committees have power to call government officials to appear before them and in sixty-three countries, committees can summon other witnesses to give evidence. Certain restrictions apply in some countries, such as limitation of these powers to investigatory or standing committees, or to the Public Accounts Committee. In other cases such as Lebanon, a special vote of Parliament is required. These powers are important in that they assist the committee in the detailed analysis of various matters which they undertake. Failure to produce documents or to appear before a committee is interpreted in many countries as an offence against Parliament and is punishable by the courts of law or by Parliament itself (see Table 4).

700

TABLE 23C. **Powers to Summon Witnesses and Request Documents**

Power	Number of Countries
Summon Government Officials	73
Summon Other Witnesses	63
Call for Documents	72

TABLE 23: ATTENDANCE AT COMMITTEE MEETINGS

Country and House(s)	23.1 Can govt officials a) Be summoned by committees b) Be committee members	23.2 Can MPs not members of a cttee attend, speak at its meetings
ALGERIA National People's Assembly (APN)	a) They may be heard on request transmitted via the APN President b) No	Standing cttees may request the participation of members of other cttees. Originators of amdts may be heard.
ARGENTINA Senate	a) Yes b) No	No provisions, but customary practice permits MPs to attend and speak.
Chamber of Deputies		Yes
AUSTRALIA Senate	a) Yes b) No	Senators may participate in public sessions but cannot vote.
House of Representatives		Representatives may attend public hearings but must withdraw when cttee is deliberating or when requested to do so by a cttee member. They cannot put questions to witnesses or take any formal part.
AUSTRIA Federal Council	a) Yes b) No	Yes
National Council		
BAHAMAS Senate	a) Yes b) No	Can attend but not speak.
House of Assembly		
BELGIUM Senate	a) Yes b) No	Yes
Chamber of Representatives		

23.3 Right to summon witnesses	23.4 Right to call for documents	23.5 Can Ministers be called before a committee
In cases of disciplinary actions	No	No
Yes	Cttees may request documents but request can be refused.	Cttees may invite Ministers but they are not obliged to attend.
Yes	Yes	Yes, under any circumstances which the cttee considers appropriate, although, if a Minister is member of a House other than the House to which the cttee belongs, leave must be sought from the Minister's House for his attendance.
Yes (if the cttee decides, they are summoned by the President of the Council).	Yes	By a simple majority vote
Yes	Yes	On matters concerning the Minister's portfolio
Persons may be consulted but only Senate cttees of inquiry can summon witnesses. House cttees may seek advice from persons or organisations on a consultative capacity.	Only cttees of inquiry	Only Parliament has the right to summon Ministers, but in practice Ministers respond to requests to appear before cttees.

Country and House(s)	23.1 Can govt officials a) Be summoned by committees b) Be committee members	23.2 Can MPs not members of a cttee attend, speak at its meetings
BRAZIL Federal Senate Chamber of Deputies	a) No, except by inquiry cttees, but they may be invited and heard b) No	Yes, but not vote.
BULGARIA National Assembly	a) Yes b) Only when they are also Assembly Members	Yes, but not vote.
CAMEROON National Assembly	a) Yes b) No	Attend with permission of cttee chairmen.
CANADA Senate House of Commons	a) Yes b) No	They may attend and speak unless otherwise stated by the House.
CAPE VERDE People's National Assembly	a) Yes b) No	Yes
CHINA National People's Congress (NPC)	a) Yes b) Govt officials elected to NPC can be members of the special permanent cttees but not of the Standing Cttee	The Head of a Delegation or a Deputy or member of the Standing Cttee who raised a question subsequently referred to a special cttee, may attend when the Head of a govt department is called to respond before the cttee.
COMOROS Federal Assembly	a) Yes b) No	Yes
CONGO People's National Assembly (ANP)	a) Yes b) No	On request of cttee
COSTA RICA Legislative Assembly	a) No, but they may be heard b) No	May attend, but only speak with Chairman's permission.
CUBA National Assembly of People's Power	a) Yes b) No	Yes

23.3 Right to summon witnesses	23.4 Right to call for documents	23.5 Can Ministers be called before a committee
Yes	Yes	Only before inquiry cttees or by a majority decision of the respective House
Yes	Yes	Yes, in context of cttee work.
Yes	Yes	For details which only he can provide.
Yes	Yes	Yes
Yes	Yes	To request advice
Yes	Yes	Yes
Yes	–	Yes
Yes	–	To provide information or defend a Bill
No	Yes	No
Yes	Yes	Yes

Country and House(s)	23.1 Can govt officials a) Be summoned by committees b) Be committee members	23.2 Can MPs not members of a cttee attend, speak at its meetings
CYPRUS House of Representatives	a) Yes b) No	Yes, but not vote.
CZECHOSLOVAKIA Chamber of Nations	a) Yes b) No	Yes, but not vote.
Chamber of the People		
DEMOCRATIC YEMEN Supreme People's Council	a) Yes b) No	Yes
DENMARK Folketing	a) No, but can be heard when accompanying a summoned Minister with his agreement b) No	Mover of a Bill may participate in debate in relation to Bill, but not vote.
EGYPT People's Assembly	a) Yes b) No	Yes
FIJI Senate	a) Yes b) No	Not normally, and cannot speak.
House of Representatives		
FINLAND Eduskunta	a) Yes b) No	No
FRANCE Senate	a) Yes b) No	Only the proposers of the Bill or amdts being considered, or the rapporteur of another cttee considering the same Bill for advice, or the special rapporteur of the Finance Cttee for the Budget, may attend and speak.
National Assembly		

23.3 Right to summon witnesses	23.4 Right to call for documents	23.5 Can Ministers be called before a committee
Yes	Yes	Yes
Yes	Yes	Yes
Yes	Yes	Yes
Investigatory cttees set up according to Const. can summon persons and papers but this is rarely done.	No, but may be requested of Ministers (see also 23.3).	Ministers can be requested to appear, and in practice always do, but could refuse.
Yes	Yes	When cttee subject is within the Minister's jurisdiction.
Yes	Yes	Yes
Experts only	Yes	Yes
No, but consultation is possible (see 28.3).	Only for public documents, by investigative cttees and by special rapporteurs with investigative powers of the Finance Cttee.	No obligation to appear except before investigative cttees, but in practice Ministers attend when requested.

Country and House(s)	23.1 Can govt officials a) Be summoned by committees b) Be committee members	23.2 Can MPs not members of a cttee attend, speak at its meetings
GABON National Assembly	a) When necessary b) -	Yes, but not vote.
GERMAN DEMOCRATIC REPUBLIC People's Chamber	a) Yes b) Yes	Yes
GERMANY Federal Council	a) Yes b) No (only State officials)	Council members and Federal and State commissioners may attend and speak but not vote.
Federal Diet	a) Yes b) No	Diet members may attend most cttees. The President, chairmen of parliamentary groups and proposers of Bills or motions under consideration may speak.
GREECE Chamber of Deputies	a) Yes b) No	Attend but not speak
HUNGARY National Assembly	a) Yes b) Yes, but not Govt members	Yes
INDIA Council of States House of the People	a) Yes, but not Ministers b) No	Varies with cttee. Members admitted may not participate in deliberations or vote.
INDONESIA House of Representatives	a) Yes b) No, unless they are also Members	With advance notification may attend but not speak.
IRELAND Senate Dáil	a) Yes, if the cttee has power to send for persons b) No	Yes, if terms of reference permit.

23.3 Right to summon witnesses	23.4 Right to call for documents	23.5 Can Ministers be called before a committee
-	Yes	-
Yes	Yes	Yes
No	No	Yes. Govt members have the right to attend and must be heard.
Only investigatory cttees	Only investigatory cttees	Yes, by majority decision.
Senior govt officials only	Yes	Yes
Yes	Yes	Yes
Yes	Yes, but the Govt may claim privileges where State interest or safety could be prejudiced.	No
Yes	Yes	Yes
Yes, if terms of reference permit.	Yes, if terms of reference permit.	Yes, if the cttee has power to send for persons.

Country and House(s)	23.1 Can govt officials a) Be summoned by committees b) Be committee members	23.2 Can MPs not members of a cttee attend, speak at its meetings
ISRAEL The Knesset	a) Yes b) No	If invited by the cttee (usually as proposer of a motion or as an expert).
ITALY Senate	a) Yes b) No	Yes
Chamber of Deputies		
IVORY COAST National Assembly	a) Yes b) No	Yes
JAPAN House of Councillors	a) Yes b) No	Attend but not speak unless invited.
House of Representatives		
JORDAN Senate	a) Yes b) No	No, except the Presiding Officer who can attend and speak.
House of Deputies		
KENYA National Assembly	a) Yes b) No	No
KUWAIT National Assembly	a) Yes b) No	Yes, with approval of cttee chairman.
LEBANON National Assembly	a) Yes b) No	Yes
LIECHTENSTEIN Diet	a) Yes b) No	No
LUXEMBOURG Chamber of Deputies	a) No, but they can be invited to make a presentation or prepare a special study b) No	No, but an absent member may nominate a replacement from his group. The Chamber President may attend and advise.

710

23.3 Right to summon witnesses	23.4 Right to call for documents	23.5 Can Ministers be called before a committee
Appearance not compulsory unless cttee provided with powers of inquiry	Yes, but submission not compulsory unless cttee provided with powers of inquiry.	Yes, for matters referred or within cttee jurisdiction.
Via the Govt for public administrators, companies, or administrations subject to Govt scrutiny or control. Via respective Presiding Officer for other witnesses.	Yes	Yes
Yes	-	Yes
Officially through the Presiding Officer	Officially through the Presiding Officer but in practice directly	Yes
Yes	Yes	Yes
Yes	Yes	Yes
Yes, before cttees of investigation.	Yes	To provide clarifications
Requires special vote of the Assembly.	Requires special vote of the Assembly.	Requires special vote of the Assembly.
Yes	Yes	Yes
No, but individuals and organisations may be consulted.	No, except in the case of a parliamentary inquiry which has full subpoena powers.	No, but they may be heard.

Country and House(s)	23.1 Can govt officials a) Be summoned by committees b) Be committee members	23.2 Can MPs not members of a cttee attend, speak at its meetings
MALAWI National Assembly	a) Yes b) No	Only by leave of the cttee
MALAYSIA Senate	a) Yes b) No	By invitation
House of Representatives		
MALI National Assembly	a) Yes b) No	Yes
MALTA House of Representatives	a) Yes b) Yes, if legislation or a motion of procedure so provides	No
MAURITIUS Legislative Assembly	a) The Public Accounts Cttee can summon, other cttees may invite b) No	Attend but not speak
MEXICO Chamber of Senators	a) Yes b) No	Yes
Chamber of Deputies		
MONACO National Council	a) No b) No	Yes, but not vote.
MONGOLIA Great People's Khural (GPKh)	a) Yes b) Yes, if they are MPs	Yes, in a consultative capacity.
NAURU Parliament	a) Yes b) No	May attend when witnesses examined but withdraw on request.

712

23.3 Right to summon witnesses	23.4 Right to call for documents	23.5 Can Ministers be called before a committee
Yes	Yes	-
Yes	Yes	To obtain a statement
-	-	Yes
Yes	Yes	Practice is that a Minister may not accept to appear when he can address the House on the subject.
Only the Public Accounts Cttee can summon.	Yes	Yes, when the Minister's experience and knowledge may be vital to a cttee's work.
Witnesses are not obliged to attend.	Yes	Cttees may invite Ministers but they are not obliged to attend.
Yes	Yes	No
Yes	Yes	Yes
Yes	Yes	Yes

Country and House(s)	23.1 Can govt officials a) Be summoned by committees b) Be committee members	23.2 Can MPs not members of a cttee attend, speak at its meetings
NETHERLANDS First Chamber	a) Yes, but authorisation of the relevant Minister is required b) No	Only when a draft is being prepared. A substitute may replace an absent member.
Second Chamber		Yes, with permission of the cttee. All Members may participate in an Extended Cttee meeting.
NEW ZEALAND House of Representatives	a) Yes b) No	Attend but not speak.
NICARAGUA National Assembly	a) Yes b) No	Attend but not speak.
NORWAY Storting	a) No, but an invitation to attend is always heeded b) No	No
PHILIPPINES National Assembly	a) Yes b) No	Yes, with cttee permission.
POLAND Diet	a) Yes b) No	Members may participate when a Bill has its 1st reading in cttee or submit written comment. Otherwise with chairman's permission but not to vote.
PORTUGAL Assembly of the Republic	a) Their attendance may be requested b) No	Yes
REPUBLIC OF KOREA National Assembly	a) Yes b) No	May attend, and speak with cttee's permission.
ROMANIA Grand National Assembly	a) Yes b) No	Yes

23.3 Right to summon witnesses	23.4 Right to call for documents	23.5 Can Ministers be called before a committee
No	No	Yes
Only by cttees charged with a parliamentary inquiry	Yes	Yes
Yes	Yes	Yes
No	Yes	Yes, but proposed through the Assembly Secretary.
No, but they may be invited.	No, but requests will normally be met.	Yes, to elaborate matters the Minister has submitted to the Storting.
Yes	Yes	Yes, for inquiries affecting his ministry.
Yes	Yes	Yes
Yes	Yes	Attendance may be requested.
Yes	Yes	Yes
Yes	Yes, from State instrumentalities.	Cttees may invite Ministers.

TABLE 23: ATTENDANCE AT COMMITTEE MEETINGS (continued)

Country and House(s)	23.1 Can govt officials a) Be summoned by committees b) Be committee members	23.2 Can MPs not members of a cttee attend, speak at its meetings
RWANDA National Development Council (CND)	a) Yes b) No	Yes, but not vote.
ST VINCENT House of Assembly	a) Yes b) No	No
SENEGAL National Assembly	a) They may be consulted with consent of the relevant Minister b) No	Yes, but not vote.
SOLOMON ISLANDS National Parliament	a) Yes b) No	Yes
SOMALIA People's Assembly	a) Yes b) Yes	No
SOUTH AFRICA House of Assembly	a) Yes b) No	May attend only when evidence is taken unless Chairman requests withdrawal, but may not speak.
House of Representatives		
House of Delegates		
SPAIN Senate	a) Yes b) No	Attend, but not speak.
Congress of Deputies		
SRI LANKA Parliament	a) Yes b) No	No
SWEDEN Riksdag	a) State officials, yes; govt officials, not obligatory b) No	No

716

23.3 Right to summon witnesses	23.4 Right to call for documents	23.5 Can Ministers be called before a committee
Yes	Yes	Yes
Yes	Yes	Yes, for political matters affecting the ministry.
Yes	No	Yes
Yes	Yes	-
Yes	Yes	Yes
Yes for standing cttees other than those for domestic matters of Parlt.	Yes (as for 23.3).	Yes
Yes	Yes	Attendance may be requested through the House President.
Yes	Yes	Yes
Yes, but no obligation to appear.	Only State authorities obliged to comply. Govt is obliged only to Cttee of Const.	Yes, but no obligation to appear.

717

Country and House(s)	23.1 Can govt officials a) Be summoned by committees b) Be committee members	23.2 Can MPs not members of a cttee attend, speak at its meetings
SWITZERLAND States Council National Council	a) Yes b) No	Authors of parliamentary initiatives are heard. Non-members may submit written proposals.
SYRIAN ARAB REPUBLIC People's Council	a) Yes b) No	Yes
THAILAND Senate House of Representatives	a) Yes b) In ad hoc cttees only	Those submitting a motion or an amdt may attend and speak. Persons assigned by Ministers may observe, requiring chairman's permission if secret.
TUNISIA Chamber of Deputies	a) No, but they may be heard b) No	Yes, but not vote.
UGANDA National Assembly	a) Yes b) No	Attend but not speak
UNION OF SOVIET SOCIALIST REPUBLICS Soviet of Nationalities Soviet of the Union	a) Yes b) Yes, provided they are also MPs	Yes. They may also vote.
UNITED KINGDOM House of Lords House of Commons	a) Yes b) No a) Yes, for select cttees but not standing cttees unless specially empowered b) No	Yes Attend but not speak
UNITED REPUBLIC OF TANZANIA National Assembly	a) Yes b) No	Yes, but not vote.

23.3 Right to summon witnesses	23.4 Right to call for documents	23.5 Can Ministers be called before a committee
Yes	Yes	Yes
Yes	Yes	Yes
Yes	Yes	Yes
Cttees may consult persons as required.	No	Cttees may invite a Minister to reply to questions orally and in writing.
Yes	Yes	Yes, to give evidence.
Yes	Yes	Yes
Yes	Yes	Yes
Yes, for most select cttees.	Yes, for most select cttees.	
Yes	Yes	Yes, when a cttee considers an issue requires political attention.

Country and House(s)	23.1 Can govt officials a) Be summoned by committees b) Be committee members	23.2 Can MPs not members of a cttee attend, speak at its meetings
UNITED STATES OF AMERICA Senate	a) Yes b) No	Attend but not speak, except with Chairman's permission in Senate cttee, or at discretion of House cttee.
House of Representatives		
VANUATU Parliament	a) Yes b) No	Only as experts
YUGOSLAVIA Federal Chamber	a) Yes b) Yes, in particular of joint bodies	Attend but not speak
Chamber of Republics and Provinces		
ZAIRE Legislative Council	a) Yes b) No	Yes
ZAMBIA National Assembly	a) Yes b) No	No
ZIMBABWE Senate	a) Yes b) No	No
House of Assembly		

23.3 Right to summon witnesses	23.4 Right to call for documents	23.5 Can Ministers be called before a committee
Yes	Yes	Yes, at cttee's discretion.
Yes	Yes	Yes
No	Yes	Yes
Yes	Yes	Yes
Yes	Yes	A Minister may appear to brief a cttee on his ministry and the matter under examination.
Yes	Yes	Yes